Casualties of Conflict

Fatalities of the War of Independence and Civil War
in Glasnevin Cemetery

CASUALTIES

OF

CONFLICT

Fatalities of the War of Independence and Civil War

in Glasnevin Cemetery

CONOR DODD

MERCIER PRESS

DEDICATION

DO SHANE – IMITHE ROMHAINN RÓ–LUATH ACH NÍ IMITHE UAINN

MERCIER PRESS

Cork

www.mercierpress.ie

© Conor Dodd/Dublin Cemeteries Trust

ISBN: 978-1-78117-728-0

eBook: 978-1-78117-729-7

Cover design: Craig Carry

A CIP record for this title is available from the British Library

Printed and bound in the EU.

Contents

ACKNOWLEDGEMENTS

Producing a book is a solitary task but one that is impossible without the support and contribution of many people. I have been very fortunate with the help I have received and kindness shown to me during the process by those I know and those I have never met. I would like to thank all those who I have been in contact with during the period of research and writing, I am very grateful to everyone.

The process of writing this book has, like many similar endeavours in the past few years, been made possible by the work of those in repositories and institutions in making source material available online. I am indebted to the staff of the libraries and archives listed in the bibliography for their hard and often thankless work. Particular thanks go to Brenda Malone and Clare McNamara of the National Museum of Ireland, Berni Metcalfe and the National Library of Ireland, Michael Foley, Cian Murphy and the GAA Museum, Derek Jones, Georgina Laragy, Ciaran O'Neill, Peter Power-Hynes, George Fonsie Mealy, Georgina Kelly, Peadar Breslin, Donal King, May Moran, Joe Baldwin of Southampton Archives and Local Studies, Ray McManus of Sportsfile, Natalie Jones of Reach Licensing, Mary Feehan of Mercier Press, the staff of the Military Archives and also the relatives of those included within this book that have contacted me or who I was able to contact. I would also like to thank all the staff of Glasnevin and members of Dublin Cemeteries Trust, past and present, who I have worked with and who not only share an interest in the cemetery but also know how special a place it is. I am particularly grateful to the CEO, Aoife Watters and Chair, David Bunworth, as well as George McCullough and John Green. Their support has made this project possible.

Finally I would like to acknowledge Liam and Mairéad who have consistently and constantly supported me. Without doubt, my greatest debt is owed to Katie, who has made everything possible. While Meadhbh and Aoibhín, whom I love dearly, have given me perspective on many things, not least the important things in life.

Go raibh maith agaibh go léir.

Introduction

Glasnevin Cemetery in Dublin is Ireland's largest cemetery with over one million burials. Its interments represent and reflect the multifaceted history of the city and Ireland but it is also steeped in political meaning and significance. Its foundation in 1832 was, in its own right, a form of political activism by Daniel O'Connell, the Catholic Association and its supporters, in the midst of the Penal Laws and restrictions in relation to Catholic burial rights. Its initial association with O'Connell provided a basis from which it developed into a cemetery that not only holds many famous interments but is also an important space of identity and meaning. In this context the national and international conflicts of the period between 1914 and 1923 had what is arguably the most significant impact on Glasnevin.

Amongst the visible legacies of this tumultuous period are the Republican and the National Army plots, as well as the subsequent burials of well-known political figures of the revolutionary period in the areas that immediately surround those plots. However, the casualties interred within that area of the cemetery tell a small part of the wider picture in relation to the legacy of the War of Independence and Civil War in Glasnevin. Naturally the focus often falls on a small number of well-known interments. These are individuals who made significant political or other contributions during the period and remain, and are likely to remain, a deserving source of interest and study. However, even a cursory examination of the names included here show that these figures make up a small proportion of the overall numbers buried in the cemetery who died as a result of these conflicts. It is also worth noting that although parts of the cemetery, such as the Republican, Royal Irish Constabulary or National Army plots, can be described as being curated spaces of political or institutional importance, the majority of those included in this book were interred in Glasnevin due to its practical function as a burial place. Beyond this, familial links to the cemetery are also in evidence through family burial plots or relations previously buried in the cemetery. It is therefore important to emphasise, that although Glasnevin has a reputation of revolutionary importance, for most of those who died in the two conflicts examined here, the cemetery was chosen due to practical or personal reasons rather than political.

In focusing simply on biographies and the circumstances of death of those killed this book has a necessarily narrow view of the revolutionary period in Ireland. As a result the significant political, social, administrative and other change of the period is somewhat obscured but glimpses are visible through the lives of those included. The use of a chronology of deaths also assists in using these biographies to track the progression and the ebb and flow of the conflicts.

Through them, we can see the expansion of urban warfare in Dublin, executions, assassinations, the Connaught Rangers mutiny in India, rural ambushes, Bloody Sunday, the Battle of Dublin, seaborne landings, the Kerry offensive, extra-judicial shootings and official executions of the Civil War and much more. The connections between events, personalities and deaths is also clear throughout, showing the, at times, parochial nature of the conflicts with their chains of events, actions and reactions. Juxtaposed with this is the representation in the book of those who were born in twenty-three different counties as well as Wales, England, Scotland, Canada and the United States of America. Likewise, although many of the fatal incidents recounted occurred in Dublin, there is also a much wider geographic representation and sense of the conflicts beyond that county. Perhaps most important are the examples that give a sense of the grief, loss and impact on individual family members left behind and, in certain cases, who also witnessed the death of their loved one.

Where possible, I have tried to include first hand accounts of the circumstances of fatalities, however, like all witness statements these can be influenced by different factors and varying accounts of the same incidents exist in many cases. The available evidence will be debated, contested and interpreted in many different ways but I have attempted to give a balanced representation of all incidents. This includes the determination of affiliation attached to every individual. This is not intended as a definitive judgment of the status of an individual, or indeed representative of their own political activities or other beliefs, which as the biographies demonstrate can be complicated. However, I have attempted to categorise all those listed. The criteria for the biographies included are those who met their deaths because of political violence or in carrying out political activities or protest. A very small number of individuals who died through apparent armed robberies or in homicides that appear to have no clear political motivation or connection have been excluded.

A visitor to Glasnevin in the nineteenth century, utilising a quotation from *As You Like It*, described that there were 'sermons in stones' within the walls of the cemetery. His description might have been more apt than he had imagined given that Glasnevin was formed as part of the garden cemetery movement earlier that century. This ethos, which had a direct impression on the early formation of the cemetery, advocated for the positioning of burial grounds as institutions of culture and heritage, an experiential and educational space that had the potential to inform visitors of the current generation and future generations. In recent years, the cemetery has returned to this function, albeit in a very different way, through its educational activities, tours and visitor centre. The ultimate aspiration of this book is to provide a basis for exploring the War of Independence and Civil War through the prism of Glasnevin. It is hoped that it will not just act as a guide for those who might visit the cemetery but also demonstrate the possibilities of using cemeteries and burial places for educational purposes and to shine a little light on personalities, incidents and events of the past.

CONOR DODD

Patrick Smyth (centre, with moustache) with other Dublin Metropolitan Police detectives outside the Dublin City Morgue following an inquest in March 1919. Courtesy of Mercier Archives.

1919

8 September 1919   **Dublin Metropolitan Police**
Patrick Smyth   *DH 225½, St Bridget's*

Patrick Smyth, a detective with G Division, Dublin Metropolitan Police, was shot on the evening of 30 July 1919, his wounds proving fatal. His shooting was the first assassination attempt authorised by IRA General Headquarters and would be a precursor to the types of operations carried out later in the War of Independence by the Squad.

Born in Co. Longford, Patrick Smyth joined the DMP in 1893 aged twenty-five becoming a member of G Division four years later. Having settled in Dublin he married Annie Bourke in 1901 and lived at 51 Millmount Avenue in Drumcondra. In the aftermath of the 1916 Rising, and early stages of the War of Independence, Smyth became well-known as an active and efficient detective, working in combating and harassing the activities of republicans. His activities had made him a source of great irritation for many leading figures in the independence movement, including Michael Collins. In March 1919, he was involved in the arrest of Piaras Béaslaí, who was found to be carrying documents of a military nature. Despite being approached, and warned not to forward evidence to the trial of Béaslaí, Smyth did so, resulting in a guilty verdict and two year jail sentence for Béaslaí. As Smyth continued in his work plans were being put in place for his assassination. James Slattery was one of four men tasked with shooting Smyth. He later recalled the events leading to the evening of 30 July 1919:

> Mick McDonnell told us that Detective Officer Smith [*Sic*]was living in Millmount Avenue and he was to be shot as he was becoming too active working against Volunteer interests. Mick McDonnell instructed me to go to Drumcondra Bridge and take with me Tom Keogh, Tom Ennis and Mick Kennedy, who knew Smith by sight. Mick McDonnell told us that Smith usually came home by tram, alighted at Botanic Avenue, and walked across the bridge. We were to wait at the bridge and shoot Smith when opportunity offered. We waited at Drumcondra bridge for about five nights. Finally we saw a man approaching across the bridge and Kennedy said, 'I think this is Smith'. I told him to make sure, but Kennedy said he could not be sure, although he thought it was Smith. I said 'If this man turns into Millmount Avenue we will shoot him', because I knew Smith was living there and between Kennedy being nearly sure of his identity and the fact that he turned

into Millmount Avenue would leave very little doubt about him. Kennedy was still undecided, but instead of turning into the Avenue, the man walked across, passed the Avenue and turned down a lane going along the back of the Avenue. After he passed us and crossed over I nearly dropped on my knees thinking I had nearly shot an innocent man, but when he turned down at the back of the houses we knew it was Smith. By this time he had gone out of range and we knew we had missed him. There was a bit of an argument then, 'I told you so' and so on ... We came back again to the bridge and after about a week we shot Smith. We had .38 guns and they were too small. I thought that the minute we would fire at him he would fall, but after we hit him he ran. The four of us fired at him. Keogh and myself ran after him right to his own door and I think he fell at the door, but he got into the house. He lived for about a fortnight afterwards. I met Mick McDonnell the following morning and he said that we had made a right mess of the job the night before, but I can assure you that I was more worried until Smith died than Mick was. We never used .38 guns again, we used .45 guns after that lesson.

It was reported that Smyth was making good progress in his recovery in the Mater Hospital despite being shot five times. He even had the opportunity to give an account of his shooting to another member of the DMP:

I was going home soon after 11 o'clock. When I got off the tram at the end of my own avenue, I saw 4 or 5 men standing against the dead wall and a bicycle resting against the kerbstone. Just as I turned the corner I was shot in the back. I turned round and said to them 'You cowards' and 3 of them fired again with revolvers at me and one bullet entered my leg. I then ran away and they pursued me to within about 15 yards of my own door and kept firing at me all the time. In all, about 10 or 12 shots were fired at me. I shouted for assistance but no one came to me except my own son. I had no revolver myself and I am glad now I had not one, as I might have shot some of them when I turned round after the first shot, and I would not like now to have done that. About a week ago, when going home one night, I noticed a similar number of men at the same place with two bicycles. As I suspected them, I did not go into my own avenue but went along as far as Millbourne Avenue, where I turned up to my own house. I cannot describe any of the men nor can I identify any of them.

Despite his initial progress, Patrick Smyth died of his wounds on 8 September 1919. Three days later, following requiem mass at Mount Argus, his remains were removed to Glasnevin for burial in what was described as a semi-private and 'simple funeral' with family, friends and some colleagues attending.[1]

1920

22 March 1920   **Civilian**
Ellen Hendrick   *DD 71, St Paul's*

Ellen Hendrick, who was born in the Coombe Hospital on 28 September 1901, was the daughter of William Hendrick, a baker and Ellen McCann who resided at 5 Kelly's Cottages. She was killed after members of the British army, who were attempting to disperse a crowd, fired shots. 22 March 1920, the day of Ellen Hendrick's death, marked the anniversary of the Battle of Tofrek, fought between the British army and Mahdist forces in Sudan in 1885. The 1st Battalion of the Berkshire Regiment was present and because of their involvement was granted the Royal title, becoming the Royal Berkshire Regiment and marked the day annually. On this occasion its members, who were stationed in Portobello Barracks, were given 150 tickets to a performance in the Theatre Royal on Hawkins Street.

In the House of Commons, the chief secretary of Ireland, Ian MacPhearson, outlined the official account of events that occurred that evening after T. P. O'Connor, the Home Rule MP, raised the issue with him:

> The 22nd of March is the anniversary day of the Royal Berkshire Regiment, and 150 were given free tickets by the battalion for the performance at the Royal Theatre. At the end of the performance the men sang the National Anthem. No disturbance occurred. The men then proceeded home in groups, singing. A crowd collected and followed, and on reaching Kelly's Corner, at about 9 p.m., the crowd commenced to throw stones at the troops. The troops were unarmed, but defended themselves, gradually moving up South Richmond Street. On reaching Lennox Street, the troops were fired on by the crowd, who used revolvers; one soldier was shot in the chest. At 9.45 p.m. information reached Royal Berks headquarters at Portobello Barracks concerning the disturbance. A cyclist patrol, under an officer, was ordered to proceed to the scene of the disturbance, and to assist the men who had been attending the theatre to return. The patrol reached the scene at about 10 p.m., and was supported by a piquet on foot. On reaching Portobello Bridge, fire was opened on patrol from direction of Portobello House, and stones were thrown by the crowd. The officer in charge of patrol, considering that his command was in danger, cautioned the crowd, and ordered them to disperse. The crowd refused to do so. The officer then ordered ten rounds to be fired, and charged the crowd, which withdrew to Fade Street. The patrol followed up the crowd as far as Kelly's Corner, where it was again fired on by civilians. A position was taken up at Kelly's Corner, and civilians in the vicinity were searched

for arms. A further reinforcement was sent to the patrol from Portobello Barracks, but nothing further transpired.

It was disputed whether the soldiers had been fired on but some witnesses noted that the gathered crowd threw stones and other objects at them. The actions of the soldiers while returning to their barracks from the Theatre Royal did little to endear them to the local onlookers and exacerbated an already tense situation. One newspaper stated that the evidence of civilian witnesses showed:

> ... their conduct was characterised by disorder and by shouting such as to cause irritation and annoyance throughout the whole of their march to South Richmond Street.

The initial melee had little risk of fatalities, as the members of the Berkshire Regiment engaged in it were unarmed. However, when armed reinforcements arrived, commanded by twenty-two year-old Lieut Thomas G.L. Dawson, the situation became much more dangerous. In his report to the adjutant, Dawson stated that:

> On the night of 22nd March 1920, I was detailed to proceed down to Dublin town and deal with a hostile mob (and rescue the theatre party) which had shot some of our men. On reaching Portobello Bridge I came in contact with the crowd who booed at us, threw bricks and fired shots. I cautioned them and they continued to fire and throw stones. I gave the order to fire and we charged the mob who dispersed towards Kelly's Corner and down the side streets. We then followed them down the main road and were fired at again at Kelly's Corner. We had no casualties in my command but three civilians were hit. We searched every pedestrian whom we met in the street but found no arms.

One of those hit was Ellen Hendrick. She was not part of the crowd that had gathered but was making her way towards the centre of the city from Rathmines. John Nolan, a civilian from Albert Place, witnessed the soldiers fire shots from Portobello Bridge and Ellen fall. As she did so, she screamed that she had been shot. The bullet had entered her chest and exited through her back severing a number of blood vessels. She was removed to the Meath Hospital but was dead on arrival. A girl, with whom she worked as a servant, originally identified her as Margaret Dowling, as she knew her by that name so there was a delay before her mother correctly identified her. Her funeral took place on 25 March from St Nicholas' church to Glasnevin. At the time, the incident drew many comparisons with the shootings at Bachelor's Walk in 1914 and the army were denounced at the coroner's inquest that took place following it.

Ellen was the first to be buried in a family grave in the St Paul's section of the cemetery. In 1944, her brother William Hendrick was buried in the same grave. William had served throughout the First World War as a member of British army with the Army Service Corps. He was one of the first to arrive in France with the British Expeditionary Force and left the army just under a year before his sister was killed. He returned to serve during the Second World War and died while still a member of the Army Catering Corps. Their grave is marked in memory of Ellen and also bears a formal marker in memory of her brother, William.

Thomas G.L. Dawson, who commanded the detachment that opened fire on 22 March 1920, served for a long period with the Berkshire Regiment and throughout the Second World War. He died in Wales in 1988 aged ninety.[1]

9 May 1920	Irish Republican Army
Francis Gleeson	*RD 35, South New Chapel*

Francis Aiden (Frank) Gleeson died on 9 May 1920 in the Mater Hospital in Dublin. Born in Liverpool in 1895 to Irish parents Gleeson was a trainee teacher and a member of the Irish Volunteers when he travelled to Ireland in 1915 in order to avoid the possibility of being conscripted into the British army. His brother later described that his decision to leave England was 'because he did not want to dishonour his soul'. Gleeson initially joined with the Irish Volunteers in Belfast before he moved to Dublin in 1919. There he lived at 34 Cadogan Road with the Holohan family. Hugh Holohan was a fellow member of Dublin Brigade, IRA and early on the morning of 19 February 1920 the house on Cadogan Road was raided by members of the British army acting on information received from the DMP. During the raid revolvers, ammunition, a bullet-making machine, notebooks and orders were found. Hugh Holohan, Francis Gleeson and two other men were arrested. The men were initially brought to Ship Street Barracks and later transferred to Mountjoy. They were briefly released but promptly arrested once again and placed on trial for possession of revolvers and ammunition. Gleeson refused to give any information to the authorities on his entry to Mountjoy and was processed under his alias, Aiden Redmond. The four men were sentenced to two months hard labour with a further month on probation. On Easter

Monday 1920 Gleeson and over sixty other IRA prisoners went on hunger strike. The numbers participating in the strike grew to over 100 and after ten days on strike Gleeson was one of a number of prisoners who were released. However within this time his health had deteriorated significantly and he was taken straight to the Mater Hospital. He remained in hospital until 3 May when he was discharged but two days later was taken back by ambulance. Suffering with acute appendicitis he was operated on but died the following day. An inquest returned a verdict that he died of 'toxaemia following nephritis and acute appendicitis accelerated by hunger strike'.[2]

28 May 1920 — Royal Irish Constabulary
Thomas Kane — *JF 233½, Garden*

Courtesy of Reach plc
(Daily Mirror)

Born in Co. Meath, Thomas Kane joined the Royal Irish Constabulary in 1891, aged nineteen, and became a member of its Mounted Force the following year. His first period with the police force lasted until 1901, when he temporarily resigned from the RIC and joined the newly raised 131st (Irish Horse) Company of the Imperial Yeomanry to serve in South Africa during the Anglo-Boer War. Following his return to Ireland at the end of 1902, he was reappointed to his position and continued to serve on horseback with the police. As time progressed, the Mounted Force of the RIC became outmoded and by 1920 it only had thirteen members including Thomas Kane, who was one of its three sergeants. It was disbanded that year and Kane was due to be appointed to a new position in Co. Limerick. On 26 May 1920, he was temporarily sent to Kilmallock where two days later a group, consisting of some 100 IRA volunteers, participated in and supported the attack on the fortified barracks there. Here the RIC detachment with Tobias O'Sullivan *(see 20 January 1921)* defended the barracks against a long and sustained attack. One of the members of the IRA who took part in the attack that night later recalled the events that led to the death of Thomas Kane:

> By the spring of 1920, the campaign against RIC barracks was well under way and successfully fulfilling its two-fold purpose of loosening the enemy's hold on the country and augmenting the arms of the Volunteers. It was decided to attack and capture Kilmallock RIC barracks. It was discovered that the normal strength of the barracks

consisted of two sergeants and eighteen men. The building was a very substantial one and all the windows were steel shuttered and slotted to enable rifle to be fired through them. In addition to a plentiful supply of ammunition, the garrison was well provided with rifle, grenade and Mills bombs. In short the police were in the position of an exceptionally strong military force with every prospect of holding out for days against even overwhelming numbers. The barrack however, had one drawback, of which great advantage could be taken by daring attackers. Situated in the main street of the village, it was a rather low, squat structure strongly built, but overlooked by higher buildings adjacent to it. This gave the attackers, provided they could occupy these buildings successfully, a dominant position over those barracks ... It was too much to hope that so strong a barrack could be carried by a short, sharp attack. It would obviously have to be besieged. This constituted the greatest part of our task, because a protracted fight would certainly lead to the possibility of reinforcements coming to the relief of the garrison. Our force was too small for the risk to be lightly regarded. All available help in the entire district was accordingly mobilised at 9 o'clock on the night of the attack and all the main roads, by-roads and railway tracks for a radius of about fifteen miles around Kilmallock were rendered impassable for any form of traffic. A prodigious amount of labour went into this work, but it was cheerfully and effectively done, and it was well indeed that it was so, for the barrack proved a far tougher proposition than we had counted upon.

About thirty men, each of whom was recommended by his local commander, were now specially selected, armed with the best of rifles, given a plentiful supply of ammunition and detailed for the direct attack on the barracks. The remaining men, to the number of about forty, armed with shot-guns and all sorts of miniature weapons were detailed to guard minor entrances and exits ... About six paces from the gable-end of the barracks, facing south-west, another building towered above it. From the roof of the building our leader was to give three flashes of a lamp which was the signal to begin the attack. All eyes were now straining towards this point. There was no sign of life or activity from the barrack and we seemed to have made our occupation of the surrounding houses without arousing suspicions. Suddenly from the roof top three flashes of light winked out into the night and were instantly answered by the roar of thirty rifles. At the same moment our leader cast a fifty-six pound weight crashing though the slates of the barrack roof. Two other fifty-six pound weights followed in quick succession, their crashing noise passing almost unnoticed in the din of rifles and bursting bombs. This unique method of breaking a fort was very effective, causing a large gaping hole in the roof. Into this opening our leader, from the roof hurled bottle after bottle of petrol. The bottles broke and saturated the roof with petrol. Then our leader hurled bombs into the breach. Each bomb burst with terrific force causing considerable damage but completely failing to set the roof on fire. Meanwhile the fight was raging fiercely all round the barrack. The large garrison had manned every loop-hole and were returning hot fire to our attack ... By means of a hose paraffin was now poured into the breach in the roof, for the best part of an hour. Then another Mills bomb hurled into the breach had the desired effect and the roof burst into a blaze ... The battle for possession of the barracks raged without intermission from midnight to 2 a.m.. At that hour our leader flashed out the 'cease fire' signal from his perch on the house top. It was almost instantly obeyed by the attackers and the only sound was from the intermittent fire of the defenders. It was a weird night and one which the participants are never likely to forget, the smoke of burst bombs and the burning roof billowing around the building, the sudden comparative quiet after the fierce noise of the conflict, the red, hungry flame shooting skyward out of the doomed building.

The garrison was called on to surrender but the reply was 'No surrender' followed by a volley of rifle and grenade fire. Instantly the three flashes of light for the 'open fire' winked out from the house-top and the battle was again in full swing. For upwards of three more hours the building, the fire of which was increasing every moment, was subjected to a continuous attack. During all this time the defenders, who showed remarkable courage and pertinacity, directed their main efforts against Clery's Hotel. They endeavoured to make this position untenable by a continuous attack ... The fight had been waged for over five hours and the entire barrack was little better than a roaring furnace. The position of the defenders was hopeless as it was quite impossible to remain any longer in the building. Once more the 'cease fire' signal flashed out. Silence again took the place of conflict. The garrison, for the last time, were called upon to 'surrender'. Their answer was 'never' followed by a few shots. The fight then recommenced and was continued up to about a quarter to six. About that hour the entire roof fell in, amidst frantic cheering from the attackers. Flames, sparks and clouds of smoke now shot skyward, giving a weird red tinge to the whole scene. The defenders had by this time made a dash to a small building in the yard of the barrack. This building like the barracks, was fortified... From this small building they put up a stubborn resistance. They fought the fight of heroes and although we were engaged in a life and death struggle with them, we readily acknowledged the magnificent stand they made in the face of an utterly hopeless situation... With daylight full across the country, our supplies of ammunition exhausted and the danger of being trapped by heavy reinforcements, our leader was forced to sound the 'Retire'. We retired in good order leaving the barracks a smouldering ruin.

Sgt Thomas Kane had been killed in the main barrack building. An inquest was unable to convene because the full jury summoned did not attend. His death was recorded as being due to 'shock from burns', however, contemporary reports described Kane as being killed by one of the bombs that was thrown into the barracks at the height of the battle. He was posthumously awarded the Constabulary Medal for his gallantry in the defence of the barracks.

His funeral came to Glasnevin on 1 June 1920 with his coffin draped in the Union flag and led by the bands of the 15th Hussars, Royal Irish Constabulary and Dublin Metropolitan Police. His wife, Teresa, whom he had married in 1905, and their children followed the hearse. Amongst those in attendance were the chief commissioner of the Dublin Metropolitan Police Lieut Col Walter Edgeworth-Johnstone and Lieut Gen. Henry Hugh Tudor. His widow, who remarried a former member of the Royal Irish Constabulary in 1922, died in 1952 and is buried with him.[3]

The funeral of Thomas Kane in Glasnevin. Courtesy of Reach/Daily Mirror.

1 July 1920   **Connaught Rangers**
Peter Sears   *SD 28, South New Chapel*

Peter Sears from Ballyshingadaun, the Neale, Ballinrobe, Co. Mayo enlisted in the Connaught Rangers at Claremorris in November 1914, following the outbreak of the First World War aged eighteen. A member of the newly formed 6th Battalion Connaught Rangers, part of the 16th (Irish) Division, he was sent to the Western Front, arriving in France in December 1915. Whilst serving with the Connaught Rangers he was temporarily attached to the Royal Engineers and specifically to one of their tunnelling companies. In the midst of the stagnation of trench warfare in France and Belgium these units of tunnellers were often given the responsibly of digging from their own trenches underneath no-man's land and beneath their enemies defensive positions where large quantities of explosives were placed and detonated. The job was not just difficult physically but also dangerous and nerve-racking as both sides mined and counter-mined. They also listened to each other's movements in the anticipation of detonating explosives to blow one another up. Sometimes they even broke through into enemy tunnels with subsequent hand-to-hand fighting in the dark with knives and bayonets. The chalky soil of northern

France lent itself well to this type of tunnelling but for Peter Sears the dust it produced resulted in significant health issues and he eventually began suffering with defective eyesight. Despite this he continued to serve during the war and in July 1918, he was transferred to the Labour Corps where he was involved in overseeing German prisoners of war who were used to carry out a variety of different labour tasks in groups known as Prisoner of War Companies. Peter Sears remained in France until February 1919 when he was discharged. However, he soon re-enlisted in the Connaught Rangers, this time the 1st Battalion of the regiment, which was stationed on garrison duty in India.

It was here on 28 June 1920 that a chain of events began leading to the deaths of Peter Sears and Patrick Smythe (*see below*). On that day, a mutiny began amongst members of the Connaught Rangers stationed in northern India. Amongst the mutineers' concerns was the situation in Ireland and the actions of British authorities in the War of Independence in their home country. The mutiny began peacefully in Jalandhar through a refusal to carry out their duties in protest and soon spread to another garrison at nearby Solon. Here events came to a violent climax when some members of the Connaughts attempted to rush the garrison armoury to capture weapons they had earlier given up. During this struggle, both Peter Sears and Smythe were fatally wounded. The mutiny of the Connaughts was quickly quashed and the participants placed under arrest and marched away to face courts martial. There was some understandable confusion during the attempted storming of armoury at Solon and differing accounts of the wounding of Sears and Smythe exist. Joseph Hawes, the *de facto* leader of the mutiny in Jalandhar, gave details of the events at Solon that were recounted to him by the leader there, James Joseph Daly, who was later executed by firing squad:

> On the day of our mutiny at Jallander the officers in Solon must have been notified of the occurrence. Rumours started to circulate amongst the men at Solon, probably through the indiscretion of some officer, but none of the men knew what was wrong at Jallander but that something had happened there. Kelly and Keenan arrived at Solon barracks and were immediately put under arrest but as they were being led away they shouted an incomplete message of the happenings at Jallander. Private James Joseph Daly who chanced to be one of those on the scene overheard what Kelly and Keenan said even though the message was incomplete Jim Daly figured out the rest for himself and took action. He immediately spread the word of the Jallander mutiny and what had caused it, about 40 of his comrades joined him and they occupied a bungalow over which in a short time flew the tricolour. This was only about one-third of the total force at Solon. Like the Jallander men the Solon mutineers were also armed. Father Baker, an Irishman and an army

chaplain, advised Daly and his comrades to hand up their arms as they were only a small party and not as strong as the Jallander mutineers. They took his advice to fight a passive resistance and their arms were handed over and put in the magazine. A heavy guard was then put over the magazine by the authorities. This magazine was built on rising ground.

That night a rumour spread in the barracks that British troops were coming in the morning to arrest the rebels. At a discussion in the canteen some of the hotter mutineers suggested taking back their arms and fighting the British. Daly who was a teetotaller himself said 'I have given my word to Fr. Baker and I won't break it'. Somebody said 'Are you afraid?' This grieved Daly who said 'fall in outside and follow me and I will show you I am no coward.' The mutineers obeyed and fell in behind Daly and advanced up the hill towards the magazine. When they reached between 20 or 30 yards of the magazine which was still on a ledge over them a sentries voice rang out 'Halt who goes there'. The men halted and Daly stepped forward a pace and said 'I'm James Joseph Daly of Tyrrell's Pass, Mullingar, Westmeath, Ireland and I demand ye are to lay down your arms and surrender in the name of the Irish Republic'. Immediately Lieutenants Walsh and McSweeney (*Sic*) who were in charge of the guard opened fire with their service revolvers at Daly. They missed Daly but mortally wounded Private Sears who though wounded rushed the rising ground and fell dying at the feet of the two officers. Private John Egan was shot through the chest but survived to later stand trial and be sentenced to death. Private Smith (*Sic*), who was not a mutineer and not of the party which approached the magazine, going to his bungalow further down the hill was shot through the head and died on the spot. Father Baker on hearing the shooting rushed to the scene and implored all concerned to take back the dead and wounded to the camp hospital. At the hospital Egan's wound was attended to and it was seen that nothing could be done for the other two men.

Lieut Desmond Thomas McWeeney, from Dublin, was one of the officers in charge of the armoury on the night of the attempted capture of the weapons. At the court of inquiry into the events of the night, he described how Lieut C.J. Walsh called for assistance and his response:

> ... about 22.00 hours, I was sitting in the veranda of the officers' mess. I heard a whistle blown, which I knew to be the alarm signal, from the direction of the magazine. I immediately ran to the magazine followed by the Guard, where I met Lieut Walsh, who told me that four mutineers had tried to rush the Sentry, and, on being cautioned by him, withdrew. I then took up a position close to Lieut Walsh, and on the south side from the men's bungalows. A few minutes after an attack was made on the Magazine by the Mutineers armed with naked bayonets. The attackers were challenged at least three or four times, but refused to stop. As a further warning, I fired two revolver shots into the air, but the attackers took no notice but came on. I then fired into the attackers, who, thereupon, withdrew. I shortly afterwards saw three men being carried on stretchers to the station Hospital, two of whom, I heard, were dead and one wounded.

Both Peter Sears and Patrick Smythe were buried in Solon and remained there until 1970 when they were exhumed and returned to Ireland for burial in Glasnevin. Both men were interred together, a short distance from the Connaught Rangers mutiny memorial in the cemetery, which had been erected and unveiled in June 1949 in a ceremony attended by some of the surviving mutineers, 1916 Rising veterans, former members of Cumann na mBan and relatives.[4]

1 July 1920 — Connaught Rangers
Patrick Smythe — *SD 28, South New Chapel*

Patrick Smythe died from wounds received during the Connaught Rangers mutiny at Solon in India (*see above*). Smythe and Peter Sears were the only two men to be killed during the mutiny and both are buried together in Glasnevin. Patrick Smythe, from Drogheda, was a regular soldier and member of the Connaught Rangers before the outbreak of the First World War having enlisted in December 1910 in Cavan. Having served at home for just over a year, he was sent to India where he remained with his regiment from 1912 to 1914 when, along with his battalion, he was recalled to Europe to take part in the war there. Smythe spent the war with his battalion, serving firstly in the fighting around the town of Ypres in Belgium in the autumn of 1914 and he was wounded in the left arm in November 1914 during the First Battle of Ypres. In December 1915, he left France arriving in Mesopotamia where he took part in the campaign there for two years, fighting against the Ottoman Empire. After a brief period back in India, Smythe and his battalion moved to Palestine joining with the Egyptian Expeditionary Force in campaigns in Transjordan and Syria where they remained until the end of the war. He re-enlisted for further service with his regiment following the Armistice and was sent to India in October 1919 where he was present in Solon during the mutiny and was fatally wounded. At least two of his comrades noted that Smythe was not an active participant in the mutiny and was an unlucky bystander. A letter to his mother Bridget on 17 July 1920 confirmed to her the death of her son:

> I regret having to inform you that a report has been received from India to the effect that your son, No. 10079 Lance Corporal Patrick Smyth [*Sic*], 1st Battalion, The Connaught Rangers, died on the 1st July 1920 from gunshot wound. No further particulars have been received in this office.[5]

9 August 1920   **Civilian**
Thomas Farrelly   *VC 77, St Paul's*

Thomas Farrelly, from Mary's Lane in Dublin, was shot dead by members of the Lancashire Fusiliers who opened fire on him, and a group of other men, gathered at the junction of Greek Street, Mary's Lane and Beresford Street, to the rear of the Four Courts, following curfew on the night of 9/10 August 1920.

Born in Dublin in 1900 Thomas was the son of Patrick and Mary Farrelly. On the night of his death, a bonfire had been lit, and a crowd had gathered, in support of the Irish-born Catholic archbishop of Melbourne, Daniel Mannix. The archbishop had been prevented from visiting Ireland by the British government due to his outspoken support for the republican movement. While the group gathered around the dying embers of a fire, they sang songs. As they sang 'The West's Awake', a routine military patrol of fifteen men of the Lancashire Fusiliers, under the command of Lieut J.A. Smith, arrived at the location. Smith later stated that he saw the group of people moving around by the light of the fire and decided to split his party into two sections. The first under his command approached via Mary's Lane and the other, under the command of Sgt Burgess, approached by Greek Street. As they advanced the latter party opened fire and the group of civilians ran. As Thomas Farrelly was approaching his nearby family home, he was struck by a number of bullets. His mother remembered being woken by the shots followed by her son shouting out 'Mother, Mother'. The fatally wounded Farrelly was taken into his home where Lieut Smith arrived shortly afterwards telling Mary Farrelly 'My God, I gave no order to fire'. In the civil inquest that followed, his death a finding was produced that stated:

> We find that Thomas Farrelly died on August 10 from shock and haemorrhage caused by bullets fired from the guns of the military on 10th inst. without justification. We strongly condemn the action of the military in empowering youths to endanger the lives of citizens and we desire to place on the record our deepest sympathy with the relatives of the deceased.

The funeral of Thomas Farrelly to Glasnevin on 13 August was a huge event and a significant political funeral. It began with a service at St Michan's before removal to the cemetery just after 14.00. His coffin was draped in a Tricolour, which had been made by Thomas in the days before his death, and was embroidered with the words 'Welcome to Dr Mannix'. Large crowds lined the route of the funeral with members of the Volunteer movement acting as marshals. Two bands led the procession with a Tricolour marked with a black cross and a horse drawn bier was used to transport floral tributes. Amongst the mourners were members of Dáil Éireann, including W.T. Cosgrave and Richard Mulcahy, Dublin Corporation and a significant representation of clergy. He was buried in the St Paul's section of the cemetery.[6]

Thomas Farrelly (inset) and his funeral on arrival at Glasnevin. Courtesy of Reach/ Daily Mirror.

3 September 1920   **Irish Republican Army**
Neill Kerr   *SD 38, South New Chapel*

Neill Kerr, an IRA volunteer, was killed in an accident during an operation involving the shipment of weapons in Liverpool, England. Born near Loughgall in Co. Armagh in 1896, he was the son of Neill and Sarah Ann Kerr. The family moved to England and lived at Florida Street in Bootle. Neill junior participated in the 1916 Rising and was a member of the garrison at Jacob's Biscuit Factory, being interned in Frongoch following the surrender. Neill, his father and many other members of his family were also active participants in the War of Independence. On 3 September 1920 Kerr, along with his father, brother, and other Liverpool IRA members were awaiting a shipment of arms and ammunition from Scotland to be sent to Dublin. While the group was waiting in the basement of a Sinn Féin Club, at 93 Scotland Road in Liverpool, Kerr was fatally wounded. Stephen Lanigan, in support of an application by Neill Kerr senior for a military pension, stated that while waiting for the consignment of arms in Scotland Road the tension increased over many hours and a gun was accidentally discharged resulting in the death of Neill Kerr. He further stated that Neill's brother, Tom, fired the fatal shot. Patrick Daly, a member of the Irish Volunteers and IRB in Liverpool, who was present when Kerr died, gave a similar account of the incident to the Bureau of Military History, albeit with one significant difference:

> On one of these few occasions on which a lorry or car was expected I remember a tragedy occurring affecting one of our members. We were waiting in a cellar for this lorry to come from Glasgow and, as the time of arrival was very uncertain, actually after waiting all day it did not come at all. But during the course of the day a member of the I.R.A., a son of Kerr, put as he thought, an empty parabellum to his head and shot himself dead.

The remains of Neill Kerr were brought from Liverpool to Dublin on the steamer *Killiney* accompanied by his father, step-mother, sister and brother. After mass at the church on City Quay, the coffin was brought, covered in the Tricolour, to Glasnevin where he was interred in the Republican Plot.[7]

30 September 1920	**Royal Irish Constabulary**
James Joseph Brady	*TE 7, South New Chapel*

James Joseph Brady in the uniform of the Irish Guards. **Courtesy of Peter Power Hynes.**

James Joseph Mary Brady was born on 9 October 1898 in 17 Corrig Avenue, Kingstown (Dún Laoghaire), Dublin. The son of Louis Brady and Anne Corless his father worked on a number of merchant navy and other vessels operating from the town. In the early 1900s Louis became one of the crew of the Commissioners of Irish Lights vessel *SS Tearaght,* later rising to become captain of another of the lighthouse service's vessels the *SS Ierne.* In January 1916, James joined the Inns of Court Officer Training Corps, giving a fake date of birth on his enlistment and the following April was enrolled as a cadet in the Dublin University Officer Training Corps in Trinity College, Dublin. Following his training, he was commissioned as a second lieutenant in the Irish Guards and sent to the Western Front for service. Following the war he joined the Royal Irish Constabulary as a cadet in February 1920 and was made a district inspector in June, being posted to Ballymena in Antrim. Soon afterwards, he wrote a letter to Dublin Castle requesting to be posted elsewhere stating that:

> I have a good station and should be sorry to lose it but I am only 22 years old and fit and I do not see why I should be up here in safety and not in the firing line where I might relieve some older man who may be nerve-wrecked and feeling the strain.

As a result, after just three months in Ballymena, he was transferred to Tubbercurry in Sligo on 11 September 1920 where the district inspector had reported sick. There he was killed before the end of that month in an ambush. John P. Brennan, a member of Sligo Brigade IRA, described the engagement:

> After the brigade had received a consignment of arms from GHQ it was decided to carry out an ambush in the battalion area of Chaffpool. In order to cause enemy activity and get enemy patrols on to the roads we raided a mail car in the early morning of the 1st September. Frank Carty took charge of the men who took up position at Chaffpool. The number of men in Carty's party, including himself, was 10. All were armed with service rifles. After waiting the whole day in position, towards evening a Crossley tender approached containing a load of police. The police officer in charge of the Crossley was District Inspector Brady who had been in the area only a short time and whose advent in Tubbercurry initiated British activities against the IRA. Brady was sitting with the driver of the car and the rest of the police were in the body of the lorry. As the lorry came opposite the position occupied by our men fire was opened on them. D.I. Brady received five bullet wounds which proved fatal a few hours later. Head Constable O'Hara was severely wounded and a Constable Browne was also wounded. The driver of the tender was able to get the tender through and reach Tubbercurry safely. None of Carty's men was injured by the exchange of fire from the police in the lorry.

Following the ambush and the death of Brady reprisals took place in Tubbercurry with homes and businesses being burned. The burnings resulted in approximately £125,000 of damage and, significantly, the loss of two creameries in the area, affecting over 1,000 dairy farmers. The funeral of James Joseph Brady came to Glasnevin on 4 October. Following mass at Aughrim Street his coffin was placed on a gun carriage and the cortege proceeded to the cemetery with a police and military guard of honour including members of the Irish Guards who had travelled from London for the occasion. Members of the RIC and DMP lined the pathways of the cemetery to the grave where the

Last Post was sounded. His parents and his uncle, P.J. Brady, a former Irish Parliamentary Party MP for Dublin St Stephen's Green, led the mourners. He was buried in the grave of his grandfather who died in 1879.

Upon hearing of the reprisals following the death of his son, Louis Brady decided to write to the parish priest in Tubbercurry, Canon Gunning. His letter was read to the parishioners the week of his son's funeral:

The funeral of James Joseph Brady on its way to Glasnevin. Courtesy of the National Library of Ireland.

The parents of James Joseph Brady arrive at the cemetery during his funeral. Courtesy of the National Library of Ireland.

Very Rev and Dear Sir,

As regards the death of my beloved son, writing on his mother's behalf and my own, I want to tell you that neither of us entertains the least feeling of ill-will towards anyone in connection with the tragedy. God's holy will be done. It was his way of bringing Jim to heaven. We forgive from our hearts whoever was responsible for this deed, wherever they came from. My wife and I were deeply grieved to learn of the reprisals that have taken place in your parish. No useful purpose is served by such conduct, and if anything could now make my poor boy unhappy it would be to know that he was the innocent cause of injury to anyone. Availing for your prayers and those of your congregation for my boy and his heartbroken mother and father.

Believe me yours sincerely,

Louis Brady.[8]

14 October 1920 — Civilian
Patrick Carroll — *XJ 300½, St Patrick's*

Patrick Carroll, a sixteen-year-old messenger boy, from Royal Canal Terrace was shot and killed during a firefight on Talbot Street in Dublin. The fight also resulted in the death of Seán Treacy, one of those responsible for the Soloheadbeg Ambush, regarded as the first military engagement of the War of Independence, and one of the most wanted IRA men in Ireland. Following the escape of Dan Breen and Seán Treacy from the house of John Carolan in Drumcondra *(see 26 October 1920)* Breen was treated for his wounds in the Mater Hospital under an alias while Treacy remained in Dublin. Two days later in the early evening of 14 October 1920, a British raiding party outside the Republican Outfitters on Talbot Street found Treacy. Following a struggle and firefight Treacy and a British intelligence officer, Gilbert Price, were killed. Two civilians Patrick Carroll and Joseph Corringham were also hit by gunfire and died.

Patrick Carroll was the son of Patrick Carroll and Eliza Duffy and was born in 11 North King Street in December 1903. Moving first to Dorset Street and then to Royal Canal Terrace in Phibsborough, Patrick worked as a messenger boy for Gilbey's wine stores in the city. On the evening of his death, he was reported to be passing by J. Speidel's butchers, at 98 Talbot Street, walking towards O'Connell Street, when he was fatally wounded and died almost instantly. He was buried in a family grave in the St Bridget's section of the cemetery on 19 October. He was one of four Carroll siblings buried in the same grave to die aged sixteen and under.[9]

Seán Treacy's body [right] on the path outside Speidel's Butchers in the aftermath of the fight on Talbot Street that resulted in the death of Patrick Carroll. Courtesy of Mercier Archives.

[Below] *Bodies being removed from Talbot Street following the gun fight.* Courtesy of Mercier Archives.

Talbot Street following the fight that resulted in the death of Patrick Carroll and Seán Treacy. **Courtesy of Mercier Archives.**

16 October 1920   **Civilian**
Peter O'Carroll   *MH 193½, St Bridget's*

In the early hours of 16 October 1920 Peter O'Carroll, a butcher aged sixty-three, was shot dead at his home 92 Manor Street, Dublin. Born in Dublin in 1858 Peter O'Carroll was an old member of the Irish Republican Brotherhood. Two of his sons, Liam and Peter, were members of Dublin Brigade, IRA, and his daughter Mary was a member of Cumann na mBan.. Although he could not take an active part in the conflict due to his age and health Peter O'Carroll bought arms and equipment from British soldiers stationed at the nearby Royal Barracks, which he passed to the Irish Volunteers and later IRA. His home and business on Manor Street had been raided a number of times and on the morning of 16 October 1920, when a knock was heard on their door, Peter and his wife Annie assumed that another raid was about to take place. Peter went down the stairs and as he opened the door he was forced backwards into the shop and shot in the head. His assailants then quickly and quietly made their escape.

Peter O'Carroll's daughter gave an account of his shooting shortly after the incident:

> At about 1.40 this morning a knock came to our door and having been often raided, particularly within the last three or four weeks, we believed they were about to search the place once more. My mother also got out of bed and looked through the window.

She noticed the forms of two or three men at the door. The night was densely dark. My father turned on the electric light in the kitchen and shop and then opened the door. After this all appeared absolutely quiet except for a slight movement of persons walking in the shop floor. There was a slight thud and then stillness. The light in the shop was put out and the door from the kitchen closed and the shop door was also pulled to on the spring lock. My mother hearing no noise suspected the raiders had gone to the back accompanied by her husband. She came down stairs and seeing the shop in darkness and quietness still prevailing, returned to her room again. After being about 10 minutes there she became uneasy and returned to the kitchen turned on the shop light and opened the door leading to the shop and there the most terrible spectacle met her eyes, her aged husband lying a lifeless corpse in a huge pool of blood. She went upstairs again and screamed from the window at the top of her voice: Murder! Murder! And kept on screaming until coming on to 3 o'clock when people in the locality heard her cries and rushed to the house.

Fr George Turley from Aughrim Street arrived to administer the last rites but O'Carroll was dead. He had been shot through the left temple at close range and died almost instantly. There had been no struggle, no noise and no loud gunshot. It was reported in the *Evening Herald* in the aftermath of the shooting that following an earlier raid on the property, during which his sons were not present, Peter O'Carroll was told '... we will come back again soon and if they are not here it will be worse for you'.

David Neligan stated that within the IRA it was believed that Jocelyn Lee Hardy had carried out the shooting. Hardy, a British intelligence officer, had served with the Connaught Rangers during the First World War. Having been captured in 1914 he spent much of the war as a prisoner before, after many attempts, he escaped to England via the Netherlands. He was sent back to the Western Front in 1918 where he won a Military Cross for gallantry and was wounded multiple times in October 1918, necessitating the amputation of his leg and gained the nickname 'Hoppy' as a result. During his time in Ireland he became a well-known and much feared operative. Neligan later claimed that:

> The same British officer figured in another murder, a fact I knew from a description of him given to Volunteers by the Carroll family, and from clues at the time. An old man named Carroll kept a locksmith's shop in Stoneybatter, a working class quarter of the city. He had two sons, active Volunteers. Carroll had a visit from a British Army officer who warned him that if his sons did not surrender at the Castle before a given date he would be shot. Carroll was found shot dead in his shop later. On his body was pinned a card: 'Spies beware, I.R.A.' Tobin brought me a slip of paper and on it was written in Collins' writing: 'Concentrate on Hardy'. That was the name of the killer. MacNamara and myself knew this man well. He was an Orangeman, with an artificial leg, on the Castle garrison and was an Intelligence Officer in the Auxiliaries and a very hostile killer.

In the aftermath of O'Carroll's killing, the lord lieutenant directed the Dublin City coroner not to hold an inquest, as a military inquiry was to be held. Members of the O'Carroll family refused to recognise the inquiry and did not attend. Annie O'Carroll wrote a letter to Dublin Corporation expressing her views:

> About 1.50 am on Saturday the 16th inst. my husband Peter O'Carroll was murdered by members of the Army of Occupation, Not content with this they placed a label on his body which maligned the living and defamed the dead. Myself and members of my family have been notified to attend an inquiry which is to be held by this same Army of Occupation. I cannot see my way to recognise this inquiry. As a citizen of Dublin I now demand that an inquest be ordered by the City Coroner in the usual way, or failing that, an inquiry be held by the Corporation whose members represent the people of Dublin. I seek not vengeance I only ask for justice and truth, trusting there is yet civilisation enough left to have my demand granted.

The O'Carroll family was informed that if nobody was available to identify the body as part of the military inquiry it would remain in the mortuary of the Richmond Hospital unburied. Due to this some members of A Company, 1st Battalion, Dublin Brigade took matters into their own hands. Liam O'Carroll recalled that:

> We entered the hospital, held up the hall porter and demanded the keys. He gave us the keys, at the same time informing us that there was no need for a hold-up, that he had just received instructions that, if anybody called for the remains, they could be handed over.

The military inquiry returned the cause of death as 'shock and haemorrhage resulting from a bullet wound inflicted by a person unknown who committed wilful murder'. Peter O'Carroll's funeral to Glasnevin took place on 19 October accompanied by a large procession. The Dublin Brigade IRA and Gaelic League were amongst those represented with Michael Staines also in attendance. He was buried alongside three of his children who had died as infants. His widow, Annie, died in 1954 and was buried in the same grave. In 2014, the story of his death was explored as part of the BBC television programme *Who Do You Think You Are?* by his grandson, actor and comedian, Brendan O'Carroll.[10]

16 October 1920   **Civilian**
William Robinson   *RG 61, Garden*

William Robinson from 47 Stafford Street in Dublin was a well-known
member of Jacob's Football Club and a British army veteran. William had
enlisted in the Royal Irish Fusiliers in 1911 being sent for a short period to
India, before being discharged in 1915. He was described as an 'honest, hard-
working, sober and respectable man'. On the night of Friday 15 October 1920
he was standing with a group of men on the corner of Capel Street and Mary
Street. Just before midnight, two men dressed in civilian clothes approached
them and asked what they were doing. The group replied that they were just
talking and were further questioned by the two men who identified themselves
as members of the Republican Police. Robinson sarcastically told them that
he could show them proof in writing that he was a Sinn Féiner if they wanted
to follow him across the road. Shortly afterwards three shots were fired and
Robinson fell with wounds to the leg and abdomen. Robinson's friends then
chased after the shooters losing sight of them at the Bridewell. They carried the
wounded Robinson to the Jervis Street Hospital where he died of his wounds
some twenty-one hours later. Remarkably, Liam O'Carroll, whose father Peter
was also shot in strange circumstances on the same night in nearby Manor
Street, heard the shots that killed William Robinson *(see above)*. William
Robinson's funeral took place to Glasnevin on the morning of 21 October, his
wife and four young children followed his coffin. His nephew, also William
Robinson, was fatally wounded at Croke Park on Bloody Sunday one month
later *(see 22 November 1920).*[11]

18 October 1920   **Irish Republican Army**
Thomas O'Rourke   *UF 89½, Garden*

On the evening of Sunday 17 October 1920 members of the Auxiliary Division
RIC carried out a raid on the Banba Hall, in Rutland (Parnell) Square searching
for those they believed were responsible for the death of Sgt Daniel Roche of
the RIC. Roche had been shot dead earlier that day on the junction of Capel
Street and Ormond Quay while he was in the city to identify the body of Seán
Treacy who had been killed three days earlier. This raid on the Banba Hall
resulted in the deaths of two people, one of whom was Thomas O'Rourke.

O'Rourke, of 5 Peter Street, Dublin, was employed at the nearby Jacob's
Factory until the 1916 Rising when he participated in the rebellion as a member

of the Irish Volunteers. Joseph O'Connor, company commander of A Company, 3rd Battalion, Dublin Brigade stated that O'Rourke had been a member of his company before 1916, and listed him as part of the Rising's Boland's Mills Garrison in the 1936 Roll of Honour. Following the Rising his activities and revolutionary education continued. In 1918, he was arrested for having stolen a copy of Thomas Carlyle's *The French Revolution: A History* in two volumes. Shortly afterwards he was again on trial and received a sentence of one year of hard labour for 'carrying firearms, namely a revolver' and 'carrying 32 rounds of ammunition'. On the evening of the raid on the Banba Hall, the members of the Auxiliary Division accompanied by an armoured car, approached the building and also secured its rear via Frederick Lane. A number of members of the IRA were present at the time and one of them, James Cahill, recalled the scene of confusion and panic in the building:

> We were ordered to assemble in Collins Billiard Room in Parnell Street. Later, as the place was suspected to be under enemy observation we were ordered to dismiss and re-assemble in The Banba Hall, Parnell Square. About half an hour later Mick Kilkelly and I were at the main entrance, Banba Hall, when we saw a lorry of Auxiliaries swing into the Square from the east side. Mick remained in the hallway, with the object of securing the door, whilst I rushed up the stairs to warn the remainder of the party

> In the excitement that ensued a member of the party left his revolver on the floor. I delayed a moment to pick up the revolver with the result that I was the last man coming down the stairs. On reaching the hallway I found that the party had gone towards the rear of the premises. Kilkelly had failed in finding any way to secure the door, and as was typical of the man, remained to cover the withdrawal of the other men. The Auxiliaries, unaware that the door was unlocked and unbolted, were endeavouring to smash it in with their rifles. As Kilkelly and I withdrew a rifle-barrel was pushed through the glass panel at the side of the door.

> When we entered the dance hall, which is at the rear of the Banba, all was in confusion. A concert had been in progress and our party, rushing through the hall, caused the audience to become excited. Seats were upset all over the place and it was with great difficulty that Kilkelly and I forced our way through the crowd. On reaching the back door we found one of our men, Loughney, frantically trying to force back the bolts which had become stuck through disuse, paint and rust. Mick Fitzpatrick, an official employed in the Banba, arrived on the scene, forced Loughney away and suggested we should return to the hall and mix among the audience.

> This line of action would certainly result in a number of arrests and the loss of practically all the Company's revolvers. I in turn forced Fitzpatrick away from the door and with bleeding hands ultimately opened the door. By that time, three of our men, Mick Kilkelly, Nick Leonard and Harry Kelly, despairing of getting out by the back door, had gone back into the hall hoping to find another exit. The first two passed their guns over to two girls, who succeeded in getting out without being searched.

They were fortunate as women searchers arrived after they had left. I was the last of our group getting around the bend in the lane at the back of the Banba, and glancing back I saw a lorry of soldiers entering the lane from Frederick Street. They were about seventy-five yards distant from us but did not observe us. Before we left the Banba an order had been given to us to re-assemble at Ballybough. The last arrivals at the rendezvous brought the information that Harry Kelly had been killed immediately outside the back door of the Banba.

The exact circumstances of the death of Thomas O'Rourke are not clear. It was reported that he was moving away from the Hall in the direction of Dorset Street when he was wounded in the chest. He was taken to the Mater Hospital where he died the following day, 18 October. He was buried five days later in the grave of his grandparents. An application by his mother for a military pension was refused on the basis that 'the wounds which caused your deceased son's death were not received during military service'. He was, however, post-humously awarded the 1916 Rising Medal and War of Independence Medal for his service.[12]

24 October 1920   Civilian
James McCormack   *TC 84, St Paul's*

James McCormack (McCormick) was shot and fatally wounded just after 21.00 on 23 October 1920 at his workplace, Farrell's Fried Fish Saloon, on North Brunswick Street. John Farrell, who owned the fish and chip shop, was James McCormack's cousin and an uncle of Thomas Farrelly (*see 9 August 1920*). John Farrell had been a member of the Irish Citizen Army and had taken an active part in the 1916 Rising, serving in the North Brunswick Street area. However he was not arrested following the surrender and took no active part as a combatant in the war of the years that followed it. Catherine Farrell, John's wife, was present on the night of the shooting and witnessed it. She described what she saw:

> Two men came into the shop about a quarter or twenty minutes past nine. One man was very tall, wearing a navy blue suit and a cap. The other wore a light suit and a trilby hat. The two stood at the counter and the smaller man asked for fish, which I gave him. When I gave him the fish he went to a side door in the shop that leads into the hall. He went out just for a minute and then walked back again. The tall man then called to James McCormack who was behind the counter and said to him 'Hands Up!' He then said, 'Come out into the hall' but James said, 'Oh no, sir, I don't own the shop'. James put his hands over his head. The tall man then put his hand to his hip pocket and pulled out a revolver and fired one shot. James staggered and the two men ran out.

When the men had gone I ran out into the street and shouted 'He is shot, he is shot!' Two soldiers and a number of civilians ran in and I went for my husband. James was conscious and asked for the priest and Father Columbus arrived from Church Street and heard his confession.

James McCormack was brought to the nearby Richmond Hospital where he was tended to by the house surgeon. The bullet had entered the left side of his chest causing significant damage and he died the following morning. Little came to light regarding the motive for his death, although it was suggested by Dublin Castle that he had been shot for defying a demand made of him to stop serving British soldiers in the shop. Catherine Farrell rejected the claim and stated that no such demands had been made. It was officially recorded that 'the deceased died as a result of a bullet wound in the abdomen inflicted by a person unknown and further that his death was caused by murder committed by two persons unknown.' John and Catherine Farrell died in 1956 and 1947 respectively, they are both buried in Glasnevin.[13]

Unknown date September/October 1920   Civilian
William Straw   TB 75, St Paul's

On 25 October 1920 the body of a man identified as William Straw came to Glasnevin for burial. His story was an unusual, unclear and mysterious one. The body had been found buried in a shallow grave, a ditch near Ballyboughal in Co. Dublin, with two bullet wounds, one in the right eyebrow and one in the chest. The chain of events leading to his death began on 20 September 1920 when Head Constable Peter Burke, a member of the Royal Irish Constabulary from Galway, was shot dead in a public house in Balbriggan. Retaliation was swift and immediate. The same night a mixed force of Auxiliaries and Black and Tans travelled from Gormanston to Balbriggan and proceeded to inflict revenge for the shooting. The result was the infamous sack of Balbriggan with houses, pubs and a factory burned and damaged. Two local men Seán Gibbons and Seamus Lawless lost their lives being bayonetted to death. In the aftermath of the sack of Balbriggan local members of the IRA became suspicious of a man known as William (or Jack) Straw who had been living on Quay Street in the town for a number of months and was thought to be a British ex-serviceman, possibly from Glasgow.

John Gaynor stated that it was the local gossip that he had led the British forces around the town on the night of the burnings and pointed out homes of the Volunteers. Gaynor had seen him on the morning of 21 September standing at some smouldering ruins laughing to himself. He asked Straw what he was laughing at to which he replied 'at the fire'. Straw was captured and taken to a building off the road between Thomandtown and Gracedieu, near Ballyboughal, where he was the subject of an IRA courtmartial. After some debate and differing viewpoints on the evidence to support Straw's guilt, it was decided that he was to be shot. It was stated that Daniel Brophy and Joseph Kelly, veterans of the 1916 Rising and members of the Fingal Brigade IRA, carried out the execution.

Some years later Joseph Lawless recounted the events leading to the shooting of Straw:

Most of the beggars who travelled around selling studs and boot laces or collecting mushrooms or crab apples in season were fairly well known as individuals, but this was a stranger who appeared quite suddenly and who gave no plausible account of himself. He became known as Jack Straw, whether this was the name he gave himself or whether it was an appellation applied by the country people I do not know, but he was viewed with the suspicion that any such stranger excited at the time. After the sack of Balbriggan the story of his appearance there in company with the R.I.C. began to circulate and Volunteer Intelligence Officers began a check-up, but now it seemed the individual had disappeared. He was reported again in the district about a fortnight later, but no responsible Volunteer Officer could manage to get sight of him until one day Dan Brophy happened to be in Lusk on business – he was at the time employed as the driver of the motor van belonging to the Swords Co-operative Society – and he was told by one of the local Volunteers that the now notorious Jack Straw had passed through the town some ten minutes earlier heading towards Corduff. Brophy did not know Jack Straw by sight and so he took his informant with him in the van and in due course passed and had identified to him the wanted man. Brophy drove on to Corduff where he called to the house of the Kelly family. Joe Kelly was the Brigade Intelligence Officer. There he found his brother Tommy Kelly, whom he informed of the situation and obtained a weapon and some cord to tie up the intended prisoner, and returning on the road he had come he accosted the supposed beggar and invited him to accept a lift in the van, which he did. The prisoner was taken to Dempsey's mill at Grace Dieu, where Brophy handed him over to Willie Dempsey with very strict instructions as to his safe custody. Willie, I believe, took this very seriously, and to ensure that he would not escape tied him to one of the heavy stanchions, which supported an upper floor of the mill. Meanwhile Brophy made contact with the Brigade Commander and a formal courtmartial of the prisoner was arranged for that night at the mill. Brophy told me afterwards that he found it difficult to convince the Brigade Commander who presided on the courtmartial that the evidence against the prisoner was sufficiently conclusive to warrant his conviction as an enemy agent, but the court finally agreed on a verdict and Straw was condemned to death. The execution was carried out later by Brophy and Joe Kelly, and in the end Straw admitted that he was in fact a British Intelligence Officer and died bravely. When Brophy asked him whether he had anything to say before he died, he stood erect and folded his arms replying: 'No, when

I undertook this mission I was fully aware of what the end might be and now I accept my fate without complaint'. Jack Shields, another of the Ballyboughal Officers, had been instructed to prepare a grave in a field on the hill north of Ballyboughal near the 'Nag's Head', but when the execution party arrived late at night they found the tools were there but no grave dug. The body was therefore placed in a dry ditch and the earth from the bank above thrown in on it. Cattle in the fields, however, stamped over the fresh earth within the following day or two and so exposed the body, which was removed by a searching party of Black and Tans a little later.

His body was found on 21 October 1920 by a passer-by who saw the sleeve of a coat sticking out of the mud in a ditch. In opposition to the rumours that had circulated, the owner of the house in which he had lodged claimed that he was 'no politician' but was very friendly with the police. His remains were brought to King George V Hospital by the RIC where Dr R.J. Rowlette carried out a post mortem. It was acknowledged as being an unpleasant task as '… the body had been buried for some time and was in fact in an advanced state of decay and maggot ridden.'

The truth of who William Straw was, where he came from, why he was residing in Balbriggan and what, if any, were his political activities is not clear. Conflicting information exists regarding his background. He is reputed to have served in the Royal Navy, or the Argyll and Sutherland Highlanders, that he had served in Mesopotamia or Palestine and that he may have been wounded but his background remains a mystery. Whatever the truth, his body was unclaimed by any family member or authority and was duly brought to Glasnevin for burial in a communal grave. His details entered in the burial register as William Straw, found in a drain in Swords, result of gun shot wounds.[14]

26 October 1920   **Civilian**
John Carolan   *VC 85, St Paul's*

John Carolan (47) was shot dead during a raid on his home in Drumcondra in October 1920. His father Robert was a head constable with thirty years service in the RIC. John trained at St Patrick's teacher training college in Drumcondra and worked as a national schoolteacher before returning to St Patrick's to take a position as a professor of science and education. In 1904, he married Bridget Leavey and together they had one son, Robert. They lived at a house on Drumcondra Road, named Fernside. Dan Breen and Seán Treacy used this home as a safe house on a number of occasions during the War of Independence. Carolan, having been introduced to them by the Fleming brothers of Drumcondra Road, whose property had been regularly used by Tipperary men who were 'on the run'. IRA member Joseph Lawless recalled that:

> On the night of 12th October a message reached Flemings from Mick Collins that there might be a raid on the premises that night and that Treacy and Breen who were in town should not stay there. The Tipperary men had not yet arrived at Flemings when the message came, so the Flemings arranged alternative accommodation in case they should arrive late. Actually when they did arrive it was almost the curfew hour and they had only just time to leave again by the back gate and get to the house of Professor Carolan, 'Fernside', on the Whitehall Road where their arrival was expected. But, all unknown, an enemy agent had observed their arrival at Flemings and had tracked them to 'Fernside' where in the small hours of the morning, a strong raiding party of military accompanied by an armoured car surrounded the house.

Desmond Ryan, who later gave a dramatic account of the events of that day in *Dublin's Fighting Story*, indicated that Breen and Treacy were aware that they had been followed from the city to Drumcondra but had thought the authorities were unaware of their presence in Carolan's residence. However, at 02.00 a raiding party under the command of Maj. George O.S. Smyth surrounded Fernside and smashed the windows of the front door to gain entry. Smyth, from Co. Down, had returned to Ireland from India to work as an intelligence officer following the shooting of his brother by the IRA in Cork. Professor Carolan made his way to the front door and was questioned by the raiders who made their way upstairs. Breen and Treacy were by now aware of the raid and were intent on making an escape. They opened fire and an intense fight ensued with numerous bullets being fired by either side. With no means of escape through the house, both men decided to attempt a get away via the window of their room. A conservatory beneath the window broke their falls, while also inflicting more wounds to them. They became separated as Treacy covered Breen's initial escape but both men managed to break out through the military cordon surrounding the house and into the night.

Three people died due to the raid, all of whom were from Ireland. Capt. Alfred White from Dublin had been shot at the entrance to the room of Treacy and Breen, followed shortly afterwards by Maj. George Smyth, the commanding officer, who had been shot through the chest and lung.

The Dublin Metropolitan Police made independent enquiries into the incident but were unable to interview any members of the raiding party. The day after the raid they took a statement from Lawrence Enright, a customs and excise officer, who was lodging in the house and was sleeping in a bedroom on the top floor of the house opposite the room in which Breen and Treacy were staying. He stated that three or four men in military uniforms with flashlights entered his room:

> … one of them said to me 'don't move or I will blow your brains out'. He then kept me covered with a revolver and pulled the bedclothes off me and threw them on the floor. He then directed me to get out of bed and he then turned out the mattress and the pillows. The military turned on the electric light in the room and immediately one of the military who occupied a position opposite the open door, fell from a shot which was fired from some person outside on the landing or stairs. The man evidently in charge of the military, ordered me to close the door, which I did, and made the door more secure by placing like a chair under the knob, as there was no key. I could not see who fired the shot into the room which struck the soldier in my room as I was behind the door which prevented me from seeing anybody who might be on the landing or the stairs. As soon as the door was closed another shot was fired through the bedroom door which penetrated it. The man in charge of the military asked me how they were to get out of the room, after they removed the wounded man out of range of fire. I suggested that they use the bed sheets to assist them in dropping from the room to the ground in front, about 12 feet. The bedroom window was then opened by one of the military and the sheets were knotted so as to make a rope, but before doing so they had a conversation with other troops outside in the front garden, asking them to enter by the hall door and approach the room by the stairs. Soon afterwards the military in my room had a conversation with other military on the landing outside the bedroom door who had apparently entered by hall door from the street. I then heard several other shots fired evidently in the house. The military that was in my room directed me to open the door, which I did, and as soon as the door was open the occupier of the house, Mr Carolan, entered my room and entered into conversation with the military in it.
>
> I was then ordered out of my room on to the landing leaving Mr Carolan behind me. I went to the landing and was ordered to put up my hands and was taken charge of by one of the military party. My back was to the wall and I was facing the open door of the back bedroom. I saw a military officer lying on the landing, evidently lifeless with his feet towards my bedroom door and his head towards the stairs. On reaching the landing I heard Mr Carolan being directed by the Military to enter the back bedroom. Mr Carolan walked out of the front bedroom onto the landing, followed by an officer and as he was about to enter the back bedroom a shot rang out and he fell forward across the door beside the dead officer. The shot which struck Mr Carolan appeared to come from the back bedroom, which was in darkness. The officer, or any of the military on the landing did not fire any shots. No person left the back room by the door, while I was on the landing. I was then ordered back to my room by the military who appeared then about to go downstairs. After the shot was fired out of the back bedroom, the shot that struck Mr Carolan. I heard the clashing of glass somewhere at the back of the premises. In about 10 or 15 minutes Dr Murray who lives next door arrived and I assisted him in dressing Carolan's injuries and he was then removed in the ambulance to hospital.

The bullet had entered the right side of Professor Carolan's neck fracturing the spine. The chronology of Lawrence Enright's account of events compares closely with those accounts of the raiding party at a court of inquiry in relation to the deaths of that night. Enright also gave evidence at this inquiry, however in contrast to the statement he supplied to the DMP he claimed that he had seen nothing of significance and did not mention Carolan being used to try to enter the bedroom from which shots had been fired. While in hospital, and despite being very weak, Carolan gave his statement of events to a newspaper reporter and stated his belief that it was a member of the raiding party who had shot him and that it was some time after he heard a crash of glass from the conservatory that he was wounded while on the landing opposite the bedroom.

John Carolan succumbed to his wound on 26 October 1920 in the Mater Hospital, the same hospital in which Dan Breen was being secretly treated for his wounds. Professor Carolan's funeral took place to Glasnevin on 29 October following mass at the chapel of St Patrick's College. Some 120 students and teachers followed his coffin, a further 100 joined them at the cemetery and his remains were carried to the grave by relays of students. Prominent among the many floral wreaths placed on the grave was one signed 'Mr R. Mulcahy T.D.'

The funerals of Maj. Smyth and Capt. White took place to Banbridge and Kingston-upon-Thames respectively. George Roupell, a Tipperary man and a Victoria Cross winner of the First World War, commanded the firing party at the funeral of White. Lawrence Enright died in May 1921 and is also buried in Glasnevin. Bridget Carolan died in 1964 and is buried with her husband. Charles Dalton, a member of 'The Squad' noted that following the raid enquiries were made and suspicion fell on Robert Pike, a former soldier who lived in the locality, as the person who had provided information about the movements of Dan Breen and Seán Treacy in Fernside (*see 18 June 1921*).[15]

| **1 November 1920** | **Irish Republican Army** |
| *Kevin Barry* | *A20, O'Connell Tower Circle* |

Kevin Gerard Barry was born on 20 January 1902 in Fleet Street, Dublin, the son of Thomas Barry, a dairy owner, and Mary Dowling, who were both originally from Carlow. Kevin entered UCD in 1919 to study medicine and at the same time was a member of 1st Battalion, Dublin Brigade, spending time on attachment to the Carlow Brigade. On 20 September 1920, he took part in an attempt by members of the 1st Battalion to capture weapons from a party of British

Courtesy of Dublin Cemeteries Trust.

soldiers on Church Street and was captured, being subsequently put on trial and executed.

Seamus Kavanagh, an officer in H Company, 1st Battalion, Dublin Brigade, recalled that the initial idea for the Church Street ambush began with conversation in early September 1920 between him and a member of G Company of the same Battalion, who noted that British soldiers called to Monks' Bakery every Monday and Thursday morning for bread rations. Having carried out some preliminary reconnaissance Kavanagh talked to Tom Byrne, the commanding officer of the 1st Battalion, to receive permission to carry out the operation, given that it was outside the immediate operational area of his company. Following further discussions with Dick McKee and Peadar Clancy (*see 22 November 1920*) the operation was given permission to go ahead. Kavanagh named twenty-five members of the company who would take part. On the morning of 20 September, they took up their positions on Church Street and around the bakery. Kavanagh later recalled what happened next:

> ... I took out my handkerchief and gave the signal to advance, saying 'We'll move in the name of God'. One of the others said 'Amen'. Having given the signal I looked to see if the men at 'D' were moving. They were. Kevin Barry still had his paper in front of him. Lieutenant O'Flanagan was moving along the wall, with S. O'Neill on the outside. As soon as they got in line with my party we advanced with them towards the rear and side of the lorry. Section Commander T. Staunton's party 'I' were advancing on the left front of the lorry and H. Murphy's party 'G' on the right front. The tailboard of the lorry was down. One of the Volunteers (not Kevin Barry) as a result probably of over anxiety, ran out in front shouting 'Hands up' and fired, it was now obvious we were in for a fight as most of the British troops were standing up grasping their rifles and watching us. I gave the order to fire, at the same time opening up myself. We drew our guns and charged, shooting as we ran forward. Some of the troops put their hands up, others returning the fire. I could see right into the rear of the lorry at this time and saw some of the British falling. I particularly noticed one soldier swinging his rifle to hit one of our men. I do not think he succeeded because this soldier fell almost immediately as if hit by a bullet.

> We could hear their bullets flying past and hitting off the walls and ground. The object of the attack failed, that of capturing firearms and it was realised by the Volunteers that to retire without losses was the only alternative and by keeping up steady firing succeeded in confining the troops to the lorry, thus helping in a successful retirement. As we fell back I looked all round to see if there were any casualties among our men but I could not see anyone lying around. I had noticed Lieutenant Flanagan (*Sic*) run by with his hands to his head just after we opened fire, and thought he might have been hit on the head by the soldier swinging the rifle. I learned afterwards he had been wounded in the head by a ricochet. As we left Church Street, Mick Robinson almost fell over a bicycle left abandoned by someone in the centre of the road. I can still hear his swearing heartily and Tom Kissane laughing equally heartily.

Unknown to Kavanagh at the time was that Kevin Barry had been left behind, sheltering under a lorry in Church Street. Archer Banks, a lance sergeant in the Duke of Wellington Regiment, who was the non-commissioned officer in charge of the lorry ambushed, gave his perspective of events that day at the subsequent trial by courtmartial of Barry:

> I was N.C.O. in charge of the Ration Lorry coming from Collinstown Camp, going to Monk's Bakery, Church Street. My party consisted of 6 armed men, two unarmed fatigue men and one lorry driver unarmed. I was unarmed. We were going to the bakery to draw bread. The lorry stopped just beyond the passage leading into the bakery. Pte Humphreys (*Sic*) who was armed was in the front seat next to the driver. The rest were in the back of the lorry. When the lorry stopped I got out, so did Pte Noble and Pte Smith, they were the two fatigue men. I went into the bakery up the passage to see if the bread was ready. Noble and Smith stayed behind. The bread was ready and I went back to fetch Noble and Smith I led the way back into the bakery and they followed. When I was in the passage I heard shots fired in the street. I should say there were about 10 shots fired. I then saw a man standing at the right corner of the passage facing me. I saw he had a revolver in his hand. He fired down the passage towards me. He fired about two shots. I don't know whether he hit Smith or Noble. I ran towards the bakery office, which is on the left as you enter the courtyard. I entered the office, I was immediately confronted by a man in the office with a revolver who pointed it at me. I struck at him with my fist and he struck back at me with the revolver and hit me on the head. He then rushed out of the room. There were two civilians in the room. I don't know who they were. I stayed in the room about a minute. They advised me not to go out or I would be shot. I then went out to the lorry. I obtained a rifle from Private Cleary. I don't know whose rifle it was, it was loaded. I then saw a civilian lying under the far end of the lorry. He was lying face downwards. He had a pistol in his hand. The accused now present is the man who was under the lorry. I covered him with my rifle and ordered him to come out and put up his hands. He did so. He dropped his pistol as he came out. I picked it up. I handed it to the driver to take charge of it. I did not examine it to see if it was loaded. I told the accused to get into the lorry. He did so. There were no civilians round the lorry when I came out of the bakery. We drove to the North Dublin Union Pte Whitehead and Pte Humphreys I found had been wounded. I handed over the accused to the N.C.O. of the Guard. The wounded were taken away for treatment. Pte Washington was dead in the lorry. The driver was out of the lorry. He showed me three rounds of ammunition, which he stated he had taken from the pistol. I examined them and two, I am sure, were flat nosed.

Three British soldiers died in the firefight, Marshall Whitehead, Henry Washington and Thomas Humphries. Washington was dead on arrival at the North Dublin Union, he had been shot through the mouth, the bullet lodging in his neck. He was aged sixteen at the time of his death, his elder brother William had been killed two years earlier in France. Whitehead and Humphries were taken to King George V Hospital where Sir William Taylor operated on them. Both had serious wounds to the stomach and lost a significant amount of blood. They died a short time later of their wounds. Kevin Barry was charged with all three deaths and found guilty in a subsequent trial. Aged eighteen he became the first person to be tried by general court martial and executed for a capital offence under the 1920 Restoration of Order in Ireland Act. Before his death, he gave a sworn statement of torture and ill treatment that he received in the aftermath of his arrest and interrogation. He was executed by hanging on the morning of Monday 1 November 1920 at Mountjoy Jail and was buried in the grounds of the prison. Nine more would follow to the same grave before the end of the War of Independence. In 2001, all ten men were exhumed, and nine of them, including Kevin Barry were reburied together in Glasnevin Cemetery.[16]

21 November 1920   Civilian
Jane Boyle   *BG 48½, Dublin*

Jane Boyle was born on 16 June 1891 at her parents' home, 56 Lower Baggot Street. The daughter of Jane Eustace and Thomas Boyle, her father worked as a coach-builder. At the time of her death, Jane was working as an assistant in a butcher's shop and was engaged to Daniel Byron, with whom she travelled to Croke Park to watch the matches taking place there on what would become known as Bloody Sunday. In the subsequent military inquiry into her death Daniel Byron, her brothers and sister made a statement to the court that they would decline to give evidence to the inquiry due to the fact that it was being held in-camera. Although Daniel Byron did not give evidence at that inquiry into Jane's death, he did give a short account of the events that day to the 1921 *Report of the Labour commission to Ireland* to which he stated:

> I was present at the football match, Croke Park, Dublin. I was accompanied by my fiancee. We were standing near the centre line of the ground opposite the grand stand. The match had been in progress about a quarter of an hour when I saw an aeroplane approach, hover over the ground, and then go away. Almost immediately afterwards I heard the sound of shots coming from the direction of the bridge outside the ground, and my fiancee, who had hold of my arm, was shot dead. A few seconds after this 'Black and Tans' rushed into the field through the gate near the bridge, and the people became panic-stricken. I saw the 'Black and Tans' ordering people to put up their hands. I saw no shots fired from the crowd.

In the aftermath of the shootings, medical help began arriving for the wounded and injured. One witness, present in an ambulance that was directed towards

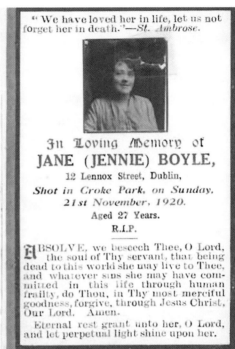

" We have loved her in life, let us not forget her in death."—*St. Ambrose.*

In Loving Memory of
JANE (JENNIE) BOYLE,
12 Lennox Street, Dublin,
*Shot in Croke Park, on Sunday,
21st November, 1920.*
Aged 27 Years.
R.I.P.

ABSOLVE, we beseech Thee, O Lord, the soul of Thy servant, that being dead to this world she may live to Thee, and whatever sins she may have committed in this life through human frailty, do Thou, in Thy most merciful goodness, forgive, through Jesus Christ, Our Lord. Amen.

Eternal rest grant unto her, O Lord, and let perpetual light shine upon her.

In Loving Memory

Courtesy of the GAA Museum.

Croke Park by the military, described his arrival there and finding Jane Boyle's body on the pitch:

> I was called out with the Ambulance to proceed to No. 11 Russell Street. On arrival at Jones Road we were halted by the Military and told to go to Croke Park Football Ground. When we arrived there we found a man inside the gates dead. We placed him in the Ambulance and saw that his leg was badly shattered. On the opposite side of the field we found a woman. She was dead. I ascertained afterwards that her name was Jane Boyle. She was placed in the Ambulance and both bodies taken to the Mater Hospital.

At the Mater Hospital Jane was identified by her brother James – she had fractures to her jaw, collarbone and ribs. The fatal injury was a bullet wound on the right side of her lower back. Her funeral, on 25 November, at St Kevin's church on Harrington Street, was attended by a large number of relatives and friends. She was laid to rest in a grave purchased by her uncle, James Eustace, in which her mother, who had died on Christmas Day 1905, was buried. Her father, who died in 1909, is buried in another family grave in the St Bridget's section of the cemetery.[17]

21 November 1920   **Civilian**
Michael Feery   *QB 75, St Paul's*

In the midst of the confusion and panic surrounding the events of Bloody Sunday at Croke Park, an unidentified body was brought to the Jervis Street Hospital. The unknown man, aged about forty, had been badly wounded in the left thigh and pelvis which resulted in the severing of his femoral artery. Five feet and six inches in height with blue eyes and a sandy moustache he was described, by an officer of the Royal Army Medical Corps who examined him, as badly nourished. The entirety of his belongings consisted of a shirt, vest, cardigan, trousers and a dark grey coat, as well as a pair of well-worn boots and a leather tobacco pouch. Most of the clothing and the boots appeared to be army issue and some were embroidered with the initials 'M.F.'. Four days passed before Bridget Feery identified the remains at the hospital as those her husband Michael Feery. In identifying him she stated:

> The last time I saw him alive was on Sunday morning, 21st November 1920, at about 12 o'clock. My husband was an ex-soldier, discharged from the Royal Marines, over a year ago. He was living with me but out of regular employment and had no work since his discharge ...

Michael Feery was born on 10 April 1870 in Dublin's Rotunda Hospital, the son of James Feery, a solicitor's clerk originally from Ennis in Co. Clare, and his wife Mary Gorman. Michael's father died in 1882 when he was aged twelve, followed by his mother in 1894. In March 1899 Michael married his first wife Anne Hutchinson, Anne had previously been married to Christopher Carr in 1892, however he had died in 1898. Michael and Anne lived at a number of addresses in Dublin and in June 1906 their son, also Michael, was born at Glorney's Buildings, off Gloucester Street in the city. Michael worked in a variety of jobs as a casual labourer, while both he and Anne took part in a side business of shebeening; producing and selling illicit alcohol. Aside from being arrested for this, Michael had some convictions for petty crimes, ranging from using profane language and loitering to the illegal possession of a pair of spectacles. Anne Feery died from tuberculosis in May 1912 at the age of thirty-eight and two years later on the outbreak of the First World War Michael enlisted in the Royal Dublin Fusiliers. Michael Feery junior went to live with his father's sister, Sarah Elston, first at Denzille Street and later Holles Street, where he remained until after his father's death. Michael senior was sent to the Curragh Camp for training with a new battalion of the Dublin Fusiliers.

While still in training news returned to Dublin that Michael's brother, Mark, who was serving on the Western Front with the Connaught Rangers, had been reported missing during an engagement in the First Battle of Ypres. Mark Feery's wife Mary died three months later leaving four children aged between six months and thirteen years. A photograph and notice placed in the *Evening Herald* over a year after he was initially reported missing stated that '... nothing had been heard of him since the battle of Mons. His wife being dead, his children and brother would be glad of any news of him'. No information was forthcoming and Michael Feery and his family were still no closer to knowing exactly what had happened to him and whether he had been killed, wounded or taken prisoner.

During the same period, Michael Feery remarried. His new wife, Bridget Campbell had a somewhat chequered past with a number of aliases, such as Olive Mills and Maggie Carroll. Michael's first phase of service with the British army came to an abrupt end in March 1915 when he was discharged after being deemed 'medically unfit' due to issues with his eyesight. The period after his discharge included admissions to the Dublin Union Workhouses and an arrest in September 1916. Soon afterwards, he left Dublin with Bridget for Liverpool where he worked temporarily as a dock labourer before enlisting in the Inland Water Transport and Docks Section of the Royal Engineers. This unit was formed to work transporting materials along canals and waterways both at home and abroad. Again Michael's time with the British army was short-lived as he was discharged after two months described as 'no longer fit'. He immediately returned to Dublin and in March 1918 enlisted once more, this time in the Royal Marine Labour Corps. One of their Irish recruiting posters described that 'Irishmen between 42 and 55 years, who are able to perform a fair day's work of hard labour, are required for the Royal Marine Labour Corps ... The work consists in loading and unloading ships either at home or in France.' Michael Feery was sent to France serving in Dieppe and elsewhere until the Armistice and was eventually demobilised in 1919. He was still wearing his army issue clothes and boots over a year later when he was killed at Croke Park. Four years after the death of Michael Feery, another unidentified body was found wearing British army clothing and boots. This time it was during the exhumation of a grave south-west of the village of Passchendaele in Belgium. The grave was marked with a cross bearing the words 'Unknown British Soldier'. Nothing further regarding the remains was known but an identity disc was found next to them. It appeared to have the surname Jury inscribed on it and a partial service number. On closer inspection it was found to be inscribed with the name 'M. Feery'. The body was that of Mark Feery, Michael's brother. Unknown to Michael and his family Mark's body had been buried by German soldiers in one of their own cemeteries following his death in 1914.[18]

21 November 1920	Royal Irish Constabulary
John Joseph Fitzgerald	*AC 64, South*

John Joseph Fitzgerald was born on 15 March 1898 in Cappawhite, Co. Tipperary, the son of a local doctor, Joseph Fitzgerald and Mary Teresa Quinlan. His father was, for most of his life, Poor Law Medical Officer for the Cappawhite dispensary district. On the outbreak of the First World War, and aged sixteen, John Joseph Fitzgerald enlisted in the British army being commissioned as an officer with the Royal Irish Regiment. Serving as a 2nd lieutenant, with responsibility for up to 50 men, he was wounded during the advance of the 16th (Irish) Division on the village of Ginchy on 9 September 1916, during the Battle of the Somme. Having recuperated he transferred to the Royal Flying Corps in February 1917, becoming a pilot with 60 Squadron. In early October 1917 while serving in Flanders Fitzgerald's plane was reported missing and he was assumed killed. However, it transpired that while flying in heavy mist he had mistaken a German airfield at Harlebeke as friendly and landed his S.E.5a fighter. He was promptly taken prisoner and his plane, a new and technologically advanced model issued to his squadron that summer, taken away for inspection by the German inspectorate for aviation. Fitzgerald was taken to a prisoner of war camp in Karlsruhe in Germany and was eventually released in December 1918 following the Armistice. After a period of leave, he resumed service as a pilot. During the Northern Russian expedition of

An identity disc worn by John Joseph Fitzgerald while he was serving with the Royal Flying Corps during the First World War. **Courtesy of Derek Jones.**

1919, also known as operation Archangel, Fitzgerald and other foreign troops participated in the Russian Civil War assisting the anti-Bolshevik White army. During this time, he was attached to a unit flying seaplanes in reconnaissance, bombing and other missions between May and September 1919 before he finally returned home and left the RAF.

Following his return to Ireland John Fitzgerald joined the RIC in June 1920, being employed as a defence of barracks sergeant. His role involved overseeing the preparation of defensive installations in police barracks in Co. Clare in anticipation of future attacks as the War of Independence progressed. He was later attached to the Auxiliary Division of the RIC as a bomb instructor. On 27 August 1920, when walking down a road whilst reading a book near Kildysart in Clare, he was held up by John Grace and Tim McMahon who were members of West Clare Brigade IRA. They were told of Fitzgerald's routine whilst in a local public house and took it upon themselves to intercept him. They captured his weapon and having told him to put up his hands, John Grace shot Fitzgerald in the leg before taking him down the road and letting him go. After some time recovering in hospital Fitzgerald took up residence at number 28 Earlsfort Terrace in Dublin to recuperate further. Whilst here, on the morning of Bloody Sunday 1920, he was shot dead by members of the IRA, under the command of Lieut Patrick Byrne of the 3rd Battalion, Dublin Brigade. Christopher (Kit) Carroll a member of the same battalion, and one of those assigned to take part in the shooting of Fitzgerald, later recounted the events of the morning at Earlsfort Terrace:

> At midnight on Saturday, 20th November 1920, I was asked by Mick Kennedy to go on a job the following morning. He told me the job was the execution of an enemy intelligence agent who resided at 28 Earlsfort Terrace. He told me that if I had any scruples or conscientious objection to going on it I need not go and that nothing the worse would be thought of me. I agreed to go. We were to bring our own revolvers and meet at the junction of Hatch St. and Harcourt St. at 8.45 the following morning, Sunday 21st November 1920.

> We assembled as arranged and each man was issued with a grenade. I was detailed to take charge of the covering party. I was to place my men at strategic points in the street and engage any enemy forces that might come along. I was to remain in position for five minutes after our attacking party had left. In my party were Joe Lynch, Jim and Kit O'Donnell (brothers), Con Conway and a lad named Jones. Paddy Byrne was in charge of the party which was to enter the house and carry out the execution. In this party were Leo O'Brien, Michael Kennedy and two brothers named Timmins. At 8.55 I moved off with my party and placed the men at strategic points. I took up position outside the door of No. 28 Earlsfort Terrace. Sharp at 9 o'clock the attacking party arrived and knocked on the door. They were admitted by a servant girl. They lost

no time in getting down to business as, almost immediately, I heard the sound of shots being fired inside the house. When the party came out Captain Paddy Byrne said to me 'Come along Kit'. I reminded him of my instructions to remain for five minutes after they had left. He said: There is no necessity for you to remain. So we all moved off together. My party was not called to action. The operation was successful.

At a court of inquiry into Fitzgerald's death the unnamed maid who answered the door of No. 28 that morning gave evidence of what happened within the house. She noted that there was some confusion on the part of the IRA group regarding the name of the person that was to be shot:

> I answered a ring at the door. There were two men outside, one asked for Mr Fitz-patrick. I replied, 'he does not live here', he said, 'Isn't he a Lieut. Col.?' I answered, 'There's no one here only Capt. Fitzgerald' and I asked if they wanted to see him. He did not reply but calling to four more men on the pavement entered the house. The leader sent one down to the kitchen and the other three upstairs. He himself remained at the door, I believe there was another outside. The leader said, 'don't be alarmed, show me his room'. I did so and about three men went up to it. I next heard Capt. Fitzgerald scream and three shots in quick succession. The party then left the house and walked away quietly.

John Fitzgerald had been shot through the right side of his neck, his chest and once through the centre of his forehead. One of the bullets had passed through his right wrist, which appeared to indicate an attempt to shield himself. His funeral came to Glasnevin on 24 November, led by the band of the RIC and followed by members of the Auxiliary Division bearing wreaths, his father, sisters and brothers. After his coffin was lowered into his grave in the South section of the cemetery the Last Post was sounded and three volleys were fired.[19]

The funeral of John Joseph Fitzgerald who was killed on Bloody Sunday. **Courtesy of Reach plc (Daily Mirror).**

21 November 1920　　　　　　　　　　　　**Civilian**
James Matthews　　　　　　　　　　　*XE 224, Garden*

James Matthews (Mathews) from North Cumberland Street in Dublin was fatally wounded in the leg during the shootings at Croke Park. The following morning, 22 November, at 9 a.m., his pregnant wife, Kate Matthews went to the Mater Hospital to identify her husband. James and Kate had married in May 1908 in the pro-cathedral in Dublin and their first daughter, Mary, was born in July. Their second daughter Kate was born in February 1911 and their third, Nancy, was born after James' death. Dr Robert Vincent Monahan who examined his body at the hospital described that he '... found on the outer side of the left leg about 3 inches above the knee joint, a small circular wound, apparently a bullet wound, and on the inner side a large ragged one about 8 inches long and 3 inches wide. There was a compound fracture of the femur and several lacerations of the muscles, nerves and arteries.' In his opinion, the latter wound was an exit wound and his death was due to shock and haemorrhage. James Matthews' funeral, along with five of the others killed at the Dublin v Tipperary match, came to Glasnevin on 25 November. He was buried in a grave in the Garden section of the cemetery. His daughter, Mary, who died four years later aged sixteen, was also interred in the same grave. Their grave remained unmarked until 2016 when, as part of a GAA project to

Nancy Dillon, the daughter of James Matthews, at the unveiling of a headstone to mark his grave in 2016. Nancy was born three months after her father was killed in Croke Park. **Courtesy of Ray McManus (Sportsfile).**

mark the graves of all those killed at Croke Park on Bloody Sunday, a newly erected headstone was unveiled on the grave. One of those in attendance was Nancy Dillon, aged ninety-five, the daughter of James Matthews.[20]

21 November 1920 — Civilian
Patrick McCormack — *UA 37, South*

Patrick McCormack (MacCormack) was shot dead by the IRA in the Gresham Hotel on the morning of Bloody Sunday as part their operation throughout the city that morning. Also shot dead in the hotel on the same day was Leonard Wilde *(see below)*. Formerly a captain in the Royal Army Veterinary Corps McCormack was born in April 1877 in Castlebar and was the son of Patrick McCormack and Kate Feeney. He was educated at Castleknock College, Trinity College Dublin and finally the Royal College of Veterinary Surgeons where he qualified as a veterinarian. Following his qualification he returned to Castlebar where the Agricultural Committee employed him. McCormack maintained an interest in horses and horse-racing throughout his life and was a member of the South Mayo Hunt and enjoyed success as an amateur jockey. He married Mary O'Connor and their only child, Grace Mary, was born in 1916. He later joined the Royal Army Veterinary Corps being given a commission as an officer due to his occupation. He was sent to Egypt where he served with the Army Remount Service, which was responsible for the purchase, training and supply of horses for the British army. Following the end of the war, he remained in Egypt and was offered a position as race starter for the Egyptian Turf Club, which he accepted. McCormack returned to Dublin in August 1920, his mother described that this trip was in connection with some work he was carrying out in purchasing a horse for a Mr Montessian of Cairo from a J.J. Parkinson. Parkinson was a breeder, horse dealer and one of Ireland's most successful trainers during his lifetime who was later made a Senator. On arrival in Dublin McCormack checked into the Gresham Hotel where he remained until his

Courtesy of Reach plc (Daily Mirror)

death. It is possible that attention was drawn to McCormack as an ex-British officer carrying his former rank within his title.

On the morning of Bloody Sunday members of D Company, 2nd Battalion, Dublin Brigade were given the task of entering the Gresham Hotel and shooting dead three men listed as suspected British intelligence officers. The small unit, of fourteen men, were under the command of Paddy Moran, who was not a member of The Squad, but was a trusted and capable leader within the IRA. The men entered the Gresham and asked to speak to the hall porter. He later recounted what happened at an inquiry into the deaths of McCormack and Leonard Wilde:

> I noticed a bunch of men muffled up about the neck and their hats pulled down over their eyes. When they got into the hotel they asked for the person in charge of the register. They said to me 'show me No's. 14, 15 & 24', so I said there was no one in No. 15. I produced the bed book and showed them no one was in No. 15. They then ordered me to take them to rooms Nos. 14, 15 & 24. I took them to No. 14 first. They tried the door and found it locked. Mr Wilde then came to the door and a few words were spoken. The next thing I heard were 2 shots. Two of the party then rushed in and some more shots were fired. They then asked me to lead them to No. 24 which I did. The door was open and they walked right in. I then heard four or five shots. They then came out and went downstairs and out of the hotel in a hurry.

Amongst those who carried out the shootings was James Cahill, who was originally from Cavan. He left a description of what happened in the Gresham that morning:

> The three groups having assembled in the vestibule, each was dispatched by the Company O.C. to its respective destination, the group of which I was a member moving off first. As we were not conversant with the layout of the hotel, I ordered the head porter to guide us to McCormack's room ... We found McCormack's bedroom door closed but unlocked. Nick Leonard and I entered the room and moved towards McCormack, who was partially sitting up in bed. He fired, the bullet passing between Nick and myself burying itself in a door jamb. We fired almost in the same instant, killing him outright.

James Cahill believed that his claim that McCormack was in possession of a weapon and was willing to use it was evidence that he was indeed an intelligence officer. James Doyle the manager of the Gresham believed differently. He later stated that '... although he had been a veterinary surgeon in the British army there would appear to have been grave doubt as to his being associated with British intelligence. While he was here, I never saw him receiving any guests. He slept well into the afternoon and only got up early when a race meeting was on. When I found him shot in his room [the] *Irish Field* was lying beside him.'

Patrick McCormack's mother corresponded with Richard Mulcahy in 1922 with the hope of trying to dismiss any claim that her son was an intelligence officer. She asked Mulcahy:

> ... if you will let me know the circumstances of my son's death or what the charges were against him. I am 75 years of age and naturally I felt deeply the loss of my only support in life, but I feel more deeply that charges of dishonourable conduct against his country should be preferred against him by people who have always known him to be a supporter of the national aspirations of the Irish people. It is only recently that an old friend let me know what was being said in reference to my son and as I have a number of important facts, which may possibly clear his name, I would feel grateful for an enquiry into the matter. Principally I rely on the point that another Captain McCormack, who lost his hand in a Clara ambush and who is reported to have sat on a court-martial at the trial of Kevin Barry, is at present in England and it is possible that my son may have been mistaken for him ... Mr J. H. Callan who is my solicitor, is a man whom I know to be very friendly disposed towards the republican movement and he examined all the effects, private documents etc. of my son and I am sure if he is questioned he will be able to assure you that nothing of an incriminating nature against the republican movement was found. My son had been appointed official starter to the Alexandria Turf Club at a salary of about £600 per year, his practice, commission on horses etc. being close to £2,000 in perspective, and as he intended going into the horse trade in a big way it was his intention to return to Cairo on 16 October but the difficulties of arranging berthage for himself and family and horses took so long that the final arrangements were not made until a few days before his death and he was to have sailed on 2nd December 1920. Mr Callan can testify to shipping correspondence. Might I mention that I am a cousin of the late Michael Davitt and a sister-in-law of the late Dr McCormack, Bishop of Galway, that in younger days I took a leading part in the 'plan of campaign' and the Land League and that my son was thoroughly Irish in his education and upbringing. I therefore find it impossible to believe that he should have been mixed up with anything discreditable and I will feel relieved beyond measure to know that you have investigated the matter and satisfied yourself that a grave mistake has been made.

Mulcahy wrote to Michael Collins regarding the circumstances of the death of McCormack. Collins in his reply stated that:

> ... you will remember that I stated on a former occasion that we had no evidence that he was a secret service agent. You will also remember that several of the 21st November cases were just regular officers. Some of the names were put on by the Dublin Brigade. So far as I remember McCormack's name was one of these. In my opinion it would be as well to tell Mrs McCormack that there was no particular charge against her son, but that he was an enemy soldier.

Mulcahy replied to Kate McCormack with a brief note that echoed Collins' statement. In her final correspondence with Mulcahy she stated that her son '...

could not have been an enemy soldier as he had been demobilised nine or ten months previous to his death'. She concluded that his death had left her 'childless and heartbroken'.

Patrick McCormack was interred in Glasnevin on 24 November in a grave in the South section. His mother, who died in 1930, is also buried in the same grave. Nicholas Leonard, one of those who shot McCormack, died in 1948 and is also buried in Glasnevin. Paddy Moran, who commanded the IRA group at the Gresham that day, was later arrested and convicted of a shooting in a different part of the city that day to which he had no connection. He was sentenced to death and executed in Mountjoy Jail (*see 14 March 1921*).[21]

Mary and Grace McCormack, the widow and daughter of Patrick McCormack.
Courtesy of Georgina Kelly

21 November 1920   **Civilian**
Patrick O'Dowd   *SD 13, St Paul's*

Patrick O'Dowd (Dowd) was born in Boyerstown, near Navan, in Co. Meath, the son of a farmer. He worked as a farmer and in April 1897 married a local woman Julia Conway. Together they lived in Boyerstown, where their first child, Patrick, was born in 1898. A short time after Patrick's birth the family moved to Dublin where Patrick worked as a bricklayer's labourer and lived at North Clarence Street. The family spent a considerable amount of time living here before moving to Buckingham Buildings in Summerhill. Patrick was shot in the head at Croke Park on Bloody Sunday and his body was taken to the Mater Hospital where his wife, Julia, identified it. His funeral took place at the Church of Our Lady of Lourdes in Gloucester Street. Aside from his relatives, a large number of his colleagues and his employer Mr Clarke, a builder based in Fairview, also attended. He was buried in a grave in which his eldest son, Patrick, who had died of influenza, was buried in 1919.[22]

21 November 1920   Civilian
Jerome O'Leary   *ZD 151, Garden*

Jerome O'Leary was born in the Rotunda Hospital in August 1910 and was aged ten when he was shot dead at Croke Park on Bloody Sunday. He was the son of Mary Jane and Jerome O'Leary, a bookkeeper. Both his parents were from Cork and met and married in 1904 while they were working in Limerick. Together they lived at Newenham Street in the city and their first daughter, Mary Angela, was born there in 1906. A second child, John, was born in 1908 but died in infancy. Shortly afterwards Jerome O'Leary senior left his job as a clerk and bookkeeper for the local council and moved to Dublin with his family where they lived at 69 Blessington Street. It was here the family remained for many years and where Jerome junior grew up. During the First World War Jerome O'Leary senior enlisted in the Royal Dublin Fusiliers and served as a quarter-master sergeant. However, he was never sent to the front and following his discharge took up a civilian position with the military accountant's office in Dublin.

After his death the body of Jerome junior was taken to the Mater Hospital where his father identified him. He had been shot through the head resulting in catastrophic injuries. Michael Foley has concluded that he was sitting on a wall behind the goal at the canal end of the football field when he was hit by one of the first bullets fired. The following year, in June 1921, Jerome's father was walking down Gardiner Place, turning onto Mountjoy Square, when three men wearing caps approached him and began firing shots at him from revolvers. The men were members of the IRA with orders to kill Jerome O'Leary senior, whom they believed to be a spy. One of them was Morgan Durnin, a section commander and member of D Company, 2nd Battalion, Dublin Brigade. He lived a short distance from the O'Leary family home and had been one of those present at the Gresham Hotel during the shooting of Leonard Wilde and Patrick McCormack (*see above and below*). After the initial shots, Jerome O'Leary fell to the ground and a further two or three shots were fired at him. Onlookers and pedestrians ran for cover as O'Leary, though wounded, managed to get up and run towards a house on the square that had its door open at the time. He sought safety within the house, No. 57, and fortuitously for him it happened to be the home of Dr James Whelan, a physician and surgeon. Dr

Whelan had been sitting in his home when his daughter decided to go out and he accompanied her to the door. The two were standing at the door when Jerome O'Leary ran up the steps towards them and Whelan, not realising what had happened, asked him what the matter was. O'Leary exclaimed, 'I am shot. My God, I have done nothing to anybody'. The doctor sat O'Leary in a chair and examined him, it appeared to him that he had escaped serious injury. In the meantime a Dublin Metropolitan Police sergeant and constable, who had been nearby, arrived at the house. They commandeered a private car and rushed O'Leary to the Mater Hospital where he was treated and recovered. Having received compensation of £700 for his wounds Jerome O'Leary senior, with his wife and daughter, left for London where they remained for the rest of their lives. The grave of his son remained unmarked until 2019 when it was marked as part of the GAA project to mark these graves, supported by Dublin Cemeteries Trust. Dr James Whelan died in 1940 and is buried in the Garden section of Glasnevin Cemetery not far from Jerome O'Leary. Morgan Durnin died in 1980 and is also buried in Glasnevin.[23]

21 November 1920 — Irish Republican Army
Thomas Ryan — *DC 86, St Paul's*

Thomas Ryan, originally from Glenbrien, near Enniscorthy in Co. Wexford, lived on Viking Road in Arbour Hill with his wife Mary Boland, who was also originally from Wexford, and his two infant daughters. An employee of the Alliance and Dublin Gas Company Thomas had joined the Irish Volunteers in 1917 and was an active member of the 1st Battalion, Dublin Brigade IRA. He took part in the raid on Collinstown Aerodrome in 1919 and worked in procuring weapons from military barracks with Peadar Breslin (*see 10 October 1922*). On the morning of Bloody Sunday Thomas was involved in an abortive attempted shooting of a suspected British intelligence officer at a house on Marlborough Road, off the North Circular Road. The intended target was not at the house raided and the operation was called off. Although a member of the IRA he was killed unarmed and as a civilian spectator at Croke Park. It is widely recounted that he was killed on the field in Croke Park while saying an Act of Contrition into the ear of the stricken Michael Hogan, captain of the Tipperary team. However, an account of his death by Hubert Joseph Murphy, a fellow member of his IRA Battalion who was also present at Marlborough Road on the morning of Bloody Sunday, stated that '... on the arrival of the British forces he escaped over the wall at the Canal end of the field. As he was proceeding along the canal he was fired on by the British and died from his wounds shortly afterwards'. The military court of inquiry into the deaths at Croke Park could not procure any evidence as to the exact place in which Thomas Ryan was found following his fatal wound. What is clear is that he died at the Jervis Street Hospital and was buried in Glasnevin on 25 November 1920. In January 1921, the British authorities issued an order to raid 56 Viking Road and arrest Thomas Ryan suspected of being an active member of the IRA. They were seemingly unaware of the fact that he was the same Thomas Ryan killed in Croke Park a few months earlier. A party of the 1st Battalion Wiltshire Regiment duly raided the house on 6 January. The only people they found in the house were Thomas' widow Mary and her sister Frances Boland.[24]

21 November 1920
John William Scott

Civilian
PH 74½, St Bridget's

John William Scott was fourteen when he was killed on Bloody Sunday 1920. His father, John Frederick Scott, and mother, Mary Chapman, married in 1905 and moved to 15 Fitzroy Avenue where they raised their family. John was born there on 9 October 1906 and was the eldest of three children. His brother, Frederick, was born in 1908 and his sister, Kathleen, in 1915. On the day of his death, John travelled the very short distance from his home to Croke Park and while there he was shot in the lower back, the bullet exiting through his chest. His body was taken to the Mater Hospital where his father identified him. He was buried in Glasnevin on 25 November in a grave in which his maternal grandmother had previously been buried. His sister, who died in 1934 from tuberculosis, is also buried in the same grave, as is his brother who died in 1994.[25]

21 November 1920
Leonard Wilde

Civilian
PC 87, St Paul's

Leonard Wilde was shot dead in the Gresham Hotel on the morning of Bloody Sunday in the same incident in which Patrick McCormack was killed *(see above)*. Born in Reading, England, in 1891 Wilde was a veteran of the First World War. He had been a student and tutor at St Michael's, a Benedictine Abbey in Farmborough, Hampshire, before joining the army. In January 1915, Wilde enlisted in the Royal Army Medical Corps at Reading and was sent to Aldershot. However, he was discharged just a week later due to poor eyesight. Six months later, he once again enlisted but this time Wilde was commissioned as an officer becoming a second lieutenant in the 1st/7th Battalion Sherwood Foresters (Notts & Derby Regiment). Sent to the Western Front in August 1915 he first joined his battalion at Ypres in trenches close to the infamous Hill 60. Wilde was evacuated, sick, in October 1915 but returned to his battalion in January 1916. He remained at the front until July when he was evacuated suffering with neurasthenia. Because of ill health he left the army and was appointed as vice consul in Barcelona in November 1916. His appointment was terminated in September 1917 in an undignified manner as he left behind him a number of significant personal debts, something that he later tried to atone for. In 1919, Wilde married Frances Rabbitts, an American from Springfield, Ohio, in Notre Dame cathedral in Paris. The ceremony was an elaborate religious one with a blessing by Cardinal Léon-Adolphe Amette, archbishop of Paris.

The exact timing of Wilde's arrival in Dublin is not clear. A letter written by Wilde, just three days before his death, gives an apparent purpose for his time Dublin:

> For some time past I have been an interested witness of the Labour Party's magnificent fight for real democracy and my object in addressing this letter to you is to beg you to be so kind as to put me in touch with those who can advise me as the best method of consecrating my life to this course. I am at present interested in the Irish question and as an eye-witness of 'George and Greenwood' administration ... From personal observation and from intimate relations with the Catholic clergy of Ireland (I am Roman Catholic). I believe it is not too late to bring into effect the Labour Party policy with regard to this country. Ireland is essentially a country of tradition-loving people and her traditions must be respected by those who govern her. My knowledge of her history might prove useful to the Labour Party and I should be happy to assist in propaganda work in England and I trust that my little quota to the settlement of Ireland may help to make the world realise that Ireland is a pillar of the Empire and Ireland is proud of her work in building and maintaining the greatest democratic Empire the world has ever known ...

Thomas Walsh, a member of Dublin Brigade, IRA, claimed that he was the one that had made the IRA aware of the name of a person that was shot in the Gresham on 21 November 1920. It is possible, given his description, that this was Leonard Wilde due to his background with the Benedictines and the reference in his letter to his connection with Irish Catholic clergy. According to Walsh there seems to have been little time to interrogate any evidence that supported the addition of this target to the list for Bloody Sunday:

Another fellow, I forget his name, he was shot in the Gresham on Bloody Sunday and it was a well-known clergyman that told me all about him. I only got it the day before and he was shot the next morning. I reported it to Collins and anything I ever reported, it was never wrong.

Interestingly James Doyle, the manager of the Gresham stated that '... Mr Wilde had been here for a considerable time before Bloody Sunday. When Archbishop Clune visited this hotel again subsequently, I mentioned the shooting to him and he told me that Wilde had been put out of Spain, that he was well-known there as a British agent.'

On the day of his death, Leonard Wilde was staying in room No. 14 in the Gresham. According to the hall porter, the party of IRA men who came to the hotel were shown to his room, which was locked, and having knocked on it Wilde came to the door and following a few words was shot dead. James Cahill, one of the Dublin Brigade present that day, gave a differing account many years later:

> Whilst proceeding along the corridor I observed a man of foreign appearance come to a bedroom door. I had a hunch that he might be one of the other two Intelligence Officers and would, if we continued on our way, take alarm, barricade himself in his room and endeavour to call for assistance. I covered him with my gun, and asked him for his name. He promptly replied, 'Alan Wilde, British Intelligence Officer, just back from Spain'. At that moment, Mick Kilkelly, whose group had been detailed to deal with Wilde, came on the scene and fired, killing him instantly. The fact that Wilde was a new arrival and probably mistook us for a British raiding party would explain his readiness to give us information regarding himself. As I moved away, I saw through a window a lorry of British soldiers patrolling slowly along O'Connell Street ...

Michael Kilkelly, in a letter to Patrick Kennedy one of the other IRA men present that day, stated that he was the *de facto* leader within the hotel that day and that Paddy Moran:

> ... also charged me with responsibility of making sure that the victims were properly creased. I am sure you recollect Moran questioning me when I came down stairs as to whether we done the job. When I said all was OK he did not believe me with the result that I had to go up stairs again with him and show him the dead bodies ...

There appears to be little evidence to support the theory that Leonard Wilde was involved in intelligence work in either Spain or Ireland. In contrast with others shot that morning, he was not brought back to England at government expense in a formal and ceremonial manner. Instead, he was buried in a grave that remains unmarked in Glasnevin.[26]

22 November 1920   **Irish Republican Army**
Peadar Clancy   *RD 35½, South New Chapel*

Peadar Clancy, born Peter, was from Carrowreagh East, Cranny, Co. Clare, the son of James Clancy and Mary Keane. A draper by trade he worked in Limerick and Cork before arriving in Dublin in 1913. He became one of the early members of the Irish Volunteers taking part in the 1916 Rising, for which he received a sentence of death, which was subsequently commuted to ten years imprisonment. He was eventually released in the summer of 1917, after which he went to work in the reorganisation of the Irish Volunteers and became an important figure within the movement. He was involved in numerous activities and operations including campaigning in the 1917 East-Clare by-election, the Strangeways prison break in 1919 and the Mountjoy break early the following year. He was also one of the leaders of the Mountjoy hunger strike in 1920.

Outside his political activities, Clancy also continued his drapery work in Dublin, opening the Republican Outfitters in Talbot Street. He became a particularly important figure within Dublin Brigade IRA and vice-commandant working closely with Michael Collins and others, including Dick McKee, in the establishment and operational activities of 'The Squad' and the Dublin Brigade's Active Service Unit.

On the evening of 20 November 1920, final preparations were being put in place for the large IRA operation the following morning. Both Clancy and Dick McKee attended a last meeting and briefing for some of those Dublin Brigade men before going to another meeting at Vaughan's Hotel. Afterwards both men retired for the night to their lodgings, the house of Seán Fitzgerald, at 36 Lower Gloucester Street. A few hours later, early on the morning of 21 November 1920 at approximately 01.30, members of F Company, Auxiliary Division, under the command of Capt. William L. King, raided the house. All three men, Clancy, McKee and Fitzgerald, were arrested and the Auxiliaries seized a number of items they suspected of being for military use including swords, equipment, clothing, a revolver target and other materials. McKee and Clancy were brought to the Company Guard Room at Dublin Castle, along with Conor Clune who had been arrested separately. Fitzgerald was transferred to Beggars Bush Barracks. Later that morning the IRA operation in the city to shoot suspected intelligence officers went ahead, followed by the infamous Croke Park shootings. That night McKee, Clancy and Clune were shot in the

Guard Room at Dublin Castle. The Castle quickly issued an official account of their deaths to journalists claiming that:

> ... The three prisoners suddenly rose to their feet and the sentry turned round on hearing the noise. One of the prisoners had a Mills' bomb in his hand, which he had abstracted from a box of bombs under a bed. This he threw at the sentry. The bomb did not explode because (unknown to the prisoner) none of the bombs had been detonated. The sentry jumped to one side and the prisoner throwing a second bomb dashed behind a pile of mattresses when the sentry fired. Another of the prisoners meanwhile had seized a rifle and fired at the other members of the guard. Both ducked behind the table, which was upset and the shot lodged in the wall. The third prisoner lifted a shovel, lying near the fire and aimed a blow at the men who were crouching behind the overturned table. The shovel crashed into the wood, but missed the men. The commander of the guard hearing the firing at this moment rushed into the room and fired. This sudden diversion enabled both his companions to rise from the table and firing together, the second and third prisoners fell simultaneously. The whole affair only lasted a few seconds.

These claims, issued by the British authorities, were disputed and according to accounts by their relatives and comrades both Peadar Clancy and Dick McKee had injuries to their bodies indicating that they had been beaten and tortured before their deaths. The injuries to Clancy were reported at the time as being:

> A bullet wound through the right temple. The bullet went through the brain and there was an exit wound in the back of the head. There were two bullet wounds on the back, one on the back of the right shoulder and one on the back of left hip. There were grazed superficial bullet wounds on the arm and forearm, probably caused by the one bullet.

The IRA suspected that Jocelyn Lee Hardy (*see 16 October 1920*) and Capt. William L. King had a hand in their deaths. Both Hardy and King had been amongst those who were due to be targeted that morning but neither were at the addresses the IRA had. King, who had arrested Clancy and McKee, was later put on trial for the murder of two civilians arising out of another incident at Dublin Castle but was acquitted (*see 12 February 1921*). The formal military inquiry into the deaths returned an official verdict that the men had died as a result of '... gunshot wounds inflicted by Aux[iliary] Div[ision] R.I.C. in execution of their duty and self defence and in preventing escape from lawful custody'.

The funerals of both McKee and Clancy came to Glasnevin on 26 November following mass at the pro-cathedral. Their coffins were draped in the Tricolour and their caps and belts placed upon them. On arrival at the cemetery, the coffins were brought to the chapel where the cemetery chaplain, Fr Fitzgibbon, recited final prayers before they were carried to a grave in the Republican Plot.[27]

Photographs of staged reconstructions taken in the guard room in Dublin Castle. The images were circulated as propangda to illustrate the British authorities claims regarding the deaths of McKee, Clancy and Clune. Courtesy of Mercier Archives.

66

22 November 1920
Richard McKee

Irish Republican Army
RD 35½, South New Chapel

Richard (Dick) McKee was born in 1893 at the home of his family on Phibsborough Road, just a short distance from Glasnevin Cemetery. He was the eldest child of Patrick McKee, a market gardener and land steward originally from Meath, and Bridget O'Leary, from Cork. Following a period living in Drumshambo in Leitrim the family returned to Dublin where they lived at Royal Canal Bank close to where Dick had been born. His father died in 1906 when he was aged twelve. McKee became an apprentice at the printers M. H. Gill & Sons, qualifying as a compositor. Like Peadar Clancy, he was an early member of the Irish Volunteers following its foundation in 1913. A member of 2nd Battalion, Dublin Brigade he served with the Jacob's Biscuit Factory garrison during the 1916 Rising. He was arrested and sent to Knutsford before being interned at Frongoch camp. Following his release, he returned to Dublin and rose within the ranks of the local Volunteer organisation becoming officer commanding the Dublin Brigade by 1918. His position within the brigade meant he was a central figure in the organisation of its operations during the 1919–20 period, including the Collinstown aerodrome raid in March 1919. Early in 1920, he left his position as a compositor with Gills turning his attention completely to revolutionary activities and worked closely with Collins in the establishment of 'The Squad' and their subsequent activities including the plans and preparations for the shootings on the morning of Bloody Sunday. Arrested with Peadar Clancy early on the morning of 21 November 1920 he was taken to the Guard Room of F Company, Auxiliary Division at Dublin Castle where, along with Clancy and Conor Clune, he was killed (*see above*).

According to the testimony of those who viewed his body before his funeral Dick McKee had suffered the most significant injuries of the three men. His sister, Maire, told Ernie O'Malley that he had wounds in both hands, along his arms and a big wound in his side as well as another in his neck. A formal description published at the time stated that McKee had:

> An incised wound below the right breast through the liver. This wound was stitched. A bullet wound on the front of the right throat. A fractured rib on the left side. There were ten skin abrasions on the face, one of which was extensive.

Following a joint funeral with Peadar Clancy to Glasnevin, both men were buried in the same grave in the Republican Plot.[28]

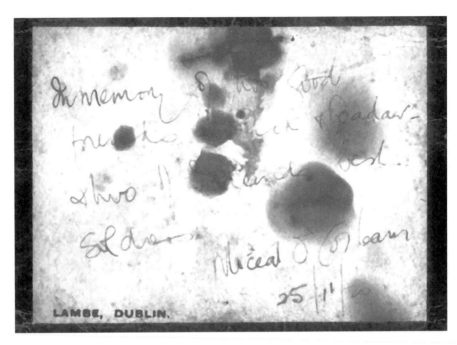

Card left on floral tribute at the grave of Dick McKee and Peadar Clancy by Michael Collins 'In memory of two good friends Dick & Peadar. Two of Ireland's best soldiers.'
Courtesy of Kilmainham Gaol Museum.

22 November 1920 **Civilian**

Michael O'Reilly *TC 87, St Paul's*

Michael O'Reilly was born in October 1904. At the time of his death, aged sixteen, he lived at 36 Temple Bar with his parents and family and worked as a messenger at Wood Quay. On the evening of 22 November 1920, Michael said goodbye to his mother Margaret and left his home for a walk with his younger brother George, aged fourteen. Together they crossed the River Liffey and were standing on Capel Street, near Grattan Bridge, where they witnessed a number of raids and searches taking place in the vicinity by members of the British army, including the 1st Battalion Lancashire Fusiliers and 1st Battalion Wiltshire Regiment. The activity attracted a crowd of interested onlookers, some of whom began jeering and booing the soldiers. George O'Reilly later recounted what happened:

> ... I went for a walk with my brother, Michael, we crossed by Capel Street and saw a lorry going up towards Parliament Street. We were then standing at the corner of Strand Street. The people in the street shouted 'Up The Rebels', I heard a shot fired and my brother dropped and then a chap carried him to the hospital. The lorry was full of soldiers wearing tin hats.

Michael was hit in the left side of the abdomen by a .303 rifle bullet that exited his body and lodged in his right arm. A number of other civilians tried to stem the flow of blood while they carried him to the Jervis Street Hospital. He was suffering badly from shock and loss of blood and although alive on arrival at 19.00, he died about fifteen minutes later. The chief mourners at his funeral to Glasnevin a few days later were his parents Margaret and Michael, his elder sister Margaret, and his brother George. A large group of his local church sodality, of which he was a member, also attended. A report by an officer of the 1st Battalion Wiltshire Regiment stated that:

> ... while investigating a charge against Pte Hampton this morning, the fact came to light that he accidentally discharged his rifle last evening while on a raid. The shot was discharged into the air while using his rifle to press back some civilians. The incident took place about 19.30 hours at the junction of Capel Street and Great Britain Street. The occurrence passed unnoticed by anyone at the time as some tenders containing Auxiliary Police who were throwing 'thunder flashes' were passing through the cordon.

The military accepted liability for Michael's death and recommended that £150 be paid to his parents as 'an act of grace'.[29]

22 November 1920   Civilian
William Robinson   *BC 86, St Paul's*

William Robinson, from Little Britain Street in Dublin, was born in 1909, the eldest child of Bridget Dwan and Patrick Robinson. He was wounded at Croke Park on Bloody Sunday aged eleven and died of his wounds in Drumcondra Hospital the following day. He was buried on 26 November, his coffin accompanied by his parents and younger sisters Kathleen and Bridget. Remarkably William was one of three members of the same family who were all civilians killed in separate incidents during the period of the War of Independence and Civil War and are buried in Glasnevin. Both his mother and father had brothers killed. Buried in the same grave with him is Edward Dwan, his mother's brother, who was killed during the Civil War aged fifteen (*see 1 July 1922*). Another uncle, William Robinson, was shot dead on the corner of Capel Street and Mary Street a month before Bloody Sunday (*see 16 October 1920*).[30]

23 November 1920   **Civilian**
Daniel Carroll   *GH 31½, St Bridget's*

Daniel Carroll died of wounds received at Croke Park on Bloody Sunday. Born in February 1889 in Co. Tipperary he worked as a grocer's assistant and lived on James Street East. By the time of Daniel's death in 1920 both of his parents were dead, his brother Denis also worked as a spirit grocer's assistant in Lucan, having only left the Dominican Order and his position as a brother a few weeks earlier. His other brother, Joseph, was employed in the Munster and Leinster Bank in Carrick-on-Suir and had returned from serving during the First World War. Having enlisted in April 1915, Joseph became an officer in the Durham Light Infantry serving on the Western Front from April 1916 and transferring to the Royal Flying Corps in 1917. Twice wounded he was also awarded a French gallantry award, the *Croix de Guerre*, whilst serving with 55 Squadron Royal Air Force. He left the RAF in January 1920 because of ill health. Daniel's sister Mary lived in Drumcondra. Having had temporary work in the Food Control Department and the Ordnance Clothing Department during the First World War, Mary found herself unemployed in June 1919 and was provided for by Daniel who gave the majority of his wages to her. Aside from spending his spare time with his sister, Daniel had few other interests or hobbies and his sister described how his only real interest outside of work was to go to Croke Park to see a football or hurling match. It was unfortunate that he was present in Croke Park on Bloody Sunday as it was unusual that he would not work on a Sunday. His employer, Martin Kennedy, travelled to the Jervis Street Hospital and visited Daniel the day after he was shot. Carroll was conscious and Kennedy recounted his conversation with him:

> He said 'wasn't it unfortunate I went'. I then asked him what happened. He said, 'I was out on the road coming home when I was shot from a lorry.' The deceased was about three years in my employment as Manager. He lived with me on the premises. I paid him a salary of one hundred and twenty pounds a year, independent of his keep. It is a custom in the license trade to get every fourth Sunday off and this was his fourth Sunday. He kept regular hours and was never out late. He was a most reliable and careful employee. His death was a severe loss to me and I will find it difficult to replace him.

Daniel Carroll was buried with his mother, Bridget, who had died in 1913. The next burial in the grave was that of Daniel's sister Mary, who died in 1963.[31]

25 November 1920   **Irish Republican Army**
Thomas Doyle   *NC 87, St Paul's*

Thomas Doyle, a member of the 4th Battalion, Dublin Brigade IRA, was aged twenty-two when he was killed on the evening of 25 November 1920 during a raid on his family home on Dolphin's Barn Street. The raiding party of Auxiliaries intended to arrest Thomas' brother, Christopher, and his brother-in-law, Patrick Byrne, both of whom were active members of the IRA and had previously served with the Irish Volunteers during the 1916 Rising. In an inquiry into the death of Thomas the officer in charge of the raiding party gave his account of what happened:

> I was in charge of a party which was ordered to arrest Christopher Doyle and Patrick Byrne. At about 17.00 hours I went to 3 Dolphins Barn Street. I knocked and entered. I was met by Mrs Doyle. I asked if Christopher Doyle or Patrick Byrne were in and she said that Byrne was upstairs. I asked if there were any other men in the house and she replied 'No'. I then went upstairs and was searching Byrne's room when I heard a shot. About five minutes later a girl came up and said a soldier was shot. I immediately went downstairs with Byrne and handed him over to someone else. I went to the back yard where I saw a civilian lying dead. Nothing could be done for him. I had only a small party and a big crowd was gathering outside. I took my party to Wellington Barracks for reinforcements. These were not available and I telephoned for a Doctor and an ambulance. I then went to the Castle to get reinforcements and returned to the house. Mrs Doyle could not be seen but Anne Doyle, her daughter, told me her brother Thomas Doyle had been killed and that the Corporation Ambulance had taken him away. She also said that a soldier in the yard shouted 'Halt, put up your hands.' The brother did not, after that a shot was fired.

The Auxiliary who fired the fatal shot stated that he had gone to the yard at the rear of the house as the raiding party arrived and noted that it was possible to leave the house via an upstairs window with the kitchen roof below. Having waited there for a number of minutes he stated that he returned to the house to warn the other members of the raiding party not to leave in their lorry without him. He stated that on returning to the yard he noticed two men climbing over walls into the yard. Having shouted a warning to the other Auxiliaries, he claimed that from the darkness he was rushed on by Thomas Doyle and having shouted 'Halt, hands up', he fired.

According to Thomas' sister Annie, her brother had been washing himself at a tap in the backyard of their house when the raiding party arrived. He had just returned home from work at the City Woollen Mills in Cork Street where he was employed as an engine man. Annie was in the kitchen when she heard somebody shout 'Hands up' followed by a shot. Ultimately the only recorded witnesses to the shooting itself were Thomas Doyle and the man who shot him. A post mortem found that the single bullet fired had pierced the front of his right lung and entered his heart, killing him almost instantly. His father identified his body and his funeral left for Glasnevin from the church of Our Lady of Dolours in Dolphin's Barn on 29 November followed by a procession including his parents, uncle, sisters and brother.[32]

29 November 1920   Civilian
James Conlan   *TA 25½, South*

James Conlan was another belated fatality of events of Bloody Sunday. A cinematograph operator aged twenty-seven, he was the son of James and Margaret Conlan and lived with his family at North Great George's Street. He was fatally wounded during an incident that evening near Westland Row in which members of the Auxiliary Division opened fire on a large group of people, resulting in the deaths of two. The exact details of the manner in which he was wounded are unclear. According to the officer in command of the Auxiliaries that evening he had received information from Dublin District Headquarters at about 21.00 that a group of about sixty men were in a drilling formation in Merrion Square. He gathered thirty of his own men and placed them in three lorries. Accompanied by an armoured car and a searchlight car they went towards Merrion Square. He later recorded his account of what then happened for a court of inquiry:

> Approaching along Upper and Lower Merrion Street I turned into Lincoln Place. In Lincoln Place I came on a party of civilians in the street in an organised formation. They were marching about. I halted the column and my men dismounted from the tenders. The crowd broke and ran in all directions. Three shots were fired in the air by my men; I don't know who fired them. My men then spread along the street and also into Westland Row and eventually to the junction of Lincoln Place and Nassau Street. I ordered my men to search every male civilian for arms or anything pertaining to the IRA. As far as I could ascertain no casualties resulted from the firing of the three shots. The male civilians were herded into groups along the street and systematically searched and as each group was finished they were allowed to go. During these proceedings a large number of people emerged from a church close by in Westland Row. The male portion of this crowd were searched, no report of arms being found was made to me. A party of about a dozen men who had been gathered from the dark Nassau Street end of Lincoln Place were lined up in the road and searched but nothing was found on them of an incriminating nature. I ordered them to get home quickly after warning them of the serious consequences likely to accrue from assembling in large numbers. They

all immediately ran down the street towards the searchlight car which was shining its lights down Westland Row. When this party commenced to run down the street several civilians jumped out from doorways at the side of the road and rushed past us in the direction in which the released men were running. About half a dozen shots were fired by my men at this party. I ordered them to stop firing and subsequently found three men wounded, two on the South side of the Street on the pavement close up to the houses and one at the junction with Westland Row on the opposite side of the street. I saw this latter man run out from a doorway in the shadow and make a dive for the street past one of my men who fired at him and I saw the man fall. First aid was rendered to the three wounded men and they were placed on tenders and taken to Mercer's Hospital. One of the wounded men while lying on the ground and evidently thinking he was going to be finished off, stated that he was an ex-soldier and had only joined the IRA under threats. The third man was too badly wounded to speak. My men were armed with revolvers and rifles. Only revolvers were fired. The man whom I saw run out of the doorway and who was shot at the end of Westland Row was wounded in the lower part of the body and was too badly wounded to speak. The man who said he was an ex-soldier had a wound in the right thigh. The third man wounded was wounded in the leg near the ankle, his wound did not appear to be as serious as the others. This was the man who stated that he had been forced to join the IRA. It appeared that the men who ran out of the shelter of the houses had evaded search and were taking advantage of the release of the others who had been searched.

No independent witness to the events that night was called by the court of inquiry into the death of James Conlan and the other fatality of that incident, William Cullinane. However, Fr O'Dwyer from Aungier Street stated that while he was with the dying Cullinane he told him that he had left the church at Westland Row following mass with a large group of people and that the men in the group were searched by the Auxiliaries there. After this they were told to run following which Cullinane was held to one side and shot. Dr Francis J. O'Donnell who treated Conlan at Mercer's Hospital noted that his right thigh had been fractured due to a gunshot wound and he had a bullet wound to his right calf. He lost a significant amount of blood. His condition somewhat stabilised but his wounds developed gangrene and he died eight days later in hospital. He was buried in a grave purchased by his mother. There appears to be no evidence to suggest that William Cullinane or James Conlan were members of the IRA.[33]

17 December 1920	Royal Irish Constabulary
Philip John O'Sullivan	*SA 27½, South*

Philip John O'Sullivan was born in Kinsale, Co. Cork on 6 August 1897 the only son of Florence O'Sullivan and Margaret Barry. Philip's father was a solicitor, a friend of Tim Healy the Irish Parliamentary Party MP, and his family was of a nationalist background. His father and uncle had founded the nationalist leaning *Southern Star* newspaper. Philip was educated at Blackrock College and had intended to join his father as a solicitor in the family practice but during the First World War he joined the Royal Naval Volunteer Reserve, serving with them as a sub-lieutenant. He had a short but eventful war serving in Italy. While engaged in submarine detection operations his boat struck a mine and sunk leaving O'Sullivan and his crew at sea on a raft for days. During the Battle of Durazzo in 1918, he volunteered to help rescue a stricken Italian ship, receiving the thanks of the Italian government and Admiral of the Italian Fleet as a result.

Philip J. O'Sullivan in his Royal Naval Volunteer Reserve uniform. **Courtesy of Jim Herlihy.**

He returned home following the war to work once again with his father and qualified as a solicitor. However, in July 1920 he decided to join the RIC and was appointed a cadet being made a district inspector in October of the same year attached to the RIC Depot as part of the Criminal Investigation Department. His work brought him to the attention of IRA Intelligence and they decided that he was to be shot. His routine was examined and on the evening of 17 December 1920, he was followed by members of The Squad on his way to meet his fiancée, Alice Moore, at Nelson's Pillar. Alice described the death of Philip:

> At about ten minutes past six on the evening of the 17th I had an appointment with Philip. I was walking down Henry Street towards the Pillar and saw Phil coming towards me, we just met, and he said something to me about hoping he was not late and I was pointing out that he wasn't at all as I was early when I heard the bang of a shot from my right and Phil fell down on his head, previously I had noticed two men in the doorway of Dowell's shop (a jeweller) who were staring hard at us and evidently watching us. The shot came from that direction. When Phil fell down at the first shot I bent over to lift him up and turn him over and a man came round from behind and pointed a revolver at Phil's shoulder as he was lying on the ground. I caught hold of the revolver and wrestled with him while he fired at the body but he got away from me and ran.

Alice had almost frustrated the attempt of the shooter to escape. Joe Leonard a member of The Squad gave a similar account of the killing:

District Inspector J. (*sic*) O'Sullivan of the Inspector General's Office was too good at decoding, so our Intelligence Officer pointed him out in company with his girl. There were two Volunteers present, one of whom was reading the Evening paper, the other shot O'Sullivan, when his girl grappled with this man, who shook her off. There was present an old flower seller sitting in the angle of a hoarding and a shop front who lifted O'Sullivan's head on her lap and was saying 'My poor boy, they have shot you' and then sensed there was a strange atmosphere around her, dropping his head on the pavement she waddled away, not praying. The Volunteer reading the paper had to be chucked by the sleeve to remind him it was time to be going, he said he never heard the shots.

O'Sullivan had been shot in the head, neck, leg and back. The bullet that entered through his left eye and exited through the right temple doing considerable damage. He had been due to be posted away from Dublin to Gorey in Wexford two weeks after his death. He was buried in a grave alongside his grandfather Dominick Barry who had been an inspector in the RIC and had died in 1907, aged seventy-three. Shortly after the death of their son, the O'Sullivans left Cork for Dublin where they remained for the rest of their lives.[34]

The coffin of Philip John O'Sullivan being carried into the mortuary chapel at Glasnevin. **Courtesy of Reach plc (Daily Mirror).**

1921

10 January 1921   **Civilian**
James Farrell   *KA 11, South*

James Farrell of 11 Prebend Street, Dublin died, according to a military court of inquiry, as a result of 'shock and haemorrhage following a wound from a bullet fired by a member of the Auxiliary Police Force whilst on duty and in self defence.'

Farrell, who was unmarried and lived with his brother, was a British army veteran of the Second Anglo-Boer War who enlisted again for service in 1917 in the Army Veterinary Corps. Having left the army, he returned to Dublin where he worked as a labourer at Broadstone railway station. Farrell became unemployed during a strike by boilermakers at Broadstone and came into casual employment, making use of his experience with horses during the First World War. One of those who employed him was Thomas Connolly, from Temple View, Broadstone, who owned a cabinet making works at Red Cow Lane and Farrell looked after his horse.

On a dark evening at about 19.00 on 10 January 1921, both men were present on North Brunswick Street when Farrell was shot dead and Connolly badly wounded. Thomas Connolly later stated to a member of the Dublin Metropolitan Police that he was walking with Farrell towards his place of business when he heard a gunshot and his companion fell. Connolly turned to see a man dressed in a fawn coloured coat and cap who then fired at him. The bullets hit him in his lower jaw, left shoulder and grazed him on the scalp. He staggered to the pathway on the other side of the road and fell. He claimed that the man in question then followed him and placed a revolver in his hand, which Connolly threw at him, before his assailant was bitten on the trousers and chased away by Connolly's terrier dog that had been accompanying him.

The DMP made enquiries in relation to the incident with I Company of the Auxiliary Division, RIC who were stationed at the North Dublin Union. The commanding officer of the company, Maj. Edward Lawrence Mills, had been placed on leave due to being in command of the mixed force of Auxiliaries and Black and Tans that had taken part in the shootings at Croke Park in November 1920. So the DMP were met by their Intelligence Officer, Capt. Herbert James

Beach who stated that following the report of the incident he made his way to North Brunswick Street where he saw the body of Farrell. Here he met D.I.3 Charles Edgar Vickers, at that time in command of No. 3 Platoon of I Company, who handed him a Smith and Wesson revolver containing one spent cartridge and four unused, which he stated he had found in the hand of James Farrell. The DMP then interviewed another member of the company, whose name was not disclosed to them, but who was present at the scene alone and stated that while undertaking confidential work two men were walking in front of him. He claimed one of them turned and fired a shot at him followed by the other who also opened fire. The Auxiliary said he returned fire on the two men in front of him, who were part of what he deemed to be a group of eight, and fired six shots. Farrell fell dead on the street with one bullet wound to the head and one to the chest. Connolly ran away and the Auxiliary claimed that others present then fired on him and he ran back to his barracks at the North Dublin Union. On reporting the incident, other members of I Company subsequently attended the scene of the shootings.

The police searched the houses of both men and found no incriminating material, no evidence was found in their clothing, and no other witnesses to the shooting could be located. The strong belief locally at the time, and relayed by newspaper reports, was that both men were not involved in any political movement and that their shootings were not justifiable. Two days after the shootings Charles Edgar Vickers was demoted to temporary cadet and his platoon was broken up. It is not clear if the killing of Farrell precipitated this action. The shooting also coincided with a complaint made by Áine Ceannt, the widow of executed 1916 Rising leader Éamonn Ceannt, who claimed that a group under the command of Vickers had stolen from her during a raid on her house in December 1920. Vickers was later court-martialled in relation to that incident and found not guilty of the charges. In February 1921 an officer on behalf of the deputy adjutant general at General Headquarters for Ireland wrote to the under-secretary for Ireland regarding the shooting of James Farrell and stated that: 'I am commanded to draw your attention to this case which does not appear very satisfactory.'[1]

14 January 1921   **Civilian**
William McGrath   *QF 56½, Garden*

William McGrath, a barrister, was shot in his home on North Circular Road in Dublin early on the morning of 14 January 1921 when a group of armed men broke through his front door and confronted him. Born in Portaferry, Co. Down, McGrath had originally worked as a journalist for the *Belfast Morning News* and later the *Freeman's Journal,* while also acting as the Dublin correspondent for the *Daily News* in the early 1900s. He left journalism when called to the Bar and worked as counsel for Dublin Corporation and other local public bodies. Due to his work he represented Dublin Corporation at the inquests for the infamous shootings at Portobello Barracks during the 1916 Rising and also the death of Thomas Farrelly *(see 9 August 1920).* He had been politically active in the 1912–14 period during the campaign for Home Rule and spoke at meetings of the Young Ireland Branch of the United Irish League but it was stated that he had taken no further part in politics following that time. However, he defended a number of prisoners who faced military trials by courts martial during the War of Independence. At the time death, he was working as chairman of the Court of Referees in the Ministry of Labour. Specifically he was involved in adjudicating in disputes relating to payments, known as 'the donation', to recently demobilised ex-servicemen of the British army. William's daughter, Maeve, described how, on the morning of her father's death, the family was awoken by loud noise:

> We heard violent knocking and banging at the front door. A few minutes later it was burst open. By this time we were all out of our beds and out on the landing. We heard the noise of men in the hall. Mother and I did all in our power to prevent daddy going down. But he did go and as he reached the last landing and was at the top of the first flight of stairs leading from the hall, five shots rang out. We afterwards found that four of them had struck him. Not a word was said and nobody saw the men in the darkness but with the light on behind him and above his head he was clearly revealed the moment he stepped on the landing. Then came the shots, he fell and the men decamped.

William McGrath's son, Donal, was also present that morning and woke a few minutes after his sister:

> I woke up about 1.30 a.m. hearing my mother and sister telling my father not to go downstairs. I called out from bed 'What's wrong?' and my mother replied, 'Someone has come in through the front door and is in the hall' or words to that effect. My mother came into my room and said 'He's gone downstairs' meaning my father. My father called out twice 'Who's there?' The light was on the landing and it was dark downstairs. I immediately heard a succession of shots downstairs, I should say about 9 or 10. We found my father sitting down on the lowest stair of the top flight. We carried him upstairs to his bedroom. My father had always a most peaceful life and had practically no enemies. He said in my presence soon after we carried him up, in answer to my mother's question, that the only reason he could have been attacked was because of the spitefulness or enmity on the part of ex-soldiers from whom he had disallowed donations. He had no connection whatever with politics.

There seemed to be no clear and obvious motive or suspect for the killing but it appeared that William McGrath had been specifically targeted. Another of those present in the house that morning stated that, 'It was neither a raid nor a robbery, they came to kill him and they did so. If he had not gone down stairs I believe they would have gone up.' William McGrath was shot in the chest, both legs and the hand and died from shock and haemorrhage. His killing bore similarities with that of Peter O'Carroll (*see 16 October 1920*) and members of the public were shocked at how such a killing could be carried out with impunity during the hours of curfew.[2]

20 January 1921	**Royal Irish Constabulary**
Tobias O'Sullivan	*CK 329, St Bridget's*

Tobias O'Sullivan, a district inspector with the RIC, was shot dead in Listowel, Co. Kerry in January 1921 aged forty-three. By the time of his death, O'Sullivan had amassed over twenty-one years of service with the RIC, joining in 1899 and rising through the ranks. He became a sergeant in 1912 and in 1920 was made a head constable in recognition of his part in the defence of an attack on the barracks at Kilmallock in Co. Limerick. On 28 May 1920, a force consisting of some 100 men of the IRA attacked the fortified barracks at Kilmallock. The men of the RIC were under the command of O'Sullivan and defended the barracks against a long and sustained attack which lasted for many hours throughout the night and burned out the barracks. The attack resulted in the death of Thomas Kane (*see 28 May 1920*) and another member of the RIC. One member of the IRA, Liam Scully, had also been killed. Five members of the RIC survived unscathed, including Tobias O'Sullivan. The attack on the barracks and the resistance put up by the members of the constabulary brought much attention. As well as being promoted O'Sullivan was also awarded the Constabulary Medal for gallantry.

In September 1920, just four months after the Kilmallock attack, O'Sullivan was again promoted and sent immediately to Listowel in Kerry. The RIC in the area was in disarray following the mutiny that had taken place that summer amongst its members in its barracks. O'Sullivan was sent to assist in taking control of the situation and to return the RIC to a position of authority within the area. The destabilisation of the police in this area had been a major coup for the IRA and O'Sullivan's new role, as well as his actions in Kilmallock, made him a target. Con Brosnan, the man who shot O'Sullivan dead, recollected the events leading up to and the day of his death:

The Royal Irish Constabulary survivors of the attack on Kilmallock barracks in which Thomas Kane was killed (see 28 May 1920). *Pictured in the centre is Tobias O'Sullivan.* **Courtesy of Getty Images.**

About the end of December or early in 1921, our Company Captain attended a Battalion Council meeting at which the battalion O/C [Officer Commanding] read an order he had received from the Brigade O/C, Paddy Cahill, to the effect that District Inspector O'Sullivan was to be shot for his part in defending the barracks at Kilmallock and the shooting of Scully. The Battalion O/C asked for volunteers for the job from each Company Captain present. Some time elapsed before anyone volunteered. Eventually, I with three other members of this company, named Jack Ahern (1st lieutenant), Daniel O'Grady and Jack Sheehan volunteered to carry out the job. Having volunteered for the job we discussed the details and the best time and place to carry it out with William O'Sullivan, our Company Captain, and members of the Battalion Staff. It was agreed between us that the best place to shoot O'Sullivan was in the town of Listowel. We had been informed of his regular movements by a number of scouts in Listowel who had been put on his trail as soon as the order was received.

Jack Ahern, Dan O'Grady and I were issued with a revolver and about seven rounds of ammunition each, while Jack Sheehan was detailed to act as scout for the occasion. We received the revolvers a couple of nights before the shooting and had a practice shot each the same night to test the effectiveness of the ammunition. Jack Ahern stayed at my house the night before. The following morning I cycled into Listowel and went into the public house of a Miss Stack which was only a short distance from the RIC barracks but on the opposite side of the street … Eventually the District

Inspector left the barracks and crossed the street directly opposite as was his custom. Sheehan immediately proceeded to walk in a line with him on the other side or the barracks side and arrived at the point opposite the window which was about 100 yards from the barracks. In the meantime O'Sullivan met someone on the path as soon as he had crossed over and stood for some moments in conversation with him, with the result that Sheehan had arrived opposite our window some time before O'Sullivan. Sheehan returned towards the barracks and once again returned to the spot opposite the window, this time O'Sullivan was outside the window.

We were sitting side by side inside the window. O'Grady and I immediately stood up and went into the street followed by Ahern. O'Grady and I opened fire together and fired about four shots each while Ahern fired about six. O'Sullivan lay dead on the pavement.

With Tobias O'Sullivan at the time of his death was his son, John, who witnessed the shooting. He had turned four the previous week. Four of the bullets fired hit Tobias O'Sullivan, he had been shot once in the face, once in the back of the head, once in the chest and once in the right arm. His body was brought to Dublin for burial and on 24 January 1921, following a service at St James' Catholic church, the funeral cortege followed a two-mile route to Glasnevin Cemetery. Members of the Auxiliary Division Royal Irish Constabulary led the cortege. The coffin, carried on a gun carriage and draped in the Union Flag, followed. General Henry Hugh Tudor came directly behind along with other officials and members of the O'Sullivan family including his widow and two sons, John and Bernard.[3]

22 January 1921	Irish Republican Army
Michael Magee	*BJ 320½, St Bridget's*

Michael Magee from 20 Ostman Place was one of the first members of the Irish Volunteers following their foundation in 1914. He fought during the 1916 Rising in the North King Street area, as part of the Four Courts Garrison, and was arrested and interned in Frongoch. After he returned to Dublin, he was selected as one of those to make up the new No. 1 Section Active Service Unit of the IRA, whose members were paid an allowance and focused solely on their revolutionary activities. On the morning of 21 January 1921, the unit, under the command of Lieut Frank Flood, took up position in Drumcondra to ambush a RIC lorry that travelled in that direction each morning from Gormanston Camp to Dublin. This ambush resulted in the death of Michael Magee and the eventual executions of four other members of the IRA (*see 14*

March 1921). Diarmuid O'Sullivan, one of the members of the Active Service Unit present that day, described how events unfolded:

On the 21st of January 1921, No. 1 Section was detailed to take up positions at Binns Bridge, Drumcondra, at 8.30 a.m. and to ambush a party of Black & Tans which usually came into the city at that time from Gormanstown. We took up positions as ordered, two of our sections at the corner of Belvedere Road, two at the corner of North Circular Road, Tommy (B)ryan (*Sic*) and myself at Leeche's public house and two on the far side of the bridge on the short road that leads in the direction of Croke Park and two at Fitzroy Avenue. The Section Commander's instructions for the attack on the Tan lorry were that the lorry was to be allowed pass through our first pair of men and when it came in line with the pair located on the north side of Binns Bridge they were to open fire on it. We were all to fire simultaneously likewise when it came abreast of our positions. The entire section remained in position until 9.30 and as no Tan lorry came our way within that time the Section Commander decided to withdraw to a position further down the Drumcondra Road in the vicinity of Clonturk Park. His reason for moving to the new position was that as the day was advancing at this time pedestrians on their way to work were becoming pretty numerous and he did not want to endanger their lives unduly. He considered that Clonturk Park area was less populous. As we were on our way to take up our new positions the Tan lorry that were waiting on passed us by. We could do nothing at the time as we were out in the open. Despite our disappointment, however, we did take up our new positions in anticipation of further Tan lorries coming our way. Tommy Brien (*Sic*) and I were at the corner of Richmond Road. The remainder of the section were behind a stone wall running along in front of Clonturk Park … After a quarter of an hour's wait in our new positions, the Section Commander decided that it would appear that there was nothing doing for that day and that consequently we were to disperse. We assembled in a group at the top of Richmond Road and we had no sooner done so when I saw a military van approaching from the direction of Whitehall. As the van came abreast of where we were assembled I threw a grenade into it. I believe we caused fatal casualties. Almost simultaneously with the arrival of the van we noticed that an armoured car and a few lorries of military were coming in our direction from the city and another armoured car and some lorries were also approaching our position from Whitehall direction. It was clear to us then that someone must have summoned the aid of the military and Tans as the place seemed to be surrounded. We saw there was nothing for it but to get out as quickly as we could, so we made our way down Richmond Road in the direction of Ballybough with the intention of cutting across country towards Clontarf. As we reached the junction of Gracepark Road we saw two tenders of Black & Tans approaching us from the Ballybough direction. We wheeled up Gracepark Road and into Gracepark Gardens. At that time Clonturk Park was open country. A Lewis gun which had opened fire at some of our section crossing Clonturk Park could have brought us under fire. In fact, one of our men, Magee, was killed as he was trying to get away. On reaching Gracepark Gardens, Frank Flood drew his revolver to burst open the lock of one of the houses which we had intended passing through out to the back and escaping to the fields around the Blind Asylum. The lock of the door jammed and the two tenders of Tans drew up in front of the porchway in which we were standing and Frank Flood surrendered. Five of us were immediately taken into custody and brought to the North Dublin Union.[4]

While they waited the men of the ASU had raised suspicions and Dublin District Headquarters had received the information that an ambush was going to take place in the area. Members of F Company, ADRIC, were dispatched with two lorries and an armoured car to search the area. On arrival in the area they were also warned by the RIC lorry that was the original target of the ambush of what was ahead of them as they continued towards Drumcondra. The Auxiliaries were under the command of Maj. W.L. King, a decorated veteran of the South African Infantry during the First World War who would later be implicated in the shooting of James Murphy and Patrick Kennedy (*see 12 February 1921*). He gave his own account of the events that followed:

> On reaching the allotments (opposite St Patrick's School) which is bounded by a low wall a shot was fired. I saw two men running away from the wall and I fired at one of them with buckshot, he fell, immediately got up and commenced to run. At this moment several shots were fired from the direction of the further side of the allotments. The fire was returned by my men and the man who I had fired at, fell and remained on the ground. One man got away into the houses, I ordered the 'cease fire' and advanced in open order across the allotments after sending parties around the flanks to search the houses in the vicinity. The wounded man was placed on the tender. Two detonated bombs were found on the ground in the line of his flight. I subsequently received a report from a member of I Company Auxiliary Division RIC stating that a patrol of his company had arrested 5 men who had run across the field and that they were in possession of revolvers and bombs.

Michael Magee had been wounded by King's initial shot and having stood again was wounded multiple times as the other members of the ADRIC opened fire. The other member of the ASU that King had spotted was Seán Burke as he attempted to help Magee. However, Burke quickly made his escape having realised that his case was hopeless. The patrol from I Company ADRIC under the command Lieut Charles Thomas intercepted the other members of the ASU at Gracepark Gardens and arrested five, Frank Flood, Patrick Doyle, Thomas Bryan, Bernard Ryan and Dermot O'Sullivan.

In the meantime, King and members of F Company, ADRIC carried Magee to one of their lorries. Badly wounded but still conscious he was questioned and gave the Auxiliaries the names and addresses of six of those that had been involved in the ambush including Seán Burke whom he described as the escaped man and explained that he could be found at the Oxford Billiard Room. Magee was then transported to the King George V Hospital. He was immediately brought to the operating theatre where Lieut Col Francis J. Palmer of the Royal Army Medical Corps from Donnybrook examined him. Palmer noted that he had lost a significant amount of blood and that he had gunshot wounds to both thighs and 'considerable smashing of bone'. A double amputation of his legs was required but Palmer considered that it would almost certainly be fatal and instead cleared what he could from the wounds. Nonetheless, Magee died of his wounds the following morning at 07.20. His funeral arrived to the cemetery on 26 January following mass at the Church of the Holy Family, Aughrim Street and he was buried in a grave purchased by his father. In the aftermath of the Drumcondra incident Robert Pike was suspected by members of the IRA of being involved in alerting the authorities (*see 18 June 1921*).[4]

30 January 1921	**Royal Irish Constabulary**
Peter McArdle	*DC 28, South*

Peter John McArdle was born in 1878 in Ballincollig, Co. Cork, the son of Michael McArdle and Jane Joyce. His father was a member of the RIC from Monaghan who was stationed there and when Peter turned eighteen he also joined the police. Posted first to Limerick he was promoted to sergeant in 1905 and was transferred to Roscommon in 1915. On the evening of 5 January 1921, Sgt John Cawley based at Strokestown RIC Barracks heard a number of shots and with some constables rushed to see what had happened. Not far from the entrance to the barracks, he found Sgt McArdle wounded and lying on the ground. He had been shot twice in the right leg but was still conscious and was brought into the barracks. There are conflicting accounts in relation circumstances of the shooting of Peter McArdle. Martin Fallon of the 3rd Battalion, North Roscommon Brigade, IRA stated that:

> Around this time there was stationed in Strokestown a Sergeant Hopkins of the RIC. Hopkins was a much-wanted man by our side and we were all anxious to get a shot at him. He had made himself notorious by his ill-treatment of our members that were made prisoners by his side ... I knew Hopkins, he was a man of 40 years of age, 6 ft. or over in height. He had steel grey hair and a moustache. One night while I was away in Ballinameen some of the column, with my consent went into Strokestown to see if they could get Hopkins. Jim Casey took charge of this party and, on entering Strokestown, they split up in parties of two or so to scout the different streets and premises for their quarry. Volunteer Brehon, who accompanied Casey, went into a publichouse next door to the barracks. This was at 8 p.m. and curfew was at 9 p.m. Brehon spotted a Sergeant of the RIC in the publichouse. He looked at him and decided he was the man they were looking for. Brehon called for a drink and, having consumed it, came out to Casey and told him that a man answering to Hopkins' description was inside. Casey said that he would know him when out the door walked the man. Casey said, 'It

is him all right'. There were no lights on the streets at this time. They opened fire on the man and shot him dead against the wall just as he was going to enter the barracks. It was the wrong man they had shot. It was Sergeant McArdle who had only come to Strokestown a short while before and against whom nothing out of the ordinary was known. Strange to relate, Sergeant McArdle answered the description of Sergeant Hopkins in every way except that he was at least 10 years older, and, stranger still, the RIC or Tans did not carry out any reprisals for his death. Hopkins was never got and served on until the RIC were disbanded.

Seán Leavy who was the commanding officer of Martin Fallon's battalion gave a different account of the death of McArdle:

On the 5th January 1921, Fallon took a portion of the column to Tarmonbarry with the intention of ambushing a patrol of police there. They could not find a patrol, so they attacked the barracks there and wounded two R.I.C. men. The garrison was strengthened by Black and Tans who were in large numbers in the country by now. The column had no casualties. The remainder of the column went into Strokestown under the Battalion O/C, Doherty, and I accompanied this force. It was our intention to hit up a lorry load of the enemy who usually went out of barracks and would be returning about this time. We had information that the lorry was out and expected to have a crack at it. We posted out men in the different streets and also men to go in to the publichouses and shoot the British that might be in them and collect what arms they had on them. We opened fire on it as it went through, but I doubt with an effect. Sergeant McArdle of the R.I.C. lived next door to the R.I.C. barracks and apparently, on hearing the firing, left his house to enter the barracks. As he had his hand on the barrack door, one of our lads went up to him and shot him.

Luke Duffy, another Roscommon IRA volunteer gave a similar account to that of Leavy. Peter McArdle was transferred to Dr Steevens' Hospital in Dublin where he died of complications associated with the wounds. Dr Robert J. Ogden who cared for him was of the opinion that '… death was due to pneumonia. I do not think that the deceased would have developed pneumonia, if he had not received the gun shot wounds'. His father, who had retired to Dublin in 1903 with the rank of head constable, organised for the burial of his son to Glasnevin.[5]

3 February 1921   Royal Irish Constabulary
Michael Doyle   *KF 220½, Garden*

Michael Doyle was one of eleven members of the RIC killed during the Dromkeen ambush in Limerick in February 1921. Born in Dublin in July 1889 he had served during the First World War as a 'rough rider'. In April 1920, he was one of a flood of former servicemen recruited to the RIC by Cyril Francis

Fleming, who would become known as 'Black and Tans'. In December 1920 he was sent to Limerick and was present there the following February when a mixed patrol of RIC, including Black and Tans, were ambushed by members of the East and Mid Limerick Brigades of the IRA at Dromkeen resulting in the deaths of the majority of the RIC patrol. John M. MacCarthy, a member of the East Limerick Brigade who was present that day, gave an account of the ambush that was published some years later in *Limerick's Fighting Story:*

> Hardly had the signal been amplified to indicate that the number of vehicles was two, than the first of them appeared around the road bend and it was quickly followed by the second, about fifty yards distant. Orders had provided for fire to be opened when the first of whatever number of lorries might comprise the convoy took the turn at the road-junction. In the event, fire was opened a few seconds before this occurred, due probably to the difficulty in judging the exact moment of the leading lorry's arrival at the road-fork ... After the opening volley, the first lorry continued along the short distance which separated it from the road-junction. To the occupants of the command post it gave a feeling akin to what must be the reaction of riflemen in a trench when confronted by a tank charging directly upon them. The lorry towered to a huge size in the eyes of the command post garrison as it thundered down the sloping road almost on to the muzzles of their rifles. Would it maintain its course and crush them in a sickening crash into the ramshackle cottage? Would its driver survive long enough to avoid the crash and take either the left or the right turn? Amazingly he did survive despite the point-blank volleys which struck his lorry from the front and both sides. Confronted by the barricades as he was taking the left-hand turn on the usual route to Dromkeen station he swerved violently to the right in an effort to take the other turn. Faced there by the second barricade, the lorry struck both it and the fence adjoining the house. Thrown, or having jumped clear, the driver, who happened to be the district inspector and another policeman, reached the adjoining field, unharmed. Aided by the fact that they alone among the R.I.C. were wearing their civilian clothes, they succeeded in making their escape, and eventually proved to be the only survivors of a total police party of thirteen. A stronger R.I.C. escort had been expected, but a reduction in the original number had probably been made at Fedamore. Of the five occupants of the first lorry three remained, one of whom had been mortally wounded and two slightly wounded at the outset. The latter two took cover at the roadside but shortly after were hit again, this time fatally.

> There were eight R.I.C. men in the second lorry, which had arrived a little beyond midway in the ambush when the first shots were fired. Having halted at once, the police began to dismount. Some were hit while doing so, others as they took up positions at the roadside. Five were killed outright and one suffered severe wounds that proved fatal some days later. Two managed to crawl into positions beneath the lorry from which they fired from behind the wheels. They refused to surrender, maintained a steady exchange of shots and might have prolonged the engagement indefinitely as they were well protected against fire from the initial positions of the attackers. A move to engage them from their own level on the actual road-bed was undertaken by Volunteer Johnny Vaughan, a Limerick city member of the Mid Limerick Column. Aided by the fire of his comrades

comrades he engaged the two policemen in a close-range duel from a new position on the roadside and he quickly put and end to this last-ditch stand of the R.I.C. remnant. The policemen who made this determined fight against hopeless odds were two of only three members of the regular R.I.C. in the police party. The others were Black and Tans.

In his account, MacCarthy did not mention the shooting of members of the RIC following their capture. But, other accounts did, including that of Maurice Meade, who along with MacCarthy was a member of the East Limerick Brigade. Meade was a former member of the Royal Irish Regiment who had been a regular soldier before the outbreak of the First World War and was one of the first members of the British army to arrive in France in August 1914. He was taken prisoner of war at a disastrous battle for his battalion at Le Pilly in northern France and later was one of those who joined Roger Casement's ill-fated Irish Brigade. Describing the aftermath of the Dromkeen ambush he stated:

> When fire was opened and we could see that all the Tans appeared to be dead, I gave our fellows the order to cease fire. I noticed then that Bill Hayes was holding his hand out and I asked him what was wrong. It seems that he had been struck in the hand by a bullet which had smashed his finger. We had relaxed at this stage and lit up cigarettes when I heard a shot and I saw a puff of smoke off the stones near where Davy Guerin was. Looking out from the window of the house we were in, I saw that someone was firing from beneath one of the lorries. I shouted to the other fellows to get out, that there was a man shooting from under one of the lorries. I fired a shot from the window myself. Then I got out on the road where I was better able to see and to shoot, and I fired at this fellow under the lorry. I could see my bullets striking the road very close to him and, after a minute or so, he came out holding his left hand up but carrying a carbine in his right hand. Davy Guerin had him covered and shouted to him as he came out 'Drop your rifle, or I'll blow your brains out'. Dropping his rifle, he came out to me with his two hands over his head but, considering his action had been treacherous, I shot him. Then O'Hannigan and someone else went walking down through the position, past where the lorries and the dead Tans were lying. They found two Tans still alive and apparently uninjured, down at the end, and they brought them back with them up to the farmyard where a courtmartial sat upon them on the spot. Five officers constituted the courtmartial. Two officers voted against shooting them, but three, which was a majority, voted for their immediate execution. We were standing nearby at the time. Donncadh O'Hannigan called me and said 'Here, Maurice, will you shoot one of them?' I agreed to do so. He gave Stapleton the job of executing the other. I took my man down the road and shot him. Then I went down to see how Stapleton was getting on, and found that he disliked the job and did not want to do it, so I took this fellow over and executed him also.

Michael Doyle died of gun shot wounds to the left shoulder and chest. His funeral came to Glasnevin on 7 February 1921 and he was buried in the Royal Irish Constabulary plot.[6]

12 February 1921   **Civilian**
James Murphy   *TD 43, St Paul's*

Members of the Auxiliary Division RIC arrested James Murphy and his friend Patrick Kennedy on Talbot Street on the evening of 9 February 1921. Initially taken to Dublin Castle they were then driven to Clonturk Park in Drumcondra where metal buckets were placed on their heads and they were shot multiple times. Patrick Kennedy was killed instantly while James Murphy died two days later of his wounds. He had been shot through the chest, collarbone, left cheek, nose and eyebrow.

James Murphy, aged twenty-four, lived with his brother, Joseph, at 22 Killarney Street in a back room of the building. He worked as an assistant at the Whiteside & Co. grocers in South Great George's Street. Murphy had been living with his brother in lodgings since 1902 and his brother stated that he took no part in political activities and was not connected in anyway to the IRA. On the night of his brother's shooting members of the 2nd Battalion East Surrey Regiment raided the Murphy's room in Killarney Street to look for evidence of the connection to the IRA. Joseph Murphy recounted the events of the evening and the account his brother gave to him of what happened:

> I saw him [James] last Wednesday, the 9th inst. about 6.30, when, after his day's work he came home for his evening meal. After he had tea he left me saying that he was going to pass a few hours at the pictures or a game of billiards. I have since ascertained that he went to the Cinema Theatre in Talbot Street, when a number of young men were held up and searched. He with others was searched and put by the soldiers on a motor lorry and brought to Dublin Castle where he was examined. Nothing of any kind of a compromising character was found on him. He had no weapons and no documents of any kind. The examination was finished at about 10 o'clock when the military authorities told him that he was released and he might go home. As it was then after curfew hour there was difficulty for anybody going through the streets for fear of the military. Accordingly the officer in charge told some soldiers to take my brother and Patrick Kennedy to their homes and leave them there and to leave my brother at 22 Killarney Street or as near to it as they could go. Instead of bringing my brother to his lodgings the military drove the motor lorry by Drumcondra to Clonturk Park. They halted the motor lorry near a field where there was unused and derelict ground. They took my brother and Patrick Kennedy out of the motor lorry brought them into the field put old tin cans over their heads put them against the wall and fired a number of shots at them. I believe Patrick Kennedy was killed almost instantaneously. My brother was hit through the tin can in his mouth, on the left cheek, on the right cheek, and through the breast. Having done this the soldiers left them and went away. Shortly afterwards two members of the Dublin Metropolitan Police on their beat in the neighbourhood heard groans on the other side of the wall, which came from my brother. They got into the field and they found Kennedy dead and my brother still

moaning and bleeding from his wounds. They brought my brother and Kennedy to the Mater Misericordiae Hospital.

At about 3.30 on Thursday 10th of February, while I was in bed in my lodgings I was awakened by the flashing in my eyes of an electric torch by an officer who asked me where was my brother. I told him I did not know, that he had not come home and that I could not understand what had become of him. He then told me to get dressed. While I was dressing the officer searched every corner of our little room, but of course with no result. With the military party were two sergeants of the Dublin Metropolitan Police and one of them told me that my brother had been badly wounded and was in the Mater Hospital. They asked me would I wish to see my brother. When I said I was most anxious to see him at once, they took me away in the motor lorry to the Mater Hospital. My brother was quite conscious and he told me the facts above stated. He assured me that when he was interrogated at the Castle his examination was perfectly satisfactory and he was released and told he might go home and it being after curfew hours directions were given by an officer that he should be sent home on the motor lorry and he got on that vehicle with the Black and Tans Auxiliary Police believing that he was going to be left at his lodgings instead of which he was brought to Clonturk Park.

A military court of inquiry, in lieu of an inquest, gathered together evidence of the events leading to the deaths of the two men. It came to the conclusion that both died as a result of gunshot wounds inflicted by Capt. William L. King, Temporary Cadet Frederick James Welsh and Temporary Cadet Herbert Hinchcliffe and that it was a case of wilful murder. All three men were members of F Company, Auxiliary Division, RIC. William L. King was the company commander and an infamous member of the Auxiliaries who had served with the South African Infantry during the First World War and received a number of awards for gallantry. He had been present at the failed Drumcondra ambush a couple of weeks before the killings of Murphy and Kennedy (*see 22 January 1921*) and their bodies were found where that incident had taken place. The court martial for the murders of Murphy and Kennedy was held in City Hall and began on 12 April, lasting for three days.

Conflicting accounts of that evening were presented during the trial. It was uncontested that having been arrested in Talbot Street that both men were brought to Dublin Castle. The crown prosecution produced a number of witnesses to the events of the night in Dublin Castle. One of these witnesses was John Joseph Connolly. Connolly was born in Wexford in 1895 and had served during the First World War with the Leinster Regiment. Rising through the ranks, he was eventually commissioned as an officer following a number of attempts. After the war, he was appointed for special duty in Dublin Castle with Lieut Col Walter Wilson, head of Intelligence for the Dublin District. Although the IRA did not target him on the morning of Bloody Sunday, Connolly became caught up in the shooting of Lieut Henry James Angliss at Lower Mount Street. When members of the IRA entered Angliss' room with orders to kill him, they found him in bed with John Connolly. Angliss was shot but Connolly was spared as the IRA men did not recognise him as a British officer and had no orders to kill him.

Frank Teeling, one of the IRA men present that day, was arrested for the shooting of Angliss and Connolly was required to give evidence at his trial. However, Connolly left for England before being forcibly returned by armed guard. Having given evidence under the anonym 'Mr C' he returned to his work in Dublin Castle. It was here that he witnessed, with others, the arrival of Murphy and Kennedy in the Castle on the night of 9 February 1921 and gave evidence for the prosecution. One witness, probably Connolly, stated that evening he saw, through a window of the intelligence office, both Kennedy and Murphy being badly beaten and questioned. At about 22.30 both men were taken out into the Castle yard and placed against a wall. One was completely covered in blood on his face while the other's head was soaked through with water. He stated that King eventually said, 'Don't knock them about anymore, they have had enough' and called out for the Ford car to be brought around. When the car came around both men were placed in the back with Hinchcliffe who held a revolver while King drove and Welsh sat beside him up front. As the car was about to leave a voice, believed to be Hinchcliffe, was heard to ask 'are you coming for a ride, we are going out to shoot'. When it came to the evidence of the defence it was claimed that both the prisoners were handed over the Military Foot Police at approximately 21.45 and told to go home. They produced other witnesses, police and auxiliaries, who stated that the bloodied men in the yard were police who had been in a fight and alibis were also provided claiming that the accused had been at raids at Talbot Street and Leeson Street and playing a game of cards. The deathbed statement of James Murphy was deemed inadmissible. Despite a seemingly unlikely series of events being presented by the defence, and accusations of witness intimidation, King and Hinchcliffe were found not guilty of murder while the charges against Welsh were dropped before the end of the trial. The case attracted a significant amount of newspaper coverage and attention, and the shootings were also raised in the House of Commons and the accused men named. Nobody was ever convicted for the killings.[7]

13 February 1921   **Royal Irish Constabulary**
John Patrick Lynch   *NA 97, Garden*

Born in Co. Mayo, John Patrick Lynch joined the RIC at nineteen in 1903. His father, James, had been a constable with the police and John followed. Stationed in a number of different counties he was finally posted to Dublin in April 1915, where he moved between Lusk, Malahide and Swords.

Early on the morning of 13 February 1921, Lynch and four other members of the RIC were on patrol between Swords and Balbriggan in a Crossley Tender. They left Balbriggan to return to Swords at 02.30. Fifteen minutes later, as they approached Ballough, near Lusk, they were spotted by Thomas Peppard, a veteran of the 1916 Rising who had served under Seán Heuston at the Mendicity Institute, and now an intelligence officer with the Fingal Brigade of the IRA. He was staying in a house near Lusk with a number of men who were on the run from the authorities and was on look out duty when he spotted the lights of the Crossley Tender in which Lynch was travelling. He later recounted the events of that night:

> … I spotted the lights of a car or lorry approaching the village. I immediately warned my comrades that the enemy were approaching. By now the vehicle had reached the village and apparently halted. I went carefully towards the village to find out what was happening and found the enemy (Tans) were raiding a public house there and had now gone towards Balbriggan. I immediately called the men whom I had been with, about nine or ten, all armed with shotguns, and made with all haste to the main Belfast-Dublin road. We had just reached Ballough crossroads and were in the act of rounding up some horses to let out on the road to cause an obstruction when a tenderload of Tans arrived. We hurriedly occupied positions and opened fire on them as they passed. They did not halt, just fired back at random as they sped away. We quickly learned that we had shot dead an R.I.C. man named Lynch who was acting as guide for the Tans that night. This man had formerly been stationed in Lusk and knew the country and the people around there. This was a bit of luck to have got him.

Despite his impressions the patrol that Peppard and his comrades had opened fire on was not entirely made up of 'Black and Tans'. Of the five men in the tender two, John Shenton and Charles Lawrence, were ex-soldiers who had been recruited into the RIC during the War of Independence, while the other three, including Lynch, were Irish born regular members of the police. The RIC men on board the tender perceived that a significant force had attacked them with some 30–40 shots being fired in their direction. In reality the number was far less but the fact that the ambushers were armed only with shotguns seemed to add to the confusion. As they drove away at speed they realised that Constable

Lynch had been hit as he had stood up and returned fire. They arrived at the barracks in Swords at about 03.00 and carried Lynch in. They called for a doctor but he was dead within five minutes of arrival. A blast of shotgun pellets had entered his left thigh and severed his femoral artery resulting in the fatal haemorrhage. John Lynch was buried in Glasnevin Cemetery on 16 February 1921. Thomas Peppard continued to serve throughout the War of Independence, and with the National Army during the Civil War. He lived to the age of 90 and died in December 1984.[8]

23 February 1921	**Royal Irish Constabulary**
Martin John Greer	*KF 221, Garden*

Martin John Greer, a constable from Roscommon, was aged twenty-seven when he was shot dead in Dublin. Greer was employed on motor dispatch duties and was in the habit of going for lunch with other RIC members from Dublin Castle to a restaurant on Ormond Quay. Unknown to them Edward Kelliher, a member of the IRA GHQ Intelligence Section, was monitoring their movements. He mistakenly believed that Greer and the others were members of the Igoe Gang, a group of intelligence officers under the command of Head Const. Eugene Igoe, who were being targeted as a priority by the IRA. He reported them to IRA GHQ and the decision was made that members of the Squad would be given the orders to shoot the men. At about 13.00 on the afternoon of 23 February 1921, they took their positions. Edward Kelliher, who had the job of raising his bowler hat as the men passed the members of the Squad, accompanied them. At 13.30 Greer left the Castle with Constables Daniel Hoey and Edward McDonagh to go for lunch. As the three men approached the corner of Parliament Street, Kelliher raised his hat and an intense volley of fire was opened. Greer and Hoey fell where they stood, while McDonagh was wounded and made a dash for a nearby tobacconist shop.

In 1950 Vincent Byrne, one of the members of the Squad present, recalled what happened on the day of the shooting. Some other accounts of IRA volunteers regarding the shooting stated that Greer and the other men were shot as it was believed that they were in Dublin to identify men who had been arrested. However, at the time he was interviewed, Byrne still believed that they were members of the Igoe Gang:

> We still did not give up hope of getting Igoe, for, a few days later, we were positioned for him again. This time, the operation was a little more successful. Information was received to the effect that Igoe and his gang went for dinner to the Ormond Hotel

between 12.30 p.m. and 1.30 p.m. The position taken up at this time was at the corner of Parliament St. and Essex St. at about 1 p.m. The signal was given that the three individuals coming down the street were members of Igoe's gang. As they came to the corner where our men were posted, fire was opened on them. Two were shot dead. The third was wounded and ran across Essex St with one of our men after him. He ran into a shop between Essex St. and Wellington Quay. He tried to jump the counter of the shop but our man was in after him and finished him off. Igoe himself, or the remainder of the gang, were never got.

One of the first on the scene in the aftermath was Const. Patrick Murray, a member of the Dublin Metropolitan Police:

… I was on duty at the crossing of Parliament Street and Wellington Quay. I heard a number of shots from the direction of Parliament Street. I turned round and saw two men fall on the footway on the east side of Parliament Street at the corner of Essex Street. I immediately went to their assistance and found both men in a dying condition, I knew them to be RIC men. They were lying close together on the footway facing in the direction of the bridge. All the people in the street ran in different directions. I looked round to see if anyone was coming to my assistance and Mr Honan, Tobacconist of 25 Parliament Street came out and told me that there was another man in his shop wounded. A clergyman, Father Kennedy of 22 Parliament Street came out and administrated to the dying men. A few minutes later the Auxiliary Police came out to my assistance. In my opinion the murderers fired from Essex St. and then ran away down Essex St., mingling with the others who ran in that direction.

Martin Greer had been shot through the head, the chest, the back, his left and right legs and right arm. He was alive but in a very serious condition when he was brought to King George V Hospital. Initially it was decided to stabilise him and treat his blood loss but it soon became clear than an operation was required to attempt to extract the bullet that had hit him in the head and lodged in his brain. The .450 Webley & Scott revolver bullet and some fragments of his skull were successfully removed but Martin Greer died before the operation could be completed. He was buried in the Royal Irish Constabulary plot in Glasnevin three days later.[9]

6 March 1921   Civilian
John O'Neill   HA 55½, South

John O'Neill was killed in 1921 on the Malahide Road when the IRA mistakenly ambushed the car that he was driving. O'Neill was originally from Quinn's Lane, off Pembroke Street, in Dublin. His mother, Mary, died in childbirth and his father James, a cab driver, was killed in an accident in 1907 when he was hit by a runaway horse at Fitzwilliam Square. Given his father's occupation John was surrounded by horses from an early age. He underwent an apprenticeship as a jockey for five years with the racehorse trainer Dick Harrison in Castleknock before emigrating to Australia in 1909 where he carried on his career.

In March 1916, he enlisted at Brisbane in the Australian Imperial Force for service during the First World War. Given his background he was sent for service with the 2nd Australian Remount Unit, caring for the horses of the Australian light horse regiments, with the Egyptian Expeditionary Force, in July 1916. Here he served in the Sinai and Palestine campaign against the Ottoman empire. He was later transferred to the 6th Mobile Veterinary Service continuing his work with horses and survived the war unscathed aside from an injury to his hand in July 1918. While driving a limber loaded with horse rations in the Jordan Valley he fell and the wheel of the limber crushed his hand. Following the armistice he spent some time with the Mechanical Transport section of the Australian Army Service Corps working as a motor driver. In July 1919, he returned to Australia from Egypt to be discharged from the army and made his way back home to Dublin. There he worked for Johnson, Mooney & O'Brien bakers in Ballsbridge, he also put the driving skills he had acquired during his war service to use, working at times as a chauffer for Edmond McGrath, a tea merchant.

On Sunday, 6 March 1921, just after 10.30, O'Neill was driving McGrath, Tom Shannon, a professional golfer, Joseph O'Dowd, managing director of Michael Murphy Ltd. shipping company and George Beattie, who worked in the Custom House, to Portmarnock Golf Club where they had intended to play. One of the passengers in the car recalled what happened on the journey:

> When opposite Donnycarney House on the Malahide Road, I heard some men shout 'Halt'. John O'Neill, the chauffeur, pulled up instantly, at the same time revolver fire was opened on us and bombs were thrown at us. Firing continued for about 2 minutes and then we were ordered out of the car. A number of men, at least 20, came towards us. I was searched and my pocket book and letters examined. The man who searched me, on seeing my name and address, told me he had made a mistake. The men then withdrew through the grounds of the O'Brien Institute … I was very upset at the time and I do not think I could identify any of the men again. During the firing John O'Neill was killed.

O'Neill had been killed instantly during the ambush, a bullet had entered his head above his left ear and exited on the right side of his face. His hands remained gripped to the wheel of the car. His funeral to Glasnevin took place on 9 March from St Andrew's, Westland Row. Due to a strike at the time, it was not possible to transport his remains to the cemetery by horse drawn hearse and therefore his coffin was placed in a private motorcar and driven to the cemetery. His step-mother, sisters and other mourners followed it. He was buried with his parents.[10]

14 March 1921   Irish Republican Army
Thomas Bryan   *A22½, O'Connell Tower Circle*

Thomas Bryan was one of six men executed in Mountjoy Jail on 14 March 1921 who are buried in Glasnevin Cemetery. A member of the Dublin Brigade Active Service Unit, Bryan was one of those arrested in the aftermath of an attempt to ambush a Royal Irish Constabulary lorry that travelled each morning from Gormanston Camp to Dublin (*see 22 January 1921*).

Thomas Bryan (Brien) was born in the home of his parents on North Brunswick Street in January 1897. The son of James Bryan and Mary Caffrey his family later moved to North King Street and then to Henrietta Street, where they lived for many years in No. 14. Thomas attended the Christian Brothers' school on North Brunswick Street and later trained as an electrician working for Hanley and Robinson electrical engineers based on Dawson Street. Bryan became a member of the Irish Volunteers and according to a pension application, he took some part in the 1916 Rising. He was arrested in early November 1917 and charged with taking part in military drilling along with a group of other men. Found guilty he was sentenced to a period of imprisonment. Initially sent to Mountjoy, he was later sent to Dundalk where he participated in a hunger strike alongside other prisoners. He was released shortly afterwards under the 1913 Prisoners (Temporary Discharge for Ill-Health) Act, commonly known as the Cat and Mouse Act.

Serving with Dublin Brigade IRA during the War of Independence, he became a member of the Active Service Unit. During the same period, Thomas married Annie Glynn, who lived in nearby Dominick Street. Their marriage took place in St Michan's in November 1920. Just a few months later Thomas was captured in Drumcondra and was placed on trial in City Hall alongside Frank Flood, Patrick Doyle and Bernard Ryan. As nobody had been killed in the attempted ambush, the men were charged with high treason. Specifically they were accused of having, as members of the IRA, assembled with the intent of 'levying war against the King' and crown forces. All the men were found guilty and were subsequently sentenced to death. Rather than write directly to his wife, Thomas decided to write to his father-in-law after his sentence was passed.

Annie's father had died when she was young and her mother had re-married her father's brother, Richard (Dick) Glynn, in 1907. Richard was a career soldier with the British army and had been a member for twenty-four years. He served in the Second Anglo-Boer War, during which he was one of the British garrison besieged in Ladysmith, and was also present in Dublin during the 1916 Rising. On 25 February Thomas Bryan wrote to Richard Glynn:

> Just a few lines hoping you and all at home are in the pink as this leaves me thank God. Well Dick my trial is over and I have received my death sentence but is not confirmed yet but that is only a matter of time. I have not told Annie my sentence needless to say and I don't know how to do so. I pray that God may give her strength to bear this heavy cross. I have asked her to inquire about a visit as my trial is over she may be allowed one. Personally I don't mind death in any form but naturally my thoughts stray to my dear little wife for as she truly said some time ago it's our women who suffer the most. I don't intend to say anything to Annie re. my sentence until I see if it is possible to get a visit. I would like to see her by herself for a while afterwards I will let her know. I wonder how she will take it. God give them all strength to bear it. Well Dick I know you will do your best to keep her spirits up, it is quite possible my sentence may not be confirmed God is good ... I remain your loving son-in-law.

Annie Bryan was pregnant at the time of Thomas' arrest and trial. Their son was born on 9 March 1921 but only lived for a day. He was named Thomas after his father. On 10 March 1921, Mary Glynn, Annie's mother, travelled to the offices of the Dublin Cemeteries Committee to arrange the burial. She described that Thomas Bryan junior had died of convulsions. The following morning at 08.30 in the morning Richard Glynn arrived at the gates of Glasnevin with a coffin two feet long, ten inches wide and eight inches deep. He walked to the Garden section of the cemetery and, due to a gravediggers' strike that was in progress at the time, dug the grave himself and interred the remains of his grandson. The following day, Saturday 12 March, newspapers carried news that the death sentence of Thomas Bryan and others had been confirmed and that he was to be executed on Monday. The same day Thomas wrote a letter to his sister, Bridget, a member of Cumann na mBan, stating that:

> I hope my darling little wife and all of you will be able to bear up under the awful burden. I want to see my wife before I go and all of you if possible.

Due to Annie's health and the advice of a doctor, she was unable to visit Thomas before his execution on 14 March. Annie Bryan never re-married. Following Thomas' death, she lived in a rented room in 38 Mountjoy Street and died of tuberculosis in the home of her parents in Dominick Street in 1930. She is also buried in Glasnevin.[11]

14 March 1921   **Irish Republican Army**
Patrick Doyle   *A 21½, O'Connell Tower Circle*

Patrick Doyle was executed in Mountjoy Jail in March 1921. He was amongst those taken prisoner with Frank Flood, Thomas Bryan and Bernard Ryan in Drumcondra (*see 22 January 1921*). From Dublin, Doyle was a carpenter by trade and a founder member of the Amalgamated Society of Carpenters, Cabinetmakers and Joiners. A talented footballer he was married to Louisa Herbert. They wed in September 1916 and he moved from Buckingham Place to live with her at St Mary's Place where he resided until his arrest in 1921. It was at his home that plans were made for the ill-fated ambush.

Their eldest child, Kathleen Mary Constance was born a year later in September 1917 followed by a son, Patrick junior, in August 1919. He died at the age of fourteen months in 1920 and was buried in Glasnevin. Patrick was an active participant in the War of Independence as a member of F Company, 1st Battalion, Dublin Brigade and had taken part in the Collinstown raid in 1919. After his capture in Drumcondra he was charged with high treason, found guilty and sentenced to death. At the time, Louisa Doyle was pregnant with twins. Before his execution, he wrote a letter to her telling how he was to be executed and said:

> ... I know you will cheer up. I die like a soldier for a glorious cause. I know you will get a shock when you read this. I want no crying or wailing of any sort, be cheerful we will all be together in a very short time. Give my love to Kathleen and the other two babies that I have never seen. You will get a visit before I am shot ...

Kathleen did visit Patrick with their daughter and infant twins on Saturday 12 March. The twins were two weeks old and had been born premature. It was Patrick's first and only time seeing them. On the journey home one of the twins, Louisa, who had been ill, died in her mother's arms. Patrick Doyle was executed the following Monday. Patrick's brother Seán died of wounds received during the burning of the Custom House (*see 30 May 1921*). His nephew, Thomas Wood, died of wounds received at the Battle of Cordoba in December 1936 while serving with the International Brigades during the Spanish Civil War. He was seventeen at the time of his death and is memorialised on a family headstone in Glasnevin.[12]

The 2001 reinterment in Glasnevin Cemetery of nine men executed in Mountjoy Jail during the War of Independence. Courtesy of Alamy.

14 March 1921   **Irish Republican Army**
Leo Patrick Fitzgerald   *RD 34, South New Chapel*

Leo Fitzgerald, a member of the 3rd Battalion, Dublin Brigade, IRA, was killed during a fight with Auxiliaries on the evening of the executions of the six men in Mountjoy Jail. The skirmish also resulted in the death of David Kelly (*see below*). Leo Fitzgerald came from a family of painters and decorators who were heavily involved in the independence movement. He was one of five brothers who served in the Irish Volunteers with the Boland's Mills Garrison during the 1916 Rising and were active members of B Company, 3rd Battalion Dublin Brigade. His sister, Sheila, was also an active member of Cumann na mBan during the War of Independence. On the evening of his death Fitzgerald's Company had been given orders to carry out patrols and protect the Battalion Headquarters at number 144 Great Brunswick (Pearse) Street, also known as St Andrew's Catholic Hall, where a battalion council meeting was due to take place. The members of B Company were told that 'All enemy to be engaged and if possible wiped out. In the event of a patrol coming into contact with enemy, all patrols to concentrate on that sector of the area to be in the fight'. At 20.15 members of F Company, Auxiliary Division, RIC, in two lorries and accompanied by a Rolls Royce armoured car proceeded to Great Brunswick Street to raid No. 144. As the Auxiliaries approached, they came under fire from the men of the 3rd Battalion, Dublin Brigade. Section Leader Richard Costigan, who was driving the leading lorry, came to a halt at the pavement next to No. 145 and the Auxiliaries returned fire. District Inspector Richard K. Caparn the commander of F Company, Auxiliary Division was in charge of the raiding party, a veteran of the First World War he had served on the Western Front. He described the skirmish that unfolded:

> I was proceeding with two tenders of auxiliaries accompanied by a Rolls Royce Armoured Car to search the premises of 144 South Great Brunswick Street. On nearing No. 144 front, rear and both sides. It was very dark and all that we could see were flashes and shadowy figures, we immediately returned the fire, stopped the tenders and got into the road. Five cadets in the leading tender were hit by the first burst of firing. The firing was very intense and at very close range. I distinctly saw one man running about fifty yards ahead, he fell apparently hit and two or three people dragged him around the corner. I afterwards found a revolver where he fell. I then noticed four bodies lying on the steps and the pavement a few doors this side of No. 144 ... I had sent back the Armoured Car for an ambulance [and] on the arrival of the ambulance I sent my five wounded Cadets to King George V Hospital, under escort and subsequently the 4 dead or wounded civilians. I raided No. 144 Great Brunswick St. which was also 'The Catholic Club' and in the first room on the right on the ground

floor a leather bag was found, being open, containing several loaded revolvers, a bomb fully detonated and a quantity of revolver ammunition was lying on the floor. For about half an hour after the first firing, sniping was maintained from corners and down the streets.

At the start of the evening Leo Fitzgerald had been paired with a younger, less experienced Seán MacBride, for whom the action on Brunswick Street would be his first significant battle. Both men were stationed on the corner of Sandwith Street and Brunswick Street, under the command of Seán O'Keeffe. Both Mac-Bride and Fitzgerald had taken up firing positions lying on the pathway and during the height of the battle MacBride realised that they were both under fire themselves:

LEO FITZGERALD, I. R. A.
B. Coy. III Battalion Dublin Brigade.
Killed in Action in Great Brunswick Street
14th March, 1921.
ar ḋeis Dé ġo raiḃ a anam.

Courtesy of The National Library. of Ireland.

> Suddenly I became conscious that there were a lot of sparks hopping off the pavement around us ... Then I realised that these were bullets hitting off the paving stones. I looked up and saw an armoured car about twenty or thirty yards away firing directly at us on the ground. By this stage I realised that our position was untenable.

MacBride urged Fitzgerald to retreat but receiving no reply he put out his hand to shake him and draw his attention, however he said that '... his head was blown to pieces, my hand full of blood and brain matter'. It was MacBride's first close experience of death. While the firing continued he retreated to the nearby Erne Terrace where he remained until the following morning and made his escape. However, not all of the Dublin Brigade men escaped unnoticed. In the aftermath of the fighting, Lieut Charles Frederick Weber, of the 3rd Tank Battalion, who was in command of the armoured car noticed a man running past his car towards Sandwith Street. He jumped from the car grabbing him and on noticing that he was carrying a pistol placed him under arrest. Weber later learned that the name of the man he had captured was Thomas Traynor (*see 25 April 1921*). The fight resulted in the deaths of two IRA volunteers, two Auxiliaries and three civilians. The body of Leo Fitzgerald was brought to King George V Hospital where a post mortem took place. He had been shot in the head, chest and right hip. Three days after his death he was identified and his body claimed by his sister. He was buried in the Republican Plot in Glasnevin.[13]

14 March 1921 **Irish Republican Army**
Frank Flood *A 23, O'Connell Tower Circle*

Courtesy of The National Library of Ireland.

Francis Xavier (Frank) Flood was born in 1901 in Emmet Street in Dublin. The son of John Flood and Sarah Murphy, his father was a constable in the Dublin Metropolitan Police. His elder brother Seán had taken part in the 1916 Rising serving in the Four Courts area while another brother had served with the British army during the Rising, later being badly wounded on the Western Front. During the War of Independence Frank was one of five brothers to serve with Dublin Brigade, IRA. An engineering student in UCD he was also a friend of Kevin Barry, with whom he was a member of H Company, 1st Battalion, Dublin Brigade, IRA. He had also been present at the ambush on North King Street following which Barry was arrested (*see 1 November 1920*). An Active Service Unit member, Flood was the Lieutenant in command of No. 1 Section on the morning that it carried out an abortive ambush on a Royal Irish Constabulary lorry that travelled each morning from Gormanston Camp to Dublin *(see 22 January 1921)*. In the aftermath Flood, along with Thomas Bryan, Patrick Doyle, Bernard Ryan and Diarmuid O'Sullivan were arrested. Although the ambush had resulted in no fatalities on the British side, Flood and the others were placed on trial for treason and found guilty. O'Sullivan, aged seventeen, had his sentence commuted but the others, including Flood, aged nineteen, were executed at Mountjoy Jail. His mother, Sarah, describing the impact of the death of her son said, in 1924, that:

> After Frank's execution, I had a nervous breakdown and had the doctor attending me for six months. My nerves were entirely shattered and this was added to by raids by Black and Tans and Military. These left me a physical wreck. I had to undergo an operation and was six weeks in a private nursing home. I was then advised by my doctor to have a complete change and was three months in the country. I am still under doctor's care and even now I am suffering from insomnia and am ordered away again ... I had four other sons in the I.R.A. on active service. They were 'on the run' and the Black and Tans were continually raiding the house for them.[14]

14 March 1921   **Civilian**
David Christopher Kelly   *HF 73, Garden*

David Kelly, manager of the Sinn Féin Bank on Harcourt Street, was also killed during the fight on Great Brunswick Street that resulted in the death of Leo Fitzgerald (*see above*). David was the youngest son of Isaac and Sarah Kelly, originally from Wicklow. He had two sisters and two brothers who survived to adulthood. He had attended the Christian Brother school on Westland Row and was a schoolmate of Patrick and William Pearse. He had begun working with the Sinn Féin bank in 1910 and lived with his sister Kathleen at the family home, 132 Great Brunswick Street. His other sister was a nun in Grimsby, while a brother, Michael, had died in Liverpool in 1918. His elder brother Thomas was a well-known Sinn Féin politician; he had been arrested following the 1916 Rising and was a councillor before being elected during the 1918 general election. Although he was a non-combatant civilian David Kelly was active politically and a member of Sinn Féin. He was well known by many in the city because of his role as bank manager of the Sinn Féin Bank. One of those within the Republican movement described his work:

> No. 6 Harcourt St. was owned by the Sinn Féin Bank, of which Davy Kelly, a brother of Alderman Tom Kelly, was manager. As a matter of fact he was the whole staff of the bank. It was in the Sinn Féin bank that we lodged all the funds of the organisation and from the time I left the organisation not a penny went astray. One time when the bank was raided and closed by the British authorities, Davy Kelly put a table and chair on the top step in front of the hall door and carried on, or pretended to carry on, as usual in defiance of the British authorities.

On the evening of his death, David Kelly left his home, having said goodnight to his sister, just as the first shots were being fired in the fight close to his home. As she heard the noise, his sister Kathleen, looked out the window but could see no sign of him. He did not return that evening and his sister began enquiring with her neighbours to try to ascertain what had happened to him. Having found no further information, she checked all of the civilian hospitals in the city but could not find anybody admitted, wounded or dead, who matched his description. The reason was that David had been taken to the military hospital in the city. On Tuesday evening, the day after his death, a member of the Dublin Metropolitan Police called to the family home to break the news to Kathleen. He had been shot in the chest and the leg and was dead on admission to the hospital. His sister, who refused to swear an oath or recognise the British military court of inquiry into his death, then travelled to the hospital to identify his body. She was presented with his belongings, the blood soaked clothes he was wearing when he died. A resolution of sympathy was passed at a meeting of Dublin Corporation the following day where he was described as a 'mild-mannered man, almost peaceful to a fault'. George Lyons, who seconded the motion, noted that:

> It appeared that those who had custody of his body regarded him as a man of great importance and significance in the Irish Republican Army. It was only fair to both sides to say that he was of no importance or significance as a fighting man, being a cripple, and the label put on his body in George V Hospital had been put there under a false idea. His death could not be regarded as a victory for anyone.

Many, including the lord mayor of Dublin, attended his funeral to Glasnevin. His coffin was brought to the cemetery covered in the Tricolour and he was buried in a grave owned by his brother Thomas, who is also interred there.[15]

14 March 1921 — Irish Republican Army
Patrick Moran — A 20½, O'Connell Tower Circle

Patrick Moran was born in March 1888 in Crossna, a townland north-east of Boyle, in Roscommon. The son of Bartholomew Moran and Brigid Sheeran he was one of eleven children. After early education, he worked and trained as a grocer and moved to Dublin. A man of many interests he was a member of the Gaelic League, as a keen sportsperson he was active in the Gaelic Athletic Association and was a trade unionist. He joined the Irish Volunteers on its foundation and participated in the 1916 Rising with the Jacob's Garrison as a member of D Company, 2nd Battalion, Dublin Brigade. He was arrested following the surrender and sent to Frongoch. He was released in the summer of 1916 and returned to Ireland to resume his political and revolutionary activities. During the final period of his life, he lived and worked in Blackrock in Dublin. Moran was active during the War of Independence with his company of the Dublin Brigade and on the morning of Bloody Sunday was given command of a group of fourteen men who were tasked with shooting three men suspected of being British intelligence officers who were staying at the Gresham Hotel. Two men, Patrick McCormack and Leonard Wilde, were shot dead (*see 21 November 1921*). Following the shootings at the Gresham, Moran appears to have travelled to Croke Park where the Intermediate Championship final was taking place between Erin's Hopes and Dunleary Commercials. Moran was chairman of the latter. The final took place before the infamous match between Dublin and

Tipperary that day. Patrick Moran spent his final week of freedom at his place of work in Blackrock and was there when he was arrested the following Friday. He was placed in a line up and identified by British army witnesses as having been involved in the shooting of Lieut Peter Ashmun Ames. This was despite the fact that he had no connection to that particular part of the Bloody Sunday operation. He was placed on trial alongside Joseph Rochford, who had also been identified by witnesses. A number of civilian witnesses came forward to give evidence that they had seen Patrick Moran at mass in Blackrock on the morning of 21 November. Despite this, he had been involved in the IRA operation that morning and an alibi that accounted for the truth of his whereabouts in its entirety would have done little to help his situation. At the end of the trials Patrick Moran was found guilty of the first charge of 'murder' and Joseph Rochford was found not guilty of the charges of 'murder and manslaughter'. Patrick Moran was sentenced to 'suffer death by being hanged'. In a letter to his sisters, Patrick expressed his surprise at being convicted:

> I've just finished writing a letter home and my word it was a hard task. I know they are sure to look on the worst side of the case and will undoubtedly feel cut up. I'm taking it for granted that you have heard the result of the trial which went against me. I was so full up of the idea of getting out of it that I hadn't given it much thought but I didn't get a chance from the other side and I thought my own counsel very slack.

May Moran, a niece of Patrick, described that on the night before his execution he told his brother Jim that he had indeed been involved in the operation on Bloody Sunday, albeit not

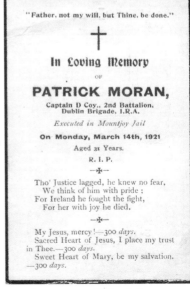

"Father, not my will, but Thine, be done."

✝

In Loving Memory

OF

PATRICK MORAN,

Captain D Coy., 2nd Battalion,
Dublin Brigade, I.R.A.

Executed in Mountjoy Jail

On Monday, March 14th, 1921

Aged 31 Years.

R. I. P.

—✠—

Tho' Justice lagged, he knew no fear,
We think of him with pride ;
For Ireland he fought the fight,
For her with joy he died.

—✠—

My Jesus, mercy !—300 *days*.
Sacred Heart of Jesus, I place my trust
in Thee.—300 *days*.
Sweet Heart of Mary, be my salvation.
—300 *days*.

Courtesy of May Moran.

the one he was convicted for, and the one thing that weighed on his conscience was that Patrick McCormack might have been unjustly killed. His execution, with five other men, took place in Mountjoy Jail on 14 March 1921.[16]

14 March 1921   **Irish Republican Army**
Bernard Ryan   *A 22, O'Connell Tower Circle*

Bernard Ryan, from Dublin, was one of those arrested following the failed Drumcondra Bridge ambush (*see 21 January 1921*) and executed in Mountjoy Jail having been found guilty of high treason. Bernard, known as Bertie, was taken into the home of Anne Ryan at Nortons Row in Dublin just eight days after his birth. Anne, the widow of a policeman, worked as a laundress and took in babies who she cared for in her home. Bernard lived the rest of his life with Anne and his adopted sister Sarah, and eventually settled at 8 Royal Canal Terrace. A tailor's presser with a keen interest in the Irish language he joined the 1st Battalion, Dublin Brigade in 1918. Recruited to the Active Service Unit he was arrested with a revolver by Temporary Cadet William Ernest Brisley, a member of the Auxiliary Division. In a letter to Michael Staines just before his death, Ryan wrote that:

> We are all reconciled to God and, in fact, we would not care to have the sentence changed, of course that is from a spiritual point of view. We know that we are wanted outside, but, while we were out, we did our best and, if we failed, it was not our fault. I have no more to say, only to ask for your prayers, but I know I can safely assume I have got them long before now. I assure you I will remember you when I go to Heaven.

Anne Ryan was one of those present at the gates of the prison as the execution of her son was carried out at 07.00 on 14 March 1921. Along with his sister, they made enquiries in an attempt to have his body released to them for burial. They were refused and he was buried in Mountjoy until his re-interment in Glasnevin in 2001.[17]

14 March 1921   **Irish Republican Army**
Thomas Whelan   *A21, O'Connell Tower Circle*

Thomas Whelan was born in October 1898 in a cottage on the Sky Road in Gourthromagh, near Clifden, Galway. He was one of thirteen children of John Whelan and Bridget Price and at the age of eighteen moved to Dublin where he boarded in a house on Barrow Street. He initially worked in Boland's Mills before being employed with the railways. A member of the Irish Volunteers and later the 3rd Battalion, Dublin Brigade IRA, he was described by Michael Noyk as '... a soft country boy with a beautiful character and a nice fresh complexion and very talkative'. Late on the night of 23 November 1920, members of the 2nd Battalion Royal Berkshire Regiment carried out a series of arrests of suspected IRA members in the area around Great Brunswick (Pearse) Street. They took in sixteen men, including Thomas Whelan. The arrests were part of a wider round up in the aftermath of Bloody Sunday. On 1 December 1920 Whelan was placed on parade at Arbour Hill and a person, who was present at Lower Baggot Street when

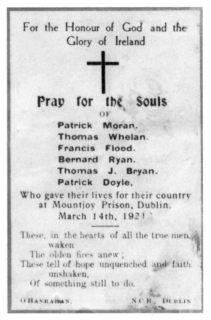

For the Honour of God and the Glory of Ireland

✝

Pray for the Souls
OF
Patrick Moran.
Thomas Whelan.
Francis Flood.
Bernard Ryan.
Thomas J. Bryan.
Patrick Doyle.
Who gave their lives for their country at Mountjoy Prison, Dublin.
March 14th, 1921.

These, in the hearts of all the true men, waken
The olden fires anew ;
These tell of hope unquenched and faith unshaken,
Of something still to do.

O'HANRAHAN.   N.C.R., DUBLIN

Courtesy of May Moran.

Capt. Geoffrey Thomas Baggally was shot, picked him out and identified him as being present there that morning. He claimed that Whelan had entered the house with the IRA party and held him up with a revolver while others shot Baggally. Whelan strenuously denied the charge and produced witnesses that described him being elsewhere that morning. Despite this Whelan was found guilty of the shooting of Baggally and being in possession of a revolver. He was sentenced to death and was executed in Mountjoy Jail.[18]

20 March 1921   **Irish Republican Army**
Dermot O'Dwyer   *RD 34½, South New Chapel*

Dermot Richard O'Dwyer was nineteen and an engineering student when he was fatally wounded while taking part in an ambush on a British army lorry in North Frederick Street in Dublin. He was the only son of Con and Katie O'Dwyer from Rossmore in Co. Tipperary. On 18 March 1921, just after 19.00, a British army ration lorry was making its way up North Frederick Street. It was a dark evening and in command of the lorry was Sgt R. W. Crouch of the 2nd Battalion Duke of Wellington's Regiment who described what happened:

> As the lorry was passing an alley about 9 men rushed out and threw four bombs at us, all of which exploded, some against the lorry. The men were in civilian clothes wearing rain coats. At the same time two men came from a doorway about 15 yards further up

A locket containing a photograph and hair of Dermot O'Dwyer who was killed in March 1921. **Courtesy of Derek Jones**

the road and opened fire on us with pistols. They were similarly dressed to the others. I immediately ordered the escort to open fire which they did, I myself shot one of the bombers. I saw another bomb explode close to one of the rebels. This man had thrown the bomb and I saw it explode just after leaving his hand. He fell down wounded.

Having returned fire, the lorry drove on and left the scene. The IRA ambush was carried out by members of 1 Company, 5th Battalion, Dublin Brigade, under the command of Lieut Edward (Ned) Kelly. One of the party, Charles Walker, later recorded his recollection of the incident:

On Friday, 18th March 1921, I was told to report at 6.30 that evening at Mark Wilson's Place, Frederick St. North. The following were amongst those present: Dan Jevins, Larrigan, Mick Dunne, Dwyer, myself, Lieut Darcy and Lieut Ned Kelly who was charge. Lieut Kelly told us we were to ambush an enemy lorry with troops which usually passed through Frederick St. each evening. He allotted us the following positions: Dwyer and two others the city end of Frederick St. Mick Dunne and Dan Jevins the corner of Frederick Street and Frederick Court. Larrigan and another man the corner of Frederick Street and Frederick Lane (North). Another man and I [were positioned on] the corner of Hardwicke St. and Frederick Court. The instructions were to throw the hand grenade first and then use the revolver and get away. On arrival at our positions, we were each given a Mills bomb and a .45 revolver with five rounds. Between 7.15 and 7.30 a heavily armed British military lorry covered with a wire cage entered North Frederick St. coming from the direction of the city. The ambush party opened fire on it. Fire was returned from the lorry which put on speed and continued on its journey. One of our men, Dwyer, was killed.

Dermot O'Dwyer was badly wounded and semi-conscious but had not been killed immediately. He was brought to the Jervis Street Hospital where it was found that he had numerous shrapnel wounds to his shoulder, torso and right leg. He had little chance of survival and died on the morning of 20 March at 01.30. His funeral took place to Glasnevin from St Joseph's Berkley Street after 10 o'clock mass on 23 March. He was buried in the Republican Plot in the cemetery. His father and mother died in 1924 and 1925 respectively and are buried in the St Paul's section of the cemetery.[19]

Above: *A certificate issued to acknowledge the service of Dermot O'Dwyer during the War of Independence.* Courtesy of Derek Jones.

Right: *A letter sent from Dermot O'Dwyer to his mother describing his experience at Croke Park on Bloody Sunday 1920.* Courtesy of Derek Jones.

28 March 1921   **Civilian**
Annie Seville   *XK 100, St Patrick's*

Annie Seville was born on 3 March 1905 at the Rotunda Hospital in Dublin. The daughter of Richard and Kate Seville she lived with her family on the north side of the city and by 1921 was working as a bead worker and living at 17 Findlater Place in a third floor flat. Her father Richard was a veteran of the British army, having served during the Second Anglo-Boer War in South Africa between 1901 and 1902 with 74th (Dublin) Company of the Imperial Yeomanry. In 1915, he enlisted for service during the First World War with the 2nd King Edward's Horse being discharged in 1916 having not served overseas. Her brother James fought during the 1916 Rising at the GPO and took part in the charge down Moore Street with The O'Rahilly. Another brother, Richard, served with the IRA during the War of Independence and took part in the attack on the Custom House two months after the death of his sister.

On the afternoon of Easter Saturday 1921 at 14.50 a Royal Air Force Crossley Tender was ambushed not far from the Seville family home. One of those present in the tender was Charles Humphrey Smith, originally a fruit farmer from Croydon in Surrey, who had joined the Royal Air Force in 1919 and was sent to 100 Squadron who were based in Baldonnel carrying out air support operations for the British army. He gave his account of events to a court of inquiry in relation to the death of Annie Seville:

> … I was proceeding along Parnell Street, Dublin in a Crossley Tender with two other airmen to get stores for the Officers Mess. None of us were armed. When we were about 100 yds. from the end of the street proceeding towards the Parnell monument a civilian stepped off the path in front of us levelling a revolver called 'hands up' and 'stop'. Immediately three or four other civilians opened fire, the driver was hit immediately and slid down in his seat. Bombs were then thrown, immediately afterwards I was thrown out of the tender. I remember getting up and falling again on the pavement just as a bomb burst in front of me. I remember nothing more until I regained consciousness in an office. At the hospital I learned from the other man who was in the tender that he had guided the car into the top of Sackville Street and stopped it.

The ambush resulted in much confusion and panic on the street with pedestrians rushing away from the scene of the attack. A stampede down Moore Street resulted in fruit and vegetables being scattered throughout the street. Annie Seville was in a room of their flat with her sister Kathleen when they heard the noise of the ambush. Annie was standing at the window and Kathleen moved to bring her away from the window but as she did, Annie fell backwards into her arms wounded. Kathleen handed Annie to their mother and ran for a priest. She was brought to the Jervis Street Hospital where it was found that she had been badly wounded on the right side of her forehead. She was conscious on admission to the hospital but soon lost consciousness and was operated on. A ricocheted bullet had hit her and the surgeon removed fragments of metal from her brain. She died later that night. Alfred Browning, the driver of the Crossley Tender was brought to King George V Hospital where he died of his wounds that evening at 18.30. The same incident also resulted in the death of another civilian, Patrick Sex *(see 6 April 1921)*. Annie was buried in the Garden section of Glasnevin Cemetery but in 1922 was reinterred in a family grave in the St Patrick's section.[20]

30 March 1921   **Royal Irish Constabulary**
Michael Hallissy   *KF 221, Garden*

Michael Hallissy was born on 29 September 1879 near Cahirciveen in Co. Kerry. The son of Denis Hallissy, a farmer and Mary Fitzgerald, he joined the RIC in November 1899 and served in a number of areas before being posted to Dublin in July 1914, four months after he had married Mary Loughnane in Tipperary. He was promoted to sergeant in August 1920 and eight months later was shot dead in an ambush beside the railway bridge crossing on Le Fanu Road near Ballyfermot. Const M. Keary who was wounded in the same ambush described the death of Hallissy:

> At Lucan on the 30th March 1921, I was detailed for a bicycle patrol in company with Sergt Hallissy and two others. We left Lucan about 11.30 hours with orders to investigate as far as possible the burning of two lorries. We proceeded by the main road to Lucan and onto Crumlin from there to the Canal bank, we crossed the canal at the 7th Lock, we turned to the right and on reaching an old mud ruined house about a quarter of a mile from the lock fire was opened up on I and Sergt Hallissy who were leading, there being a distance of about 50 yards between ourselves and Head Constable Mulrooney and Constable Neill. I was dismounting when my bicycle was hit which caused me to tumble into the ditch at the side of the road, before I was able to get up Sergt Hallissy fell on top of me exclaiming 'I am done', these are the only words he spoke. On getting up I found Sergt Hallissy was dead.

Patrick O'Connor, a twenty-year-old member, of the Active Service Unit of the IRA was one of those who carried out the ambush on the RIC bicycle patrol. He gave this account two months before he died in 1953:

> … the local Volunteers of the Company became fairly active in seizing British Military

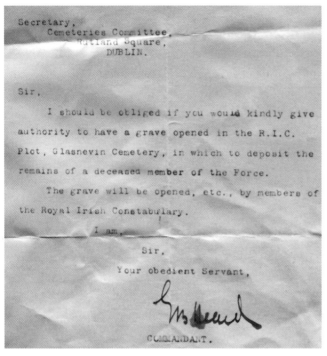

Transport wherever it could lay hands on it and destroy it either by fire or by putting it out of action by smashing it up. One day a lorry was taken down to Bluebell Lane in the vicinity of the Nugget Factory at Bluebell and destroyed by burning. Four RIC men went down to examine this truck. We were in the vicinity at the time and decided that we would attack this RIC party. We took up a position near the railway bridge at Ballyfermot and as the RIC were returning to their station at Lucan, we ambushed them, killing two and wounding one. The British military arrived on the scene in a short time and we withdrew as quickly as we could.

Letter from the Royal Irish Constabulary relating to the organisation of the burial of Michael Hallissy. **Courtesy of Dublin Cemeteries Trust.**

Michael Hallissy had been shot in the back on the lower part of the right hand side. The bullet had lodged in his body, severing an artery and resulted in death due to haemorrhage. A bullet had also hit him in the right leg. He was buried in the Royal Irish Constabulary plot in the cemetery.[21]

4 April 1921   **Civilian**
John Burke   *KA 107, Garden*

John Burke was four when he was fatally wounded near St Mary's Place. The young boy lived with his parents at 11 Lower Wellington Street and his father, also John, was employed as a labourer at the Royal Barracks. On the afternoon of 2 April 1921 Pte Henry Edward Cherry, of the 615th Motor Transport Company Royal Army Service Corps, was driving a motorcycle with a sidecar passenger, Pte Reginald James of the same unit. The two men were destined for Broadstone railway station and as they turned the corner from Dorset Street into St Mary's Place they saw a group of four men in close proximity.

One of the men pointed a revolver in their direction and fired. James returned fire and a bomb was then thrown in his direction, which exploded behind the motorcycle. Cherry accelerated and left the area as quickly as possible and on arrival at Broadstone rang the orderly room at the North Dublin Union to report the ambush. At the time of the ambush, John Burke was walking on the footpath with his grandmother, Bridget Fraher. Both had been wounded and taken to the Mater Hospital. While there, Bridget gave a description of the short event:

> I heard some reports from the direction of the Picture House and then a loud explosion. There was a lot of smoke. I saw two soldiers in a motorcycle and sidecar driving very fast towards Broadstone. They were firing towards their rear. Something struck my thigh and the little boy fell also. He was bleeding from the head. We were both taken to the Mater Hospital where I am now. I was struck as the soldiers were passing me and I don't think that the shots that shot the boy and me could have been fired by them.

At the hospital, it was discovered that a stray bullet had hit John and entered his head just behind his left ear. It caused significant damage to his brain, an operation was preformed but he died on 4 April at 11.20. His grandmother, Bridget Fraher, died in 1943, and is also buried in Glasnevin.[22]

6 April 1921   **Civilian**
Michael Daly   *CI 275½, St Bridget's*

Michael Daly was born on 1 August 1889 in Tipperary, the son of William Daly and Hanora Treacy. His father worked as a stonemason and bricklayer and the family moved to Dublin while Michael was still young. Michael worked as a painter for Mr Hull of Ringsend Road and was a talented footballer. A vice-captain of Glasnevin AFC he lived at 17 Crampton Buildings with his sisters and brother whom he helped support. He was aged thirty-one when he was killed during an ambush on Harcourt Street in Dublin. On the evening of 6 April 1921, a lorry, with men of the 2nd Battalion Worcestershire Regiment under the command of Lieut E.F. Twiney, was travelling from Portobello Barracks to the North Wall when it was ambushed between Harcourt Road and Harcourt Street. Sgt T.C. Harrell, one of those in the lorry, recalled:

> I saw a man throw a bomb which burst about 15 to 20 yards away from the lorry. Fire was immediately opened on to him with what effects I could not say as the lorry was still moving until it got to Harcourt St. Station, when my attention was attracted by men firing behind the pillars of Harcourt St. Station. Fire from my side was opened

on to them, then the lorry moved on and turned about near the High School and came back. I noticed two civilians lying apparently wounded near the Electric Car Standard and as we got close to these civilians one pulled himself along the ground and threw a bomb. I fired at him and hit him.

As the ambush unfolded Michael Daly was walking up Harcourt Street with his friend John Brady who worked as station foreman in Broadstone Station. Brady described the death of Daly:

… Michael Daly was a very old and intimate friend of mine, whenever I was not engaged on duty in the evening time I met him by appointment. I was in his complete confidence and he was a steady temperate man and never took any drink and as far as I know he took no part in politics, his whole ambition was racing, football and dancing. On the 6th April I met him at the Billiard Room in Fleet Street within a few hundred yards of his residence. A game of billiards was suggested but he said owing to it being a fine night he would go for a walk. It was decided we would go to the Rialto to look at some new houses he was painting. We proceeded from there up Grafton Street, up Harcourt Street finally arriving opposite Harcourt Street Station on the right hand side going towards Portobello. We were practically beside 52 and 53. When we arrived opposite the station a military lorry came round Harcourt Road into Harcourt Street. I heard a shot fired from Harcourt Road end and Michael Daly said to me those fellows are firing. Then there was a volley fired from the lorry and when the lorry came opposite 54 which is nearer to Harcourt Road there was a loud explosion I said Mick lie down and come up here on the steps. I went to 53 door and he went to 52 and we both laid down … The firing was still continuing from the lorry. I saw Daly about this time falling on his back out on the front of the door his head was next to the street and his feet next to the door. I asked him was he hurt, he made no reply. When I saw him before he fell he was partly kneeling facing towards the city and when he fell he rolled over on his left side and his head was more towards Harcourt Road. I was beating the bottom of the door to attract attention to get in. I was let into No. 53 where I remained.

Terence McGlynn and Daniel Carew, both part of the ambush party, had been killed. Pte A. Fryer and Pte A.E. Crow had opened fire from the lorry on Michael Daly believing that he was one of the attackers and killed him instantly. He had suffered catastrophic injuries to his skull and brain. The British army court of inquiry in relation to his death returned a verdict that they were responsible and that he died '… from shock and haemorrhage following injuries to the brain caused by gun shot wounds inflicted in Harcourt Street during an attack on a patrol of the 2nd Bn. The Worcestershire Regiment in the execution of their duty. The court is further of the opinion that the death was accidental and that the deceased was not doing any illegal act at the time of his death.'[23]

6 April 1921   **Civilian**
Patrick Sex   *TH 72½, St Bridget's*

Patrick Sex died of wounds received during the same ambush on a Royal
Air Force Crossley Tender that resulted in the death of Annie Seville (*see 28
March 1921*). He was forty-one, married with ten children and living in Lower
Dominick Street at the time of his death. He worked for John O'Doherty
who owned a butcher's shop at 63 Parnell Street. O'Doherty noted that as the
ambush began Sex was attending a customer in the shop and that following
the explosions several bomb fragments entered the shop. O'Doherty heard him
say, 'I am struck'. Exactly what had happened was unclear to him. Patrick Sex
was brought to the Jervis Street Hospital soon after the ambush and here it was
noted that he had been wounded in the left thigh. His condition deteriorated
and an operation was performed on 4 April. A piece of shrapnel from a bomb
was removed from his leg. However, the following day he began to suffer with
tetanus due to the wound and he died on 6 April at 21.30. His funeral took
place to a family grave, owned by his mother, on 11 April, overshadowed by a
public display of mourning in the city that day for Archbishop William Walsh
who had died on 9 April and was also buried in Glasnevin.[24]

13 April 1921   **Royal Irish Constabulary**
Patrick Joseph Neary   *EJ 62, Dublin*

Patrick Neary, a constable with the Royal Irish Constabulary, was fatally
wounded in an accident in Dublin Castle on 1 April 1921. Neary was the
driver of a C Company Auxiliary Division Crossley Tender that had stopped at
the Castle. Section Leader Henry Playle who was in charge of the tender gave
his account of what happened to Neary at an inquiry:

> At Dublin Castle on the 1st April 1921 at 13.05 hours I was in charge of a Crossley
> Tender. I placed my Winchester repeating gun in front of the car, leaning against the
> instrument board muzzle upwards, there was one round in the breach and the hammer
> was unlocked. Constable Neary was in the driver seat (being the driver of the car).
> Tem. Cadet Robinson and Lycette, Sec. Leader Tesseyman, Tem. Cadet Davies and
> Knight were standing outside on the near side of the car. I had my back to the car,
> about 2 feet away from the door. The car had been standing stationery for about ½
> an hour with the engine running. I heard a report and looking around found Const.
> Neary had been wounded. I jumped into the car and found he had wounds in the left
> hand and left side of the head. I assisted to bandage him and sent him to hospital. On
> examining the gun afterwards, I found that the hammer had been damaged by the fall.
> The gun was on the ground. The vibration must have caused it to fall.

Ernest Lycette another member of the ADRIC present that day, and who was sitting in the back of the Crossley Tender, gave evidence to the inquiry that he saw nothing until he heard the shot and on turning saw Neary wounded and a Winchester repeater on the ground. In an account of his career in the British army and Auxiliary Division that Lycette wrote in 1966 for his children and grandchildren, he gave a different account of what happened:

> In the morning, we got a cup of tea and perused the orders of the day to see if we were on duty. Unfortunately, I was on patrol and we had to report to the Castle for orders. Section Leader Quale (*sic*) was in charge, with five other cadets and we had to be at the vehicle park at 8 am. The leader had been recently issued with a new powerful gun, which was a heavy 12 bore, I think. He was climbing down the lorry step, when he either hit the butt of the rifle or mishandled it somehow, anyway it let off one 'bang'. The driver of the lorry was killed and as I was standing in front of the lorry I was hit by some shot but did not realise until one of the other men said 'Look, Ernie, blood'.

Const. Neary was brought to King George V Hospital were he was examined by Lieut Col F. J. Palmer of the Royal Army Medical Corps. Palmer described him as bleeding from several wounds to the head and left arm and 'though conscious was wildly excited and almost maniacal'. An operation was immediately performed and Neary's left index finger amputated. He had five wounds to his head, some of the fragments of shot remained in his skull and not all could be removed. Bleeding was halted and his condition improved for a number of days, however over time he deteriorated and died on the afternoon of 13 April. A post mortem found that a small fragment of shot and a button, likely to have been from his cap, had lodged in his brain and that these were the fragments that doctors were unable to remove with surgery. A court of inquiry returned the verdict that Const. Neary had died '… from gun shot wounds accidentally caused by the discharge of a Winchester Repeater Gun'. Col R.D.F. Oldman, commanding 24th Infantry Brigade added his opinion that the culpable negligence of Henry Playle was responsible for the death of Neary and that he should be dealt with by disciplinary measures.[25]

19 April 1921   **Royal Irish Constabulary**
Stephen Kirwan   *KF 221½, Garden*

Sgt Stephen Kirwan was fatally wounded during a brief encounter with members of the Fingal Brigade IRA at a pub in Ballyboughal in north Co. Dublin. Born in Ferns, Co. Wexford in 1877 Kirwan had joined the RIC in 1898 and was stationed in Balbriggan from 1920. On 19 April 1921, some men of the local Fingal Brigade of the IRA had planned to attack an RIC patrol, however the patrol never arrived and the IRA stood down. Some of the IRA members made their way to Connor's public house in Ballyboughal. While here a small group of RIC, acting on information, made their way to the pub. Although the members of the Royal Irish Constabulary had been called to the pub it would appear that the encounter that followed took both the members of the IRA and the RIC by surprise. One of the RIC men described what he perceived he had witnessed:

> On the 18th April 1921, I accompanied Sgt Stephen Kirwan in a motor car to Ballyboughill. On arriving at Ballyboughill at about 5.45 p.m. the car pulled up outside Connor's public house and the Sgt went into the premises by the back entrance having told myself and Constable [redacted] to wait in the car. Three civilians named White, Wilson & Donnelly were standing outside the premises when we arrived and they went inside the yard about three minutes after the Sgt. At about 5.55 p.m. I heard about 12 shots in rapid succession from the direction of the yard. Constable [redacted] and I immediately ran to the yard and found the door fastened. We opened fire

A photograph of Stephen Kirwan taken early in his career with the Royal Irish Constabulary. **Courtesy of the Kirwan Family.**

over the wall and then saw the Sgt coming out by another door. I saw that he was bleeding from a wound in the head. He said that he was shot in the stomach, that he was done, and that the red fellow with the moustache had shot him. Seeing that Sgt Kirwan was in a serious condition we returned at once to Swords. Later in the day I saw the man, White, wounded in bed at the Post Office, Ballyboughill. The man Wilson whom I saw going into the yard shortly after the Sgt went in, is a red haired man with a moustache.

According to Edward Connor, the proprietor of the pub, Kirwan entered the building through his kitchen. The sergeant asked some questions, declined a drink and then exited through the door back into the yard where the shooting began. The three men named by the constable as being present were Peter White, Patrick Donnelly and James Wilson. In the brief firefight Sgt Kirwan had been shot through the right armpit, the bullet exiting on the left side of his torso. The red haired man with the moustache who had shot him was James Wilson, a veteran member of the Irish Volunteers who had served at the Mendicity

Institute during the 1916 Rising. In the exchange of fire, Stephen Kirwan had wounded Peter White, captain of the Swords Company, Fingal Brigade, IRA.

In the aftermath of the incident Kirwan was bundled into their car by the other members of the constabulary and sped towards Swords. As they travelled, they came upon Dr Christopher Grimes from Malahide and the occupants called upon him to give assistance to Kirwan. Grimes found him to be in great pain and suffering with shock and stayed with him in the car as they returned to Swords. Having had the opportunity to assess the wound Dr Grimes had him sent to King George V Hospital where a medical officer of the Royal Army Medical Corps saw him. While here his brother Charles, also a member of the RIC, visited him and Stephen explained to him what had happened, telling him, 'I am done Charlie'.

Peter White was taken to the local post office where he was seen by a local priest and doctor. White told the doctor that 'Kirwan did for me' and asked him 'am I dying or will I get over it?' Despite the best efforts of other members of the Fingal Brigade, White was captured and also brought to King George V Hospital. Peter White died there on 19 April at 18.20. Stephen Kirwan died just over four hours later in the same hospital leaving a pregnant widow and nine children.[26]

25 April 1921	Irish Republican Army
Thomas Traynor	*A 23½, O'Connell Tower Circle*

Thomas Traynor was born in Tullow, Co. Carlow in 1882. At a young age he moved to Dublin where he worked as a bootmaker and in April 1902 married Elizabeth Davis in the Church of St Nicholas of Myra Without on Francis Street. An early member of the Irish Volunteers he served during the 1916 Rising with the garrison at Boland's Mills under the command of Joe O'Connor and, according to him, was wounded during the fighting there. Traynor was arrested in the aftermath of the Rising and imprisoned in Wakefield Prison before being moved to Frongoch. Following his release in the 1917 general amnesty, he returned to Dublin where he lived in McCaffrey's Estate, Mount Brown and worked at his bootmaker's shop at Merchant's Arch. During the same period, in the midst of the War of Independence, Traynor was a member of B Company, 3rd Battalion, Dublin Brigade, IRA and was captured carrying a gun following the skirmish at Great Brunswick (Pearse) Street on the evening that six executions had taken place in Mountjoy Jail (*see 14 March 1921*). Thomas Traynor was placed on trial on 5 April 1921 accused that he '...

feloniously, wilfully and of his malice aforethought did kill and murder Cadet Francis Joseph Farrell'. He was also charged with the death of Cadet Bernard J.L. Beard. Traynor's presence with a gun at the scene of the fight that resulted in the death of Farrell and Beard was deemed enough for him to be put on trial by association. Lieut Charles Frederick Weber, of the 3rd Tank Battalion, gave evidence at Traynor's trial of his arrest:

> On the evening of the 14th March 1921, I was detailed with my armoured car to go on a raid at 144 Great Brunswick Street Dublin. I was on the back of the Rolls armoured car. There were two tenders in the convoy besides the armoured car. The tenders were conveying Auxiliaries. We left the Castle at about 8 p.m. the two tenders led the way and my armoured car followed. We went along Dame Street by Trinity College and into Great Brunswick Street. The convoy slowed down just before the leading car reached No. 144 Great Brunswick Street ... All the convoy were closed up. My car was just beyond the corner where Upper Sandwith Street meets Great Brunswick Street. I then heard a sudden burst of small arms fire from the direction of the head of the column. On the back of the armoured car with me was Lieut. Fryer of the Tank Corps also Capt. Crang of the Auxiliaries. My car was then fired on by groups of men standing at the corners of the cross streets immediately in my rear. We all replied to the first with our pistols. I don't know if we hit anyone. We fired at the points where we saw the flashes. The night was dark and the street was badly lighted. I emptied my pistol. I saw a man running by my car on the pavement on my right. He came from the direction of the head of the convoy. I jumped off the car and caught him at the corner of Great Brunswick Street and Upper Sandwith Street. I collared him and brought him down. He was on his back and I was on top of him. I had his right wrist held in my left hand. He had an automatic in his right hand and I called for help. Capt. Crang came and I took the pistol out of the man's hand. The accused now present was the man. We put him into the armoured car and I ordered the car to convey the prisoner to the Castle.

Following the evidence of a number of military and Auxiliary witnesses Traynor responded to the accusations made against him:

> I carry on a small business here in the city, assisted by my two boys. I have a wife and 10 children. Under these circumstances it takes me all my time to earn enough to keep them. I have never been yet asked by the Republican party to take any active part in the present activity, but as an old member I was in the Army in 1916. I would be considered a proper person to do a message. The pistol in question was left in at my place on the Monday with the words: 'Bring this to 144 Great Brunswick Street at about 8 o'clock and you will find someone there to take it from you'. I proceeded to 144 at about 10 minutes past. I had just crossed Brunswick Street on the right hand side and as I advanced about 4 or 5 yards towards 144 a military car passed me and stopped just in front of me opposite 144. Just then firing broke out. I stood up against the railings and when the firing ceased a little I took the thing out of my pocket and ran back towards Sandwith Street. I was caught on the corner of Sandwith Street.

Thomas Traynor was found guilty of the charges placed before him and was sentenced 'to suffer death by being hanged'. His sentence was confirmed on 21 April 1921 and was to be carried out four days later. The day before his execution, he received a large number of visitors including his wife and family members. The following morning in the hour before his death Thomas Traynor attended mass, took communion and said prayers with the prison chaplain and assistant chaplain. As 08.00 approached his arms and feet were tied by the executioner, he was blindfolded and his face covered. It was reported that his last words were 'Lord Jesus receive my soul' as the doors of the scaffold dropped. Outside the walls of the prison a large group of members of Cumann na mBan recited the rosary in Irish and Elizabeth Traynor was overcome with emotion. Thomas Traynor was buried that afternoon in a simple wooden coffin within the prison walls in a grave adjoining Kevin Barry and the others executed previously in the prison during the War of Independence. His widow, Elizabeth, was left with ten children to care for, the youngest of whom, Sheila, was aged just five months. Elizabeth lived to the age of ninety-two, dying in England in April 1973.[27]

7 May 1921   Civilian
William Curry   TD 88, St Paul's

William Curry, aged thirteen and from Upper Erne Street, died after a bomb explosion close to his home in Dublin. At around 14.00 on the afternoon of 7 May 1921, Curry was playing with four other boys, three of whom were also from Erne Street. According to contemporary accounts, the boys entered the railway at the rear of Westland Row Station. While there William Curry happened across a bomb in a railway building, the pin was pulled and it exploded. All of the boys were injured but William Curry was the most seriously wounded. He was brought to Sir Patrick Dun's Hospital by ambulance. On arrival he was examined by a doctor who found that he had been wounded multiple times by shrapnel around his legs, waist and in his chest. His right hand, in which he had held the bomb, was also badly damaged. He was alive on arrival at the hospital but died three hours later of his injuries. Interestingly William's father, William Curry senior, was a member of the IRA and, through his job as a fireman and sailor travelling between Dublin and Liverpool, was involved in the importation and conveyance of weapons during the War of Independence.[28]

14 May 1921   **Civilian**
James Brennan   *GB 38, South*

On 18 May 1921, three funerals came to Glasnevin of those who had died
four days earlier on 14 May due to separate incidents during the War of
Independence. The first, at 11.35, was that of ten-year-old James Brennan from
Mary Street in Dublin. James had been wounded in an incident in Dublin on
the afternoon of 13 January 1920. That day members of the British army had
parked their lorry on Aston Quay, parallel with Westmoreland Street, and had
begun inspecting motor permits. Towards the end of their patrol, and as the
soldiers attached a confiscated motorbike and sidecar to their lorry, a shot rang
out. Witnesses to the incident included two journalists Ernest Townley of the
Daily Express and Charles Green of the *Manchester Guardian*. The latter in
describing what he saw stated that:

> I was walking along Aston Quay in the direction of Westmoreland Street in company
> with Mr Townley of the *Daily Express*. I was about 100 yards from Westmoreland
> Street, I saw a lorry drawn up at the corner on the right hand side of the road as I
> approached. When I got up to it I saw a crowd round the tail board which I could
> see had been lowered. The front of the lorry was practically in line with the entrance
> to Westmoreland Street and the parapet of the bridge. I made my way through the
> crowd and walked along the pavement between the lorry and the houses. Mr Townley
> stayed at the back of the lorry. When I was about half way round the corner going into
> Westmoreland Street I heard a report from behind me and coming from the direction
> of the lorry, at the same time on my left side I was conscious of a kind of gust of wind
> on the left side of my face. I only heard one shot fired that evening. On hearing the
> shot and after taking a couple of paces I turned round and looked at the lorry. I saw a
> boy lying on the pavement between me and the lorry, his feet were towards the corner
> of the pavement. I saw a soldier get out of the lorry and go towards the boy. I turned
> round again and looked up Westmoreland Street where I saw a woman lying at the
> curb on the right hand side as you leave O'Connell Bridge. The boy was about 5 yards
> from the lorry and the girl about 15 yards. When I passed between the lorry and the
> houses the soldiers in the lorry were holding their rifles horizontal ... Previous to the
> firing there was no disturbance of any kind between the soldiers and the civilians, in
> fact the utmost good humour prevailed. The number of persons in front of the lorry
> was slightly more than would be normal. I noticed a pool of blood close to the boy's
> head whilst he was lying on the pavement.

A number of witnesses, including Ernest Townley and James Kibbey, a civilian
who lived in Ivy Buildings and was slightly wounded, also stated that they
only heard one shot being fired. The officer in charge of the lorry maintained
that none of his soldiers had been responsible for the shot that had been fired
and that he could account for all of the ammunition that had been issued

to his men that day. No witnesses came forward that saw any shot or shots being fired that day. James Brennan died in a coma four months after he was wounded in the head. It was officially recorded that he died '... following an abscess of the brain due to gunshot wound inflicted by some person unknown guilty of wilful murder'.[29]

14 May 1921	**Royal Irish Constabulary**
Joseph Coleman	*KF 221½, Garden*

The two other funerals to Glasnevin on 18 May 1921 took the form of a double funeral that afternoon for two members of the Royal Irish Constabulary both killed four days earlier, one in Dublin and one in Cork. Both men were buried together in the same grave within the Royal Irish Constabulary plot of the cemetery. Joseph Coleman was born in London in 1894 and worked as a groom before joining the Royal Irish Constabulary in March 1903 and served in stations in Limerick, Belfast and Clare. In April 1915, while stationed in Quilty he married Anna Healy, the daughter of a doctor from Miltown Malbay. That June he was transferred to Cork and was promoted to the rank of sergeant in February 1921. At about 15.00 on Saturday 14 May 1921 Coleman entered Buckley's public house in Midleton to buy groceries. He was followed by a group of men of the IRA who shot him multiple times. Some constables who had heard the shooting rushed to Buckley's and found Coleman wounded on the floor. When it became apparent that Coleman was badly wounded some of the members of the constabulary made their way towards the local Catholic church for a priest. While on their way they were ambushed. Some years later John Kelleher of the Midleton Company, 4th Battalion, Cork No. 1 Brigade, IRA, later recalled the incidents of the day:

> Saturday 14th May 1921 saw another attack made in Midleton. So far as I can re-member orders were received from Brigade Headquarters in Cork that an R.I.C. man should be shot in every town in the battalion area. Early on that day, Sergeant Coleman of the R.I.C. was shot dead in a public house in Midleton. At about 2 p.m. two Black and Tans were proceeding down the town when they were ambushed by three I.R.A. men, Jackeen Ahern and Tom Buckley from the Midleton Company and Tom Riordan from the Lisgould Company. The three lads lay in ambush behind a low wall at the end of the town. They had rifles which were brought in by Mick Murnane of Coppingerstown. Fire was opened on the 'Tans' at about 150 yards range, both of whom were killed and their guns captured. Another policeman named Sergeant Gleeson narrowly escaped, although fire was brought to bear on him too.

The two other men killed were Constables Thomas Cornyn and Harold Thompson.[30]

14 May 1921	Royal Irish Constabulary
Robert Redmond	*KF 221½, Garden*

On the same day that Sgt Joseph Coleman was shot dead, a gunshot was heard at Frankfort Cottages off Killarney Street in Dublin at approximately 22.15. An unidentified man was found dead with a wound to his head in what was described by a newspaper as 'mysterious circumstances'. The body was removed by ambulance to the Mater Hospital and here a paper leave pass was found on his person that identified him as Temporary Constable Robert Redmond who had been granted leave from Beggar's Bush Barracks for three days from 13 May.

Robert Redmond was born on 27 April 1878 in Ballykillageer near Woodenbridge, Co. Wicklow, the son of Thomas and Maria Redmond. In later life, he moved to north Dublin where he worked as a general labourer and resided near Santry. In August 1898, he married Anne Shields in the Catholic church in Fairview and they had seven children. On the outbreak of the First World War in 1914 he enlisted in the newly formed 8th Battalion, Royal Dublin Fusiliers and was discharged after three months, being described as 'not likely to become an efficient soldier.' He re-enlisted the following month, this time in the Connaught Rangers but deserted from them in August 1915 before enlisting once again, in the Royal Irish Rifles, that October. He stayed with this regiment until March 1916 when he absented himself from the army once again. This time he was arrested and sent for trial, however he escaped custody only to sign up again, with the Royal Irish Regiment on this occasion. The British army soon identified him and his former activities and in June 1916 he was sentenced by a Field General Court Martial to one year of detention after he was found guilty of being absent without leave, losing his equipment, escaping and fraudulently enlisting himself in the army. Redmond did not serve his full prison term and deserted once more in November 1916. In June 1917, he enlisted for a final time in the 17th Battalion Scottish Rifles and that October his wife, Anne, died aged thirty-three in the North Dublin Union and was buried in Glasnevin Cemetery.

In July 1918, Redmond married Mary Anne Moore, a seamstress from Duleek in Co. Meath. He continued his service with the Scottish Rifles until March 1919 when he was discharged without having served overseas. On 3 January 1921, he joined the Veterans and Drivers Division of the Auxiliary

Division, Royal Irish Constabulary on the recommendation of the district inspector in Duleek. He served as a temporary constable with the Auxiliaries at Beggar's Bush Barracks in Dublin and on 13 May 1921 he was granted leave for three days. He returned home to his wife and son, John Joseph, who had been born that month one year earlier. The following day on 14 May, he was shot dead at Frankfort Cottages. In the immediate aftermath of the shooting a confidential report was written by an unidentified member of II Section, C Company, 2nd Battalion, Dublin Brigade, IRA, and sent to the battalion adjutant. It described the death of Robert Redmond:

> While out on Intelligence Patrol on Sat 14/5/21 we saw a man who aroused our suspicions. My companion was lucky in getting into his company. Afterwards we held him up and searched him and found an ex-soldier's badge in his pocket. We demanded a confession from him which he refused to give. We then took off his belt, put it around his neck and proceeded to strangle him and not until he got blue in the face did he admit that he was a Black and Tan on weekend leave and promised if we stopped to give us some information. We took him away with us to _____ [blank] and I put my revolver to his head and asked him to give us the information or say his prayers he refused to tell us anything and as it was coming near curfew I had no other alternative but to fire. He fell and I leant over him and put another round into him. We then made good a retreat.
>
> Signed H Cpl. Sec *II*[31]

17 May 1921   Civilian
Charles Cox   *CD 81, St Paul's*

Charles Cox, a bricklayer and Dublin Corporation employee, was killed when he was caught in the crossfire of an ambush on a military car near Newcomen Bridge. He was the son of John P. Cox, a bricklayer, builder's foreman and councillor. Charles, aged thirty-six, lived at Riley's Avenue, Mount Brown, with his wife Margaret, whom he had married in 1912 and their five children, ranging in age from eight years to three weeks. Based in the Corporation Works in Stanley Street, Charles was carrying out work at Kearn's Shop on the day he was killed. It was stated that as a military car containing three British soldiers crossed Newcomen Bridge there was an exchange of fire. Whilst returning fire one of the soldiers shot Charles and he collapsed, wounded in the back. He was brought by ambulance to Jervis Street Hospital but was dead on arrival, the bullet lacerated his spinal cord. The official British General Headquarters report relating to the incident stated that:

About 4 p.m. this afternoon a Ford box car containing troops was fired on at Amiens St. The fire was returned but the result is unknown. No military casualties.

His funeral, with a large attendance, came to Glasnevin three days later. He was interred in a grave with his daughter, Margaret, who had died a year earlier, aged one, from whooping cough.[32]

21 May 1921
John Byrne

Civilian
FD 9, St Paul's

On the afternoon of Saturday, 21 May 1921, two men entered the Jervis Street Hospital and made their way to the St Joseph's Ward and the bed of John Byrne who had been seriously injured in a shooting the previous day. Without being questioned, they placed Byrne on a stretcher, carried him to a courtyard outside the hospital and shot him multiple times in the head before escaping. Byrne, from 44 North Brunswick Street, Dublin, was the son of John and Lucy Byrne and like his father worked as a shoemaker. From an early age he had suffered with a limp and was known as 'Hoppy'. Dublin Brigade IRA suspected that Byrne was providing information to the authorities and on 20 May orders were issued to B Company, 1st Battalion to arrest him.

After his capture, Byrne was taken to the headquarters of the IRA's Active Service Unit at Great Strand Street where he was interrogated. That evening Byrne was taken to nearby Mary Street and shot. Remarkably, however, his wounds proved not to be fatal and he was taken to the Jervis Street Hospital for treatment. His potential recovery left the IRA in a precarious situation. Not only was Byrne in a position to identify those who had intended to kill him, he was also aware of the location of the ASU headquarters. Paddy Flanagan the commanding officer of the ASU issued orders that Byrne was to be 'liquidated' as soon as possible and at 14.15 that day two men of the ASU entered the Jervis Street Hospital wearing no disguise and commandeered a stretcher from an orderly before making their way to Byrne's bed. They placed him on the stretcher before carrying him downstairs and outside into the hospital court-yard and shot him in the head a number of times. The close proximity of the gun barrel to his face resulted in scorch marks to his skin.

Thirty minutes after the incident his wife, Bridget (neé Mitchell), whom he had married in January 1920 in Terenure, arrived to visit her husband only to be informed of the audacious manner in which he had been killed. The killing of Byrne caused outrage and shock, not only amongst the public, but also the medical profession and more importantly for the IRA, the Sisters of Mercy who threatened to desist from secretly giving medical treatment to IRA volunteers. The intervention of Michael Collins and a promise that there would be no repeat of such an action was required to stabilise the situation. John Byrne's funeral came to Glasnevin three days after his death and he was buried in a grave owned by his brother-in-law.[33]

25 May 1921	**Civilian**
John Byrne	*FK 129, St Patrick's*

On 25 May 1921, one of the most dramatic events during the War of Independence in Dublin was played out at the Custom House, the prominent eighteenth century building on the Dublin quays designed by James Gandon. On that day, a large contingent of over 100 members of Dublin Brigade IRA made an attack on the building. It was targeted as one of the most obvious symbolic structures of British rule in Ireland and from it was directed a wide range of government services and departments including administrative elements of taxation in the country. The destruction of what was described by Oscar Traynor as 'the administrative heart of the British Civil Service machine in this country' would inflict a symbolic blow for the IRA and have a significant monetary impact for the British government in Ireland. Although the operation proved to be a success for the IRA, with the Custom House being destroyed by fire, it came at a very heavy cost with a large proportion of the IRA members who took part in the action being captured and many casualties being incurred. Oscar Traynor, officer commanding Dublin Brigade IRA, was responsible for the operation and later gave details of the preparations for the attack and how the day unfolded:

> As the target was in the 2nd Battalion area it was decided that the actual destruction of the building would be entrusted to that unit. Commandant Tom Ennis was appointed to take sole control of the party within the building. The 2nd Battalion was reinforced by the addition of the 'Squad', a party of about twelve men who were attached to the D.I.'s department, as well as some men of the Active Service Unit. To the 1st Battalion was allotted the task of protecting the outside of the building. In the event of a surprise attack by enemy forces the Battalion was to engage them with grenade, rifle and machine gun fire ... To the 5th Battalion, the Engineers, was given the very important task of cutting off from all communications, telephonic, or otherwise, the Custom House with the outside world. This was a highly technical job and the most skilled men of the Engineers were called on to carry out this work ... The preparation for the main task of destruction brought about the necessity for a number of lesser actions ... It also necessitated the holding up on an oil concern and their staff for some

considerable time, the commandeering of motor lorries to bring the tinned paraffin to the Custom House precisely on time. When this lorry arrived at the back entrance to the building which is opposite Lower Gardiner Street, the men detailed for the inside operation entered, at the same time taking with them from off the lorry a tin of paraffin. The building was also entered from the Quays and Beresford Place entrance opposite Liberty Hall. In this way the number going in by any one door was not excessive and it was hoped would not arouse suspicion ... Within the building each Captain had been allotted a landing and all the offices on that landing to deal with. His job was to see that every person employed on that floor was sent down to see that every person employed on that floor was sent down the main hall where they were kept under the vigilant eyes of the men of the Squad and the A.S.U. With this part of his task completed, he was then to see that every office on his landing was thoroughly saturated with paraffin oil ... When the job of saturation had been completed, the officer was to report to Commandant Ennis on the ground floor and the actual firing was to take place on an order given by him consisting of a single blast on his whistle. Two blasts were to signify the completion of the job and the withdrawal of all men to the ground floor.

Everything went perfectly as per plan, except that just before all the floors had given the officer commanding the 'OK' or 'All ready' signal, someone blew two blasts on a whistle and all sections retired to the main hall. One officer reported that he had not completed his task of saturation. The commandant sent him and his men back at once to finish the job. The few minutes loss here was the difference between the successful retirement of all the participants and the arrival of large numbers of enemy forces in lorries and armoured cars. These forces swept into Beresford Place at exactly 1.25 p.m., just five minutes after the time allotted in the plan for the completion of the operation. They were immediately engaged on entry to Beresford Place by the 1st Battalion units with volleys of revolver shots and the throwing of a number of hand grenades. For some unknown reason the machine gun which our men were to have mounted inside the Custom House doors at the far end of Beresford Place did not come into action ... the Squad in the Custom House had gone into action with their parabellums and Mauser automatics with still further disastrous effects to the Black and Tans who were attempting to storm the main back entrance. Before I managed to get away I saw several bodies lying around the entrance immovable and, as far as I could see and judge, dead.

The official special intelligence report compiled by the Auxiliary Division Royal Irish Constabulary gave their perspective in trying to counter against the IRA action:

An urgency call was received by F. Coy Aux. Div. R.I.C. that the Customs (*Sic*) House was being attacked by armed men. Immediately a relief force dashed out under the command of the officer commanding the company and other officers. This force consisted of 3 tenders and 1 armoured car. As the first two tenders entered Beresford Place and were proceeding in the direction of the front entrance of the Customs House a heavy hail of fire was opened on them from the windows of the Customs

The Custom House on fire on 25 May 1921. **Courtesy** of Mercier Archives.

House, the railway line and the adjoining street corners. The tenders immediately halted to get into action and as the crew dismounted from the second tender bombs were thrown at them from the railway line over head. Six Cadets sustained wounds, two slight. Taking what cover they could find the remainder of the party replied to the hostile fire and brought a Lewis gun into action on the windows from which the heaviest firing seemed to come. A party of rebels made a dash from the front door of the Customs House and endeavoured to escape through the cordon, which we had thrown round the building. They were armed and fired at us as they ran. They were brought down some shot dead and some wounded. Others made sorties at intervals and were quickly dispatched. All these had guns on them when picked up. On arrival at the Customs House it was noticed that the upper portion of the premises was ablaze. Reinforcements were phoned for and the Fire Brigade summoned. When the firing abated entry was effected by the entrance at the riverside. By this time Q Coy had arrived and assisted in strengthening the cordon and searching the premises and rounding up or shooting all persons found inside.

All the documents and papers had been pulled out on to the floors, the furniture upset and smashed and the lot, as well as the walls and passageways soaked with paraffin and petrol. The whole of the centre of the building was well ablaze and progress had to be made carefully. As the search party moved through the corridors the rebels still in the building retreated. T/Cadets Sparrow and Corson got on the trail of five of them and eventually rounded them up at the Stationary Department. These men seeing no hope of escape surrendered. On searching the passageway from which they came the cadets found seven revolvers and bombs. These prisoners were in most cases heavily sprinkled with paraffin and petrol. They, with others who were rounded up in the building, were taken to the Castle. During the firing a number of men and women came out of the building and were put under guard until matters settled down. Those that were subsequently identified as Customs House staff were released and the remainder sent to Arbour Hill. The fire in the meantime was gaining great headway and seemed to defy the efforts of the Brigade. Several attempts were made to save what articles we could from the conflagration. A gallant attempt was made to save a large number of stamps but the fumes beat back the search party. The Company returned to the Castle at 14.30 hours.

Daniel McAleese was one of the civilian employees present in the Custom House that day. He was taken by surprise by the sudden entrance of the men of Dublin Brigade into the building:

Around 1 p.m. on that memorable day in May 1921, I was lunching as usual with three Civil Service colleagues in the dining room of the Custom House. This room was situated on the ground floor convenient to the Beresford Place entrance. There were about a dozen other diners in the room at the time as well as the manageress and one or two waitresses. The table at which I sat was furthest from the door partly facing the door and the counter behind which the manageress was engaged. My colleagues and I had already partaken of a first light course and, while waiting for the next, were engrossed in conversation. Suddenly, the normal tenor of the room was disturbed by loud and determined voices from the direction of the door shouting 'Up, Up, Up'. I looked towards the door and saw that three young men had entered the room with pointed revolvers and had ordered all the occupants to put their hands up. All in the room complied with this order. With our hands extended above our heads, we were marched out in single file to the corridor where we joined a number of others both of the staff and the public. Meanwhile, several young men passed us carrying tins of petrol. One of the leaders announced that the Custom House was being set on fire and warned us against causing any commotion. The crowd in the corridor grew as the upstairs rooms were vacated by the staff. At an early stage, I inquired from one of the leaders whether we would be permitted to return to our official rooms to recover our coats or other private property. After a short consultation with one of his men, he announced that we would be given five minutes for this purpose, but added that anyone who acted suspiciously or who tried to take away official documents would be summarily disposed of. I raced upstairs to my room where my colleague had remained at work until I should return to relieve him. 'Bill', I shouted, 'get your hat and coat quickly. The I.R.A. have raided the building and are about to blow it up'. Bill was a phlegmatic young man and thought I was perpetrating a joke. Nevertheless, he looked up, nibbling the end of his pen between his teeth, and inquired what I was talking about. At that very moment two armed men entered the room carrying petrol tins. One of them covered us while the other proceeded to work on the windows. I explained that permission had just been given to us downstairs to return to our room to obtain our private belongings. Within a minute, Bill and I with our possessions left the room hurriedly and raced downstairs towards the Beresford Place entrance door. Here were assembled all the members of the several staffs, one D.M.P. man in uniform, together with members of the public who were engaged on business calls in the Custom House when the raiders entered and who were not permitted to leave. The crowd was a mixed one, male and female. Everybody was frightened and nobody knew what was happening outside as the exit was barred. Occasional reports of rifle or revolver fire could be heard and some of the womenfolk became very restive. The position inside worsened quickly as smoke from the upper rooms began to billow downstairs. The upper rooms were now heavily on fire and as the thickened smoke descended to our congested quarters in the corridor, the atmosphere became almost unbearable. There were shouts and screams to open the door. At this stage there was heavy machine gun and rifle fire outside The crowd inside now became panicky; hysteria raged. Caught between smoke and fire inside and incessant gunfire outside, the crowd kept clamouring to get outside. As the smoke and fumes became almost overpowering, the Volunteers tried to quieten the people, telling them that all would be well and that they would shortly be allowed to leave. This advice was of little avail as the smoke drenched downstairs in an unending column, accompanied by the crackling of burning woodwork. It is impossible to envisage how the crowd of half demented individuals would have acted had the double danger to their lives continued. Almost imperceptibly however, the, gunfire outside decreased in volume, Being further away from the exit door, I did not actually hear the orders given, but the door was unblocked and the women folk led the way out of the building. As I had already taken my private property in a small attaché case from my room, I now remembered that I had a bicycle which I had left in the building a few yards away from this particular exit. I managed to lay hands on the bicycle and then joined the tail-end of the queue as it emerged into the open. Being semi-blinded by smoke, it was a few seconds before I glimpsed the scene outside. Those in front of me had their hands up and, as we descended the few steps into the foreyard, there were five or six Black and Tans covering us with rifles and revolvers. Fifty yards or so further away, i.e., at the junction of Gardiner St. and Beresford Place, there were several armoured cars as well as numerous soldiers kneeling with their rifles trained on us. In my efforts to put my hands up and, at the same time, hold on to my bicycle and attaché case, I stumbled down the steps. Immediately, one of the Black and Tans shoved a revolver into my ribs and threatened to shoot me. I struggled up and followed the tail of the crowd which was heading in the direction of Upper Abbey Street. I passed several dead civilians on the way. Just as I got under the railway bridge a heavy fusillade opened up. All of us dropped to the ground and sought shelter between the cobblestones. For at least five minutes (or so it seemed) the armoured cars and machine guns pumped bullets towards the exit from the Custom House, which we had just left. There seemed to be a crossfire as if bullets were passing in both directions over our heads. Presumably this heavy firing was occasioned by the Volunteers emerging from the Custom House in an attempt to fight their way through the military lines. The firing gradually subsided, but members of the Black and Tans, in a kneeling or stooped position, with guns drawn, mingled with our crowd, threatening to shoot if they saw the slightest movement. The firing, which had become somewhat sporadic, finally ceased. After a short interval, heads which had been pressed as close to the paving stones as it was possible for them to be, began to move, to rise and to turn around. The tension was easing.

The eventful attack on the Custom House was over in about an hour, the fire that had been set burned for several days. In the aftermath of the destruction, the task began of identifying and burying the dead. One of the bodies, an unknown man found dead at the scene, was brought to King George V Hospital just after the fighting had ended at the Custom House. The man had two wounds to the chest and a smaller wound on his back, at his right shoulder. The body was identified as James Kelly, a labourer from Lower Gardiner Street, by his wife, Bridget Kelly. Having seen the body of her husband she confirmed that it was James making a formal statement on Friday 27 May 1921:

> I identify the body I have just seen as that of my husband James Kelly. He was 38 years old, he was a casual labourer. He never mentioned politics and had nothing at all to do with them as far as I know. He was out of work and looking for it when he met his death. He served in the Navy for a short period during the Great War. He was in the South African War and served 13 years in the Connaught Rangers.

Bridget made her way to Rutland Square and the offices of the Dublin Cemeteries Committee where she arranged for the burial of her husband in the grave of his great-grandfather, NE 183 Garden. She then bought her mourning clothes and a shirt for him to be laid out in. The following day just before 13.00 in the afternoon Bridget received a letter signed by her husband and sent from Arbour Hill Detention Barracks asking her to send him a pipe and some tobacco. Bridget immediately made her way to Arbour Hill, although she was not allowed to see the man who claimed to be her husband as she did not have a permit. She gave the guard a plain sheet of paper and pencil requesting that the James Kelly in question write the names of all their children in order of their ages. The paper came back to her with the names correctly listed. Her husband had been one of those rounded up in the aftermath of the Custom House fighting. Bridget quickly left for the police station to inform them of her mistake, lamenting the fact that the shirt she had bought for her resurrected husband was now on the body of an unknown man.

It was a short time before it was established that the unknown man was John Byrne, a twenty-seven-year-old poulterer from Killarney Street. He was identified by his sister Eileen who noted that he cycled past the Custom House four times each day on the way from his home to work and back. At 13.00, as the attack on the Custom House began, he was returning home for his lunch break and was unlucky enough to be wounded. It was officially found that John Byrne died as a result of 'shock and haemorrhage caused by bullets fired by some person or persons unknown, accidental death'. He was buried on 2 June 1921.[34]

25 May 1921   **Civilian**
James Connolly   *QB 76, St Paul's*

James Connolly was another civilian casualty of the burning of the Custom House. Aged fifty he resided in Lower Gardiner Street with his wife Mary Anne Connolly and was employed as a quay labourer for the coal merchants, Messrs Heiton & Co. on Custom House Docks. Working directly opposite the Custom House placed Connolly amongst the fighting as it developed. Little was revealed about the exact circumstances that led to his death in a court of inquiry that followed it. The only evidence given was by his wife, who identified him, and by the doctor who received his body at King George V Hospital. The latter confirmed that a bullet that had entered the left side of his chest and exited on the right caused his death. The inquiry returned an opinion that 'James Connelly (*Sic*) died of shock and haemorrhage caused by bullets fired by some person or persons unknown – accidental death'. His wife Mary Anne arranged for his funeral to Glasnevin, which took place on 30 May 1921.[35]

25 May 1921   **Irish Republican Army**
Patrick O'Reilly   *PH 85, St Bridget's*

Patrick O'Reilly (Reilly), a captain in the 2nd Battalion, Dublin Brigade, IRA, was one of two brothers killed in the action at the Custom House in May 1921. From Wellesley Place, off Russell Street, and adjacent to Croke Park, his father Thomas, a compositor, died in 1901, leaving his widow to care for five sons and a daughter. All five brothers were active members of the IRA during the War of Independence, while the family home at Wellesley Avenue was regularly used as a meeting place and arms dump by 2nd Battalion, Dublin Brigade facilitated by his sister and mother, both named Sidney. Patrick was dead on admission to hospital following the fight at the Custom House and the doctor who received him noted that he had four irregular wounds on the right side of the chest and similar wounds on his forehead, mouth, left thigh and forearm, from a bomb or bullets. Harry Colley of Dublin Brigade, IRA, recalled the loss of both brothers:

> I had the melancholy duty of going to St Agatha's Church, North William Street, to receive the remains of Paddy O'Reilly, Quartermaster, 2nd Battalion, who had been killed in the Custom House battle. After the majority of the relatives and friends were gone, his brother Tom, opened the coffin for me and showed me where poor Paddy

had, apparently, been finished by a bullet through the head. There was a small bullet entrance wound in the side of his nose, which plainly showed scorching, indicating that the gun, presumably an automatic, had been placed right at his head when fired. He told me also that there was another corpse in King George's Hospital which he was sure was that of Stephen, his younger brother, who was Assistant Adjutant of the 2nd Battalion. Stephen was a brilliant young lad, only 16 years of age, who had already contributed profusely, in verse and prose, to Brian O'Higgins' *Banba*, a national paper for youths. Tom had been afraid to inform his mother but, unfortunately, it was too true, and the next evening I had to repeat my melancholy duty for Stephen.[36]

25 May 1921   **Irish Republican Army**
Stephen O'Reilly   ***PH 85, St Bridget's***

The younger brother of Patrick O'Reilly, Stephen was nineteen when he was killed at the Custom House. Stephen O'Reilly (Reilly) was born on 13 July 1901 and never met his father who had died that April. A commercial traveller for newspapers, he was assistant adjutant of 2nd Battalion, Dublin Brigade when he was killed. His unidentified body was brought to the King George V Hospital where it was labelled 'No. 4' and examined by a Royal Army Medical

The memorial cards of brothers Patrick and Stephen O'Reilly who were killed at the Custom House. Courtesy of Derek Jones.

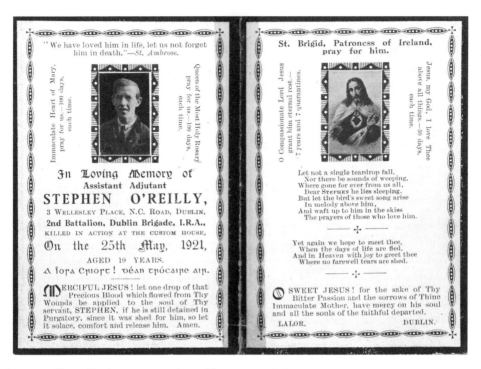

Corps officer. In his report, the officer stated that:

> Life was extinct on admission. On examination I found two small wounds in the left groin. One large wound on the outer side of the left thigh. Two wounds in the left upper arm. Five small wounds in the back. In my opinion these wounds were caused by bullets. There was also a superficial wound on the forehead about 1 inch in length, not involving the skull, probably caused by falling. Death was due to shock and haemorrhage as the result of the above wounds.

A military court of inquiry returned a verdict that Stephen O'Reilly had died of 'shock and haemorrhage caused by bullets fired by Crown Forces in execution of their duty, justifiable homicide.' Both Stephen O'Reilly and his brother Patrick were buried together in the St Bridget's section of the cemetery.[37]

27 May 1921   **Civilian**
John Congdon   *UB 16, St Paul's*

John Congdon, a plumber, was born on 15 May 1885 at 192 Phibsboro Road, the son of William Congdon, an upholsterer, and his wife Ellen Halligan. He was living with his mother and other family members at Lower Glengarriff Parade when he was fatally injured during an ambush on 15 May 1921. Just after 11.00 on the day in question Congdon was standing at the corner of

Ignatius Road and Dorset Street with Michael Derwin, a bricklayer from Ignatius Road, and James Byrne, a corporation labourer from Elizabeth Street. Derwin described what happened next:

> On 15th May 1921, about 11.30 hours I was standing at the corner of Dorset Street and Ignatius Road with Congdon and Byrne when I saw a lorry approaching from Drumcondra. Almost as soon as it had passed me I noticed a bomb rolling across the road towards the pavement where I was and it exploded about 12 feet from me and wounded me in the groin and foot. I don't know what happened after but I heard a lot of firing. I was then picked up and brought to the Mater Hospital.

The IRA had ambushed a lorry carrying members of the 1st Battalion King's Own Regiment on a return journey from Collinstown Aerodrome. Lance Cpl Godwin and Pte Hedgecock who were in the lorry saw bombs being thrown at them from the vicinity of Leech's Public House, one of which did not explode. John Congdon was badly injured by the explosion and received numerous shrapnel wounds to the abdomen and legs. He was taken to the nearby Mater Hospital. The nature of the shrapnel injuries meant that there were no exit wounds and the metal remained within his body. After an operation that removed a large piece of metal from his abdomen his condition appeared to stabilise for a number of days until 23 May when he became delirious and four days later he was operated on once more. Gangrene, abscesses and infection had taken hold in his wounds and he died at 15.30 on 27 May 1921, two hours after the completion of the operation. He was buried in a grave in the St Paul's section of the cemetery that already held his father who had died in 1911.[38]

30 May 1921	Irish Republican Army
Seán Doyle	*RD 34, South New Chapel*

Seán (John Joseph) Doyle, a member of the IRA's Dublin Brigade Active Service Unit, died of wounds received during the burning of the Custom House (*see 25 May 1921*). Born in Dublin in 1887, Doyle worked for Dublin Corporation and was a veteran of the 1916 Rising, having served in the North King Street area during Easter week. In August 1919, he married Elizabeth Ward in the church of St Laurence O'Toole and their daughter, Kathleen, was born one year later in August 1920. Doyle was wounded in the aftermath of the fires being set in the Custom House as the IRA volunteers attempted to remove themselves from the area. James Slattery who was with Doyle at the time later stated that:

... All the men who were upstairs taking part in the burning of the Custom House crowded down to the main hall. Nobody was keen on going out, but I was anxious to go out because I did not think I would stand a chance if I was arrested. I tried to get the lads to burst out with me. A few of them did but the Tans opened fire when we got outside the door. Seán Doyle, whose brother had been executed, broke through. He did not want to be arrested because he knew he stood no chance. When we were about half-way across the square there was a burst of machine gun fire and I was hit on the hand. I called Doyle, who was slightly in front of me and I saw blood trickling down his chin. I told him to keep going in the direction of Gardiner Street. Later in the day, I was talking to Seán Doyle and he told me that he got into a car and was taken to the Mater Hospital. He was in the Mater before me. He told me he had been shot through the lung ... On the night of the burning of the Custom House or the night after it, a party of British military and medical men came to the Mater Hospital and examined our charts. The nun warned me beforehand to pretend I was asleep if they came. I pretended to be asleep and they looked at the chart. They looked at Doyle and a few days afterwards Doyle died. I think the shock of seeing the military, assisted by his wound, caused his death.

Seán Doyle had been admitted into hospital under an alias. Alexander Joseph Macauley Balyney the surgeon who treated Doyle following his admission to the Mater Hospital described that he developed pneumonia arising from complications due to his wound. He died at approximately 10.00 on 30 May. He was interred in the Republican Plot in Glasnevin on 3 June 1921. His brother Patrick Doyle had been executed in Mountjoy a short time before his death (*see 14 March 1921*). His widow, Elizabeth, died in 1985 and is buried in a grave in the St Bridget's section of Glasnevin.[39]

3 June 1921   Civilian
Joseph Miller   *BD 88, St Paul's*

Joseph Miller, a carpenter who lived in South King Street with his wife and two children, was fatally wounded during an ambush that took place on Harcourt Street on 29 May 1921. At 11.00 that morning he left his home to go to church, followed by a visit to his wife, Mary Ellen, who was in hospital in Harold's Cross. As Miller walked down Harcourt Street towards the corner of Cuffe Street, a party of Auxiliaries in two lorries passed him and not long afterwards he heard explosions. The Auxiliaries, members of C Company from Portobello Barracks, had been ambushed at St Stephen's Green. Lieut R. V. Taylor who was in charge of the group stated that:

I was in the first car which was nearing York Street from Harcourt Street when a series of shots followed by an explosion were heard, the car was on the point of being turned when bombs were thrown and revolver fire opened from Stephen's Green which was replied to by the occupants of both tenders. Fire was not opened by any member of my party until the bomb was thrown from Cuffe Street, when one Cadet fired at the thrower who was running away down Cuffe Street.

This temporary cadet was Harold Lucas, a twenty-four year old former soldier from Sussex in England, who had been appointed to C Company of the Auxiliaries that February. He claimed that as his lorry passed Cuffe Street a man threw a bomb in their direction and shots were fired from the direction of Harcourt Street. Lucas said that he opened fire with a revolver on the person he believed to be the bomb thrower at a distance of about ten yards and was not sure if he had hit him or not. Michael Hourihan, a member of the Dublin Metropolitan Police, who arrived on the scene shortly after the ambush made enquiries and could only find one person wounded, Joseph Miller. He explained to Hourihan that he had heard the explosions and began to run in the opposite direction down Cuffe Street. He then felt a blow as he was wounded, a .45 revolver bullet entering his right thigh. Miller had no involvement in the ambush.

He collapsed and was taken by onlookers into the Ivanhoe Hotel, before being removed to the nearby St Vincent's Hospital where Dr T.W.T. Dillon, the house surgeon, assessed his condition. Due to the fact that Miller was suffering from shock, it was decided not to operate until the following day to try to remove the bullet. The operation was carried out successfully and as well as the bullet a piece of shirt was also removed from his wound. Although it had initially been reported that Miller's condition was improving, and he even had the opportunity to talk to newspaper reporters about the ambush, his wounds became infected and gas gangrene took hold. He died at 03.00 on the morning of 3 June 1921. 'Diminished resistance due to alcoholism' was also recorded as a factor in his death.[40]

4 June 1921   **Civilian**
Henry O'Rourke   *S 69, Garden*

Henry O'Rourke, from 6 Cornmarket in Dublin, an eighteen-year-old labourer, was shot dead on East Arran Street. On the evening of 4 June 1921, he left his house to purchase a pair of boots. When he arrived at Capel Street, a fight had broken out between two men and a large crowd gathered to watch it unfold. As they did so, a patrol of Auxiliaries arrived on the scene and the crowd scattered. DI3 William F. MacKenzie, a Canadian born member of R Company, Auxiliary Division, was present on the day and gave his own account of events leading to the death of Henry O'Rourke:

> At about 10.20 p.m. on Saturday 4th June 1921 I accompanied a patrol of R Coy. Auxiliaries in two Crossley Tenders. We were proceeding east along the North Quays. At the end of Capel Street we saw a crowd of about 50 civilians. They ran as soon as they saw us, up Capel Street in Mary's Abbey where we shouted to them to halt and fired over their heads. They still refused to halt and turned into East Arran Street. Twenty or thirty shots were then fired into them with service revolvers and two men were seen to fall. The remainder made good their escape through passages and side streets. The ambulance was sent for and the body removed.

O'Rourke was lying on his back in an archway. The ambulance was called for from a nearby public house and he was brought to the Richmond Hospital but was dead on arrival. A bullet had entered the right side of his back and exited on the left side of his chest damaging his liver and heart. He was buried in Glasnevin four days later.[41]

7 June 1921 **Irish Republican Army**
Edmond Foley *A24, O'Connell Tower Circle*

Edmond Foley from Duntryleague, near Galbally, in Co. Limerick was executed in Mountjoy Jail in June 1921 in the last executions there during the War of Independence. The eldest child of William Foley and Margaret Keogh, Edmond was born on 23 November 1895 in Duntryleague where his father worked as a farmer. Foley was an active member of the Galbally Company of the East Limerick Brigade and the chain of events that led to his execution began on 13 May 1919.

On that day Seán Hogan, a well-known IRA member, was rescued from RIC custody on a train at Knocklong Railway Station in Limerick. Hogan, who had taken part in the Soloheadbeg ambush in January 1919 with, amongst others, Dan Breen, Seán Treacy and Seamus Robinson, had been captured in Tipperary a few days earlier and moved by the RIC to Thurles Barracks. On 13 May, Hogan was due to be moved to Cork by train. Treacy, Breen and Robinson, on learning of his arrest, planned an escape attempt and decided that the train station at Knocklong presented the most opportune place to stage the break, due to its distance from any constabulary station. They were to be assisted by five men of the East Limerick Brigade, including Edmond Foley. Edmond O'Brien, from Galbally, who took part in the rescue, gave a dramatic account of what proved to be a desperate struggle at Knocklong Station:

... we started for Knocklong, and on the way, I think, both John Joe and Seán Lynch contacted Ned Foley of Duntryleague who also came along and was subsequently executed in Mountjoy for his part in the fight. We all arrived at Maloneys in Lackelly some time about three thirty in the afternoon, where we met Seán Treacy, Dan Breen and Seamus Robinson. After a consultation there it was decided that we should divide the party and that Seán Lynch, Jim Scanlon, my brother John Joe and Ned Foley would proceed to Emly station, and, as quietly as possible board the train there with a view to discovering in what compartment the prisoner and his escort were travelling. As transpired subsequently, these men did their work very effectively ... The train stopped at the station, and on looking at the carriages I saw at once the four Galbally lads at the window of a carriage. I moved quickly towards where they were, and the first one I spoke to, as he happened to be nearest to me at the time, was my brother ... he whispered quickly to me 'They are in the next carriage'. I moved rapidly towards where Seán Treacy was, and said to him, 'here they are in the next carriage'. He did not hesitate for a moment but gave the order to come ... I followed, drawing our guns as we mounted the train. I was immediately followed by the other lads, in what order I do not remember. The corridor was on the left side of the train, the side next to us, and we moved swiftly down along the corridor to where, as had been indicated to us, the prisoner and his guard were located, down about three or four compartments from where we entered. I saw Seán's left hand dropping, as he passed, to the handle of the compartment door, which was of the sliding type, it slid along a track, and simultaneously out of my right eye I saw the police and the prisoner inside. Seán having slid the door clear, the two of us wheeled in and ordered 'hands up'. We had the police covered with our guns and for a moment I thought it was going to be a bloodless victory. Then I noticed that one of the R.I.C., the only one wearing a revolver, had it drawn and was pointing it at the prisoner, whereupon I instinctively and immediately blazed at him, shooting him dead. What happened then is rather vague in my memory, but I remember Seán Treacy in handgrips with a powerful sergeant, and I remember being on the floor for a period. I remember Seán Lynch, Jim Scanlon and Foley coming into the compartment... The struggle was then hand to hand. I remember my gun was knocked out of my hand after a couple of shots and I could not reach it ... Treacy and the sergeant, Wallace I think was his name, were in deadly grips swaying to and fro in their efforts to overcome each other. In the midst of the pandemonium, we asked the prisoner to move out, and, handcuffed as he was, he fought his way out from the escort, striking at them with his manacled hands. The carriage was very crowded all this time and I remember seeing Jim Scanlon and Seán Lynch wrestling the rifle from Constable O'Reilly and bouncing it off his head until he covered down, seemingly unconscious, on the floor of the carriage ... In the meantime, Constable O'Reilly, who had been knocked out by Seán Lynch and Jim Scanlon, had crawled along the floor of the carriage on to the platform, and opened fire with his rifle on those who were still within the carriage. Dan Breen seemingly was coming into the station at this point, and they opened fire on one another at long range. O'Reilly's bullet, I heard afterwards, hit Dan in a part of the body that disabled his right arm and knocked the gun out of his hand, but Dan picked up the gun with his good arm, and, though he failed to hit him, forced O'Reilly, by his furious fire, to retreat and leave the platform. O'Reilly before firing at Breen had wounded Treacy, Jim Scanlon and myself in the carriage. The fight was a very close melee for, as there was such a number in the small compartment, most of it was necessarily hand to hand.

The men of the IRA had managed to break Hogan free and escape, albeit at a significant cost. Seán Treacy and Dan Breen had been badly wounded and the action would result in two executions. Nonetheless, the escape of Hogan was a significant victory for the IRA. Const. Michael Enright from Limerick, who had been shot by Edmond O'Brien, died immediately. Sgt Peter Wallace, wounded in a struggle with Treacy, later died of his wounds. Edmond Foley was arrested in September 1919. Following two civil trials that failed to reach a verdict a military court martial convened in Dublin on 15 March 1921 to hear evidence against Foley, Patrick Maher, a member of the IRA who had no part in the incident, and Michael Murphy, from Knocklong. All three were accused of the deaths of Sgt Wallace and Const. Enright. Concluding six days later the court martial found Murphy not guilty and both Foley and Maher guilty. Both men were sentenced '... to suffer death by being hanged'. The sentences were carried out in Mountjoy on 7 June of the same year.[42]

8 June 1921	Civilian
Charles Mullins	*OC 89, St Paul's*

Charles Mullins, a stonecutter from Sandwith Street, was born in Dublin and in 1894 had married Kate (Catherine) Kelly, the daughter of a fellow stonecutter from Great Brunswick (Pearse) Street. He was wounded during an ambush on a Royal Irish Constabulary lorry that took place at Great Brunswick Street on the afternoon of 8 June 1921. There was significant confusion during the ambush and narratives of the chronology of events are disjointed and unclear. Sgt Richard Ryan, who was in command of the RIC lorry, in his account of the ambush stated that:

> At about 12.30 hours we turned from Hanover Quay into Brunswick Street. About 50 yards from the corner revolver shots were fired at us and then about 6 bombs thrown at us. One of these exploded in the lorry. Five of the police in the lorry were wounded. We fired back with rifles at a group of about 15 armed civilians who lay down or fell. The lorry went to the fire station and then turned round. A military lorry then came along and the occupants helped us to dress the wounded. A second military lorry then came and I went with it to the place from which we had been fired at and on arrival saw the fire brigade ambulance leaving. The military stopped it and I saw one woman in it. None of the occupants of my lorry were in possession of any bombs, nor did the occupants of the military lorries throw any.

The skirmish lasted for some twenty minutes and resulted in at least six other civilians and five members of the Royal Irish Constabulary being wounded. Charles Mullins had received a wound to the stomach and died of his injuries in Sir Patrick Dun's Hospital. His cause of death was recorded as 'shock and haemorrhage due to wounds caused by bomb splinters'. He was buried in Glasnevin on 11 June 1921 in a grave purchased by his wife. Another of those wounded during the incident, thirteen-year-old William Gorman, died of his injuries and is also buried in Glasnevin *(see 14 June 1921)*.[43]

14 June 1921   Civilian
William Gorman   *M 82, Garden*

William Gorman, aged thirteen years, died of wounds received in the same incident in which Charles Mullins was killed on 8 June 1921. He was the son of William Gorman from 134 Townsend Street and worked as a donkey driver for a business on Tara Street. At the time of his fatal wounding, William was making his way from his home on Townsend Street to visit his sister who was in Sir Patrick Dun's Hospital. He was caught in the middle of the ambush on Great Brunswick Street and was wounded by bomb fragments that fractured his skull and entered his brain. An operation removed some of the fragments but he died of his wounds on 14 June in King George V Hospital. A court of inquiry returned a verdict that he died from '... meningitis and cerebral abscess caused by a fragment of a bomb which fractured his skull and lodged in his brain. That this bomb was thrown at a Police lorry in Brunswick Street, Dublin at about 12.30 hrs. on 8th June 1921 by one of a party of civilians who are guilty of wilful murder.[44]'

18 June 1921   Civilian
Robert Pike   *R 90, Garden*

Robert Pike, a former soldier, was shot dead outside Fagan's public house in Drumcondra in the presence of his wife Mary (née Barnwell) whom he had married in 1902 and lived with at the nearby Tolka Cottages. Pike had worked as a labourer for Dublin Corporation before he enlisted in the British army at the recruiting office in Great Brunswick Street in March 1917 and was given a position as a quarry man with the Royal Engineers. Having served on the Western Front he was discharged following the end of the war, suffering with bronchitis, and returned home to Dublin to his wife and six children. Described by British authorities following his death as a 'loyal subject' and 'a strong anti-Sinn Féiner', he came to the attention of the IRA who suspected him of being an informer. Charles Dalton, a member of The Squad, described Pike as:

> … a member of the tinker class and lived in Tolka Cottages, Drumcondra, I believe he was an ex-soldier who had been in the world war and he was conveying information to the Crown forces. There was an unconfirmed statement that he had reported on Dan Breen's and Sean Treacy's movements from Fleming's of Drumcondra to Fernside. (*see 26 October 1920*)

It was also rumoured that Pike was involved in warning the authorities of the ill-fated Drumcondra ambush (*see 22 January 1921*). Patrick Redmond, a veteran of the 1916 Rising and assistant company intelligence officer for F Company, 2nd Battalion, Dublin Brigade, IRA, spent a significant amount of time watching the movements of Pike and later claimed that it was on foot of his information that it was decided he should be shot. While Pike was standing with his wife and another man outside Fagan's public house in Drumcondra on the evening of 18 June 1921, a man cycling past jumped off his bicycle came towards Pike and took out a revolver. He told Mary Pike to stand back and then fired two shots at her husband, before cycling off in the direction of Whitehall. The bullets, one entering through the right side of his neck and the other through his forehead, caused catastrophic injury and instant death. His body was removed to the Mater Hospital and, on 22 June, he was buried in the Garden section of Glasnevin Cemetery. Patrick Redmond died in 1965 and is also buried in Glasnevin.[45]

19 June 1921   **Civilian**
Michael Martin   *OF 66½, Garden*

Michael Martin was aged four when a bomb that was thrown during an ambush of a British army lorry on Capel Street on 18 June 1921 fatally injured him. Catherine Mahon and Elizabeth O'Brien (*see 21 June 1921*) also died of wounds received during the ambush. That evening as the soldiers proceeded up Capel Street a number of bombs were thrown at their lorry, which was under the command of twenty year old 2nd Lieut Alan D.S. Steele of the 1st Battalion Wiltshire Regiment. One exploded underneath the lorry and others to its rear. Seven civilians were hit by the bomb fragments, one of whom was Michael Martin who was playing outside his house, No. 66. Mary Radburn, his aunt, was the first member of his family to find Michael wounded. She recalled the events of that evening:

> I went to Mrs Martin's house, 66 Capel Street, at about 17.00 hours I went out to a laundry, when I left I saw Michael Martin playing in the street just outside his front door. I had just returned, a few minutes after 17.00 hours when I heard a terrific explosion in the street, my first thought was for the child and I ran out again into the street but could not see the boy. I was told by someone, I cannot say who, that Michael was in a vegetable shop. I went there and found him. I picked him up in my arms and ran to his home, this was during a lull in the firing. I saw him attended to and returned home. I did not see him again alive.

Michael was brought to the Jervis Street Hospital where Dr Thomas Oakey examined him and found that he was suffering from a wound to his lower back. A fragment of the bomb had entered his bowel. At the same time that the ambush occurred, Michael's father, Patrick, had returned home from work. Following the incident, he heard that his son had been wounded and made his way to the hospital to see him. He found his son injured and his only and final words to him were 'Father take the bandage off'. He left his son that night and went home, when he returned the next afternoon to visit him he was informed that he had died at 12.30. A court of inquiry returned a verdict that Michael Martin had '… died as a result of shock and haemorrhage caused by a fragment

The aftermath of the ambush on Capel Street on 18 June 1921 which resulted in the deaths of Michael Martin, Catherine Mahon and Elizabeth O'Brien.
Courtesy of Getty Images.

of a bomb thrown by a person or persons unknown … such person or persons being, in the opinion of the court, guilty of wilful murder'.[46]

20 June 1921   Irish Republican Army
Edward Fox   O 92, Garden

Edward Fox from 29 South Cumberland Street was born in 1898, the son of James and Elizabeth Fox. Residing with his parents and siblings, he worked as a boilermaker with Grace's in Grahams Court, off Temple Street. During the War of Independence, he joined the IRA and due to his skills, he became a member of 5th Battalion (Engineers) Dublin Brigade. In 1921, he was fatally wounded having been shot at Corbett's public house, just a short distance from his own home on South Cumberland Street. In the military inquiry that followed his death, the press were not given access. The internal transcripts were also redacted and civilian witnesses anonymised. The person identified as shooting him was recorded as 'X'. Neither was an unusual measure, however, the full story of the death of Fox proved particularly interesting.

James Kennedy, from Harcourt Place, was in the pub on the day of Edward Fox's death. He saw Fox and 'X' enter and explained that they came in at about 15.00, had a drink and that they then '… went away and returned about 4 p.m. and had another drink. I was in the snug when I heard an explosion in the shop. I went in to see what it was and saw Fox and 'X' finish their drinks and leave. I then heard another shot outside in the street.' No witnesses to the fatal shot gave evidence, however, Patrick Fox, a cousin of Edward, was standing nearby and described that: '… I heard a shot. I looked up and saw a man staggering and fall to the ground near Corbett's public house in the carriage way. I went to the Chapel at Westland Row to fetch a priest. I did not know it was my cousin Edward Fox at the time who had been shot.' At the same time, Edward's family also heard the shot that killed him at their home in South Cumberland Street. His brother James recalled that:

> At about 4 or 4.30 p.m. on the 19th June 1921, I was sitting on my mother's bed in the front drawing room at 29 South Cumberland St. Dublin. I heard a shot fired in the street outside. My sister went over to the window and looked out. She turned round and said 'Sonny is shot', meaning my brother Edward. I then went over to the window and saw my brother on the road rolling on to his face. There was no one near him at the time. I went back to look after my mother whilst my sister left the room.

That sister, Mary Dillon, stated that from the window 'I saw "X" bending over my brother. He then ran away. I went out to my brother and stayed with him until he was taken away in a pony-cart. I heard everybody standing about say that "X" had shot my brother. I was too excited and too upset to note who the people were who were saying this'. Edward Fox was taken to the nearby Sir Patrick Dun's Hospital where Dr Margaretta Tate Stevenson treated him. She noted that he had a bullet wound in his back above his left shoulder blade and that the bullet had lodged on the right side of his neck. Fox was operated on soon afterwards and the .450 revolver bullet removed. He was transferred to King George V Hospital at 19.00 and died of his injuries early the following morning. The court of inquiry into his death returned a verdict that he died of 'Gunshot wounds inflicted by some person or persons unknown guilty of wilful murder'.

This, however, was not the end of the story of Edward Fox. A note, dated 20 July 1921, and appended to the inquiry file detailed that 'X', the man who had killed him, was working for Dublin Castle:

> 'X' is one of our agents (GXVMCA), Fox was a friend, as soon as this happened 'X' went to DD [Dublin District] & reported accident, 'X' was told to clear out from Castle as his going there jeopardised his position as agent. Nothing has been heard of him since he may have been done in by SF [Sinn Féin] or he may be at his job. Above told me by Gen. Boyd & Chief told me to lock this away.

It also identified 'X' as Danny or Daniel Whelan from Lower Mount Street. Following the shooting, instructions were given to F Company, Auxiliary Division to begin a search for Whelan. They subsequently went to Whelan's home address on Lower Mount Street with two lorries and an armoured car but the search came to nothing. Whelan's mother, Margaret, was the only member of the family present. It is not clear when Daniel Whelan began working for Dublin Castle and providing intelligence to them. His home had been raided by the military as early as November 1919. Dismissed from his position as a junior clerk in an office on College Street, Whelan had subsequently bombed the offices in June 1920 and made an arson attack upon it the following month. A few weeks later, an order was issued for the raid of Whelan's home and his arrest. Within the order, he was described as 'a dangerous man'. Early on the morning of 6 August the door of his home was broken down and the house was searched but no trace of Whelan was found. Maj. Frank Carew, an intelligence officer, eventually arrested him on 23 January 1921 and he was placed on trial in March for both attacks in a Field General Courtmartial in Kilmainham. Three witnesses gave evidence including one that stated that Whelan had met him in the days after the explosion and admitted the bombing, telling him that he was sorry for what he had done. However, before the trial had formally concluded, and Whelan had given his evidence, an adjournment was made and he was found not guilty being released but immediately taken back into custody again.

Unknown to Dublin Castle in the aftermath of the killing of Edward Fox was that Whelan had not been 'done in' but he had been captured by the Irish Republican Police and put on trial for the shooting of Edward Fox. Col John Quinn described what happened at the subsequent republican trial:

> Acting on instructions issued by the O/C 3rd Batt. Dublin Brigade Daniel Whelan was arrested by some members of B. Coy. 3rd Batt. several days after the shooting occurred, the arrest was reported to the Batt. O/C who ordered the prisoner to be tried by courtmartial (the court consisting of officers from the Batt.) on the charge of murder. During the trial it was proved from the evidence produced that there had been a row between the deceased and the accused inside the 'Beerhouse' known as Corbetts' at the top of Sth. Cumberland St. where the shooting occurred and that the accused had drawn a revolver. As there was no evidence produced to show that the shooting was other than accidental the accused was found not guilty on the capital charge. It was recommended by the court that the accused be examined as to his mental condition. The proceedings and findings of the court were duly reported to the Batt. O/C for confirmation and he issued instructions to have the accused medically examined. This examination was carried out by a qualified M.O. and as a result of the examination the accused was formally committed to the Richmond Asylum where he was detained for some time and subsequently released.[47]

21 June 1921   **Civilian**
Catherine Mahon   *OC 37, St Paul's*

Catherine (Kate) Mahon died of wounds received in the same ambush that resulted in the fatal injuries received by Michael Martin (*see 19 June 1921*). Mahon worked as a housekeeper and lived at 13 Royal Canal Terrace in Phibsborough. She had been in town shopping when she was caught up in the attack on Capel Street. Following the ambush, she was also brought to the Jervis Street Hospital with Michael Martin. There it was found that she had received nine different wounds and had lost a significant amount of blood. Shrapnel from the bomb had hit her left lung, left abdomen, right buttock and right arm. Her left leg had also been peppered with shrapnel resulting in wounds all over the leg and a large gaping wound in her left thigh containing two pieces of metal. She was in much pain and died four days after the ambush. On 24 June 1921, she was buried in a family grave in Glasnevin owned by her brother.[48]

21 June 1921   **Civilian**
Elizabeth O'Brien   *BC 89, St Paul's*

Elizabeth O'Brien (née Cassidy), known as Bessie, was the third of those buried in Glasnevin who died of wounds received during the Capel Street ambush of 18 June 1921 *(see above)*. Elizabeth was born in October 1890 in Bow Street, Dublin and at the time of her death resided at 21 Green Street with her husband Thomas O'Brien, whom she had married in 1913. After she was wounded during the ambush she was brought to the Mater Hospital. While at the hospital she explained to her husband what had happened to her. He subsequently gave her account at a court of inquiry into her death. He stated that: 'She told me that on hearing an explosion she ran out after my son Willie, the military were at the time firing from the direction of Dorset St. suddenly she felt a blow in the hip and fell down, she did not remember anything else till she found herself in hospital'. Unknown to the court was that Thomas O'Brien was a member of the IRA and it was his company that had carried out the ambush in which his wife was fatally wounded. Oscar Traynor described that Thomas had resisted the temptation to warn his family to stay away from the location of the planned ambush and it was only on returning to his home, a short distance from the ambush site, that he was informed of her fate. The court returned a verdict that Bessie O'Brien died '... from shock and internal haemorrhage, caused by injuries received in Capel St. on 18/6/21, during an ambush of the Crown Forces. In the opinion of the Court there is no evidence to show who caused the injuries, but that the deceased was accidently shot during the ambush'. Elizabeth was buried in Glasnevin on 24 June 1921.[49]

3 July 1921   **Civilian**
Daniel Duffy   *JK 130, St Patrick's*

Daniel Duffy was born on 12 August 1873 and was the son of Daniel and Bridget Duffy from Engine Alley in Dublin. In April 1900, he married Mary Anne Kearns, known as Annie, and moved to live with her at 28 John Dillon Street. Two years later, in 1902, he began working as a fitter in the engineer's department of the Guinness brewery. On the evening of 3 July 1921 a British army curfew patrol was located at the junction of the South Circular Road and Clanbrassil Street and it was here that Daniel Duffy was shot dead at approximately 22.45. The member of the patrol that fired the fatal shots later gave his account of the events that night:

> I was placed on guard facing Harold's Cross Bridge by the officer i[n]/c[ommand] [of the] armoured car. I had orders to halt everyone coming from Harold's Cross Bridge. I had orders to challenge three times and then fire if the person I challenged did not halt. I saw the deceased walking from Harold's Cross Bridge. He was about 50 or 60 yards away from me when I first challenged. I shouted 'halt', and then he turned back toward Harold's Cross Bridge. I challenged him twice more (three times in all) and then I fired at him. He fell down and I ran up to see what had happened and then went back and fetched the Corporal and laid the deceased on his back and found he was hit in the back. The deceased was carried into a house and died about 10 or 15 minutes after in the presence of a Priest and a Doctor. I am absolutely positive that he was walking when I fired.

Bridget Fitzpatrick who was a resident of 12 Upper Clanbrassil Street, the house that Duffy was brought to, and where he died, gave a differing account of his death. She was standing at the hall door of the house and witnessed Daniel Duffy drop some flowers that he was holding and stopped to pick them up. She heard an order to halt, some further shouting and then a shot was fired. She described that she was positive that Duffy was standing still when he was shot. James Dunne who lived at No. 10 on the same street also witnessed Duffy drop some of the flowers on the ground before stooping to pick them up and continue a little further down the road. He said he then turned back in the direction he had come from and walked back at the same pace. Dunne also heard orders to halt followed by a shot after which Duffy fell forward. The bullet had hit his back and entered his abdomen. A court of inquiry into his death returned the finding that he had died '… from shock and haemorrhage following a gunshot wound inflicted by a member of the Crown Forces in the execution of his duty, i.e. when on curfew patrol, the shot being fired owing to the deceased failing to obey an order of the Curfew Patrol to halt'. Daniel Duffy's son, Christopher, identified Daniel's body at the Meath Hospital and on 7 July his funeral took place to Glasnevin. His widow, Annie, died in 1943 and is buried in the same grave.[50]

3 July 1921 **Civilian**
Kathleen Kelleher *SL 283, St Patrick's*

On the evening of 2 July 1921 Kathleen Kelleher, aged seventeen, was fatally wounded in the Phoenix Park by a bullet fired from the gun of Const. John McCansh of the Royal Irish Constabulary. Kathleen was born on 5 May 1904, the daughter of Patrick Kelleher, a tailor originally from Co. Kerry and Bridget McGuinness. She worked as an embroidery and carpet maker and before her death had been employed by the Dun Emer Guild. The guild, established by Evelyn Gleeson, made a range of items inspired by the Celtic revival and promoted Irish skill and materials. On the afternoon of 2 July, Kathleen had left her home at Muckross Parade with a friend, Bridget Price, and the two walked to the Royal Irish Constabulary Depot. There Kathleen met with McCansh, whom she had met on a number of previous occasions, and they went for a walk in the Park. The only surviving witness to the fatal wounding of Kathleen Kelleher was McCansh who gave his account at a court of inquiry into her death:

> ... we went for a walk near the Military Camps. We then sat down among the trees. We had been sitting there some time and the pistol in my hip pocket was hurting me. I took it out with the intention of putting it into my breast pocket when it went off. The bullet struck the girl I was along with and hit her in the head. I saw what I had done and jumped up and went towards a soldier who was sitting under a tree not far off and told him to see what I had done. I afterwards learnt that this was Pte Dysom, Rifle Brigade. I turned round and saw two Sgts. approaching and I also told them the same. One of them asked me for the pistol and I gave it to him. They both took me up to the Military Camp. There was no quarrel of any kind between us then or at any other time. She did not say anything after she was shot.

Kathleen Kelleher had been shot on the left side of her head and was taken to Dr Steevens' Hospital where she died early the following morning from her injuries, having never regained consciousness. Soon after the incident, news returned to the Kelleher home that she had been injured. Due to curfew it was the following morning before Kathleen's brother John, a discharged member of the British army, found that she had died. John McCansh was arrested but later continued to serve with the Royal Irish Constabulary, being sent to Limerick in November 1921. Having left the constabulary, he emigrated to Canada. Kathleen Kelleher was buried in a grave with her father, who had passed away in 1915, and sister Mary who died of meningitis aged three. Kathleen's mother, Bridget, died in 1932. Within her lifetime, Bridget had witnessed the deaths of all five of her children as all Kathleen's remaining siblings died in the 1920s. Gertrude in 1923, aged thirteen and both John and Annie in 1927, of tuberculosis.[51]

12 July 1921   **Cumann na mBan**
Margaret Keogh   *MI 276, St Bridget's*

Margaret Keogh, from Stella Gardens in Ringsend, was fatally injured at her home on the evening of Saturday 9 July 1921. Born in 1900 she was the daughter of Margaret Mulvany and Michael Keogh. Her father was a baker from Dublin and her mother was from Swords, they had married in 1898. At the time of her death, Margaret was the second eldest of ten surviving children. She was employed as a clerical assistant in the Acme Works of the printers Hely & Co. at Dame Court. She was also a member of Cumann na mBan, a captain of the Croke camogie team and a member of the Irish Clerical Workers' Union. Newspaper reports described that on the evening of her death Margaret and her brother, Thomas, were the only members of the Keogh family awake at their home when there was a knock at the door. Margaret went to the door and was heard to shout out 'Mother, mother, I am shot'. Thomas Keogh ran to the door and carried his sister to the kitchen where he saw that she was wounded in the side. She was taken to Sir Patrick Dun's Hospital where her condition initially improved before she lost consciousness and died at 04.00 on the morning of 12 July. Before dying, Margaret Keogh made a statement describing that she had opened the door but could not see anybody standing outside. As she went to close the door, she felt a sting in her side. She said she had no idea who fired the shot.

There was little light shed on the identity of a potential perpetrator. A neighbour noted that shortly before the shooting somebody had knocked on the door of the home of a man who was described as being 'on the run' but was stopped from entering. Her death appeared to bear similarities with the curfew shootings of Peter O'Carroll and William McGrath. However, a family account described the circumstances of her death in a very different manner to what was made public at the time. According to Margaret's elder sister the home of the Keogh family was a store for IRA arms and ammunition. On the night that Margaret was wounded there was an attempt to move the weapons due to the fear of a potential raid. In the course of the move, a bullet that had fallen into a fire, exploded and its shrapnel hit Margaret. The attempt to keep this information from authorities and public knowledge proved successful. The funeral of Margaret Keogh came to Glasnevin on the morning of 14 July 1921. Her coffin was covered with a Tricolour and the cortege, which was large, attracted many onlookers and interested members of the public. The hearse was followed by members of Cumann na mBan, the GAA and work colleagues. She was buried in a grave in which her brother Patrick, who had died aged one, was previously interred.[52]

8 September 1921
Michael O'Brien

Fianna Éireann
JK131, St Patrick's

Michael O'Brien, a member of Fianna Éireann, died of an accidental gunshot wound received while training in Killester Lane, Dublin. The son of James and Rose O'Brien, both from Co. Meath, he was aged eighteen when he was killed. At the time of his death, he was living at Duke Street and was employed as a canteen worker in Trinity College Dublin. Along with other members of Fianna Éireann, under the command of Hugh Mehlhorn, O'Brien was present at Killester on the evening of 8 September 1921 during shooting practice. While training the revolver that O'Brien was handling accidently discharged and he was wounded in the right groin. The bullet inflicted significant damage and came to rest in his pelvis. A member of the Fianna ran to a nearby shop were they asked a grocer's assistant, James Connolly, to call an ambulance. O'Brien was brought to the Mater Hospital but was dead on arrival. His funeral came to Glasnevin on 13 September 1921.[53]

11 November 1921
James Henry Doyle

Irish Republican Army
M 76, Garden

James Doyle was an early member of the Irish Volunteers who served during the 1916 Rising at Earlsfort Terrace and Boland's Mills. He was interned and released in the 1917 amnesty and later, during War of Independence, served as a 1st lieutenant with 5th Battalion (Engineers) Dublin Brigade IRA. Originally from New Street in Dublin he married Marcella Irwin in January 1921. The exact circumstances of his death are unclear, however his widow in her pension application, which was successfully awarded, stated that while he was involved in moving weapons from an arms dump a gun discharged and wounded him in the head resulting in his death eight hours later in Mercer's Hospital. Contemporary newspaper accounts of the incident reported that the fatal shot was inflicted in his own bedroom at his home in 13 Parliament Street where he, his wife and nine month old son occupied rooms on the third floor. In the days before his death, Doyle had lost his job working as a sheet metal worker constructing gas meters. On the morning of his death, he went to the Labour Exchange before returning home. It was also claimed that he was 'depressed through recent lack of employment'. His sister, who resided on the floor above, discovered him wounded and called for help, after which he was removed to Mercer's Hospital. James Doyle was still alive but died at 19.00 that evening. An inquiry returned a verdict that his death was 'caused by intracranial haemorrhage which was caused by gun shot wounds accidentally inflicted by himself'. Some 200 members of the IRA marched behind his coffin to Glasnevin where his coffin, draped in the Tricolour, was taken to the mortuary chapel and then to his grave in the Garden section of the cemetery.[54]

1922

4 February 1922   **Civilian**
Edward Reid   *FD 90, St Paul's*

Edward Reid, a cattle driver from Upper Dominick Street, was shot and fatally wounded in the abdomen on the night of 3 February 1922. His shooting followed an argument outside a pub on the corner of Findlater's Place and Marlborough Street. A revolver was drawn and fired and two men in British army uniforms fled from the scene chased by angry onlookers. Reid was taken to the Jervis Street Hospital where he died of his injuries. An in camera military court of inquiry into his death was held, rather than a public inquest, which drew criticism at the time. Pte Ronald Hampshire a member of the 615th Company, Royal Army Service Corps, based at the Royal (Collins) Barracks was subsequently acquitted of murder in a general court-martial. Edward Reid's funeral to Glasnevin was a large affair attended by many people involved in the cattle trade in Dublin and cargo workers from the North Wall, where his mother and family lived.[1]

2 March 1922   **Royal Irish Constabulary**
John Cotter   *DD 91, St Paul's*

John Cotter, a sergeant in the Royal Irish Constabulary, was shot in Phibsborough on the afternoon of 2 March 1922 and died that evening in the Mater Hospital. Cotter was born in Co. Clare on New Year's Day 1885, and joined the RIC in 1906. He first worked in Offaly before being transferred to Tipperary. In November 1914, he married Bridget Keane, a local schoolteacher and daughter of an RIC sergeant. During the War of Independence, Cotter was promoted to sergeant and was stationed at Roskeen, west of Thurles. While there the barracks, which he was in command of, was subject to an attack by the IRA and Cotter organised its successful defence. In January 1921, he was transferred to the RIC Depot in the Phoenix Park and lived with his family in a house at Cabra Park, near Dalymount Park.

On the afternoon of 2 March 1922 John Cotter was walking through St Peter's Lane, which connects Cabra Park and St Peter's Road. As he approached St Peter's Road, three men, dressed in caps and trench coats, who had been watching Cotter, confronted him. It was reported that one of the men said 'that's him' before they began firing with revolvers. He was shot in the neck, chest and abdomen. People in the vicinity who heard the shots came to the scene and saw Cotter lying on the ground in a state of collapse. He was conscious and was brought to the Mater Hospital but never recovered from his injuries.

The reason for his shooting was never clearly identified although the only motive appeared to be political. His constabulary service record notes his cause of death as 'shot dead by S. Féiners'. Patrick Kinnane, a member of 2nd (Mid) Tipperary Brigade, IRA, claimed that Cotter was identified as being present with a group described by the IRA as the 'Thurles police murder gang' on the night of 25 October 1920. That night a group of masked men visited houses with the intention of shooting suspected IRA members. The group killed two men, Michael Ryan and William Gleeson, and badly wounded Jeremiah Kinnane, the brother of Patrick. However, Patrick Kinnane did not connect that incident with the later shooting of Cotter. The funeral of Sgt Cotter came to Glasnevin on 4 March 1922 from the church of the Holy Family, Aughrim Street. His coffin was carried on a gun carriage and followed by members of the Royal Irish Constabulary and Dublin Metropolitan Police, along with their bands. He left a widow and three children, aged five, four and three.[2]

3 March 1922 — Civilian
John Maxwell Sullivan Green — *EF 29, South New Chapel*

John Maxwell Green, known as Max, was born in September 1864 the son of

Max Green, chair of the Irish General Prisons Board. **Courtesy of Reach plc (Daily Mirror)**

James Sullivan Green and Anne Comerford. His father, a barrister, was from Cork where the ancestral home of the Green family was Air Hill, near Fermoy. Max Green was educated at the Catholic University School on Leeson Street and then Trinity College Dublin, while he also studied civil engineering at the Royal College of Science for Ireland between 1882 and 1885. Having qualified, he served a year-long apprenticeship under the well-known engineer Bindon Blood Stoney, before becoming involved in engineering work related to the construction of railways. This included work on the New Ross extension branch of the Dublin, Wicklow and Wexford Railway and the Kanturk and Newmarket Railway. He continued in this work until 1897, when he was appointed as an engineering inspector for the Irish General Prisons Board. In 1907, his career took a significant change when John Campbell Gordon, the earl of Aberdeen, appointed him as his private secretary during his second term as lord lieutenant of Ireland. He was also elected a member of the Dublin Cemeteries Committee, the operating body of Glasnevin Cemetery, in May 1910. Max Green remained working in the vice-regal lodge for five years when he left to become chair of the Irish General Prisons Board.

In January 1913, he married Johanna Redmond, a daughter of the Irish Parliamentary Party leader John Redmond from his first marriage to Johanna Dalton. The marriage garnered much interest and was reported on prominently in newspapers in Ireland, England, the United States and beyond. Max and Johanna had two sons, twins, Max and Redmond. His job became a much more difficult one in the years that followed the 1916 Rising with the imprisonment of many political prisoners. He was subjected to criticism for his oversight of the Irish prisons system and the treatment of republican prisoners, particularly following the death of Thomas Ashe in 1917. As a son-in-law of John Redmond, he was also a natural political target. However, during the War of Independence he came to be viewed by many as a conciliatory figure. One journalist noted in the aftermath of his death that he had interviewed him at his office in Dublin Castle in relation to the treatment of political prisoners. Green '... went to the very greatest trouble to explain the position as definitely as possible and it was not hard to see that he had intense sympathy for those to whom the journalist's queries appertained and was keenly anxious to do all in his power to respect their point of view and have their claims acceded to.'

The war also affected the Green family outside of Max Green's work. Katherine Barry Moloney recalled a remarkable interaction they had with her brother, Kevin Barry, and the IRA during the summer of 1920 while spending time at Aughavanagh in Wicklow:

> ... a special messenger came with orders to the local battalion to burn down John Redmond's house in Aughavanagh, as there was information that it was about to be occupied by British troops. Naturally Kevin wangled in on the job. When they arrived at Aughavanagh, Max Green and his wife, Joanna Redmond were in occupation. They were naturally very angry but the Volunteers explained the necessity for the action and Kevin acted as negotiator between Max Green and the special messenger. The upshot of it was that Max Green gave his word of honour that no British troops would occupy the house. It was spared by the IRA and it was never occupied by British troops.

The same summer Johanna was reported to the Home Office for having contacted Queen Mary whom she asked to make a request to King George V to intercede and release Terence MacSwiney shortly after he began his hunger strike in Brixton Prison.

Max Green continued in his position with the Prisons Board until his death in 1922. On that morning of 3 March, three members of the IRA, Laurence Dowling, James O'Neill and another man carried out an armed robbery on Molesworth Street. Their target was a case of cash that was carried every Friday from a bank to the Ministry of Labour. Having held up the carriers, they left the scene with a portion of the money in a case. They escaped in the direction of the Shelbourne Hotel but having been intercepted threw away the money they had stolen and turned back towards Dawson Street. As they were pursued, the men split up. Laurence Dowling ran towards St Stephen's Green and crossed the road towards it as people shouted 'stop the robber'.

As he did so, Max Green was walking through the park and was exiting near the Lady Grattan drinking fountain opposite Dawson Street. Hearing the calls to stop Dowling, he put out his arms and a shot was fired. Max Green fell fatally wounded. He had been hit in the chest and the bullet had lodged in his ribs. Dowling continued running and made it as far as Adelaide Road before he was caught. In the meantime, James O'Neill had been arrested closer to the scene of the robbery.

Both men were put on trial for stealing the money 'by force and violence' and having 'feloniously, wilfully and with malice aforethought killed and murdered one Max S. Green'. The trial garnered much public and media interest but exhibited issues that blighted a policing and justice system in transition. On two occasions, juries were unable to agree and reach any verdict. In June 1923, Laurence Dowling pleaded guilty to a charge of 'robbery under arms'. During his plea, he stated that he was acting under orders. Mr Justice William Dodd sentenced him to ten years imprisonment. Jim O'Neill pleaded not guilty to armed robbery and after another two trials, a verdict could not be reached. He was released from custody in April 1924 and later emigrated to Canada.

Max Green was buried in Glasnevin on 6 March 1922 following a funeral mass in St Mary's church on Haddington Road. The date was also the fourth anniversary of the death of Johanna Green's father, John Redmond. Amongst those in attendance were his brothers, the Redmond, family, the Marquess of Aberdeen and Temair and John Dillon. He was interred in a grave directly behind the mortuary chapel. Before the year was out Johanna was also buried in the same grave. She died in December 1922 aged thirty-five leaving their twin sons orphaned at the age of nine.[3]

7 April 1922
Cornelius Luke Cregan

Irish Republican Army
UH 34 ½, St Bridget's

Cornelius Cregan was nineteen at the time of his death. An engineering student, he was born in June 1902, the son of Maurice and Elizabeth Cregan, and had joined the IRA in 1918 being a member of 4th Battalion, Dublin Brigade. Cregan, from Tyrconnell Road, Inchicore, was accidentally killed during the Truce period. He was fatally wounded in Inchicore while he was on duty guarding an IRA arms dump. He had returned to the guardroom when the rifle of a comrade was accidentally fired and he was hit. The bullet severed his spinal cord and he was brought to Dr Steevens' Hospital where he died from his injuries. He was buried in a family grave in the St Bridget's section of the cemetery.[4]

9 April 1922
Martin O'Neill

Irish Republican Army
QD 34½, South New Chapel

Martin O'Neill, a sergeant major attached to the quartermaster general's stores was accidentally shot and fatally injured early on the morning of 9 April 1922. On the day of his death, O'Neill was sitting with other men in the day room of the recruiting offices on Great Brunswick (Pearse) Street. Capt. John O'Keeffe, a member of the National Army, took his Colt automatic pistol out of his left pocket when it fired and the bullet hit O'Neill. O'Keeffe said that he believed that the trigger had caught on his gloves, which were also in his pocket. Martin O'Neill had been an active participant in the War of Independence with the 3rd Battalion, Dublin Brigade and was badly wounded a year earlier during the fight between the IRA and Auxiliary Division on Great Brunswick Street, not far from the scene of his death (*see 14 March 1921*). Remarkably, it was John O'Keeffe who, at that time, carried him to safety under heavy fire. It was stated that although O'Neill had not formally enlisted in the National Army at the time of his death he was part of those forces then under the control of the Richard Mulcahy. His funeral came to Glasnevin on 11 April 1922. His coffin was draped with the Tricolour and covered with a wreath of lilies and O'Neill's cap. He was interred in the Republican Plot.[5]

10 April 1922   **Anti-Treaty Irish Republican Army**
Michael Sweeney   *SD 39, South New Chapel*

Michael Sweeney, a motor mechanic from Harold's Cross Road and a member of the IRA, was shot and fatally injured at the junction of Grafton Street, Suffolk Street and Nassau Street by a member of the National Army.

Born in December 1900, the son of Hugh Sweeney and Bridget Byrne, Michael Sweeney joined the Irish Volunteers and at the age of fifteen participated in the 1916 Rising as a member of the South Dublin Union garrison. A member of the 4th Battalion, Dublin Brigade IRA he later joined the Dublin Brigade's Active Service Unit during the War of Independence. In May 1921, Sweeney took part in an ambush at Conway's halfway house on the Crumlin Road. At the beginning of the attack, Sweeney threw a homemade grenade that bounced off a lorry and back onto the road. It exploded and badly injured him. He was brought by bicycle as far as Harold's Cross and then brought to the Mater Hospital for treatment. He was left with a limp and scarring on his leg due to his wounds. He opposed the Anglo-Irish Treaty and was arrested in February 1922 being sent to Mountjoy Jail where he participated in a hunger strike.

On the day of his death, Michael Sweeney was in a lorry under arrest and travelling back to Mountjoy from Beggars Bush Barracks, where he was the subject of a court-martial. He was not handcuffed as he was an officer in the IRA.

A report described that his death occurred when Sweeney tried to escape from the lorry as it slowed in traffic. Having pushed a private to one side, he placed his hands on the back of the lorry to jump off. After he swung himself over the back of the lorry a struggle began, a shot was fired from a revolver, and Sweeney was wounded. The bullet hit him in the back of his neck, injuring his spinal cord and passed through his right lung. He was brought to hospital where he died of his injuries. The official statement issued following his death described that:

> Volunteer Sweeney was being conveyed in custody from a court-martial at Beggars' Bush Barracks when he attempted to escape while passing through College Green. There was a tussle as the prisoner got out of the lorry and he fell, wounded through the back. The prisoner was taken immediately to Jervis St. Hospital where he was medically attended and the Last Sacraments administered. He died shortly afterwards.

In the subsequent inquest into his death Sweeney's mother, Bridget, described that her son had been in ill health since he was wounded in the ambush in 1921. He had been lame as a result and also weak from hunger strike, which contradicted the account of an energetic attempt to escape custody. Nicholas Timmins, a newsboy, stated that he was on the corner of Suffolk Street and Grafton Street when he heard a shot and a lorry stop. He then saw the driver get out of the lorry and push a man, who was hanging from the rear of the lorry, back in. By coincidence, another of those that witnessed the shooting was the republican, feminist and trade unionist, Helena Molony. She described hearing what she thought was the noise of a gun being fired before Michael Sweeney, who was hanging from the back of the lorry, was pulled back into it. Two other witnesses claimed that although Sweeney was making an effort to escape he was still under the control of the guards, who had a hold of him under the arms, when the fatal shot was fired.

On 12 April, Michael Sweeney's remains were brought from the Jervis Street Hospital to his home where a large group of volunteers, estimated at 1,500, marched. Members of Sweeney's Active Service Unit acted as pall-bearers and as a guard of honour. A large crowd attended his funeral, from Mount Argus to Glasnevin, two days later. Amongst those present were Cathal Brugha, Liam Mellows, Oscar Traynor and Séamus Dwyer *(see 20 December 1922)*. He was interred in a grave in the Republican Plot. Helena Molony, who witnessed his death, died in 1967 and is buried in a grave in the Republican Plot close to Sweeney. Michael Sweeney's elder brother, George, was killed in November 1917 during the Battle of Passchendaele, aged nineteen whilst serving in the British army as a member of the Royal Munster Fusiliers. He died during an early morning advance in terrible conditions, north-west of the village of Passchendaele, in the infamous battle of the same name. His battalion reached their objective, but after two hours were forced to return to their original starting point. Over 100 men of the Munster Fusiliers died in the two-hour action.[6]

29 May 1922	Anti-Treaty Irish Republican Army
Thomas O'Brien	*PH 243, St Bridget's*

Thomas O'Brien from Crampton Buildings was in his early twenties when he was accidentally shot dead during the occupation of the Four Courts. During the inquest into his death it was recounted that on 29 May 1922 Patrick Byrne, a fellow member of the anti-Treaty forces occupying the Four Courts, was standing outside the room occupied by Thomas O'Brien with his bayonet fixed to his rifle. O'Brien exited the room and on seeing Byrne in the 'on guard' position, with his rifle fixed, O'Brien smiled and raised his hands. In response, Byrne raised his rifle in jest and believing it to be unloaded, pulled the trigger – O'Brien fell dead on the floor without saying a word. The fatal bullet had passed through his heart. His funeral came from the church on Clarendon Street following mass. In attendance at the cemetery were some 500 anti-Treaty IRA members. He was buried in a family grave in the St Bridget's section.[7]

27 June 1922
Daniel Lyons

National Army
RD 35, South New Chapel

Daniel Lyons died from burns received after an explosion while manufacturing incendiary bombs in Beggars Bush Barracks on 25 June 1922. Although he was not a formally enlisted member of the National Army, he had been recruited by Col Joseph Dunne to work with the Chemicals Branch of the National Army for about a month before his death. Lyons was from Charleville Avenue, North Strand, and during the War of Independence had been a member of F Company, 2nd Battalion, Dublin Brigade, IRA. He took over command of the company following the burning of the Custom House. During the same period, he was also active in the manufacturing of explosives on Peter Street for the IRA. His work involved making a type of explosive known as Irish cheddar. This led to him being recruited to work with the Chemicals Branch of the National Army following the split leading to the Civil War. On the day he was fatally injured, Dunne was carrying out work refining potassium chlorate in a temporary hut in Beggars Bush. Two of these huts had been set up for the manufacturing of incendiary bombs. When the explosion occurred the roof was blown off the shed in which he was working and the windows shattered. Lyons staggered out of the hut with his hands over his face. He had been badly burned on his head, chest, back and shoulders. He was taken to St Vincent's Hospital where he died from his injuries two days later. Lyons was buried in the Republican Plot in Glasnevin becoming the first and only person associated with the National Army to be buried in it before the opening of the National Army's own dedicated plot.[8]

28 June 1922   **Civilian**
Patrick Cosgrove   *GD 32, St Paul's*

Patrick Joseph Cosgrove from Lower Dominick Street was fourteen when he was shot on the corner of George's Hill, near the Four Courts, on the first day of the battle of Dublin. Born in March 1908, and one of twin brothers, he was the son of Mary Lacy and Edward Cosgrove. His twin brother, Edward, died aged four months. After he was wounded Patrick Cosgrove was brought to the Richmond Hospital where he died from his injuries. He was buried in a grave in the St Paul's section of the cemetery where his father, who pre-deceased him in 1918, was already buried.[9]

28 June 1922   **Civilian**
Thomas Fitzgerald   *UC 66, St Paul's*

Thomas Fitzgerald was fifteen when he was killed on the opening day of the Battle of Dublin. The son of Peter Fitzgerald, an engine fitter, and Mary Mullen, he was born in his family home in Belview (Bellevue) Buildings in Dublin. The family later moved to Marrowbone Lane where his father died in 1919. Thomas was shot in the abdomen during the fighting in Dublin and was brought to Mercer's Hospital where he died. He was buried in Glasnevin on 1 July 1922 and was buried in a grave in which his father and brother had been previously interred. His mother died in 1965.[10]

28 June 1922   **Civilian**
Laurence Freir   *EH 213, St Bridget's*

Laurence Joseph Freir was born in September 1900 at the home of his parents on Arran Quay. His family moved to 33 Merchant's Quay soon after his birth and Laurence lived there for the rest his life, following the career path of his father and grandfather to become a confectioner. His father, George Freir, died in 1919 and the following year his mother, Catherine Ellis, married Dennis Lynch, a widower. Laurence was wounded outside 34 Merchant's Quay during the opening stages of the Battle of Dublin and was brought to Mercer's Hospital where he was examined and found to have been hit three times. He died from his injuries, the fatal wound being a bullet that entered his lung and liver. On the same day, both Laurence's mother and stepfather were also brought to hospital suffering with gun shot wounds. Laurence Freir was

A barricade at Farrell's undertakers on Marlborough Street in 1922. The beginning of the Battle of Dublin had a significant impact on the funerary process in the city. Farrell's, who often brought funerals to Glasnevin, were prevented from continuing their work. **Courtesy of The National Library of Ireland.**

interred in a grave in which father and two other siblings had been previously buried in the St Bridget's section of the cemetery. His mother and stepfather died in 1929 and 1930 respectively and are buried in the St Patrick's section of the cemetery.[11]

28 June 1922   **Civilian**
Elizabeth Gorman   *OH 153, St Bridget's*

Elizabeth Gorman, neé Banks, was a fifty-four-year-old widow from Greek Street who was fatally wounded in the lung by a bullet fired during the fighting in Dublin. She was brought to the Jervis Street Hospital and was alive on arrival but died of her injuries shortly afterwards. She was buried in a family grave in the St Bridget's section of the cemetery on 5 July 1922.[12]

28 June 1922   **Civilian**
James Hurley   *BD 101, St Paul's*

James Hurley, a labourer from 21 Upper Kevin Street, was killed outside the Jervis Street Hospital during the Battle of Dublin. At 16.45 on 28 June 1922, five anti-Treaty fighters dressed in civilian clothes with bandoliers and weapons proceeded from Middle Abbey Street to Liffey Street and turned onto North Lotts where they took up a position at barricades erected at the ruins of Cahill's printers. Soon afterwards, a Crossley tender with a similar number of National Army soldiers drove up Middle Abbey Street and stopped at the Jervis Street Hospital. All the soldiers entered the hospital except one who remained in the lorry. Interested onlookers gathered around the lorry and as they did so, the anti-Treaty volunteers came back towards Abbey Street via Abbey Cottages and opened fire on the vehicle. The group of onlookers rushed away but James Hurley who was standing nearby was hit and fell on the pathway. After a few minutes, he was brought into the hospital but was already dead.[13]

28 June 1922   **Civilian**
Michael Keogh   *PE 154½, Garden*

Michael Keogh, from Little Strand Street, was fatally wounded in the arm and abdomen during the Battle of Dublin and died in the Jervis Street Hospital. He was in his 40s at the time of his death and had worked as a general labourer. He was buried in a family grave on 3 July 1922.[14]

28 June 1922   **National Army**
Thomas Mandeville   *KD 79, South New Chapel*

Thomas Arthur Mandeville was son of Henry Storry Mandeville and Mary Bartley. His father, originally from England, served as an officer in the Royal Navy from 1856, resigning his commission a few months before his death in 1878. Mandeville, a civil engineer, was killed whilst serving as a colonel commandant with the National Army. On the afternoon of 28 June 1922, Mandeville was with three other men in a Ford car leaving Dublin. Travelling towards Beggars' Bush Barracks they were ambushed as they crossed Leeson Street Bridge turning left onto Mespil Road. A number of men, standing at the corner of the bridge opened fire and bombs were thrown at the car. The short but intense attack caused significant damage with some of the bombs entering the car exploding at the feet of the driver. Thomas Mandeville was wounded on the left side of his body and in his legs and was brought to the Baggot Street Hospital where he died of his wounds that evening. It was stated that his last words to his brother were 'Harry, I forgive them from the bottom of my heart'. One other officer in the car, Michael Vaughan *(see below)* also died from his injuries.

It was reported in the aftermath of his death that Thomas Mandeville had served with the IRA during the War of Independence and taken part in a number of ambushes. However, whether he participated in active service or not is unclear. Contesting this report, a friend of Mandeville wrote to the *Irish Independent* stating that:

> He never participated in any ambush. Anybody who had the privilege of knowing poor Tommy Mandeville knows that he was one of the gentlest creatures that ever lived and would not harm a fly. He was engaged in his occupation as one of the civil engineers attached to the Free State when he met his tragic fate and his death is deeply deplored by all who knew him. His emphatic declaration that he freely forgave his attackers is typical of the man.

He was buried alongside Michael Vaughan in the National Army plot in Glasnevin. At the time of his death, Mandeville's only living relative was his brother Henry with whom he resided at Lower Pembroke Street. His parents and his siblings, two of whom predeceased him, are buried in the south section of the cemetery. It was theorised that a reason, amongst other possibilities, for the shooting of Noel Lemass in 1923 was his involvement in the ambush that led to the deaths of Mandeville and Vaughan.[15]

28 June 1922   **Civilian**
James Shine   *FG 128, Garden*

James Shine, a retired corporation employee aged in his seventies, was killed at Beresford Street on the corner of North King Street. A stray bullet hit him when he was walking to his home at 91 Upper Grangegorman from mass. His body was brought to the Richmond Hospital and he was buried in Glasnevin on 3 July 1922.[16]

28 June 1922   **Civilian**
James Tyrrell   *DD 101, St Paul's*

James Tyrrell, aged seven, was shot in the intestine during the Battle of Dublin and died from his injuries in the Mater Hospital. The son of John Tyrrell and Jane Redmond from 3 Tramway Cottages in Phibsborough he was born in March 1915 in the Rotunda Hospital. The exact circumstances of his wounding are unclear but he was listed as being wounded in the first casualty list of the battle. He was buried in Glasnevin on 1 July 1922.[17]

28 June 1922   **National Army**
Michael Vaughan   *KD 79, South New Chapel*

Michael Vaughan, an officer in the National Army, was fatally wounded alongside Thomas Mandeville (*see above*) in an ambush at Leeson Street Bridge on the opening day of the Civil War. Vaughan, originally from Clare, served with the IRA during the War of Independence and was a staff captain at the time of his death, attached to the Survey Department and based in Beggar's Bush Barracks. Before joining the National Army, he worked as an assistant at Tunney's public house and grocery in Ringsend. During the ambush, Vaughan was hit in the back and died of his wounds that evening in St Vincent's Hospital.[18]

29 June 1922   **Fianna Éireann**
William Clarke   *UD 102 St Paul's*

William Clarke from Lower Gloucester Place was nineteen when he was killed during the Battle of Dublin. A member of 1st Battalion, Dublin Brigade, Fianna Éireann he had served during the War of Independence. He was shot dead at the rear of a building on North Great George's Street by a National Army sniper.

The circumstances of his burial give some sense of confusion that existed at the cemetery as the battle developed. The morning after his death William Clarke's body arrived at the cemetery for burial in a delivery van, accompanied by another van with armed anti-Treaty combatants. No prior arrangements had been made and they ordered the cemetery staff to open a grave, which they did, in the St Paul's section of the cemetery. One of those present was the Fianna Éireann officer and anti-Treaty commander Seán Harling who, in response to a request from the cemetery staff, submitted a note stating that 'I Commandant Gen. Seán Harling do hereby authorise the burial of Private W.

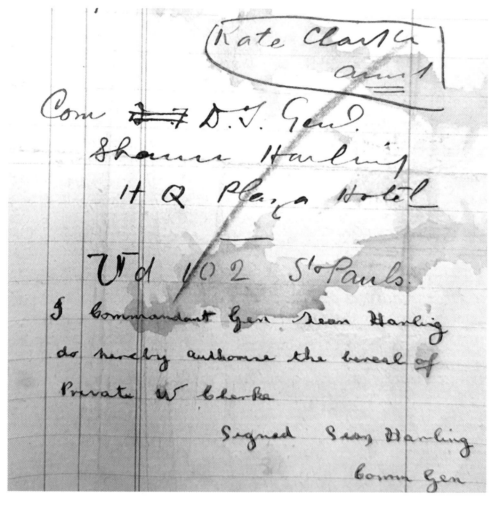

The hastily written note presented at Glasnevin Cemetery with the body of William Clarke. It includes the details requested by the cemetery staff to identify him. Courtesy of Dublin Cemeteries Trust.

Clarke.' William Clarke was duly buried and Harling was required to retro-spectively fill out an interment order.

He did this stating that Clarke had been killed on Hill Street and that his next of kin was his aunt Kate (Kathleen) Clarke. When Seán Harling died in 1977, he was also buried in the same grave that had last been opened when he had travelled to the cemetery in the midst of the Battle of Dublin.[19]

29 June 1922   **National Army**
Patrick Lowe   *KD 80, South New Chapel*

Patrick, or Paddy, Lowe from Portland Street North in Dublin was fatally wounded while serving as a quartermaster sergeant with the National Army in the Four Courts area during the Battle of Dublin. He was shot in the chest and died on his way to the Mater Hospital. With his brother James, he had been an active member of the IRA in Liverpool during the War of Independence. Due to his activities he was arrested and interned in Dartmoor Prison in March 1921, being released in February 1922. He was subsequently deported from England and on arrival in Ireland enlisted in the National Army. He was shot on Capel Street while serving with the Dublin Guard. He was buried in Glasnevin on 6 July 1922.

Patrick's brother James was a friend of Anthony Deane *(see 17 September 1922)*. Deane had also been deported from England for IRA activities. Following Deane's death Jimmy Lowe went to visit him, unaware he had been killed. Having knocked on Deane's door Lowe was dragged inside and beaten by plainclothes detectives. According to John Pinkman 'when Jimmy told them his brother Paddy had been killed [with the National Army] they took their hands off him and became sympathetic.'[20]

29 June 1922   **Civilian**
John Murphy   *PL 285, St Patrick's*

At noon on 29 June 1922, John William Murphy was wounded in the chest by a sniper's bullet while on North King Street. He was brought to hospital but soon died. Murphy was twenty-six at the time of his death and was a publican who operated premises at 42 North Cumberland Street, which was also his home.

A few months after his death, in October 1922, a young man named Owen

Kelly was arrested having broken into Murphy's home on North Cumberland Street. Kelly had stolen property belonging to Murphy, including a suit, an overcoat and some blankets. Kelly pled guilty in court. While there the judge asked Kelly if the suit he was now wearing was the same one that he was now charged with having stolen, the property of the late John Murphy. Kelly responded that it was, resulting in an outburst of laughter in the court.[21]

29 June 1922   **Civilian**
Patrick James White   *TD 102, St Paul's*

Patrick White from Benburb Street was a porter who worked for Watson's shirt factory. He was fatally wounded in the lower abdomen while standing outside a shop on North King Street. Aged nineteen, he was taken to the Richmond Hospital, where he died on the same day.[22]

30 June 1922   **Civilian**
William Byrne   *RD 102, St Paul's*

William Byrne, originally from Capel Street, lived on Upper Abbey Street with his wife, Marion Murray, whom he had married in 1908 and family. He enlisted in the British army during the First World War before being discharged and returned to his work as a carpenter. On Friday 30 June 1922, he left his home at about 15.00 and was not seen again by his family. His wife searched for him, initially without success, but eventually found and identified his body at the Richmond Hospital. He had suffered a bullet wound to the abdomen but nothing further was known about the circumstances in which he was killed. His funeral came to Glasnevin on 5 July.[23]

30 June 1922   **Anti-Treaty Irish Republican Army**
John Cusack   *PD 102, St Paul's*

John Joseph Cusack, also known as Jack, was nineteen years old when he was fatally wounded whilst serving on the anti-Treaty side at the Four Courts. Born in January 1903 he was the son of Patrick Cusack and Mary Alice Thompson and at the time of his death was employed as a messenger at the vegetarian restaurant on College Green. He had been an active member of Fianna Éireann during the War of Independence and was transferred to the 3rd Battalion, Dublin Brigade, IRA before the Truce.

Taking part in the Civil War, he was part of the group that occupied the Four Courts and was present when the National Army began the assault there. Matthew McDonnell a member of the Four Courts Garrison stated that:

> This man or rather boy was badly wounded whilst defending his post in the Courts. He was brought to the Richmond Hospital where he died the following day 30th as a result of wounds. He and a man named Wall … were the only two mortally wounded men in the Courts attack.[24]

30 June 1922   **Civilian**
Thomas Daly   *QD 102, St Paul's*

Thomas Daly worked as an attendant at the National Museum of Ireland, Kildare Street and also as caretaker of the building in which he lived, 17 Eden Quay. On the evening of 30 June at approximately 21.00 Daly was looking out a window on the upper floors of the building while combatants were fighting in the area. He was struck in the head by a bullet and died almost immediately. His wife who was also present was wounded in the left arm. He was buried in Glasnevin on 5 July 1922.[25]

30 June 1922   **National Army**
Thomas Hogan   *KD 79, South New Chapel*

Thomas Hogan from Tipperary was fatally wounded during the Battle of Dublin whilst serving as a private in the National Army. The son of Margaret A. Cahill and James C. Hogan, a farmer, he lived with his parents and siblings in Athassel House, Persse's Lot, Golden, Co. Tipperary. During the First World War, he served with the British army as a member of the Machine Gun Corps. After his discharge he joined the IRA in Tipperary, serving during the War of Independence and enlisted in the National Army in May 1922. In 1933 his mother stated that her son:

> … was a member of the late lamented Denis Lacey's column in Sth. Tipp. in 1920–21 after his return from Mesopotamia where the Irish soldiers of that time created terrible trouble over the British treatment in Ireland. My son being an expert mechanic and engineer, at the personal request of Denis Lacey, worked for his column repairing guns, making ammunition etc. during the year 1921 at Kilsheehan near Clonmel. Being in Dublin in June 1922 rather than taking any active part in the Civil War of that month he volunteered as a Red Cross driver of the National Army and was killed in O'Connell St. after the fall of the Four Courts on the evening of June 30th whilst driving a Red Cross ambulance from Jervis St. Hospital into O'Connell St.[26]

30 June 1922   **National Army**
John Lewis   *UK 314½, St Bridget's*

John Joseph Lewis, from Stafford Street in Dublin, was serving as a private in the National Army when he was fatally wounded during the Battle of Dublin. The son of John Lewis and Catherine Byrne he was born in January 1899 and before joining the army had worked as an assistant to a bootmaker and also delivering parcels for Clery's department store. The report of an inquest at the time of his death recorded that he was shot in the back of the head and died at the Bolton Street Technical Schools. A pension application by his family stated that he had been killed at Williams & Woods on Parnell Street. He was buried in a family grave in the St Bridget's section of the cemetery.[27]

30 June 1922   **National Army**
Patrick McGarry   *KD 79, South New Chapel*

Patrick McGarry was born in March 1899 in Bluepool, Kanturk, Co. Cork, the son of Ellen Linehan and Dominick McGarry. He worked in the tailoring trade before joining the National Army during the Civil War. Stationed at the Curragh with the 1st Southern unit he was fatally wounded in the back on 29 June 1922 at Cole's Lane during the Battle of Dublin. He died of his wounds in the Mater Hospital and was buried in the National Army plot in Glasnevin.[28]

30 June 1922   **Anti-Treaty Irish Republican Army**
Matthew Tomkins   *YC 87½, Garden*

Matthew Tomkins (Tompkins), from George's Quay in Dublin, was killed whilst serving as a member of the anti-Treaty IRA during the Battle of Dublin. He was originally a member of Fianna Éireann and later Dublin Brigade IRA and had served during the War of Independence. He was hit by a burst of machine-gun fire on Parnell Street while crossing the junction from North Great George's Street to Marlborough Street in an attempt to move from Barry's Hotel to the Gresham Hotel. Shot in the chest he was brought to the Mater Hospital, but was dead on arrival. At time of his death he was attached to a first aid unit and was aged twenty-one.[29]

30 June 1922   **National Army**
James Walsh   *KD 80, South New Chapel*

James Walsh, from Killaloe, near Callan, in Co. Kilkenny, was the son of Patrick and Margaret Walsh, whose father was a shepherd and farm worker. During the First World War, Walsh served in the British army and following his discharge spent some time in England working in a factory before returning to Ireland where he joined the National Army. He was fatally wounded in the head during the fighting around the Four Courts and his body was taken to the Jervis Street Hospital.[30]

1 July 1922   **National Army**
David Bain   *KD 79, South New Chapel*

David Bain (also recorded as Behan) was the son of George Bain and Julia Redmond. His father, a cabinetmaker originally from Scotland, and mother had married in Dublin in 1892. David, their second child, was born on 8 January 1897 at the family home in Sandwith Terrace. The Bains later settled in Courtney Place in Ballybough and David worked as a telegraph messenger. Following the outbreak of the First World War, he enlisted in the British army in September 1914 at the age of seventeen. Serving with the Irish Guards, he arrived in France in March the following year and remained with his regiment until his discharge in June 1918. Having returned home to Ballybough, he worked for the American Oil Company in North Wall before he enlisted in the National Army in March 1922. Bain was stationed in Howth and later in Wellington Barracks serving with the rank of sergeant major. He took part in the fighting around the Four Courts during the Battle of Dublin and was shot in the leg and the chest on 30 June 1922. He was taken to the Richmond Hospital where he died of his wounds the following day and was buried in the National Army plot in Glasnevin on 5 July 1922.[31]

1 July 1922   **Civilian**
Edward Dwan   *BC 86, St Paul's*

Edward Dwan, aged fifteen, was shot in the head and fatally wounded near his home on Grenville Street during the fighting in Dublin. Born in November 1906, he was the son of Joseph Dwan and Mary Dooley. The same bullet that killed Dwan also struck and killed Patrick Meehan *(see below)*. He died of

A letter relating to the burial of Edward Dwan. During the fighting in Dublin in 1922 the operations of Glasnevin Cemetery and its offices in Rutland (Parnell) Square were severely impacted. **Courtesy of Dublin Cemeteries Trust.**

his injuries in the Mater Hospital and was buried in a family grave in the St Paul's section of the cemetery. Edward was the third of three civilian family members to be killed within two years of one another in different incidents and buried in Glasnevin. His nephew, William Robinson, who was killed at Croke Park, aged eleven, is also buried in the same grave *(see 22 November 1920)*. His brother-in-law, also William Robinson, was killed in October 1920 on Capel Street *(see 16 October 1920)*.[32]

1 July 1922
Patrick Meehan

Civilian
RB 82½, St Paul's

Patrick Meehan, a labourer aged in his early twenties, was shot and fatally wounded close to his home on Grenville Street in Dublin and died in the Mater Hospital. He was killed by the same bullet as Edward Dwan *(see above)*. Both their funerals came to Glasnevin on the same day, 6 July 1922, and they were buried in graves not far from one another.[33]

1 July 1922   **National Army**
Richard Reid   *KD 80, South New Chapel*

Richard Reid, from Cuffe Street, was serving as an acting sergeant when he was fatally wounded in the chest during the fighting in the O'Connell Street area of Dublin. He died in Jervis Street Hospital and was buried in the National Army plot in Glasnevin on 6 July 1922.[34]

2 July 1922   **National Army**
Luke Condron   *KD 79, South New Chapel*

Luke Condron from Blackhall Place was killed while serving as a captain with the 1st Battalion, 2nd Eastern Division, National Army during the Civil War. Born on Queen Street in Dublin in 1894 he was a veteran of the 1916 Rising, having served with the Four Courts Garrison. Following internment, he was released and served during the War of Independence. He worked in the Goods Store, of Kingsbridge Railway Station.

Condron was wounded on the South Circular Road, near Wellington Barracks, where he was based, during an ambush. He received a gunshot wound to the back and died in the Meath Hospital. His coffin, borne on a gun-carriage, was brought to Glasnevin on 6 July 1922 from the church on Arran Quay. The procession was led by the army's piper's band with an advance guard and met with the coffins of five other National Army soldiers for the final journey to the cemetery and interment. A newspaper described that '... crowds watched the mournful procession, the whole scene being very impressive particularly as it passed through the ruined O'Connell St. On top of one of the mourning carriages was a large floral cross. Many other beautiful wreaths were carried. On approaching the cemetery, the band played a funeral march. After a short service in the chapel, the coffins were laid in a large grave in the National plot in which three officers were interred on the previous day. Father Fitzgibbon officiated at the graveside ... three volleys were fired over the grave and the Last Post was sounded by a bugler.'[35]

2 July 1922   **National Army**
Joseph Stewart   *KD 81, South New Chapel*

Joseph Stewart from Blantyre in Scotland was a private in the Dublin Guard who was fatally wounded during the fighting around the Four Courts in the

Battle of Dublin. Wounded on 1 July 1922 he died of his injuries the following day in the Jervis Street Hospital. Stewart came from a family of coal miners and lived in a house in Baird's Rows in Blantyre before joining the National Army. He was buried in the National Army plot following a joint funeral with two other members of the National Army.[36]

3 July 1922   **Anti-Treaty Irish Republican Army**
Charles O'Malley   *BC 51, South*

Charles O'Malley, a veterinary student and the younger brother of Ernie O'Malley, was killed during the Battle of Dublin, aged eighteen. Charles was born in Castlebar in February 1904, the son of Luke Malley and Marion Kearney.

While Charles was still young, the family moved to Dublin where they lived on Iona Drive. During the Civil War, he was a member of F Company, 2nd Battalion, Dublin Brigade, IRA. He was shot while defending a post on O'Connell Street and died of his wounds in the Jervis Street Hospital. Ernie O'Malley, writing to Liam Lynch who had expressed his condolences on the death of Charles, stated that: '... to tell the truth I did not miss his loss so much as I did not know him very well. I met him so few times in the Courts before the attack. He was a good kid and died game.' Charles O'Malley's funeral came to Glasnevin on 6 July 1922, the first burial in a grave in which his parents and brother Ernie would later be interred.[37]

4 July 1922   **Civilian**
Henry Hynes   *UB 47, Dublin*

Henry Hynes a labourer from Lower Gardiner Street, was shot dead at the corner of Parnell Street and O'Connell Street. He had left his home to purchase tobacco when he was killed. An inquest found that he had died of 'shock and haemorrhage due to the laceration of brain following a bullet wound'. He was buried in Glasnevin on 8 July 1922. Hynes was a former member of the British army, having served during the First World War. He was born in January 1881 and in 1906 married Ellen Kane with whom he had a family.[38]

5 July 1922   **National Army**
John Fitzsimons   *KD 81, South New Chapel*

John Fitzsimons was serving as a sergeant in the National Army when he was accidentally shot and killed in July 1922. From Newcomen Court in Dublin, he was the son of Patrick Fitzsimons and Jane Fagan and had been a pre-Truce member of Dublin Brigade, IRA. He was one of three brothers that served with the National Army during the Civil War.

A coroner's inquest heard that on the day of his death Fitzsimons was on duty when he decided, with another soldier, to go to a pawnbroker's shop on Francis Street to buy a pair of binoculars. The proprietor, Thomas Cummins, invited the two men to tea and John Fitzsimons left his revolver on the table. There was subsequently some conversation regarding the weapon and when Fitzsimons picked up the weapon to explain about the mechanism, the gun fired and the bullet passed through his head and hit the ceiling.[39]

6 July 1922	National Army
John Keenan	*KD 81, South New Chapel*

John Keenan, a veteran of the War of Independence, was serving as an adjutant in the 2nd Battalion, Dublin Guard at the time of his death. As a civilian, he had previously worked as a shipwright's helper in Guinness Brewery. During the initial fighting in the Battle of Dublin Keenan had been wounded in the chest and arm but had quickly returned to duty. An inquest heard that on the evening of his death he was on duty at a post on Vicar Street. According to Sgt William Conway, who was on duty there at the same time, a discussion began about the double action of a Colt .45 revolver. John Keenan lifted the Colt, which he appeared to believe was unloaded, pointed it at his head and pulled the trigger. The revolver fired and Keenan was killed instantly.[40]

6 July 1922	Civilian
Leo Walpole	*IF 131½, Garden*

Francis Leo Walpole, known by his middle name, was born on 26 October 1891 on Elizabeth Street, off Clonliffe Road. The son of Robert Walpole and Rose Sharkey his family later moved to Gardiner Street and then to 23 North Great George's Street. Leo had enlisted in the British army in 1915 and served on the Western Front from December that year. He was discharged from the army in 1919, suffering with wounds that he had received. He returned home to North Great George's Street and it was here in July 1922 that he was fatally wounded. On the day in question at 17.45 Walpole's mother was preparing a cup of tea for him when she heard him exclaim that he had been hit. He was standing a few yards back from a window in the house when he was struck in the abdomen by a bullet. He staggered to his sister, who called for an ambulance, and the St John's Ambulance brought him to Mercer's Hospital. Here he was treated but the bullet had caused damage to his liver, intestines and stomach and he died soon afterwards of shock and haemorrhage. He was buried in a grave next to his father who died in 1921.[41]

7 July 1922   Anti-Treaty Irish Republican Army
Cathal Brugha   *SD 34½, South New Chapel*

Charles William St John Burgess, Cathal Brugha, was born in his family home on Richmond Avenue in July 1874. He was one of fourteen children of Thomas Burgess and Maryanne Flynn. He joined the Gaelic League in 1899 and gaining an interest in Gaelic culture, learned Irish and began using his Irish name. In 1912, he married Kathleen Kingston in the Roman Catholic church in Rathgar. He was a member of the Irish Republican Brotherhood and joined the Irish Volunteers on their foundation in 1913. As an officer and adjutant of the 4th Battalion, Dublin Brigade, he took part in the Howth gun-

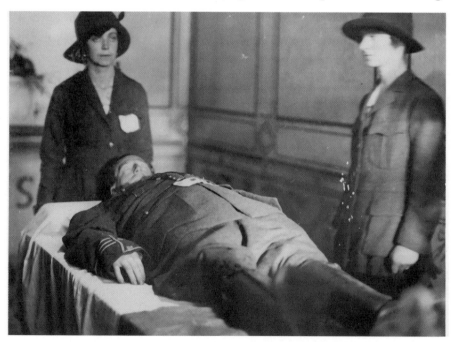

The body of Cathal Brugha lying in state at the Mater Hospital.
This image is reproduced with the kind permission of the National Museum of Ireland.

The remains of Cathal Brugha being carried from the mortuary chapel to the Republican Plot flanked by members of Cumann na mBan.
This image is reproduced with the kind permission of the National Museum of Ireland.

The funeral of Cathal Brugha at Glasnevin. Courtesy of Getty Images.

running. During the 1916 Rising he fought at the South Dublin Union and was very badly wounded multiple times. He was hospitalised as a result and remained in treatment following the surrender. His health was affected for the remainder of his life as a result.

Following the Rising, Brugha became an increasingly active and important figure in the republican movement. He was involved in the reorganisation of the Irish Volunteers and effectively made chief-of-staff in 1917 whilst also being elected to the Sinn Féin executive. The following year, Brugha helped spearhead an IRA plot to assassinate members of the British cabinet. The assassinations were to be carried out if conscription was extended to Ireland to assist the British war effort during the First World War. He travelled to London with a group of volunteers to carry out the plan and remained there until autumn 1918. He visited the House of Commons on a number of occasions developing the plan. However, the threat of conscription receded with the collapse of the German army on the Western Front and he returned to Dublin.

He was elected during the 1918 general election in the Co. Waterford parliamentary constituency, taking 75% of the vote. Brugha was subsequently made ceann comhairle and temporary president to the first Dáil. He was replaced in the latter position by Éamon de Valera in April 1919 and was appointed as Minister for Defence. During the War of Independence Michael Collins, as IRA Director of Intelligence, and Brugha had a number of disagreements in relation to policies and activities. In particular, Brugha took issue with the IRB, which he had left following 1916, holding influence over the IRA and other issues that could lead to the authority of Dáil Éireann being superseded in relation to the war. Brugha also advocated targeted and principled military actions by the IRA.

He was wholly opposed to the Anglo-Irish Treaty and launched a stinging attack on Michael Collins during the Treaty debates in the Dáil in January 1922. Following the approval of the Treaty, he was replaced as Minister for Defence. Taking part in the Civil War, he fought during the Battle of Dublin from 28 June 1922 and served in the O'Connell Street area. There he remained, along with many other anti-Treaty fighters, until the situation and their positions became untenable in the face of a persistent and determined opposition by the National Army. He remained one of the bitter-enders and on 5 July, as it proved impossible to remain any longer, evacuated his position. It was during these final moments that he was fatally wounded. There are varying accounts of the exact circumstances of Brugha's wounding, Cumann na mBan member Linda Kearns, stated that:

... Cathal had a revolver in each hand and he kept on shouting 'no surrender'. He was shot in the hip, the femoral artery being severed. I was beside him, but was not hit. To give the Free Staters their due, I don't think they wanted to kill him and aimed low. But as he was a small man, he was struck higher than they expected and in a vital part. The ambulance came at once and took him to the Mater, he lived for two days ...

Regardless of the exact circumstances of his wounding, the injuries he sustained proved fatal and he died in the Mater Hospital on 7 July 1922. His funeral to Glasnevin came from St Joseph's church, Berkeley Street and made a circuitous route around the city before arriving at the cemetery. On passing through O'Connell Street the cortege stopped at the place where Brugha had made his final stand and prayers were recited. He was interred in the Republican Plot.

Following Brugha's death Michael Collins writing to a friend stated that many, in his position, would not have forgiven Brugha for the manner in which he challenged him during the Treaty debates but that '... I would forgive him anything. Because of his sincerity I would forgive him anything. At worst he was a fanatic, though in what had been a noble cause. At best I number him among the very few who have given their all that this country, now torn by civil war, should have its freedom. When many of us are forgotten, Cathal Brugha will be remembered.'[42]

23, Suffolk Street,/
D U B L I N.
9th July, 1922.

Mrs. Cathal Brugha requests that, apart from family relations and intimate friends, the chief mourners and the Guard of Honour should include only the women of the Republican movement. She makes this request as a protest against the "immediate and terrible" Civil War made by the so-called Provisional Government on the Irish Republican Forces.
She does not desire the presence of any of the representatives of the Free State or its officials at the Funeral.

NOTE - This does not exclude the general public from attending the funeral.

A notice issued on behalf of Caitlín Brugha prior to the funeral of her husband Cathal.
Courtesy of Derek Jones.

8 July 1922   **National Army**
John Byrne   *KD 81, South New Chapel*

John Byrne, a sergeant in the Dublin Guard, died of wounds received in Harold's Cross on the night of Saturday, 8 July 1922. That day Byrne was stationed with a number of other soldiers at Harold's Cross Bridge. The men were being sniped on from the direction of Greenmount Lane across the canal. Byrne took it upon himself to see if he could locate the snipers. He took his Webley revolver and a few minutes later the National Army soldiers who had remained at their post heard a number of shots being fired. They then went towards the direction of the shooting where they found Byrne fatally wounded at Factory Lane just off Greenmount Lane. He had been shot in the thigh. He was buried in the National Army plot in Glasnevin on 12 July 1922.[43]

8 July 1922   **National Army**
John Dunne   *KD 81, South New Chapel*

John Dunne, from Spencer Street, North Strand was accidentally killed at Swords in north Co. Dublin whilst serving as a quartermaster sergeant in the National Army. He had previously served as a member of 1st Battalion, Dublin Brigade, IRA, during the War of Independence and had spent time interned in the Curragh. On the day of his death Dunne was one of a party of National Army soldiers that stopped at Taylor's public house in Swords. An inquest heard that as one of the party was taking a revolver from their pocket, the gun fired and the bullet hit Dunne. He was brought to the Mater Hospital but pronounced dead on arrival.[44]

8 July 1922   **National Army**
John Kennedy   *KD 81, South New Chapel*

John Kennedy, a sergeant major in the National Army was fatally wounded in fighting on O'Connell Street during the Battle of Dublin. Kennedy, from Fishamble Street, was a former member of the British army. He had served with the South Wales Borderers on the Western Front and later in Germany following the end of the war. After his discharge, he returned home to Dublin and worked in the Cantrell Cochrane mineral water factory on Nassau Place. During the Civil War, he enlisted in the National Army and served as a Lewis

R. I. P.

SERGEANT JOHN KENNEDY,
I.R.A.
Who died on Saturday, 8th July, 1922,
from wounds received in action in
O'Connell Street, Dublin.

Left: *John Kennedy in the uniform of the South Wales Borderers while on the Western Front during the First World War;* Right: *Memorial card.* **Courtesy of the Douglas family.**

gunner. On the first day of the Battle of Dublin, he reported for duty at 06.00 and during a lull in the fighting at 14.00 went to the pro-cathedral where he married his fiancée Mary Douglas. A few days later, on Monday 3 July, he was wounded outside the Provincial Bank while fighting on O'Connell Street. Shot in one of his lungs and suffering with severe blood loss, he was taken to the Jervis Street Hospital. He died five days later of 'shock and haemorrhage complicated by gangrene'. His widow, Mary, never re-married, she is also buried in Glasnevin.[45]

8 July 1922   **National Army**
Gerald O'Connor   *KD 82, South New Chapel*

Gerald Joseph O'Connor was the son of Patrick and Kate O'Connor and lived on Usher Street in Dublin. He worked as a law clerk and later a furniture dealer before joining the National Army. A transport driver he was travelling with a party of National Army soldiers when he was killed during an ambush at Kilreecle Wood, near Gort, in Co. Galway. An official army account described that a sniper killed O'Connor just after a group of anti-Treaty IRA had surrendered. Gerald O'Connor left a widow, Frances, whom he had married in September 1915, and three children.[46]

8 July 1922   **Civilian**
William Saunders   *HD 102, St Paul's*

William Saunders, aged fifteen, was a pipe-maker's apprentice who worked at Kapp and Petersons. He was fatally wounded on Thursday 6 July 1922 at Cross Guns Bridge, near Mountjoy Jail. The son of Ernest Saunders and Elizabeth Brennan, he was born on 3 March 1907. Between 20.00 and 21.00 on the evening that he was wounded William was standing at Cross Guns Bridge with his friend Henry Wright from Belvedere Place. The two were waving their hands at prisoners in Mountjoy to attract their attention.

Earlier that evening William had visited the prison along with Catherine Penrose from Fownes Street. Catherine's son, John, was imprisoned there and they had hoped to visit him. Having been denied entry William went to the canal behind the prison and along with Henry Wright tried to gain the attention of prisoners shouting, 'Penrose, are you there?' while standing on top of a small shed. After about ten minutes, shots were fired and William Saunders fell to the ground. It appeared that guards at Mountjoy had fired the bullets. Two people who lived nearby came to William's assistance and having placed a blanket over him brought him to the Mater Hospital. Here his father visited him and William told him he would be fine as he only had a wound to his back. However, his wounds were severe, he had been shot through the lungs the bullet entering on the left side of his chest and exiting on the opposite side. He died two days later of his injuries. A coroner's inquest found that he had died of 'shock and haemorrhage the result of shots fired by a person or persons unknown'.[47]

11 July 1922   **Anti-Treaty Irish Republican Army**
Patrick O'Brien   *SD 38, South New Chapel*

Patrick (Paddy) O'Brien died of wounds received during fighting in Enniscorthy, Co. Wexford in July 1922. A high-ranking member of the anti-Treaty IRA, O'Brien was from Pim Street in Dublin and the son of Patrick O'Brien senior, a dock labourer, and Mary Anne Kane. He had served during the 1916 Rising, alongside his brothers Larry and Denis, in the vicinity of the South Dublin Union. Before the rebellion, Patrick was employed as a clerk in the Junior Army and Navy Stores in Dublin but subsequently worked as a storeman with the Dublin Port and Docks Board. During the War of Independence, he rose through the ranks of the IRA taking charge of C Company, 4th Battalion, Dublin Brigade. He took part in the successful jailbreak of Frank Teeling, Ernie O'Malley and Simon Donnelly from Kilmainham in February 1921. He was later appointed assistant director of training with IRA GHQ under the command of Emmet Dalton who held the position of director of training.

During the Truce, O'Brien was placed in charge of a training camp for Dublin Brigade IRA at Cobb's Lodge in Glenasmole in south Dublin and following the Treaty was one of those who occupied Beggar's Bush Barracks. He ultimately took the anti-Treaty side in the Civil War and during the occu-

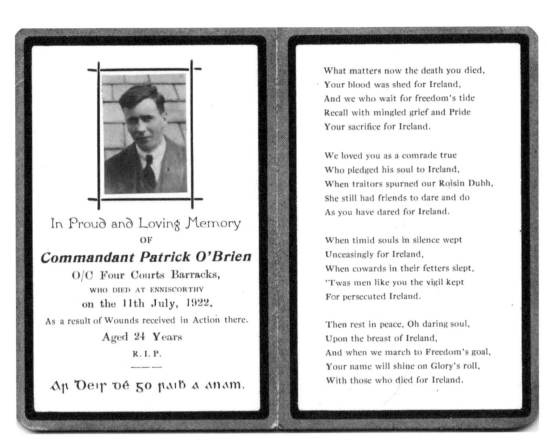

Memorial card of Patrick O'Brien. **Courtesy of Fonsie Mealy Auctioneers**

pation of the Four Courts was made officer commanding the anti-Treaty garrison. He remained in his position until wounded by shrapnel during the National Army assault in June. Following the fall of the Four Courts, O'Brien was one of a group of anti-Treaty fighters who evaded capture and eventually made their way to Wexford via Blessington. Here a mixed force of anti-Treaty IRA attempted to capture control of Enniscorthy castle, and the town, from a National Army garrison. On 5 July, a full assault to capture the castle took place. During the advance, Patrick O'Brien was fatally wounded at Friary Place by a National Army sniper located in the castle. Another anti-Treaty soldier, Maurice Spillane, was killed in the same incident. It was reported that O'Brien was shot in the lung. He was removed to the County Home in Enniscorthy where he died on 11 July. He was interred in the Republican Plot in Glasnevin three days later.[48]

| **20 July 1922** | **Civilian** |
| *Margaret King* | *TD 103, St Paul's* |

Just after 21.00 on the evening of 20 July 1922, two National Army touring cars were travelling towards Dublin when they were ambushed at Rialto Bridge. The cars continued to the church at Dolphin's Barn where they claimed, having been fired upon again, they left their vehicles and began to return fire. It was at this time that Margaret King, a draper's assistant, was walking in the area with her sister Ellen as she travelled home to the nearby Rehoboth Terrace (Place) and was shot. The bullet hit her in the chest. She was placed in a car and brought to the Meath Hospital where she died five minutes after arrival. She was buried in Glasnevin on 24 July 1922.[49]

| **20 July 1922** | **National Army** |
| *William Joseph Finlay Philips* | *KD 82, South New Chapel* |

William Philips was born in 16 Lower Kevin Street in November 1897, the son of William Philips and Annie Finlay. The family later moved to St Kevin's Cottages and during the War of Independence William was a member of K Company, 3rd Battalion, Dublin Brigade, IRA. In 1921, he was sentenced to ten years in prison for being in possession of a revolver. His sentence was later commuted. During the Civil War, he was a sergeant major in the National Army and at the time of his death he was serving with a detachment of the

Interment order for the burial of Margaret King. Courtesy of Dublin Cemeteries Trust.

Dublin Guard under the command of Comdt Tom Flood in Killaloe. A contemporary newspaper report notes that he was accidentally shot dead.[50]

22 July 1922   **National Army**
Thomas O'Connor   *KD 82, South New Chapel*

Thomas O'Connor from Rialto Buildings in Dublin was accidentally killed
at Beggar's Bush Barracks in July 1922. O'Connor had served with 4th
Battalion, Dublin Brigade, IRA, during the War of Independence and had
been employed in Crean's Soap Factory on North King Street. On the day of
his death O'Connor was one of a number of soldiers that returned to Beggar's
Bush Barracks having carried out raids. As he got out of the Lancia armoured
car in which he was travelling, the butt of his rifle struck the door of the car
and fired. O'Connor was wounded and taken to St Vincent's Hospital where
he died.[51]

23 July 1922   **National Army**
John Joseph Martin   *KD 82, South New Chapel*

John Martin was a seventeen-year-old member of the National Army who was
accidentally shot and killed at Mountjoy Jail in July 1922. The son of Mary
McManus and John Martin he was born in September 1905 in their home
on Constitution Hill in Dublin and later lived with his family on Wellington
Street. He was a member of Fianna Éireann during the War of Independence.
On the night of his death, Martin was on escort duty at the gate of the prison
when his rifle accidentally fired and the bullet hit him in the head. He was
killed immediately.[52]

24 July 1922   **National Army**
Thomas McMahon   *KD 83, South New Chapel*

Thomas McMahon, from Arran Quay in Dublin, was killed during an ambush
in Co. Wexford. He had previously served in the British army, having enlisted
in October 1914 and was a member of the Royal Army Medical Corps until
August 1917 when he was discharged. He never served overseas. Following
his discharge, he worked for a period as an insurance agent before joining the
National Army.

On 24 July 1922, McMahon was one of a number of members of the
National Army who were on a train from Wexford that was ambushed as it
approached Killurin Railway Station. The train, which was also carrying civilians

and anti-Treaty IRA prisoners, was halted by a blockade on the line. Almost immediately, an attacking force of anti-Treaty IRA, under the command of Bob Lambert, opened fire. Those in the train were in an extremely vulnerable position, beneath the ambushers, who had placed themselves in an elevated position on the railway embankment. National Army soldiers attempted to exit the train but found that the doors were locked, leaving them to climb out of the windows. Those who successfully left the carriage returned fire towards the anti-Treaty IRA while the latter continued to rain fire down on the carriages.

Approximately thirty minutes after the first shot had been fired Bob Lambert made the decision to begin a tactical retreat and the fighting ended. During the ambush, Thomas McMahon was shot through the lung and a bullet shattered his right hand. He died of his wounds shortly after admittance to hospital. Another member of the National Army, Maurice Quirke *(see below)*, was also killed and another, Michael Campion *(see 27 July 1922)*, died of wounds he received.[53]

24 July 1922	**National Army**
Patrick O'Hara	*KD 82, South New Chapel*

Patrick John O'Hara, a member of the National Army, was the son of Patrick O'Hara and Elizabeth Kelly. He was born in January 1897 and lived all his life in Abercorn Terrace, Inchicore. He worked as a body maker, or coach builder, before joining the National Army in May 1922 and had previously been a member of 4th Battalion, Dublin Brigade, IRA. On the night of 22 July 1922, O'Hara, and another member of the National Army, John Cooke, were stationed at Thompson's Garage on Great Brunswick Street. The two men decided to go to Butt Bar, near Butt Bridge, and on arriving there saw another National Army soldier, Private Byrne, drunk and brandishing his revolver in the pub. Cooke and O'Hara persuaded Byrne to leave. Having taken him outside the pub, he ran away saying that he was going back to barracks. Later O'Hara and Cooke met Byrne once more, this time on Lower Abbey Street. John Cooke gave an account that Byrne pointed his revolver in his direction while attempting to cock it. He said that he and Byrne struggled with one another and a shot was fired which hit Patrick O'Hara in the abdomen. He died two days later of his injuries in the Jervis Street Hospital.[54]

24 July 1922
Maurice Quirke

National Army
KD 82, South New Chapel

Maurice Quirke was killed during the Killurin train ambush along with Thomas McMahon *(see above)*. He was born in Longford in July 1898, the son of Maurice Quirke and Teresa Connolly. In November 1907 Fr William Fitzgerald, a priest in Longford, brought Maurice before the local Petty Sessions Court claiming that he had found him '... wandering and without proper guardianship on the public streets ...' Maurice was sent to Artane Industrial School where he was ordered to remain until 1914. His mother later moved to Dublin and resided with him and her daughter, Christina, at Lamb's Court (Cottages), off James Street. Here they lived in the front room of a tenement and

Courtesy of Southampton Archives and Local Studies

it appears that by this time Maurice Quirke senior had died. As a result, Maurice junior was the primary source of income for the family as his mother was without work and Christina Quirke was deaf due to extensive burns she had received in St Vincent's Industrial School, Goldenbridge. Before joining the National Army Maurice worked with the Merchant Navy as a deck boy and also served for a period as a member of the Royal Dublin Fusiliers, being discharged in 1919. Having joined the National Army he served as a private in B Company, 2nd Battalion, 2nd Eastern Division. During the ambush at Killurin, he was shot through the neck and died of his injuries. He was buried in the National Army plot on 27 July 1922.[55]

27 July 1922
Michael Campion

National Army
KD 83, South New Chapel

Michael Campion was sixteen when he was fatally wounded in the Killurin train ambush in Wexford *(see 24 July 1922)*. Born in September 1905, in the home of his family at Belview (Bellevue) Buildings, he was the son of Margaret Byrne and Michael Campion. Before joining the National Army, he had worked as a coachbuilder's apprentice for a company on Westland Row. During the Killurin ambush, Michael Campion was shot in the arm and lung and died of his injuries three days later in St Vincent's Hospital in Dublin. He resided on Nicholas Avenue, off Church Street, at the time of his death.[56]

28 July 1922   **National Army**
John Deasy   *KD 83, South New Chapel*

John Deasy, a member of the Volunteer Reserve Dublin Guard, was killed in an ambush in Mayo. The son of James Deasy and Annie Blood he was born in the home of his family, 71 Rialto Buildings, in January 1903. Before joining the National Army, he had worked for William Ryan, a grocer based on Thomas Street. On the day of his death, Deasy was part of a body of soldiers moving from Newport to Crossmolina when they were ambushed by the anti-Treaty IRA at Bracklagh, north-east of Newport. During the subsequent fight, John Deasy was killed. Frederick Graydon, a fellow National Army member *(see below)* and Edward Hegarty, an anti-Treaty volunteer, also died.[57]

28 July 1922   **National Army**
Frederick Graydon   *KD 83, South New Chapel*

Frederick Graydon was killed in the same ambush as John Deasy *(see above)* near Newport, Co. Mayo. Born on New Year's Day 1900 Graydon, from Bray in Co. Wicklow, was the son of Laurence Graydon and Lizzie Byrne. He had served during the First World War as a member of the 7th (South Irish Horse) Battalion Royal Irish Regiment and was discharged in November 1919. Having returned home, he was recorded as being of no fixed abode. Graydon appears to have used the alias 'Thomas Tracy' or 'Lally' when enlisting in the National Army. This led to some confusion after his death. It is possible that his use of an alias stemmed from convictions in 1920 and 1921 for obtaining money through false pretences and being 'found in an enclosed area for an unlawful purpose'. For the latter he was sentenced to three months hard labour. His funeral, a joint one with John Deasy, came to Glasnevin on 2 August 1922 and both were buried in the same grave in the National Army plot.[58]

30 July 1922   **National Army**
Patrick Kinsella   *KD 83, South New Chapel*

Patrick Kinsella, from Capel Street in Dublin, was a member of the Dublin

Guard and was killed during the fighting leading to the capture of Tipperary town. On the afternoon of Saturday 29 July 1922, the Dublin Guard advanced into the town via Spital Street and the Abbey Grammar School. The anti-Treaty IRA mounted a significant defence near the latter location resulting in National Army casualties and their withdrawal. The following morning the advance was continued. The progress of the offensive was gradual and marked by close quarter fighting, particularly at the junction of Main Street and Bridge Street. However, by early that afternoon the town was in possession of the National Army, who suffered three fatal casualties in the fighting that weekend. One of these was Patrick Kinsella who was shot in the stomach. Before joining the National Army, he worked for D'Arcy's Brewery driving a dray and had married his wife, Mary Kinsella, in May 1922. Mary was pregnant at the time of her husband's death.[59]

1 August 1922	Anti-Treaty Irish Republican Army
Harry Boland	*SD 37, South New Chapel*

Harry Boland was born a short distance from the cemetery in the home of his family on Dalymount Terrace in April 1887. The son of Catherine Woods and James Boland, his parents had earlier returned to Dublin from Manchester. His father was a Fenian, GAA member and staunch Parnellite. James Boland died unexpectedly at a young age in 1895 when Harry was seven. His funeral to Glasnevin was a large affair and representative of his standing as a well-known and politically active figure. Funds raised in the aftermath of his death helped provide for the Boland family.

Harry followed his father becoming a member of the GAA and the IRB while he also joined the Gaelic League. He excelled in the GAA, being a member of the Dublin County Board and later a Dublin County chairman, a post previously held by his father. On the field, he played for the Dublin team that reached the 1908 All-Ireland senior hurling final in 1909. He joined the Irish Volunteers in 1913 and took part in the 1916 Rising. During Easter week, he initially held a post at Goulding's fertiliser factory at Fairview Bridge, before moving to Gibney's wine merchants on the corner of Richmond Avenue. Here he remained until Wednesday when he joined the garrison at the GPO. He was one of the last to leave the building towards the end of the week and the surrender. He was sentenced to ten years imprisonment but was released following the general amnesty in 1917.

During the period that followed Boland built on his reputation as an increasingly important republican leader, focusing on matters political and

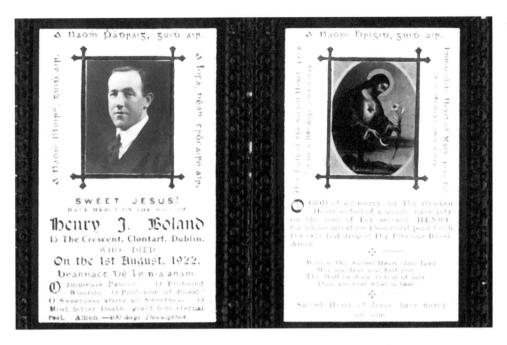

Memorial card of Harry Boland. **Courtesy of Fonsie Mealy Auctioneers.**

propaganda. He was elected in the 1918 general election in the South Roscommon constituency and in line with Sinn Féin's policy of abstentionism became a member of the first Dáil. His relationship with Michael Collins, whom he is reputed to have introduced to the IRB via Sam Maguire in London in 1909, also developed during this time. Both were members of the executive of Sinn Féin and within the leadership of the IRB. David Fitzpatrick described the two as continuing to '... consort, wrestle, hurl and tipple while on the run'. They also collaborated in the escape of De Valera from Lincoln Gaol in 1919. Later the same year Boland travelled to the United States, where he remained for much of the War of Independence, assisting in a campaign of arms smuggling, fundraising, propaganda and political organisation with mixed results.

His relationship with Collins soured in 1921, in both political and personal terms. Collins had consolidated a position of authority in the absence of Boland while also winning the affections of Kitty Kiernan who had been a romantic interest of both men for a number of years. Harry Boland voted against the Treaty and during the Civil War, early on the morning of 31 July 1922, he was surprised by a National Army raiding party whilst staying in the Grand Hotel in Skerries in north Co. Dublin and was fatally wounded. There are differing accounts and opinions of the exact circumstances of his shooting and whether it was accidental or intentional. In the official report issued by National Army

GHQ it was claimed that:

> ... when accosted in his bedroom he [Boland] made an unsuccessful attempt to seize a
> gun from one of the troops and then rushed out to the corridor. After firing two shots
> at random and calling on Mr Boland to halt it was found necessary to fire a third shot
> to prevent escape. Mr Boland was wounded and was later taken to a city hospital ...

Alive but badly injured, Boland was taken to St Vincent's Hospital. He had
been shot in the lower part of his chest but was conscious and able to speak.
Boland's sister stated that he told her before his death that he had been shot
by an old comrade who had been in Lewes Gaol with him. He slipped out of
consciousness at around midday on 1 August 1922 and died that night. His
funeral came to Glasnevin from the Carmelite church on Whitefriar Street on
4 August and was led by members of Cumann na mBan. He was interred in
the Republican Plot.[60]

2 August 1922	**Civilian**
Muriel Bruton	*BD 103, St Paul's*

Muriel Bruton (née Thomas) was born at 42 Lower Clanbrassil Street on 2
January 1900 the daughter of Richard Thomas and Emily Kavanagh. In
September 1919, she married Patrick Bruton, a butcher from 6 Lower Dorset
Street, and together they lived at South Dock Street. On Tuesday 1 August
1922, Muriel and Patrick were walking together down Great Brunswick Street
on their way to the Theatre Royal. As they passed by Thompson's Motor Car
Company, at number 19–20, a small National Army guard under the command
of Sgt Edward O'Brien was standing on the pathway talking to each other and
inspecting revolvers in their possession. Muriel heard one of the soldiers ask
'What sort of one have you?' followed by a reply and then a shot. The soldier had
taken a captured bulldog revolver from its holster believing it to be unloaded.
It was fired towards the ground and the ricochet from the pathway hit Muriel
Bruton. She was brought to Mercer's Hospital and she died the following day.[61]

2 August 1922	**National Army**
Patrick Reilly	*KD 84, South New Chapel*

Patrick Reilly (sometimes O'Reilly), aged twenty-two, was killed in action in
Tralee, Co. Kerry following the landing of over 400 National Army soldiers

at Fenit on 2 August 1922 from the *SS Lady Wicklow* as part of the offensive to capture Kerry. From Lower Gardiner Street in Dublin, Reilly worked as a coal hawker before joining the National Army. A member of the 2nd Battalion Reserve, Dublin Guard, he was shot dead by a sniper on Rock Street in Tralee. Describing the circumstances surrounding his death, the acting command adjutant in Southern Command stated that:

> Deceased was attached to the Dublin Guard and was among the party who first entered Kerry at the Fenit landing. The Guards were subjected to considerable sniping instantly [when] they got ashore at that port and until they secured possession of Tralee. O'Reilly was shot dead during the fight in Tralee, near the Munster & Leinster Bank, by a sniper who had taken up position in O'Hara's shop at Moyderwell.

He was one of nine men killed in the Kerry offensive to be buried together in Glasnevin following a large public funeral. The bodies of the men were returned to Dublin on board the same ship from which they had landed in Kerry, the *SS Lady Wicklow*. In charge of the ship was Louis Brady, father of James Joseph Brady *(see 30 September 1920)*. Having sailed up the Liffey with its flag at half-mast the *Lady Wicklow* docked opposite Commons Street where the coffins were taken ashore. They were received by a National Army

August 1922 – A coffin is carried during the joint funeral to Glasnevin of nine members of the National Army killed in Kerry. Courtesy of Getty Images.

guard of honour and transported to Portobello Barracks where they were met by Michael Collins, Richard Mulcahy, Gearóid O'Sullivan and other officers.

On Monday, 7 August 1922, requiem mass was held in the library of the barracks for the deceased men and attended by relatives, with many dignitaries present. The following day the nine coffins were brought to Glasnevin for burial. Large crowds lined the route of the funeral procession. A newsreel captured the funeral travelling over O'Connell Bridge and the burial at Glasnevin. A newspaper reporter described the scene at the cemetery:

> From as early as 10 o'clock immense numbers congregated in and around Glasnevin Cemetery. They waited patiently until the advance guard of the mournful cortege was seen approaching a few minutes before one o'clock. A melancholy attraction was the huge grave made to receive nine bodies which had been opened in what has now come to be regarded as the Army Plot, situated in the space on the right close to the entrance gates ... A few minutes before one o'clock the shrill strains of the pipes playing a sweet but mournful Gaelic lament announced the arrival of the first section of the funeral. The gates, which had been locked, were thrown open and, preceded by the guard of honour, with their arms reversed, five horse hearses and three motor hearses filed slowly in towards the Mortuary Chapel. Here the honoured remains were received by Rev. Fr Fitzgibbon C.C., chaplain. The scenes as the coffins were borne from the chapel to the grave were affecting in the extreme, many of the relatives, and not a few of the general public, bursting into tears. The coffins having been laid side by side were reverently covered, three volleys were fired, 'Last Post' sounded and the last earthly tribute had been paid to the heroic dead.[62]

3 August 1922   **National Army**
William Carson   *KD 84½, South New Chapel*

William David Carson was born in January 1903 at Rosapenna Street in Belfast the son of David Carson and Mary Catherine Hart. His father had a long career as a member of the British army rising through the ranks of the Royal Irish Rifles, becoming an officer during the First World War serving with the 36th (Ulster) Division Base Depot. Following the war, David Carson became a chief inspector with the Ulster Special Constabulary. William Carson also joined the British army but purchased his discharge to join the National Army. Serving as a corporal with the 3rd Battalion, Dublin Guard he was fatally wounded in the abdomen during the fighting around Pembroke Street in Tralee. He died of his injuries in the Kerry County Infirmary. He was one of the nine men killed in the Kerry offensive to be buried together in Glasnevin following a large public funeral *(see 2 August 1922)*.[63]

3 August 1922   **National Army**
Michael Farrell   *KD 84, South New Chapel*

Michael Farrell, a corporal and machine gunner with the 2nd Eastern Division, was killed during the fighting around Pembroke Street in Tralee. Originally from James's Place in Dublin, he was the son of Hugh and Annie Farrell. Before joining the National Army, he worked as a labourer and lived at East James's Street where he had moved having married Annie O'Hara in July 1915. He was one of nine men killed in the Kerry offensive to be buried together in Glasnevin in a joint funeral *(see 2 August 1922)*.[64]

3 August 1922   **National Army**
Frederick Gillespie   *KD 84½, South New Chapel*

Frederick Gillespie was born on 21 October 1898, in the home of his family, on St Ignatius Road in Dublin. The son of Mary Hennigan and William Gillespie, a baker, his family moved shortly after his birth to the nearby Glengarriff Parade to live with the Hennigan family and later to Kenmare Parade, where he lived until his death in 1922. Working as a ship caulker Frederick joined the Irish Volunteers in 1918, serving as a member of B Company, 2nd Battalion, Dublin Brigade. He joined the National Army in February 1922 at Beggar's Bush Barracks following its handover by the British army. A member of the Dublin Guard, he served at the Four Courts during the Battle of Dublin and embarked for the landing in Co. Kerry in August. Paddy Daly, who commanded the Dublin contingent that landed at Fenit, stated that:

> When the Dublin Guard were formed in February 1922 we only accepted men with pre-Truce service in Volunteers, Fianna Éireann or Citizen Army. We were about 400 strong by July 1922. The draft that left for Kerry on August 2nd 1922 was composed of 200 Dublin Guard and 200 recruits of all sorts, many of them had no previous service and no training and of course they soon all called themselves Dublin Guard. On the way to Kerry by the *Lady Wicklow* we selected N.C.O. [non commissioned officers] from the Guards, among them was Frederick Gillespie.

As it transpired Paddy Daly was a few yards from Frederick Gillespie when he was hit by Lewis gun fire in the initial skirmishes in Tralee on Rock Street. He was one of nine men killed in the Kerry offensive to be buried together in Glasnevin *(see 2 August 1922)*.[65]

3 August 1922   **National Army**
Patrick Harding   *KD 84, South New Chapel*

Patrick Harding was nineteen when he was killed during the fighting in Tralee, Co. Kerry. Before joining the National Army, he worked as a messenger for Boyd and Goodwin's Chemists on Merrion Row, while also repairing bicycles at his home where he lived with his grandmother. From East James's Street, he had joined National Army on 17 May 1922 and was a medic attached to the Dublin Guard. He died of head wounds received whilst attending to the wounded and was buried in Glasnevin in the National Army plot *(see 2 August 1922)*.[66]

3 August 1922   **National Army**
John Kenny   *KD 84, South New Chapel*

John Kenny, from Coombe Street in Dublin, was killed in action during the fighting in Tralee following the National Army landing at Fenit in Kerry. The son of James and Ellen Kenny he worked as a dairyman before enlisting in the British army in June 1921. He served with the Royal Dublin Fusiliers until his discharge in July 1922. It appears that he then immediately enlisted in the National Army and was sent to Kerry the following month. In January 1922, he married Elizabeth Molloy who was also from Coombe Street. His wife was pregnant at the time of his death and in October 1922 gave birth to a daughter, Bridget. He was one of nine National Army members buried together in Glasnevin *(see 2 August 1922)*. John Kenny was aged nineteen at the time of his death.[67]

3 August 1922   **National Army**
Thomas Joseph Larkin   *KD 83, South New Chapel*

Thomas Larkin, from Howth in Co. Dublin, was a member of the Dublin Guard killed in action following the National Army landing in Kerry in August 1922. The son of James and Annie Larkin of Shielmartin Cottage, Bailey, Howth, he was a carpenter and also worked as a porter for the Great Northern Railway in Amiens Street Station. Before the Truce, he had been a member of 2nd Battalion, Dublin Brigade, IRA, for six weeks before enlisting in the National Army on 28 April 1922 at Marlborough Hall in Glasnevin. He was killed during the fighting on Castle Street in Tralee. He was buried in Glasnevin following a joint funeral with eight other men *(see 2 August 1922).*[68]

3 August 1922 — National Army
James O'Connor — *KD 84½, South New Chapel*

James O'Connor, from Lower Summerhill in Dublin, was seventeen when he was killed in action in Kerry with the Dublin Guard during the summer offensive in 1922. The only son of Thomas and Bridget O'Connor he had served for a period during the War of Independence with 1st Battalion, Dublin Brigade, IRA. An apprentice welder he enlisted in the National Army in March 1922 and was shot dead in the fighting in Tralee. O'Connor was one of those interred in Glasnevin following the large public funeral for National Army members killed in Kerry *(see 2 August 1922).*[69]

3 August 1922 — National Army
Patrick Quinn — *KD 84, South New Chapel*

Patrick Quinn was one of the first casualties suffered by the National Army following their landing at Fenit in Co. Kerry in 1922. Originally from Rialto he worked as a labourer at Guinness Brewery before enlisting in the British army during the First World War. He served as a pioneer in the Royal Engineers using Gibney as an alias surname. During that war, he suffered a bullet wound to the left leg, although this would appear to have been accidentally received. He was discharged in January 1919 and returned home to Dublin. There he lived in the front parlour of a tenement on Poole Street with his wife, Teresa Mills, whom he had married in December 1915 and his three daughters born in 1917, 1919 and 1922. During the Civil War, he enlisted in the National Army taking part in the landing at Fenit and was killed instantly near Kilfenora after a bullet hit him in the back of the neck. His name was initially incorrectly reported and the confusion resulted in his widow being informed of his death the day he was buried in Glasnevin with eight other National Army members *(see 2 August 1922).*[70]

4 August 1922   **Civilian**
Hyacinth D'Arcy   *ED 8½, South*

Hyacinth D'Arcy was shot and killed by the National Army at the junction of Lower Liffey Street and Bachelors Walk, opposite the Ha'penny Bridge. D'Arcy lived on Clanbrassil Street, where he was born, and also where he worked as a wholesale chandler at the time of his death. The city coroner held an inquest into his death at Mercer's Hospital. The inquest heard that Capt. Herbert Halpin, based in Portobello Barracks, had taken a group of five men in plainclothes to Lower Liffey Street with orders to search for a particular motorbike and sidecar. While there, they noted Hyacinth D'Arcy standing with a similar motorbike on Bachelors Walk. Halpin requested D'Arcy's details, which were given and he then placed him under arrest but did not physically restrain him. After about five minutes D'Arcy proceeded to walk away and Halpin shouted for his men to stop him. The officer stated that D'Arcy was given a warning before shots were fired over his head and then a shot was directed at him. That bullet hit him on the left side of his torso and entered his lung. It was surmised that D'Arcy might have been suspicious of the men who had held him up, given that they were not in uniform, had not fully identified themselves or given the reason for his arrest. He was buried in Glasnevin on 8 August in a family grave.[71]

6 August 1922   **National Army**
Brian Houlihan   *KD 85, South New Chapel*

Brian Houlihan was serving as a staff captain in the National Army when he was killed in an ambush at Castleisland in his native Kerry in 1922. A well-known figure in the independence movement Houlihan was a veteran of the Rising and War of Independence and was a member of the Irish Republican Brotherhood. In 1914, he had joined the Irish Volunteers and became a member of B Company, 2nd Battalion, Dublin Brigade. Injuries he had received limited his direct involvement in warfare, however, he was successful in procuring guns and ammunition from members of the British army for the IRA during the War of Independence. He was also a member of the Active Service Unit and a close friend of Peadar Clancy. In April 1922, he married Margaret (Peg) Murray from Dunmore in Galway. During the

Civil War, he served at the Four Courts Hotel during the Battle of Dublin before leaving for Kerry with the Dublin Guard under Paddy Daly.

On the day of his death, Brian Houlihan was part of an escort for a food supply convoy travelling between Tralee and Castleisland when it was ambushed. He was hit by what was reported as a dum-dum bullet and later died from his wounds. Paddy Daly described that he was wounded in a location where he previously had surgery on injuries he received when he was beaten during an IRA operation to limit betting in Croke Park at the behest of the GAA. It was Daly's opinion that the wound he received would not have been fatal had it not been for those previous injuries. His funeral arrived at Glasnevin on 10 August 1922 from the church of Our Lady of Refuge in Rathmines and was attended by a large crowd.[72]

8 August 1922   **National Army**
Edward Coughlan   *KD 85, South New Chapel*

Edward Coughlan, from Upper Mercer Street and a member of the National Army since April 1922, was fatally wounded at Amiens Street Station on 23 July 1922. On that day, Coughlan was on duty with Pte Michael Joseph Coyle. The men were together, unarmed, on the steps of a bridge leading to premises of the Dublin and South Eastern Railway when three shots were fired. The shots came from the direction of the signal cabin and Coughlan was hit in the left leg. Shortly afterwards National Army soldiers at the station came under a further attack that lasted approximately fifteen minutes. Edward Coughlan was taken to the Jervis Street Hospital where his leg was amputated. He died due to complications on the night of 8 August 1922 and was buried in the National Army plot in Glasnevin.[73]

8 August 1922   **National Army**
Patrick Maguire   *JD 79, South New Chapel*

Patrick Maguire, from Brankill (Flood) near Belturbet in Cavan, was killed following the National Army landing at Passage West in Cork in August 1922. Before joining the National Army in March 1922 he had worked on his father's small farm. After his enlistment he was initially sent to Swanlinbar in Cavan before being assigned to take part in the landing in Cork in August 1922. Following the landing at Fenit in Kerry the National Army turned its attention to Cork city, which was in anti-Treaty hands. Their plan to take the city involved amphibious landings, the largest of which, with 450 men, was to take place at Passage West from where they intended to advance west.

The men, under the command of Emmet Dalton, travelled from Dublin on Monday 7 August on board the commandeered ships *Arvonia* and *Lady Wicklow*. The latter had only recently returned from Kerry with the coffins of the soldiers killed in the fighting there. The ships arrived at their destination early on the morning of 8 August under the cover of darkness. The *Arvonia*, which held the majority of the National Army contingent, was the first to land as soldiers disembarked to gain a foothold at the dock. The initial landing saw a brief defence by the surprised anti-Treaty men who were tasked with holding Passage West from such an attack. However, the National Army quickly consolidated their positions and took hold of the town. The subsequent advance on Cork saw more intense fighting and casualties. Amongst these were seven National Army soldiers who were killed in this offensive and subsequently buried in Glasnevin, Patrick Maguire was one, along with brothers Frederick McKenna and Gerald McKenna, William Nevin, Christopher O'Toole, Patrick Perry and Henry Quinn. Their remains were returned to Dublin and to Portobello Barracks.

Many onlookers watched on the streets as the coffins draped in Tricolours travelled to the cemetery in a military procession. At the cemetery a guard of honour was formed at the mortuary chapel where a short service was performed before the men were buried in the National Army plot. In some cases, before the interment, the flags covering their coffins were returned to their families, while in others they remained in situ as they were lowered into the grave and a volley of shots were fired followed by the Last Post.[74]

8 August 1922   **National Army**
Frederick McKenna   *JD 80, South New Chapel*

Frederick McKenna was the elder of two teenage brothers who were killed during the landing at Passage West in 1922. Born in April 1904, he was eighteen at the time of his death. The son of Mary Jane McCullough and Alfred George McKenna, his father was a medical doctor and surgeon. Originally from Galway, Alfred McKenna studied at Edinburgh before moving to Belfast. It was there that Frederick and his younger brother Gerald were born, as well as two other siblings, an older brother and younger sister. During the First World

War, their father had served as a captain in the Royal Army Medical Corps and their eldest brother Robert was a pilot in the Royal Air Force.

The family remained in Belfast until after the end of the war and then moved to Phibsborough in Dublin. While living there, Frederick and Gerald enlisted in the National Army and were sent to Cork in August 1922. Their mother received a notification that her sixteen-year-old son, Gerald, had been killed in action and on the day of his funeral to Glasnevin travelled to the mortuary at Portobello Barracks to view his body before the ceremony. While there she noticed another, unidentified, body and realised that it was her other son Fred. Both Mary Jane McKenna and her only surviving son, Robert, were described as being overcome with grief. Their father is not recorded in newspaper reports as having attended their funerals. Mary Jane McKenna died in 1957 and is buried with her husband in a family grave in the St Bridget's section of Glasnevin Cemetery.[75]

8 August 1922   **National Army**
Gerald McKenna   *JD 80, South New Chapel*

Gerald McKenna was the younger brother of Frederick McKenna (*see above*). Both were killed together following the Passage West landing. Gerald was aged sixteen at the time of his death and was born in June 1906 in Belfast. He is buried in the same grave as his brother in the National Army plot.[76]

8 August 1922   **National Army**
William Nevin   *JD 79 South New Chapel*

William Nevin was forty when he was killed following the landing at Passage West in Cork. His address was given as Marietta Lodge, which was a lodge attached to Marietta, a house off Breffni Road in Sandycove, owned by Michael Bannon. His next-of-kin at the time of his death was his mother and step-father.[77]

8 August 1922   **National Army**
Christopher O'Toole   *JD 79, South New Chapel*

Christopher O'Toole, a private in the National Army, was killed at Rochestown in Cork following the landing at Passage West. Before joining the National

Army, he was employed as a carter by Mr Mooney of Clarendon Street. His step-father also served in the National Army during the Civil War. He was buried in Glasnevin on 14 August 1922 following a joint funeral with the other soldiers killed in Cork earlier that month.[78]

8 August 1922 — National Army
Patrick Perry — *JD 79, South New Chapel*

Patrick Perry from Brookfield Terrace in Blackrock, Co. Dublin was born in March 1896 the son of Mary McGrath and William Perry. Enlisting in the Irish Guards in December 1914 Patrick Perry served on the Western Front and ultimately left the British army in October 1918. He was one of a number of siblings who served during the First World War. One brother, also a member of the Irish Guards, was killed in 1918. Following Patrick's discharge, he returned home to Dublin and began a relationship with Rose Byrne who lived in Blackrock.

In 1911, Rose had married James Mooney, also from Brookfield. Together they had three children, the youngest of whom died in infancy. James Mooney had enlisted in the British army in 1915 and survived the war, however the family never reunited. Rose later stated that James had abandoned them or that she had been forced to leave him. Regardless, as James Mooney was still alive, Rose Mooney and Patrick Perry were unable to marry. Patrick later travelled to Greenock in Scotland seeking work and while there was employed as a labourer in a ship-building works. Rose travelled with him and together they had two children, born in 1919 and 1921. During the same period, Rose began referring to herself with the surname Perry.

Having returned to Dublin Patrick Perry joined the National Army in July 1922, being made a sergeant in the Dublin Guard. The following month he was part of the contingent that landed at Passage West and was killed in action at Rochestown during the advance to Cork city. Patrick Perry's mother and siblings attended his funeral to Glasnevin as his next-of-kin. Rose only heard of his death on the day he was buried. That day, she was in the Cork Street Fever Hospital having been admitted from the Dublin Union as both their children were suffering with whooping cough. She was taken into employment at the hospital and a doctor there, unaware she was not legally married to Patrick Perry, wrote to the Department of Defence in an attempt to help claim money for her. Worried that she might lose her job Rose then wrote a letter herself to the Department explaining her circumstances:

Sir, Please pardon me taking the liberty of writing to you. I want to ask you a great favour. I expect you will have a letter from a gentleman concerning me, about money. I am a maid here and one of the ladies asked me had I got no money yet after my husband being killed so I said no. They think here I was married and I want to ask you would you please let them think so, I would have to leave the place if they found me out and I have got a nice post here. I was unfortunate enough to be foolish but I suffered for it, I got a very bad husband and I had to leave him and then I went and lived with the man that was killed in Cork. I want to atone for the past and be good so I ask you if you get any letters concerning me and money matters that you will send some answer that will put them off. The man's name was Sergeant Patrick Perry, I was living with him for 4 years and I hope and trust that you will look after the poor little children and God will reward you.

A weekly pension was initially awarded to Rose Perry backdated to Patrick's death in August 1922. However, the pension became subject to an internal debate within the Ministry of Defence regarding the rights of 'unmarried wives' and children considered 'illegitimate' to claim the dependents' pensions of deceased soldiers. This was precipitated by the attempts of Patrick Perry's mother, Mary, to receive his dependent's pension. In her correspondence she claimed that Rose, and ultimately her grandchildren, had no right to any money that was due to be granted as, in her own words, he '... was not legally married to the woman he was living with, as her husband was and is still alive'. A statement from Fr McCarthy, the parish priest in Blackrock, stating that she was Patrick's immediate next-of-kin, reinforced Mary Perry's letter.

Rose Perry's allowance was discontinued in March 1924 and was not reinstated after a prolonged deliberation involving the chief state solicitor. A onetime compensation award of £50 was granted to Patrick Perry's mother. With no employment or income, Rose Perry and her two older children went to live with her mother in Blackrock. Patrick Perry's children, aged four and six at that time, were placed in St Brigid's Orphanage on Eccles Street by Rose where she contributed towards their subsistence.[79]

8 August 1922   **National Army**
Henry Quinn   *JD 79, South New Chapel*

Henry Quinn was seventeen when he was killed during the National Army landing at Passage West in Cork. He was born in the Rotunda Hospital in Dublin in September 1904, the son of Henry Quinn and Esther Ledwidge. Henry was their eldest child and they lived at a number of addresses in Dublin. At the time of his death, they were living in a house on Upper Wellington

Street. Henry joined the National Army in July 1922 and was part of the contingent sent from Dublin to Cork on board the *SS Arvonia* the following month.

It was recorded that, during initial landing at Passage West, Quinn was shot in the face and killed instantly. Due to a lack of formal means of identification, he was initially identified by the name recorded in a prayer book that he had on his person when he was killed. Due to this no next-of-kin were contacted and he was buried in Glasnevin under the name Thomas Lynch. In 1924, after a lack of any contact from her son, Esther Quinn began making enquiries as to what had happened to him. She was initially told, due to a clerical error, that her son was alive and had been discharged from the army in January 1924. Esther Quinn made her own attempts to discover the fate of her son and a soldier who served with him confirmed that he had been killed in Cork. The National Army realised their mistake having confirmed that no person with the name Lynch had been sent with the contingent to Cork. As a result, Henry Quinn was finally acknowledged as the person who had been buried in Glasnevin in 1922.[80]

8 August 1922   Civilian
Patrick Whelan   *MD 104, St Paul's*

Patrick Whelan was a former soldier, suffering with shell shock, who was fatally wounded by a sentry at Mountjoy Prison. Whelan had enlisted for service in the First World War with the Royal Field Artillery and arrived on the Western Front in September 1915. Later sent to Salonika he suffered with shell shock and bouts of malaria while serving with the rank of acting bombardier. He was discharged from the army in 1918 one week before the armistice. In Dublin, he lived at Upper Gardiner Street and St Teresa's Place in Glasnevin. He worked as a watchmaker. His sister later stated that he had continued to struggle with his health and was suffering from a nervous breakdown at the time of his death. His mother Bridget also said '… his mind was disturbed owing to shell shock during service in Salonika'. Just after midnight on the morning of 16 July 1922 Whelan made his way towards Mountjoy Prison with the intention of visiting a prisoner. As it was dark and out of visiting hours he was challenged by a sentry to halt, which he did, and then challenged to raise his arms, which he did not. The sentry fired at Whelan and he fell to the ground. The prison's medical officer tended to Whelan and he was removed to the Mater Hospital.

Here it was found that the bullet had ruptured his bladder, this eventually led to toxaemia and his death the following month.[81]

9 August 1922   **National Army**
Edward McAvoy   *KD 84, South New Chapel*

Edward McAvoy, a member of Kildare Brigade National Army was killed in action in Co. Wexford. From Kerrera Street, off Crumlin Road, in Belfast he worked as an engine driver before joining the National Army during the Civil War and was stationed at Ferrycarrig in August 1922. Due to repeated attempts by the anti-Treaty IRA to destroy Ferrycarrig Bridge, a vital connection for communication between Dublin and Wexford, it was decided to place a contingent of fourteen National Army soldiers in the pub and shop of John McDonald. The building gave a clear vantage over the whole bridge.

Early on the morning of 9 August, the National Army troops were awoken by the sounds of shots. It was quickly apparent that they were under attack by a large contingent, later estimated at over 100, and they took up positions to defend their building. In an inquest, it was stated that McAvoy was at a front window when he was wounded after about thirty minutes fighting. He cried out, 'I am hit boys' before falling to the floor. He died shortly afterwards. His final words were reported to be 'Lord Jesus, have mercy upon me. Fight on, boys'. After over an hour of fighting the National Army soldiers surrendered, their weapons were taken and their attackers released the men and left the scene of the fight. The inquest found that McAvoy had died of 'shock and haemorrhage [the] result of [a] bullet wound through thigh, fired by some person or persons unknown whilst deceased was in discharge of his duty.'[82]

11 August 1922   **National Army**
William Purdy   *KD 85, South New Chapel*

William Purdy was born in the United States of America. He had served with the Canadian Expeditionary Force during the First World War and was accidentally killed in Abbeyfeale, Co. Limerick, while a member of the National Army in 1922.

William Purdy was born in Newark, New Jersey in July 1889. His father, Hugh Purdy, was a Unitarian from Down and his mother, Margaret Martin, was a Presbyterian from Longford. They had married in New Jersey in 1887.

The family returned to Ireland not long after the birth of William and they lived in Holywood, Co. Down, where his father, a builder, had a business. William emigrated to Quebec in Canada in 1912 and remained there until September 1914 when he enlisted in the Canadian Expeditionary Force. On his enlistment, he described himself as a nurse and was assigned to the No. 1 Canadian General Hospital. After a period in England Purdy and his unit was sent to Étaples in France in May 1915 where they dealt with the sick and wounded coming from the front. His hospital had capacity for over 1,000 patients at any given time. While in Étaples, Purdy began suffering health issues in July 1915 and was returned to England in September being diagnosed with neurasthenia. He was discharged in February 1917. A description of his health at the time of his discharge stated that his 'nervous system seems to be debilitated, he had large and small tremors, is very nervous, has hesitation of speech, easily excited, sleeps poorly, nausea after eating, shortness of breath on exertion or excitement ...'

Following his discharge, Purdy returned to his family in Holywood. He may have never disclosed the reason for his discharge to his parents as his mother believed that he had been wounded in the leg during his time at the front. William worked with his father in his building business until they were vigorously boycotted due to the nationalist views of the family. Forced to abandon their business in Holywood the family moved to Belfast where they opened a toy factory. The factory was successful but the family were forced out of business once again in 1920, this time due to the Belfast pogroms. Then William Purdy moved south to Dublin where he lived in Clontarf. During the Civil War, he joined the National Army serving as a sergeant in the Dublin Guard. A description of his death stated that:

> The Dublin Guard left Newcastle West and arrived in Abbeyfeale on the 10th August 1922. On the morning of the 11th they received orders to advance into Kerry. C Company, to which the deceased belonged, was formed in two ranks on the street. Prior to advancing the deceased was in the supernumerary rank. A shot rang out and Purdy fell mortally wounded. Captain Stapleton, who has since been killed, was O/C of the Company. He inspected the rifles but placed no one under arrest.

It appeared that William Purdy had been shot with his own rifle. He was buried in the National Army plot in Glasnevin on 14 August 1922.[83]

19 August 1922   **National Army**
Christopher Hynes   *JD 80, South New Chapel*

Christopher Hynes, from Stella Gardens in Irishtown, was a member of B Company, 2nd Dublin Guard and was accidentally killed in Limerick in August 1922. A bottle blower, he had served in the British army during the First World War as a member of the Army Service Corps. A report regarding the circumstances of his death described that Hynes was '... in the kitchen of Cleeves Factory, Bruree on the 19th August 1922. At about 10 p.m. on this date a comrade named Cleary entered the kitchen having returned from a patrol. Cleary removed the magazine from his rifle and placed the magazine in his pocket. The bolt was open and he closed it and pulled the trigger. A round which had been left in the breech and forgotten by Cleary consequently exploded, the bullet entering Hyne's head killing him instantly.'[84]

19 August 1922   **Anti-Treaty Irish Republican Army**
Daniel Kane   *RB 32, Garden*

In August 1922, two men brought the body of an unidentified man into the morgue in Dublin and informed the caretaker, Michael Brophy, that they had been stopped between Sally Gap and Glendalough in Wicklow and were told to bring the body there. The men then left. There was no identification with the body and only a small handkerchief, two pencils and a comb in the man's pockets. There was a bullet wound in the left shoulder of his body and an exit wound in his back. At an inquest, Mrs Bridget Kane, from Ranelagh Road, identified the body as that of her son Daniel Kane. She had last seen him on 14 August. The inquest concluded that no further information could be garnered regarding the circumstances of his death and returned a verdict that he died of shock and haemorrhage following a bullet wound inflicted by a person or persons unknown.

Daniel Kane had in fact been killed while serving as a volunteer with the anti-Treaty Irish Republican Army. He was fatally wounded during an attack on a National Army post in the Glenmalure Valley. Two other anti-Treaty men were captured. Kane had served as a member of 3rd Battalion, Dublin Brigade, IRA, during the War of Independence having joined in 1921. He was posthumously awarded a service medal for his participation in the War of Independence.[85]

21 August 1922   **National Army**
Michael Daly   *JD 80, South New Chapel*

Michael Daly was born in February 1890 in 13 Towerview Cottages, opposite Glasnevin Cemetery. Michael's father, Thomas, worked as a labourer in Glasnevin Cemetery and lived in one of these cottages provided by the cemetery to their employees and families. The Daly family later moved to Scally's Cottages off Lower Mayor Street, close to the docks, where Michael worked from as a sailor. In August 1911, he married Catherine Lawlor in the church of St Laurence O'Toole. The couple initially lived on Lower Sherriff Street where their first child Thomas was born in 1912. After a few years, they moved once again, this time to Leland Place, off Commons Street where they were living when Michael Daly enlisted in the National Army during the Civil War.

While serving with the Machine Gun Section, Dublin Guard during the Kerry offensive Michael Daly was wounded on 12 August at Castleisland. He died nine days later in Tralee Infirmary and his body was returned to Dublin. His funeral was held on 25 August in the church in which he had married eleven years earlier. The cortege to Glasnevin was led by the Dublin Guard pipers and he was buried in the National Army plot a short distance from the house in which he had been born.[86]

21 August 1922   **National Army**
Michael Finnegan   *JD 80, South New Chapel*

Michael Finnegan, from Upper Gloucester Street in Dublin, was killed during an ambush in Tipperary in August 1922. He had previously been a member of Fianna Éireann and the 5th Battalion, Dublin Brigade IRA, during the War of Independence. He worked as an engine man before joining the National Army in 1922. A staff sergeant he was posted to Kilkenny and on the day of his death Finnegan was travelling in a Ford car from Kilkenny to Clonmel in Tipperary. Also in the car were four other members of the National Army, including its driver Richard Cantwell from Clogh in Kilkenny and Col Comdt Frank Thornton, a veteran of the 1916 Rising and intelligence officer in the War of Independence who was an important figure in IRA GHQ then.

The group stopped at Carrick-on-Suir before proceeding on towards Clonmel. On the outskirts of Clonmel, as they drove towards a dip in the road beside the railway bridge of the Limerick Junction and Waterford line before

Redmondstown, they were ambushed. A hail of machine-gun and rifle fire was directed at the car by members of the anti-Treaty IRA who had located themselves behind a tree that had been felled and placed across the road. Both Michael Finnegan and Richard Cantwell were killed, being hit numerous times. One report stated that '... both when found later were literally riddled, in both cases their legs were smashed in pieces and they had extensive wounds in the back and arms'. Frank Thornton was badly wounded, being hit many times. The two other occupants of the car escaped unscathed but were taken prisoner. An anti-Treaty IRA unit, under command of Jack Killeen, carried out the ambush. Following the fall of Clonmel in early August the anti-Treaty IRA in the area had divided into flying columns and the Killeen column had been formed on 14 August 1922. They harassed National Army troops in the area and carried out a number of ambushes, this being their second.

When the firing ceased the anti-Treaty IRA administered first aid to Thornton and Jack Killeen stopped a passing cyclist giving him a note to bring to the officer commanding the National Army at Clonmel telling him that there was a wounded officer at Redmondstown. The National Army dispatched an ambulance and they found Killeen still waiting there with several of his men. When the doctor got out of the ambulance Killeen said, 'tell Colonel Prout I am sorry Colonel Thornton is wounded'. Killeen and his men then helped place him in the ambulance and dispersed. Thornton, though very badly injured, survived. When he had recovered sufficiently he had to be informed that his brother, Hugh Thornton (*see 27 August 1922*), and his close friend and comrade, Michael Collins (*see 22 August 1922*) had both been killed in separate incidents.

Frank Thornton died in 1965 and is also buried in Glasnevin, a short distance from where Michael Finnegan is buried. Richard Cantwell is buried in a family grave in the churchyard of St Patrick's church in Clogh. Michael Finnegan left a widow, Christina, whom he had married in 1920, and one child, a son named James. Christina Finnegan died in 1982 and is buried in Glasnevin.[87]

22 August 1922	National Army
Michael Collins	*GD 82, South New Chapel*

Michael Collins was born at Woodfield, Sam's Cross in Co. Cork in October 1890 he was the youngest child of Michael Collins senior and Mary Anne

O'Brien. At the age of fifteen, Collins left for London, working in a number of clerical positions with a stockbrokers and the Board of Trade. During his time in London, he was involved with the GAA and Gaelic League and was sworn into the Irish Republican Brotherhood before joining the Irish Volunteers on their foundation in 1914. He was also appointed to administrative roles within organisations gaining valuable experience and contacts. Collins returned home to Ireland in early 1916 and there he became close to Joseph Plunkett, to whom he acted as ADC during the Easter Rising at the GPO.

Following the surrender, Collins was arrested and eventually imprisoned alongside fellow rebels in Frongoch. He became a well-known figure in the prison camp and following his release in December 1916 was poised to advance his position within the independence movement. Key to this was his subsequent work with the Irish National Aid and Volunteer Dependents' Fund and the IRB. Within a year, Collins had risen to become a member of the Sinn Féin executive. His growing importance was publicly demonstrated by his involvement at the funeral of Thomas Ashe in Glasnevin Cemetery in September 1917, where he delivered a succinct but effective graveside oration. In it he simply stated that, 'Nothing additional remains to be said. That volley which we have just heard is the only speech which it is proper to make above the grave of a dead Fenian'. Collins positioning was made all the more symbolic by the fact that two years earlier Patrick Pearse had delivered his famous oration at the funeral of Jeremiah O'Donovan Rossa in almost the exact same spot.

In March 1918, Collins became adjutant-general of the reorganised Irish Volunteers and the following month was arrested in Dublin and charged with having made a seditious speech in Longford. He spent three weeks in prison before being given bail and absconding. The arrests of Sinn Féin leadership arising from the so-called 'German Plot', of which Collins had forewarned others and he avoided, left him in a position of influence and power becoming central to the organisation of Sinn Féin during the 1918 general election and ultimately their success. Elected unopposed in Cork South during that election he took his seat in the first Dáil and became Minister for Finance in April

Cars with floral tributes arrive outside Glasnevin during the funeral of Michael Collins.
Courtesy of the National Library of Ireland.

Mourners at the graveside of Michael Collins. Courtesy of the National Library of
Ireland.

1919. His organisation of the Dáil loan and positions held in the IRB and IRA helped cement Collins' influence and leadership within the independence movement, both political and physical.

During the War of Independence Collins was instrumental in the development of IRA intelligence networks and activities. He established a group of assassins, known as The Squad, who targeted members of the Dublin Metropolitan Police and suspected British intelligence officers. His activities also extended to the organisation of jail breaks and arms importation. Following the Truce, Collins was selected by the Dáil as one of those who would negotiate with the British government. In October 1921 Collins he became engaged to Kitty Kiernan. The Anglo-Irish Treaty was signed in December 1921 and during the split in opinion that followed Collins led in supporting the agreement he had helped negotiate.

The reconciliation of opinion proved impossible, and in June 1922, faced with an increasingly difficult situation, Collins ordered the bombardment of the Four Courts, which had been occupied by anti-Treaty volunteers, beginning the Battle of Dublin and the Irish Civil War. He formally moved into the role of commander-in-chief of the National Army leading the military campaign on the pro-Treaty side during that war. On 22 August 1922, while travelling in west Cork he was shot and killed during an ambush at Béal na Bláth. Emmet Dalton, who was travelling in the Collins convoy when it was ambushed gave an account of the events leading to his death on a visit to the location some years later. He stated that when the ambush began:

> He [Collins] and I got out and some people got off the Crossley Tender and we lined up on a ditch ... it was a small ditch ... it gave you cover from the angle from which the firing was coming ... this was obviously a very bad position, there was no area for retreat, there was only one thing that we could have done [which] was drive on which I said to the Commander in Chief I said 'drive like hell', but he elected to stop here and fight them you see, so we did. There was a motorcyclist on advance, a scout, he was followed by the Crossley Tender and then we came in our touring car and behind us came the Rolls Royce [armoured] car. We were stretched out ... it was a continuous bend, the spot where we were, one continuous bend of bank and the various other members were sheltered down there and they were firing obliquely across [towards the ambushing party] ... After about ten minutes of our engagement here he [Collins] got up, he saw a movement, and he moved to the back of the armoured car, used it as protection to have a better sight of what was happening on the hill above. Then he moved from there up around the bend out of my vision but he was firing from up there and I was firing from here ... I thought I heard a voice calling me and I jumped up and at that stage [Seán] O'Connell had come up the road to me and he said where's the big fellow, so I said he's around the corner, or around the bend, and we both went up there and he had been shot, he was lying there with a very gaping wound to the back of his head. I called the armoured car back and we lifted him and took him onto the

side of the armoured car, with the armoured car between us and their firing positions, got him to the position of the side of the road and under protection of the armoured car I bandaged the wound and O'Connell said an act of contrition to him. I knew he was dying if not already dead, so we did the best we could to cover it up ... it was a very large wound, an open wound, in the back of the head and it was difficult for me to get a first field aid bandage to cover it when I was binding it up, it was quite obvious to me with the experience that I had that it was a ricochet bullet, it could only have been a ricochet or a dum-dum ...

The National Army party left the scene and the body of Michael Collins was moved into the touring car with Dalton holding Collins with his head on his shoulder on the journey back to Cork city. The location of Collins death was a short distance north from his place of birth almost thirty-two years earlier. His body was returned by boat to Dublin where his burial was arranged. On 28 August 1922, his funeral came to Glasnevin from the pro-cathedral. Thousands of people lined the streets to watch the imposing procession as it made its way to the cemetery that Collins had visited just a few days earlier for the funeral of Arthur Griffith. He was interred in the National Army plot amongst its other members who had died since the outbreak of the Civil War.

Delivering the graveside oration Richard Mulcahy stated that:

... we bend today over the grave of a young man not more than thirty years of age who took to himself the gospel of toil for Ireland, and of sacrifice for their good, and who has made himself a hero and a legend that will stand in the pages of our history with any bright page that was written there. Pages have been written by him in the hearts of our people that will never find a place in print. But we lived, some of us, with these intimate pages and those pages that will reach history, meagre though they be, will do good to our country and will inspire us through many a dark hour ...[88]

23 August 1922   **National Army**
Thomas Kavanagh   *JD 80, South New Chapel*

Thomas Stanislaus Kavanagh was born in November 1899 and was the son of Bernard Kavanagh and Louisa Mary Greer from George's Place, Dublin. Thomas and his family later moved to King's Avenue and then to Sherrard Avenue where he resided at the time of his death. Before volunteering to serve with the National Army, he worked as a messenger and carter. In August 1922, while serving with the Dublin Guard at Kilcummin in Co. Kerry Thomas Kavanagh was wounded in the head and back during an ambush. He subsequently died of his wounds. His funeral to Glasnevin was a joint one with

Thomas White (*see 27 August 1922*). His coffin was taken from Portobello Barracks to the cemetery accompanied by a band and guard of honour.[89]

26 August 1922   Fianna Éireann
Seán Cole   *GB 82 ½, South*

Seán (John Joseph) Cole from Lower Buckingham Street was shot dead alongside a fellow Fianna Éireann member, Alfred Colley (*see below*), in August 1922. Their deaths were amongst the first of a series of extra-judicial killings to take place in Dublin in the midst of the Civil War. They were both shot dead at Yellow Lane, near the modern Collins Avenue, in Whitehall.

Seán Cole was born in July 1902 at the home of his family on Foster Terrace in Dublin. He was the eldest child of James Cole, a bookkeeper and the son of a farmer from Cavan, and Julia Byrne, the daughter of a cabinetmaker from Portland Row. At the time of his death, Cole worked as an apprentice electrician for Thomas Dockrell & Sons, where his father was also employed. He had joined Fianna Éireann in 1917 and remained with them following the Truce, taking the anti-Treaty side during the Civil War. He rose to the rank of commandant, which he held at the time of his death.

On 26 August 1922, Seán Cole and Alfred Colley had attended a meeting at Charlemont House regarding the decision to create an Active Service Unit within the Dublin Brigade of Fianna Éireann. Following the meeting of the members of this unit, Cole and Colley left to walk in the direction of home. At Newcomen Bridge, the two were stopped and searched by men in trench coats and hats. A boy, Vincent Raftery, stated at the inquest into their deaths that he was at the bridge that day and recognised Seán Cole sitting in a black motor car with another person, whom he did not know and that there was a man beside them with a revolver in his hand. He also stated that he saw a National Army uniform beneath the trench coat of one of the men in the car. The car drove away at about 17.30.

Approximately twenty minutes later Annie Sheppard, who was making her way home to Grenville Street from her place of work at Yellow Lane, saw a motor car with a number of men in it. Shortly afterwards she heard a number of shots being fired. She ran across a field in the direction of where she had heard the shots coming from and found two bodies lying near each other. One of them she recognised as Alfred Colley as she had known him.

Another woman, Annie Halpin, who was also with Annie Sheppard, confirmed her description of what had happened. She also described the men who were at the scene of the killings as wearing trench coats with hats pulled down to their eyes. Although it was not recorded at the inquest, *The Irish Times* reported that witnesses who had seen the car arrive at Yellow Lane described two men trying frantically to escape from it. The car drove a short distance up the Lane and stopped at a gate that led to a field. One of the men in the car attempted to open the gate but failed. At this point, the two prisoners in the car once again attempted to escape but were held and had revolvers pointed at their heads. It further described that after one last attempt to break away, which failed, both Cole and Colley '... then seemed to have given themselves over to their fate. They sat on the roadside moaning and were apparently in a dreadfully distressed state. One was heard to ask in terror "What had they done?"' The young men were then placed sitting, one at each pier of the gate, and shot. Those who had shot them then ran back to the car and left the scene. The bodies were left slumped and sitting against the gate. Seán Cole had been shot four times, once in the head and three times in his body.

Some at the time considered the killings an indiscriminate retaliation following the death of Michael Collins less than a week earlier. This was a view shared by British intelligence. A report made in September 1922 described that the killings were probably a reprisal for his death. It further stated that on the day of the deaths of Cole and Colley a sergeant of the Cameronians (Scottish Rifles) heard the shots that killed them. On arriving at the scene, he witnessed six men, 'three in Provisional Government uniform and three in trench coats' who got into a car and drove away. In the aftermath of the killings, rumours were circulated that both Cole and Colley had been shot as they had intended to depart the anti-Treaty side. There was little evidence to support such a theory and Fianna Éireann strongly denied it. In a letter to the Cole family Barney Mellows, adjutant general of Fianna Éireann, described the events of that day as he believed them to have happened:

> The staff here investigated as far as is possible the circumstances of the deaths and find that Sean and his comrade Alf Colley attended on the 26th inst. at an ordinary parade of the northern city section of the Dublin Fianna fixed for 3 p.m., the place being Charlemont House, Marino. At the conclusion of the meeting Sean and Alf Colley were picked up by armed men in the vicinity of Newcomen Bridge, taken near 'The Thatch' and there, without any preliminary, foully and callously murdered. In view of the cruel insinuations which had been passed by slanderers' mouths throughout the city that the two boys died by the hands of their comrades we take this opportunity of characterising the statement as a cowardly lie which has evidently been spread to cover the tracks of the real murderers ...

Seán Cole's funeral to Glasnevin on 30 August 1922 was a public and military one with members of Fianna Éireann and Cumann na mBan in attendance. Amongst the attendees was Seán Harling, Fianna Éireann Dublin Brigade commandant, who was arrested by members of the Criminal Investigation Department following the funeral. Some years later he recalled his subsequent interrogation and what he suggests was tension between the CID and National Army intelligence in relation to the attribution of blame for the deaths of Cole and Colley and other killings during the period:

> On the day of the funeral of the two officers I took complete charge, on arrival at Glasnevin No. 1 A.S.U. took over the outposts, one of the runners reported that the graveyard was surrounded by Free State troops. I informed Madame Markievicz of the position and she ordered me to make an attempt to get away I left and made my way to the lower end of the graveyard and crossed the river Tolka at the village of Finglas with Mr Thomas O'Donohue and Miss Dorothy Redican. Miss Redican took my Webley revolver and concealed it on her person, shortly after we got a lift as far as Hart's stores on Finglas Road. We walked to Phibsboro corner where we were surrounded by C.I.D. I was arrested and taken to Oriel House, on arrival I was interviewed by Capt. Ennis and Inspector Mooney, they spoke a lot about the shooting of my subordinate officers and did everything in their power to convince me that the C.I.D. was not responsible for those shootings. I refused to discuss the matter, they left the room, and were away about ten or fifteen minutes, when they returned I was told I was free to go. This amazed me and I remarked 'shot while trying to escape', I was however immediately released. The [pension] board will understand the apparent inconsistence of the C.I.D. releasing a known Fianna officer if they take into consideration the extraordinary position in Dublin at that time, feeling among the civilian population was high over the murder of men in and around Dublin. The C.I.D. which was a police organisation were being charged with those crimes but maintained that it was Army intelligence officers who were responsible, consequently there was considerable antagonism between C.I.D. and Army intelligence.[90]

26 August 1922   Fianna Éireann
Alfred Colley   BA 21½, *South*

Alfred Leo Colley, commandant of the 1st Battalion, Dublin Brigade, Fianna Éireann, was shot dead at Yellow Lane in Whitehall in August 1922 alongside Seán Cole (*see above*). Born in August 1901 at the home of his family on Amiens Street, he was the son of William Colley and Annie Walsh and had taken an active part in the War of Independence as a member of Fianna Éireann. At the time of his death, he resided at 113 Parnell Street and was working as a tinsmith. It was reported at the inquest into his death that he been shot once in the head, once in his spine and twice in his body. His funeral to Glasnevin took place on the same day as Seán Cole but was a private event. He was buried in a family grave in the South section of the cemetery.[91]

27 August 1922   National Army
Cyril Joseph Lee   *JD 81, South New Chapel*

Cyril Joseph Lee, born in 1895 in Toronto, Canada, was killed during an ambush in Cork while serving with the Dublin Guard as a second lieutenant. Lee had previously been a member of the British army. He had joined up in August 1914 and took part in the Gallipoli landings as a sergeant in April 1915. He was wounded in August 1915 and following treatment was commissioned as an officer in the Royal Irish Regiment and sent to the Western Front. During his time there, he was wounded in the head in October 1916 and wounded in the leg in April 1918. He returned to England for treatment for this latter wound and while there, in May 1918, he married Ethel Upton in Liverpool. The war left its marks on his body with visible scars, a bullet remaining in his leg and shrapnel wounds on his back, hip and head, while his hands suffered with tremors. His poor health led to his discharge in August 1918, however, Lee decided not to accept his enforced retirement from the British army. Instead, he immediately enlisted once again on having arrived in Cork. This was despite him having to join with the rank of private. On this occasion, he was a member of the 2/1st Duke of Lancaster's Own Yeomanry, who were at that time stationed in Kerry. He stayed with them until May 1919 when he was demobilised but he did not remain a civilian for long. He enlisted once more in the British army in July 1919. This time he joined the Leinster Regiment, remaining with them until February 1922 when he was discharged once more.

During the Civil War, he joined the National Army and served in Cork. On 27 August 1922, Lee was in charge of a small party of soldiers from the 1st Cork Reserve based in Macroom. The men, in a Ford lorry and car, were tasked with carrying out reconnaissance work around Clondrohid and Garranenagappul. As they crossed a bridge entering Clondrohid, a large party of anti-Treaty IRA ambushed the group. Being fired upon from their left the National Army soldiers dismounted their vehicles and returned fire. As they did so another group, located in a house in an elevated position on their right, also attacked them. At this time, Cyril Lee was fatally wounded being shot in the head. The remaining National Army members continued fighting for a considerable period until reinforcements arrived from Macroom.

They eventually rushed the house and found that the anti-Treaty fighters had begun retreating leaving three Mauser rifles, five revolvers and 550 rounds of ammunition. In the meantime, Cyril Lee was taken to Macroom where he died a few hours later. The following day his remains were removed from Williams' Hotel and his coffin, covered in the Tricolour, was carried by four National Army officers and members of the Red Cross for almost a mile before being placed in an ambulance and brought to Cork for return to Dublin. He was buried in the National Army plot on 2 September 1922. Although he was married at the time of his death, he was described as single and his mother was recorded as his next-of-kin for the purpose of his pension and effects.[92]

27 August 1922	**National Army**
David O'Shea	*JD 81, South New Chapel*

David O'Shea, from Whitworth Road in Drumcondra, was fatally wounded in an ambush while serving as a driver in the National Army attached to the Transport Section, Limerick Command. Before joining the National Army, he had worked as a waiter in Cruises Hotel in Limerick. On Saturday, 26 August 1922, O'Shea was one of a small group of National Army soldiers travelling in two lorries from Nenagh to Limerick. As they approached Ballywilliam, outside Nenagh, an explosion rang out as the first lorry ran over a mine. The force of the blast lifted the lorry up and into the air. The anti-Treaty IRA who had positioned themselves at different points around the ambush site then opened fire simultaneously on the soldiers. The men in the first lorry bore the brunt of the attack as the second lorry had warning of the ambush and its occupants sought cover. David O'Shea was badly wounded in the back and died the following day of his injuries. His funeral, to the National Army plot in Glasnevin, took place on 31 August 1922 following mass at the church of St Francis Xavier on Gardiner Street. His next-of-kin was his widowed mother Mary O'Shea, née Brennan. David O'Shea was her only son. She emigrated to New York in 1928 and died there in 1943.[93]

27 August 1922	**National Army**
Hugh Thornton	*JD 81, South New Chapel*

Hugh Thornton was born in April 1897 at the home of his family on Peter Street in Drogheda. The son of Hugh Thornton and Mary Harte, his father worked as a painter. The family later moved to Liverpool where they lived on

Royston Street in Edge Hill. From there, Hugh, along with three siblings, Frank, Patrick and Nora, travelled to take part in the 1916 Rising. Hugh fought as part of the GPO garrison during the Rising and was subsequently sent from Richmond Barracks to Stafford Prison and then Frongoch. In September 1916, while imprisoned there he was sentenced to 168 hours closed confinement for refusing to answer with his name and number and giving guards a false name.

Immediately after the completion of this sentence, there was an attempt to compel him, and three other Irish prisoners in Frongoch, to serve in the British army. The men were deemed liable for conscription as they had been resident in Great Britain after August 1915. He was sent to the 65th Training Reserve Battalion in Kinmel Park, Rhyl, in north Wales. He refused to sign his enrolment papers and when a sergeant major ordered him to remove his civilian clothes and put on a uniform he refused saying, 'I am not going to put on khaki'. As a result, Hugh Thornton was placed on trial by court martial for disobedience and sentenced to two years imprisonment with hard labour. The sentence was later commuted and he was discharged in December 1916 with his character being described as 'bad, refused to serve'.

Having been released in 1917, Hugh Thornton returned to Ireland and travelled to Bandon where he took part in activities with the IRA. In 1919, he was subject to an order barring him from living in, or from entering, Munster and he returned to Dublin where he became intelligence officer with 2nd Battalion, Dublin Brigade, IRA. He took the pro-Treaty side during the Civil War and joined the National Army. He was promoted to the rank of captain and served in Cork where he was killed in August 1922.

Following his death newspapers initially stated that Hugh Thornton was passing through Clonakilty in a Lancia car with other National Army soldiers when they were fired upon, he was hit in the neck and died almost instantly. It was later reported that this was incorrect and a military inquiry found that his death was accidental and had taken place while he was travelling from Bantry to Skibbereen. This later account stated that it was an accidental discharge of a rifle during this trip that led to his death. His remains were returned to Dublin by sea and a large crowd attended his funeral to Glasnevin. Less than a week before Hugh Thornton's death, his brother Frank was badly injured following an ambush in which Michael Finnegan was killed (*see 21 August 1922*).[94]

27 August 1922   **National Army**
Thomas White   *JD 80, South New Chapel*

Thomas White was seventeen and serving with the National Army when he was accidentally shot dead by Pte Christopher Whelan in Wexford Barracks. White was born in March 1905 in Dolphin's Barn, the son of Thomas White and Harriet Hickey, and later lived on Emmet Road in Inchicore. In an inquiry following White's death, Christopher Whelan described the circumstances leading to the fatal injury:

> I was in the guardroom with some others, Thomas White came in after being at Mass. It was about twelve o'clock, as far as I know. One of the men in the room was showing me how to slope Arms, different to the way I was taught at the Curragh. We came to 'standing load' when I pulled back the bolt. I looked into the magazine and breach and saw it was empty. I then shoved the bolt home again, presented arms and fired. This man alongside me said that I could fire properly in that position or words to that effect. I then got 'order arms' after which I left the rifle back in the rack. We then had a discussion about the different ways of drilling. I then turned round and picked up what I thought was the same rifle. I thought every rifle was empty as I saw the men unload as they came in. I again went through the same drill as before and came to firing position, when I pulled the trigger and was horrified to hear a shot ring out and deceased fall. A man took the rifle from me and someone rushed in and asked what was wrong. I said that I had shot a man and I asked some of the men to go for a priest. The Sergt of the Guard and Sergt D. Jordan then came in and escorted me to the cell where they locked me up.

It was described that after White's death Christopher Whelan 'exhibited signs of insanity' and was dismissed from the army by his commandant.[95]

28 August 1922   **Criminal Investigation Department**
John Murray   *HD 105, St Paul's*

John Joseph Murray from Temple Buildings in Dublin was a driver with the Criminal Investigation Department in Oriel House who was fatally wounded in an ambush in Deansgrange, Co. Dublin, in August 1922.

Born in 1892, Murray had enlisted in the King's Royal Rifle Corps for service during the First World War in December 1914 and served with that regiment on the Western Front. He was later transferred to the Mechanical Transport Section of the Royal Army Service Corps and suffered a gunshot wound to his left foot. He was discharged from the army in December 1918. He returned home to Dublin and was employed during the Civil War as a driver with the Criminal Investigation Department, utilising the experience he had gained during the First World War. On Friday 25 August 1922, Murray was driving a party of men to Deansgrange to make arrests. They first visited the home of Thomas O'Toole at Kill of the Grange, whom they arrested, before proceeding towards Deansgrange. Here, when approaching the house of the second man they intended to arrest, the CID members were attacked.

During the initial engagement, Murray was wounded in the right leg and Thomas O'Toole shot in the shoulder. Murray and the other men left their car and took up a position in a house on the opposite side of the road where they exchanged fire with the ambushers for some forty-five minutes. Despite being wounded, John Murray took an active part in the skirmish until reinforcements arrived from Dún Laoghaire and the ambushers escaped. John Murray was initially taken to Monkstown Hospital for treatment. He was then sent to St Vincent's Hospital where Dr W. R. Cussen found that a bullet had entered through his right calf and exited at his knee. His leg soon became gangrenous and on Sunday, a decision was made to amputate it. He died the day after the operation. On 31 August his funeral arrived at Glasnevin, a number of wreaths were placed on his coffin, including one from Oriel House, and thirty members of the CID followed the hearse. His mother, Ellen, who died in 1929, is also buried with him.[96]

30 August 1922	National Army
Albert Cottle	*JD 81, South New Chapel*

Albert Redvers Cottle, a sergeant in the National Army, was killed following a land mine explosion near Watergrasshill in Co. Cork. He was born in 1902 in Taunton, Somerset, England, the son of Bessie and William Cottle and appears to have travelled to Ireland to enlist in the National Army. On 30 August 1922, Cottle was one of a party of National Army soldiers on patrol between Cork and Fermoy. He was in the lead vehicle, a Crossley tender, under which a land mine was detonated as they approached Tobereenmire Bridge. The vehicle was described as having been 'blown to pieces' and three of its occupants were injured. Albert Cottle received the most severe wounds, with damage inflicted to his head and face. He was taken to the North Infirmary in Cork where he died that day of his injuries. On enlistment he gave his address as 25 Grattan Street in Dublin, however, he gave no information regarding his next-of-kin. This resulted in his parents only being informed of his death following their own enquiries in October 1922.[97]

1 September 1922   **National Army**
Joseph Hudson   *JD 81, South New Chapel*

Joseph Hudson from Denzille Lane in Dublin died of wounds received while serving as a member of the Dublin Guard. He was born in November 1897, the son of William Hudson and Anne Wilson. He had previously been a member of the Royal Army Service Corps between March 1916 and February 1919 and was wounded in the abdomen, leg and hand during his time in the British army. Hudson was shot in the abdomen near Mitchelstown in Cork in late August 1922 and died of his wounds in Fermoy Hospital on 1 September 1922. His wounds were described as having been accidentally inflicted. He was buried in the National Army plot in Glasnevin on 5 September 1922 following a funeral mass at St Andrew's, Westland Row.[98]

1 September 1922   **National Army**
Michael Behan   *FJ 252, St Patrick's*

Michael Behan from St Paul's Street in Dublin was killed during an attack on National Army soldiers at the City Club in Cork in September 1922. Born in Dublin in December 1900, he was the son of Michael Behan and Catherine Whelan. During much of his early life, the family resided on Blackhall Place, off Ellis Quay. Behan had enlisted in the army six weeks before his death and was sent to Cork. On 1 September 1922, he was present with a number of other soldiers who were waiting outside the City Club on Grand Parade. At about 10.00 the men were told by an officer to fall in and collect their pay. They were standing, unarmed, adjacent to the National Monument when fire was opened by men positioned on the opposite side of the River Lee on Sullivan's Quay. The attack lasted five minutes and about a dozen National Army soldiers were hit. Behan was killed instantly, having been shot in the head. His body was brought to Mercy Hospital. Thomas Conway (*see below*) was killed in the same incident and others, such as James Yeates (*see 14 September 1922*), were wounded. Michael Behan's body was returned to Dublin and he was buried in a grave in the St Patrick's section of Glasnevin.[99]

1 September 1922   **National Army**
Thomas Conway   *JD 82, South New Chapel*

Thomas Conway was born at the home of his parents, Robert and Bridget Conway, on Francis Street, Dublin, in November 1892. His parents were originally from Sligo and Thomas became a slater like his father. Robert Conway died in 1905 and the family subsequently moved to St Augustine Street where they remained for many years. Following the outbreak of the First World War Thomas Conway enlisted in the British army and being 4 feet and 11 inches tall he joined the 12th Battalion South Lancashire Regiment which was a bantam battalion that consisted of men below the normal minimum height requirement for the British army. In October 1915, he deserted, but was later arrested and returned. He never served at the front during the war. During the Civil War, he enlisted in the National Army and was a private in the Curragh Reserve. On 1 September 1922, Conway was fatally wounded during the attack at the City Club in Cork that also led to the death of Michael Behan (*see above*). Conway was hit by one of the first bursts of fire and was wounded in the head and chest. He was buried in the National Army plot on 5 September 1922.[100]

1 September 1922   **National Army**
John Doyle   *JD 81, South New Chapel*

John Doyle, a member of the National Army from St Patrick's Villas, Ringsend Road, was accidentally shot dead while on duty at Baldonnel Aerodrome. Christopher Kennedy, a bugler and fellow member of the National Army, fired the fatal round. Kennedy later stated that:

> I had been tricking with Vols. Doyle and Shelly and had just come in from escort. I forgot that there was a round in the breech. Vol. Doyle went out to wash himself and I unloaded my rifle. As Vol. Doyle came into the room I forgot that there was still a round in the breech and pulled the trigger, the bullet struck Vol. Doyle.

John Doyle's mother died a few months later and his father, Thomas, described that '... since the time of my son's death, which occurred so suddenly, she had never been the same. She took his death very much to heart and it really hastened her end very much'.[101]

1 September 1922   National Army
Nicholas Ward   *JD 82, South New Chapel*

Nicholas Ward from Fingal Street in Dublin was serving as a member of the National Army when he was killed in an ambush at Watergrasshill in Co. Cork. On the day of his death, Ward was one of a party of soldiers who had travelled to tow the remains of a lorry destroyed in a mine explosion back to Cork city. On their return, the soldiers halted having run over another mine on the road that had failed to detonate. The bomb then exploded as one of the party was examining it, although he survived unscathed. Following the explosion the soldiers were fired on by a concealed group. Fire was returned and during the fight and Nicholas Ward was killed, being hit in the head. He died a short time later of his injuries.[102]

2 September 1922   National Army
Robert Hempenstall   *JD 82, South New Chapel*

Robert Hempenstall, a member of the Dublin Guard, from North Summer Street was killed accidentally in Newcastle West in Limerick. He was born in the home of his parents at Kelly's Court, off Patrick Street, in Dún Laoghaire in July 1898. Before joining the National Army, he had worked as a cleaner for the Midland and Great Western Railway. He was interred in the National Army plot on 6 September 1922. His father, who died in 1906, and mother, who died in 1921, are buried in Deansgrange Cemetery.[103]

4 September 1922   Anti-Treaty Irish Republican Army
William Somers   *RB 43, Dublin*

William Somers was born in July 1903 the son of Bernard Somers and Mary Meehan. He was born in the family home on Jervis Street and remained living there until his death in 1922. He worked for James Duffy and Company Limited, publishers, at their premises on Great Strand Street as a machinist. However, he had been out of work in the period immediately before his death, having been charged with armed robbery. A pre-Truce member of the IRA he took the anti-Treaty side during the Civil War and was a volunteer with C Company, 3rd Battalion Dublin Brigade. On the night of his death, William Somers was in a fish and chip shop on Capel Street when two National Army soldiers arrived and began to search people. As they came closer to William Somers, he took out a revolver and fired at one of the soldiers, Frederick Dunne, who fell wounded. Dunne's companion quickly returned fire and William Somers was hit, being fatally injured. His body was brought to Mercer's Hospital. It was described that Bernard Somers '... got hysterics the night William was shot and that he lamented ever after'. He died suddenly, apparently after a heart attack, in the Somers home on Jervis Street seven months later. Mary Somers died in 1957. Both are also buried in Glasnevin.[104]

11 September 1922 — National Army
John Lydon — JD 84, South New Chapel

John Francis Xavier Lydon was born in Galway in January 1897, the son of John Lydon and Ellen Shore. His father was a well known figure in the city and later the proprietor of Lydon's woollen mills. John Lydon junior began studying medicine in 1913 but enlisted in the British army in 1915 and served on Western Front. When demobilised he returned home and went to Dublin to complete his medical degree. He joined the IRA during the War of Independence and later enlisted in the National Army. Serving with the medical corps he was one of the first to land at Fenit in August 1922. On the day of his death, John Lydon travelled to Tralee to board a boat. However, he missed the boat and travelled by bicycle to Blennerville where he hoped to catch it as it passed there. At Blennerville, he met Comdt Eamonn Horan who was travelling in a car with some patients who were also due to take the boat but had similarly missed it at Tralee. Lydon gave his bicycle to Horan and went to the town to buy some cigarettes. In the meantime, Horan had become suspicious of some men around the area and ordered Lydon back to join the boat. As Horan returned a party of men shot at him and he fired back one shot from his revolver. He then rushed for his car where Lydon joined him. The occupants of the car drove along the canal bank where it was ambushed. Many bullets hit the car and Lydon was fatally wounded in the abdomen. Despite being under heavy fire, the driver succeeded in returning the damaged car to the County Infirmary in Tralee. John Lydon's body was brought to Dublin where he was interred in the National Army plot in Glasnevin. His family were not present at his funeral as they had not received notification of his death due to issues with telegraph wires being cut.[105]

11 September 1922   **National Army**
Michael Magee   *JD 83, South New Chapel*

Michael Magee was born in October 1902 in Belfast, the son of James Magee, a hairdresser, and Mary Ann O'Kane. He grew up on Lake Street in the city and when he was aged two his father died in the Belfast Workhouse as a result of 'delirium tremens and cardiac failure'. Michael worked as a messenger and when he was aged fourteen enlisted in the British army in Belfast. He served for a brief period with the Royal Irish Fusiliers before being discharged. He then worked for a period in the shipyards before enlisting in the National Army. Serving with the Dublin Guard, as a driver, he was killed at Dysart near Castleisland in Kerry when he was shot in the head during an ambush. On the evening of his death Magee was part of a convoy of soldiers under Capt. O'Donnell who were travelling from Tralee to Castleisland with rations and mail when they were attacked. He was buried in Glasnevin on 20 September.[106]

12 September 1922   **Anti-Treaty Irish Republican Army**
Seán McEvoy   *IC 80, South*

Seán (John Anthony) McEvoy was born in December 1900 the only son of Ellen Connaty and William McEvoy. His father, a grocer and publican, and mother lived at City Quay at the time of his birth but later resided at a number of different addresses around the city. At the time of his death, Seán McEvoy was a medical student at University College Dublin and a serving captain with Dublin Brigade Active Service Unit of the anti-Treaty IRA. On the day of his death, McEvoy, with another man, carried out an ambush on a lorry of soldiers on the South Circular Road. The National Army issued an account of the incident that stated:

> About 5 p.m. a lorry containing troops passing along the S[outh] C[ircular] Rd. in the direction of Wellington Barracks was attacked near Curzon St. A bomb was thrown at the troops, which missed its objective, but passed through the plate-glass window of the newsagency of Mr Jas. Williams, exploding in the shop and causing much damage. In the subsequent firing a girl, aged seven years, named Maureen Carroll, was wounded in the side and taken to hospital. Some officers who came on the scene at the time of the occurrence gave chase to the ambushers who ran down Heytesbury St. into Bishop St. They were captured and disarmed when their revolvers were found to contain 10 spent cartridges. While being walked to Cross Kevin St. both prisoners bolted and endeavoured to get away. The troops opened fire and one irregular was wounded. He died following admission to hospital. The second irregular, though wounded, got away.

McEvoy was taken to the Adelaide Hospital and was alive on admission but died approximately twenty minutes later. He had been shot in the back with the bullet entering his lung. He was interred in a grave next to his mother, Ellen, who had died in 1917.

At the inquest into his death evidence was given by James Geoghegan from Peter Street that on that evening he heard a number of shots and saw a National Army soldier running in his direction. He heard the soldiers call on men that they were chasing to halt and then began firing at them. The men being chased then stopped and were searched by the National Army who took the two men towards Bride Street. A few minutes later, he saw the men running and being fired at once again. He saw Seán McEvoy fall to the path and went to help him but was warned away at gunpoint by the National Army. Another witness, Annie Kavanagh, from Bishop Street was brought forward by Michael Comyn, who was representing anti-Treaty IRA GHQ. Kavanagh stated that she had seen the two prisoners being marched down the street and badly beaten and suggested that in her opinion the soldiers had let them run away and then shot them. Comyn presented Annie Kavanagh as an independent witness whom, he said, had only come forward 'impelled by a sense of public duty'. Although those at the inquest were not aware of it, she was not devoid of any political connection. Her son James was a member of the anti-Treaty IRA and at this time was imprisoned in Tintown internment camp in the Curragh, having been arrested in the aftermath of the Battle of Dublin. Through his solicitor William McEvoy stated to the inquest that he appreciated the difficulties that the National Army faced and wanted to make clear that he blamed them in no way for the death of his son as they were only carrying out their duty. A verdict was passed that Seán McEvoy had died as a result of '... shock and haemorrhage, caused by a bullet wound inflicted by National troops in the execution of their duty'.

Later that week *Poblacht na hÉireann War News,* an anti-Treaty publication, carried another account of the death of McEvoy by the second man involved in the ambush that day whom it named as Fergus Murphy:

Seán and I ran for it but when Seán was hit we both surrendered. Our guns were taken and the C.I.D. man wanted to shoot us both. When we proceeded a little way towards Kevin Street, reinforcements of the enemy arrived including two more C.I.D. men. One of the C.I.D. men fired three shots at me from a revolver but missed me. I took cover in a doorway I saw the first mentioned C.I.D. man firing deliberately at Seán's head. He hit him in the neck. Then the officers of the party attempted to prevent the C.I.D. man from shooting me and in the confusion that followed I escaped.

The same publication criticised William McEvoy's statement that he did not blame the National Army for the death of his son and wrote that '... this unnatural father turned his son out of his house for defending the Republic against the Black and Tans and has always been a bitter enemy of the independence movement.' However, the words inscribed by William on the grave of his son does not seem to reflect the sentiment of a man ashamed of his involvement in the republican movement. It states: 'Erected to the memory ... of my fond and only son Seán McEvoy, A.S.U. [Active Service Unit] Capt. 4th Batt. D.B. [Dublin Brigade] I.R.A. who died for Ireland (at Bishop St) 12 Sep. 1922 aged 21 ...'[107]

14 September 1922	**Anti-Treaty Irish Republican Army**
Francis Derham	*JD 82, South New Chapel*

Francis Derham was born in the Rotunda Hospital in October 1904, the son of Francis Derham senior and Margaret McCormick, from Church Street. He enlisted in the National Army at the age of seventeen and fought during the Battle of Dublin. He was also a member of the Dublin Command fife and drum band. Francis Derham was fatally wounded on 14 September 1922 when he was accidentally shot in the foot while in the guardroom at Harcourt Street Station. He died of his injuries in the Meath Hospital. His father was also a member of the National Army.[108]

14 September 1922	**National Army**
Henry O'Reilly	*JD 82, South New Chapel*

Henry O'Reilly from Cork Street in Dublin was serving as a private in the National Army at the Ordnance Survey Barracks in the Phoenix Park when he was wounded following the accidental discharge of a fellow soldier's rifle. Shot in his right side he was removed to Dr Steevens' Hospital where he died of his injuries on the same day.[109]

14 September 1922	**National Army**
James Patrick McCann	*JD 83, South New Chapel*

James McCann, from Hamilton Street, Govan, Glasgow, died of wounds received during an attack at the City Club in Cork in September 1922. He had been a member of Fianna Éireann in Scotland from 1917 and in 1921 joined the Scottish Brigade, IRA. He joined the National Army a month before his death, having travelled to Ireland to enlist. On the day he was fatally wounded, McCann and others were waiting for their pay when ambushed. The attack lasted five minutes and about a dozen National Army soldiers were hit including Michael Behan *(see 2 September 1922)*. James McCann died of his injuries in Mercy Hospital twelve days later. James Yeates, who was also wounded in the same attack also died on the same day *(see below)*.[110]

14 September 1922	**National Army**
James Yeates	*JD 83, South New Chapel*

James Yeates (Yates) from Capel Street in Dublin died of wounds received in September 1922 in Cork. Yeates was a former member of the British army who enlisted in 1915 and served until 1919, being wounded on one occasion in the leg. On his return to Ireland, he worked as a van man in the fruit markets and in July 1921 he married Brigid Delaney in the pro-cathedral. They had one child together. Following his enlistment in the National Army, he was sent to Cork, where he was stationed at the City Club on Grand Parade and was fatally wounded there *(see 2 September 1922)*. Yeates' wounds were particularly severe. He was brought to hospital where he was operated on and his right leg was amputated. His condition initially improved but it worsened soon afterwards and he died on the evening of 14 September 1922.[111]

16 September 1922	**National Army**
Edward Crabbe	*JD 85, South New Chapel*

Aged twenty-two at the time of his death Edward (Edmund) Crabbe was born in March 1900, the son of Alice Foster and John Crabbe from Thomas Street in Dublin. Edward and his family later resided on City Quay. His father was a sailor and Edward was connected to the sea throughout his life working as a trimmer on a fishing ship and also with the Merchant Navy. In August 1917, he enlisted in the Royal Navy and served until November 1918 spending time on *HMS Albion*, a guard ship based on the Humber in northern England. John Crabbe assisted the IRA during the War of Independence by helping ship weapons from England to Ireland before enlisting in the National Army during the Civil War. Edward also enlisted in the National Army becoming a

sergeant major. He was killed during the Glenamoy ambush in Mayo in September 1922.

Following a successful attack on Ballina on 12 September 1922, members of the anti-Treaty IRA broke up into columns and dispersed into the countryside. On Thursday 14 September, a small group of National Army soldiers, under Brig.-Gen. Neary, left Ballina and travelled to Bangor and towards Glencullen. On their way, they were fired upon and engaged with some anti-Treaty IRA, taking a number of prisoners. The National Army soldiers then made their way to Glenlossera Lodge. They surrounded the building and found it to be in the hands of a sizeable group of anti-Treaty men. By this time, it was late evening and Neary sent a dispatch rider for reinforcements, which never arrived, and he abandoned his position early the following morning. Neary then moved to Crossmolina and gathered more troops, before coming back to the same area once again.

In the meantime, the anti-Treaty IRA had been reinforced with additional men under Michael Kilroy and positioned themselves in anticipation of a National Army assault. A fierce fight soon materialised and following the initial action members of the National Army, including Edward Crabbe, identified a house where they believed Michael Kilroy was situated and surrounded it. It was reported that an attack on the house was held up due to civilians being present within it. Meanwhile the anti-Treaty IRA attacked those National Army members surrounding the house with intense volleys of fire. It was during this fight that Edward Crabbe was killed. Newspapers stated that he had been hit with dum-dum ammunition and badly injured. His body was brought to the workhouse in Ballina before being transferred to Portobello Barracks via Broadstone Railway Station. He was buried in the National Army plot on 21 September 1922.[112]

16 September 1922   **National Army**
William Murphy   *JD 83, South New Chapel*

William Murphy, Daniel O'Brien and Patrick O'Rourke were three of seven members of the National Army who were killed in September 1922 following a mine explosion at Carrigaphooca in Cork. Murphy was from Esker in Co.

Longford and his father, also William, was a farmer there. On the day of his death he was one of a number of soldiers that proceeded from Macroom to Carrigaphooca where an explosive mine was reported at the bridge. They had begun to remove the mine when a large explosion took place. The noise of the explosion reverberated around the area and the seven men in the National Army party were killed instantly or fatally wounded. The highest-ranking casualty was Col Comdt Tom Kehoe, a member of The Squad during the War of Independence. The injuries suffered by the men were described as 'horribly catastrophic'. A description of the incident stated that:

> ... a flying column from Macroom, in the charge of Commandant Peadar O'Conlon, penetrated the Clondrohid and Carrigaphooca districts in search of irregulars, equipment, etc. Close by the Carrigaphooca bridge a mine was located in the road. It being the duty of the officer in charge to remove all road mines as he advanced he had the wires cut and it being considered safe to remove the mine then he ordered one man to remove it. The earth was cleared around the mine and Comdt O'Conlon in company with Comdt Thomas Keogh approached the position where it lay. The former ordered four men to procure a cross-cut from one of the cars and cut the trees near the bridge. The men procured the cross-cut and just as they were returning by the exposed mine, the man who had done the clearing round it put down his hands to lift it. Just as he raised it the mine burst and there was a terrific explosion.

Unknown to the men tasked with the removal of the explosives was that beneath the mine a mills bomb, or grenade, had been placed with the pin removed. The pressure applied to the safety lever of the grenade by the weight of the mine prevented its detonation, however, on the removal of the weight above it the grenade was detonated resulting in the explosion of the mine itself. The remains of the men who were killed were brought to Williams' Hotel in Macroom for transfer to Dublin. William Murphy, Daniel O'Brien and Patrick O'Rourke were buried together in Glasnevin on 19 September in the National Army plot.[113]

16 September 1922	**National Army**
Daniel O'Brien	*JD 83, South New Chapel*

Daniel O'Brien, a captain in the National Army, was also killed in the Carrigaphooca Bridge explosion (*see above*). From Macroom in Cork, O'Brien was serving with a Dublin detachment of the National Army at the time of his death. Before joining the National Army he had worked as an engineering instructor for Wexford County Council. He was employed as an engineer by the army and was it was for this reason that he was present when the attempt was made to defuse the Carrigaphooca bomb.[114]

16 September 1922   National Army
Patrick O'Rourke   *JD 83, South New Chapel*

Patrick O'Rourke, from Longford, was killed in the same mine explosion as William Murphy and Daniel O'Brien. He had previously served for a brief period with the British army, having enlisted in 1920 at nineteen. He was discharged the following year and worked as a labourer before joining the National Army. His next-of-kin was his mother, Mary.[115]

17 September 1922   Civilian
Patrick Brady   *XA 14, Dublin*

Patrick Brady from South King Street was shot dead at St Stephen's Green in September 1922. On the evening of his death, it was reported that shots were fired at a National Army tender as it approached the corner of York Street. The assailants quickly fled avoiding capture. However, as the soldiers returned to barracks their sergeant noticed a man walking at pace past Stephen's Green towards Grafton Street. They called on him to halt but he fled, running towards South King Street. The soldiers gave chase and fired shots in the air before firing directly at him.

In their description of the incident the National Army stated that it was at this point that the person they were chasing grabbed another man, who was walking ahead of him, and used him as a shield. This man, Patrick Brady, was subsequently hit and fatally wounded. The National Army then arrested the younger man who surrendered after Brady had been hit. He was found to be carrying a fully loaded Webley revolver with a small quantity of spare ammunition. He gave his name as Denis O'Dea and his address as 52 South Richmond Street. He was the son of Michael O'Dea, a former member of the Royal Irish Constabulary. Denis had served with Dublin Brigade IRA during the War of Independence as a teenager before taking the anti-Treaty side during the Civil War. Unknown to the National Army was that O'Dea was on his way to take part in the attack on Oriel House that resulted in the death of Anthony Deane (*see below*). It is not clear if he was involved in the initial attack on the National Army tender or his presence at Stephen's Green was happenstance.

After he was wounded, Patrick Brady was taken to the nearby St Vincent's Hospital where he died of his injuries. Another man, James Kehoe, also from South King Street, who was wounded during the affray, was also taken there. However, his wounds were less serious and he made a full recovery. Patrick Brady was in his late fortiess and working as a wine porter and glass warehouseman at the time of his death. He had previously lived at Upper Stephen Street and in October 1900, he married Mary Graham and settled on South King Street. Mary died in 1916, aged thirty-three, leaving Patrick as a widower and their children.

Although he appears to have been a bystander during this incident Patrick Brady was previously associated with the Irish Volunteers. In August 1917, he was arrested when Sgt Patrick Smyth (see 8 September 1919) raided 44 Parnell Square, then headquarters of the Volunteers, and seized a large quantity of arms and ammunition. Brady was described as one of four men who were '... in charge of the premises and appeared to be on guard there'. Patrick Brady was buried on 20 September 1922, in a different grave to his wife, but in the same section of the cemetery in which she had been buried six years earlier.

Following his arrest Denis O'Dea was interned in Newbridge Barracks. While there, O'Dea began to organise plays on a temporary stage in the dining hall. It was his first time acting and his interest developed. Following his release, he and other former IRA internees staged plays in Dublin to help raise funds for the dependents of Republican prisoners. In the 1920s, O'Dea decided to follow his aspiration to become a professional actor and forged a successful career leading from the Abbey to Hollywood. He starred in movies by John Ford and Alfred Hitchcock, as well as Disney productions such as *Treasure Island* and *Darby O'Gill and the Little People*. He died in 1978, still living in the same house on South Richmond Street that had been his home in 1922.[116]

17 September 1922	Criminal Investigation Department
Anthony Deane	*HD 106, St Paul's*

Anthony Deane was born on 13 September 1895 in Sheskin, Co. Mayo, the son of Anthony and Anne Deane. On the evening of Sunday 17 September 1922, at 21.45, Joseph Sherlock, a member of the Criminal Investigation Department, answered the door of their headquarters at Oriel House. Two men at the door stated that they wished to report a car stolen and Sherlock brought them into the inquiry office where Inspector Michael Finn and Anthony Deane were also present. The two men then took out revolvers and a struggle ensued with

Sherlock. Bullets were fired, one of which passed through the collar of Sherlock's coat. Anthony Deane was hit in head and back by two bullets, and was killed almost instantly. Following the exchange of fire, the two men escaped from Oriel House, running in the direction of Westland Row Railway Station chased by CID members. Anthony Deane was brought to St Vincent's Hospital but was dead on arrival. He was buried in Glasnevin three days after his death in a formal ceremony with three volleys fired over his grave and the Last Post sounded.[117]

17 September 1922	**National Army**
John Lynn	*JD 84, South New Chapel*

John Lynn, from Nisbet Street, Glasgow, was a member of the Glasgow IRA during the War of Independence who travelled from Scotland to join the National Army. A mechanic in Parkhead Forge before the Civil War, Lynn was stationed at Bushfield in Tipperary on the day of his death. That morning he was one of a party of eighteen National Army soldiers who were walking towards Boher Roman Catholic church in to attend mass. They had almost reached the church when they were ambushed. Pte Thomas Maguire gave an account to a newspaper of the attack. He had seen a head pop above a ditch and was looking closely when he saw another. He shouted a warning to his colleagues, but they quickly came under fire. The account stated that:

> Several of the troops fell but their companions threw themselves down in the shallow drains at each side of the road, pulled in the wounded and started to reply to the irregular fire. Their position was impossible, lying in nettle-filled drains, with the irregulars in good cover 30 yards away, firing straight down on them from a position above their heads. The din was appalling. A rapid vicious crackle of rifle fire, punctuated by the cries of the wounded and the thunderous roar of rifle grenades used by the irregulars. Pte Maguire was alone on one side of the road. He started to crawl to better cover. He had heard five or six of his companions cry out that they were wounded and recognised that not only was their position untenable but that there was no cover near them anywhere to retreat to. As he edged along the lane his cap was caught by some briars. While trying to extricate it he was seen and five or six irregulars fired at him. One bullet smashed through the steel clasp of his pocket book and buried itself in the papers inside, another pierced his thigh. He sustained a compound fracture in the upper part of his left arm from a bullet. Cpl Kehoe, realising that he would have to surrender to save the party from annihilation cried out 'we surrender'. A voice from the irregular position cried, 'come out of that'. Cpl Kehoe again put up his hand and said 'we surrender'. He half raised himself and then fell riddled with bullets. The firing continued but the position was impossible and a few moments later Pte Maguire called out his intention of surrendering and crawled out with his hands up. His companions hesitated slightly and then followed suit.

Following their surrender, the men were stripped of their equipment, ammunition and weapons. Despite the impression given by this account, the ambush was not an entirely one-sided affair and the National Army had engaged in a prolonged fight. The skirmish resulted in the deaths of three members of the National Army and one member of the anti-Treaty IRA. The latter was sixteen-year-old Thomas Hayes from Nenagh. John Lynn had been killed instantly. He was shot multiple times. One bullet had entered through his left shoulder blade, and travelled through his lung, exiting via his abdomen. He was also shot in the head, right shoulder and the jaw.[118]

18 September 1922	**National Army**
Bernard Gray	*JD 84, South New Chapel*

Bernard Gray, a sixteen-year-old member of the National Army, from Fairfield Street, Govan, Glasgow was killed at Coachford in Co. Cork. A report described that Gray had cleaned his rifle with a type of flammable liquid and when he fired it, the gun exploded inflicting fatal injuries to his face. His cause of death was recorded as 'laceration of brain caused by bullet from his own rifle which burst'. Another account described his death as having occurred in the midst of a small attack on the post at which he was stationed. He was buried in the National Army plot in Glasnevin on 23 September 1922.[119]

22 September 1922	**National Army**
James Kennedy	*JD 85, South New Chapel*

James Kennedy was born in July 1894 at the home of his parents on Sir John Rogerson's Quay. In August 1916, he married Katie Forde, from Merchants Cottages, East Wall and moved to live there. He had worked as a sailor before joining the National Army. On the day of his death, Kennedy was travelling with a small group of National Army men in a Crossley tender from the North Wall into the city centre. As the lorry came to O'Connell Bridge, it turned left onto Eden Quay and there was a loud explosion. A bomb had been thrown at the lorry and the men within it immediately fired shots in return. The lorry sped away and Sgt Maurice Byrne, who was one of those present in the lorry, noticed that James Kennedy had not moved and had blood coming from his face. He was dead, a fragment of metal had hit him and entered his brain. Shrapnel had also hit and wounded four other men.

In Byrne's opinion, the bomb had been thrown from Mooney's public house on Eden Quay or nearby. Later that day a small group of armed men entered Mooney's public house on Eden Quay, and took away a barman, Michael Neville, who was an anti-Treaty IRA volunteer. Neville's body was later found near old Killester graveyard. He had been shot multiple times.[120]

Courtesy of Southampton Archives and Local Studies.

22 September 1922   **National Army**
William Warren   *JD 84, South New Chapel*

William Warren was shot dead by a sentry in Howth in September 1922. Before joining the National Army, he had worked as a dairy boy and lived with his aunt, who was also his foster mother, at the rear of 78 Leinster Road. Serving with 4th Battalion, 1st Dublin Brigade, he was shot by Pte Devine, a fellow member of his battalion. Devine later stated that on the night of 22 September 1922 he was on sentry duty near Howth Tower when somebody approached his post. He then described that '… I called on him to "halt" and repeated the order three times and also a fourth time, adding that I would fire, but he still kept on without halting. I fired from the hip at random and as it turned out afterwards my aim unluckily was only too true. I might add that it was a night of pitch darkness and it was impossible to distinguish a uniform or what way a person was dressed.' William Warren had been shot in the head and died instantly. His funeral to Glasnevin was a joint one with James Kennedy (*see above*).[121]

24 September 1922   **Civic Guard**
Charles Eastwood   *VF 81, St Paul's*

Charles Eastwood was one of the first members of the Civic Guard, later An Garda Síochána, to be killed. Aged nineteen at the time of his death, Eastwood was accidentally shot by a colleague at Ship Street Barracks on 20 September 1922. He died four days later. On the day he was wounded Eastwood was on guard duty at Ship Street when a colleague, Guard Leo Herde, came to visit Guard Maguire who was on duty with Eastwood. In a report to the Minister for Justice regarding the matter, Eoin O'Duffy described that:

> ... Eastwood was on the stairs, and when Herde was coming to see Maguire, the former said 'You're not coming up here Leo' in a joking way, at the same time pointing his revolver at Herde. The latter knowing Eastwood well, and that he was only joking pulled out his revolver and pointed it at Eastwood, and forgetful of the fact of its being loaded, pressed the trigger, when a shot discharged, the bullet striking Eastwood in the chest. He was taken to Mercers Hospital where he was treated, and on the next and succeeding days showed signs of improvement that his recovery was expected, but I regret to say, he took a turn for the worse and died early this morning ...

O'Duffy was satisfied that Eastwood's death was accidental and that Herde had been badly affected by the killing. He had him released from custody. A coroner's inquest found that he had died from 'shock and haemorrhage caused by a bullet accidentally fired from a revolver'. Charles Eastwood's shooting, along with other serious firearms incidents led O'Duffy to decree in September 1922 that arms were only to be used while on duty and when necessary. This was quickly followed by a commitment to disarm the force. Charles Eastwood's funeral took place on 27 September. Following mass at St James' church a party of the civic guards, with their pipers' band, headed the cortege to Glasnevin. Fifty-two other members of the guards followed behind. He was buried in a grave in the St Paul's section of the cemetery with his mother and father who predeceased him.[122]

26 September 1922 — National Army
Bernard Murphy — JD 84, South New Chapel

Bernard Murphy, a member of the Voluntary Reserve of the National Army, was shot and killed in Victoria Barracks, Cork, in September 1922. From Upper Mercer Street in Dublin, he had served during the First World War with the British army as a member of the 11th Mountain Battery, Royal Garrison Artillery. He fought with the Egyptian Expeditionary Force during the Sinai and Palestine campaign and was discharged in September 1919, suffering with malaria as a result of his service. After his return home to Dublin, he worked as a general labourer and in September 1921 he married Catherine McDermott (neé O'Donnell), who was a widow. He enlisted in the National Army in July 1922 and on the day of his death was engaged in delivering rations to a number of National Army posts in Cork City as part of an escort party. According to an officer, it was on his return to Victoria Barracks that he was accidentally shot while jumping from the army tender in which he had travelled. He had been shot through the heart and his death was deemed accidental. Bernard Murphy's funeral took place at Whitefriar Street church on 29 September 1922 after which his coffin, covered in the Tricolour, was led to the National Army plot by the pipers' band from Beggars Bush Barracks. Amongst the mourners following were his wife, four sisters and two of his stepchildren.[123]

27 September 1922   **National Army**
Thomas Murray   *ID 79, South New Chapel*

Sgt-Maj. Thomas Murray, a member of the Dublin Guard, stationed at Lismore Castle was accidentally killed in September 1922. Originally from Lower Bridge Street in Dublin he had married Sarah Murphy in July 1921. He was killed on the afternoon of 27 September 1922 when, while preparing to go on duty, his Thompson gun accidentally fired and he was fatally injured. His widow later emigrated to the United States where she lived in Newark and remarried in 1925.[124]

28 September 1922   **National Army**
Edward Noone   *ID 79, South New Chapel*

Edward Noone, from Middle Gardiner Street in Dublin, was serving as a sergeant with the Dublin Guard when he was killed at Rathmore in Co. Kerry in September 1922. On the day of his death, Noone was on sentry duty on the eastern side of the town when some other members of the National Army, who were unarmed and on a walk, approached him to talk. As they did so they were all fired upon by the anti-Treaty IRA as part of a co-ordinated attack on the town and the Dublin Guard who were garrisoned there. Noone was killed instantly and the other men talking to him were wounded. His body was brought initially to the Mercy Hospital in Cork and then returned to Dublin for burial in Glasnevin. Noone had previously served with the Royal Irish Rifles during the First World War. He initially arrived in France in November 1915 and in 1918, while serving with the 1st Battalion of his regiment, was awarded the Military Medal for his gallantry in action. He was discharged from the British army in June 1919 and had married Christina McMahon in the pro-cathedral in January 1920.[125]

28 September 1922   **National Army**
Patrick O'Brien   *JD 85, South New Chapel*

Patrick O'Brien was a private in the National Army, based in Portobello Barracks. A former member of the British army he lived at Baggot Terrace, off Blackhorse Avenue. On the night of 22 September 1922, O'Brien was on patrol in a Lancia armoured car in the area around Amiens Street. At about 03.00 the car, under the command of Sgt George McCarthy stopped near Amiens Street Post Office. After some time there, they saw a Ford car come out of a side street with no lights on and followed it to Newcomen Bridge. Here the men in the armoured car ordered the Ford to stop and it did. A man in civilian clothes got out but the car quickly sped off. According to evidence given at the inquest of Patrick O'Brien, the armoured car followed the car and as it turned a corner they saw a similar Ford driving back in the direction they had come from. The armoured car pulled up and McCarthy opened fire. One of the first bullets shattered the windscreen and another hit one of the occupants.

The Ford stopped and the occupants got out, having shouted that they were members of the National Army. It transpired that the Ford that the armoured car had fired at contained three officers of the National Army from Portobello Barracks and a driver. Sgt McCarthy had mistaken the Ford car containing the officers for the one he was chasing. One of the officers asked to speak to the sergeant in charge of the armoured car but it sped away with the officers firing shots at it as it left the scene. In the midst of the confusion, Patrick O'Brien was wounded. He was brought back to Amiens Street and eventually to the Jervis Street Hospital where he died of his wounds six days later. George McCarthy was later questioned by the officers in relation to the events of that night, they stated that '... he could not give a proper explanation as to what happened, as he had lost his head'. It was never ascertained who fired the shot that killed Patrick O'Brien. He left a widow, Annie, whom he had married in 1921.[126]

5 October 1922   **National Army**
Patrick Byrne   *ID 79, South New Chapel*

Patrick Byrne, the son of Richard Byrne, a vegetable dealer, and Julia McGrath was born in January 1897 in Donnybrook where he grew up living in The Crescent. In 1915, he enlisted in the British army and served with the Royal Irish Rifles for three years. Following his discharge, he returned home to

Dublin and later enlisted in the National Army. Serving as a machine gunner, he was posted to Cork. On 4 October 1922, Patrick Byrne was one of a group that were travelling on foot to Clonakilty from Dunmanway. The soldiers, under the command of Seán Hales, were nearing the village of Ballygurteen when they were ambushed. Heavy fire was opened by members of the anti-Treaty IRA on a hillside overlooking a bend in the road and the National Army returned fire. During the skirmish, Patrick Byrne was badly wounded and was brought to Dunmanway Hospital where he died of his injuries the following day. It was reported that one other member of the National Army was also killed, while five were wounded. He was buried on 9 October in the National Army plot.[127]

7 October 1922 — Anti-Treaty Irish Republican Army
Brendan Holohan — *YG 165, Garden*

On 11 October 1922 the funerals of Brendan Holohan and Eamonn (Edwin) Hughes, both aged seventeen, came to Glasnevin following a funeral mass at the pro-cathedral. Their bodies, along with that of Joseph Rogers, had been found near Red Cow with all three having been shot multiple times. Their coffins were draped in the Tricolour and covered in flowers and wreaths. Members of Cumann na mBan marched alongside the hearses on the journey to the cemetery where volleys were fired over their graves and the Last Post sounded.

Brendan Michael Holohan was born in August 1905, the son of Michael Joseph Holohan and Delia Mullen, who were both originally from Galway. At the time of his birth, the Holohan family were living in a house in Victoria Terrace in Clontarf and his father was employed as a buyer for Clery's department store. The family later moved to Drumcondra where they resided on St Patrick's Road and Brendan was employed as a clerk in Arnotts. He joined the anti-Treaty IRA in April 1922 and served with 2nd Battalion, Dublin Brigade under the command of Tom Burke. On the night of 6 October 1922 at 22.30 Joseph Rogers, Brendan Holohan and Eamonn Hughes left the home of the latter on Clonliffe Road. It was recorded at the inquest into their deaths that they had paste, brushes and Republican handbills with them and that they had intended to hang these notices up around the locality. Their commanding officer, Tom Burke, later stated that they were carrying out an intelligence patrol that night. Regardless, the three were spotted by officers of the National Army and arrested close to the home of Hughes. The officers were travelling in the area in a car and two of them were Charlie Dalton, then deputy head of National Army GHQ Intelligence, and Nicholas Tobin, a staff captain and brother of Maj.-Gen. Liam Tobin. It was reported that handbills carried by the three announced the targeting of members of the pro-Treaty forces, and those supporting them, who lived in the Drumcondra area. Essentially the notices were a direct threat towards Charlie Dalton and Nicholas Tobin, who both lived in the vicinity. The handbills stated that:

> Any person employed by the Free State Force, either in mufti or in the vicinity of Drumcondra on or after Sunday October 8, 1922, shall be shot at sight. This warning applies to the Murder Gang, otherwise known as the Military Intelligence Department, and so-called C.I.D. men, or to any persons who have been giving information, also to any person found giving information, or helping same.

The notice was signed 'Irish Republican Defence Association' and came with a further warning that anybody found tampering with the notice would '... be drastically dealt with'. Having been arrested and placed in the car, Holohan, Hughes and Rogers were not seen alive again that night by any independent witness who came forward. The men of the National Army claimed that after the arrest they had brought the three to Wellington Barracks, they were handed over to Capt. Stephen Murphy for interrogation and that he had them released almost immediately.

The following day at 05.00 the bodies of Brendan Holohan, Eamonn Hughes and Joseph Rogers were found by passers by in a quarry near Mount St Joseph's Monastery on the road from Red Cow to Clondalkin. Two of the three were already dead, but one was still alive. It was reported that the latter had attempted to make his way out of the quarry as there were marks of blood along one side of it where he had made his way before collapsing. He died before an ambulance arrived. All three had been shot multiple times. People who lived in the area described hearing gunfire around midnight. The subsequent inquest into the deaths garnered great public interest and much coverage with ill-tempered exchanges between both sides. However, it provided little clarity in relation to the timeline of events leading up to their deaths. It returned a verdict that they had died of 'gunshot wounds inflicted by some person or persons unknown'.

Charlie Dalton continued to serve with the National Army until 1924 when he was involved in the Army Mutiny of that year. He died in 1974. Nicholas Tobin was shot dead four days after giving evidence to the inquest for the Red Cow deaths (*see 21 October 1922*).[128]

7 October 1922   **Anti-Treaty Irish Republican Army**
Eamonn Hughes   *PH 173, St Bridgets*

Eamonn (Edwin) Hughes was shot dead at Red Cow in October 1922 alongside Brendan Holohan (*see above*). Born in the Rotunda Hospital in October 1904, Eamonn was the second child of Mark John Hughes, a civil servant, and Annie Julia Brady, a music teacher. His only sibling was his elder brother Gerald. He was a childhood friend of Brendan Holohan and the two had lived a few doors away from each other on St Patrick's Road before the Hughes family moved to nearby Clonliffe Road. He joined Fianna Éireann in December 1920 and later transferred to the IRA during the War of Independence in May 1921. This was the same month that his brother, Gerald, who was also a member of Dublin Brigade IRA, was arrested at the Custom House.

The pro-Treaty side claimed that on the night of his death Hughes was carrying a revolver when he was arrested. A description published in a newspaper before his identification showed that his body was found with a wristwatch inscribed 'E.H. Drumcondra 1922'. In his pockets were money, a cigarette case with one Abdulla brand cigarette, a comb, keys, rosary beads and religious medals.[129]

8 October 1922   **National Army**
John Hunter   *ID 79, South New Chapel*

Sgt Maj. John (Seán) Hunter was shot by Frank Teeling, a fellow member of the National Army, on 6 October 1922 at Gormanston Camp and died of his wounds two days later. Hunter was a veteran member of Dublin Brigade IRA from Irvine Terrace, North Wall and had participated in Bloody Sunday and the Great Brunswick Street fight in March 1921. One of those present on the day of Hunter's fatal wounding described what he saw that day during a subsequent inquiry:

> On the 6th October, about 3.30 p.m. Lieuts Foy, Teeling and Transport Driver and myself were in a Crossley tender. We were going down to the Pumping Station. The car was outside the Transport Office. Sgt Maj. Hunter came over to the car and was talking to Lieut Teeling. They were joking. The next thing I heard was a shot and I saw Sgt Maj. Hunter lying on the ground. He was put into the car and taken over to the hospital.

An inquest returned a verdict that Sgt Maj. Hunter had died of 'septic pneumonia consequent of a bullet wound accidentally received' and Frank Teeling was cleared of any culpability. A few months later, Teeling shot dead William Johnson, a member of Citizens' Defence Force, because he took exception to him bringing a bag of tomatoes into the bar at the Theatre Royal. He was found guilty of manslaughter for that shooting and was sentenced to eighteen months imprisonment. Frank Teeling died in 1976 and is buried in Glasnevin.[130]

9 October 1922
Charles Kearns

National Army
ID 80, South New Chapel

Charles Kearns, from Crocus Street in Belfast, was the son of Annie Gorman and Charles Kearns senior. Born in March 1902 he had been a pre-Truce member of the IRA and was aged twenty when he was killed in Cork while serving as a sergeant in the National Army. His body was returned to Dublin and he was buried in the National Army plot after a funeral mass in Rathmines church. He was described as having been killed in action in an ambush in Cork.[131]

10 October 1922
Peadar Breslin

Anti-Treaty Irish Republican Army
RD 34, South New Chapel

Peter (Peadar) Breslin, originally from New Street in Dublin, and later Mount Temple Road, was shot dead at Mountjoy Jail in October 1922. He was one of four brothers involved in the independence movement and the elder brother of Christopher Breslin who was also killed during the Civil War (*see 3 April 1923*).

Peadar was born in 1887, the son of James Breslin and Johanna Phelan from New Street in Dublin. He had been a member of the Irish Volunteers from its inception in 1913. He was also an active member of the Craobh Colmcille branch of the Gaelic League and the Gaelic Athletic Association. He participated in the 1916 Rising, fighting in the Church Street area and on 25 April he took part in the unsuccessful attempt to occupy Broadstone Railway Station with a small group of other Volunteers. He was arrested following the surrender and was initially sent to Stafford Gaol, before being interned in Frongoch.

He took part in the War of Independence as a member of the 1st Battalion, Dublin Brigade, rising to become the officer commanding A Company.

Courtesy of the Breslin family.

Dick McKee described Breslin as being 'peculiarly adapted' to guerrilla warfare and he took part in many operations. One of the most significant of these was the Collinstown Aerodrome arms raid in 1919. Seán Lemass described that '... if there was anything that distinguished him [Breslin] from all the men around him, it was his tremendous capacity for work and his transparent honesty of character ...' In January 1921, Peadar married Anne Callender. Both families knew one another and Anne's brother, Ignatius, was a veteran of the 1916 Rising and a member of the same branch of the Gaelic League. Two of Anne's other brothers were killed fighting on the Western Front with the British army, one of whom died of wounds during Easter week 1916. Her mother ran the Lucan Restaurant on Sarsfield Quay which was frequented by leaders of the Rising and she also prepared Patrick Pearse's final meals before his execution. Peadar Breslin took part in the Civil War as a commandant with the anti-Treaty IRA and was one of those who took part in the occupation of the Four Courts. He was subsequently arrested and imprisoned in Mountjoy where he died in October 1922.

Breslin was killed in an incident that also led to the deaths of three other men. The three others who died were National Army guards. It was stated at an inquest into his death that on the day of the death of Peadar Breslin an attempt was made by Republican prisoners to escape from C Wing in Mountjoy Prison. Many of the prisoners on this wing had been arrested as members of the Four Courts garrison during the Battle of Dublin. An official account described that as breakfast was delivered to the prisoners they rushed the gates to their wing and overpowered the guards. Shortly afterwards a number of shots were fired. One of the National Army guards, who was wounded in the incident described that some of the prisoners were armed with revolvers and had begun firing. A number of shots were fired between the two parties and the skirmish lasted approximately fifteen minutes before the escape attempt was subdued. In its aftermath, four men lay dead. Three were National Army guards and the other was Peadar Breslin. His body was found in a cell, which was not his own, on the ground floor of the wing. A Webley revolver with three empty and two live cartridges was described as being found in the same cell. However, a member of the military police stated that it was his belief that Breslin had not placed it there and there were other prisoners in the cell. Peadar Breslin had been killed instantly. A bullet had hit him in the skull, entering or exiting through his left eye. His body was brought out of the prison wing on a stretcher and removed to the Mater Hospital. All of the C wing prisoners and their cells were searched following the escape attempt. The army reported that amongst the materials found were three revolvers, a grenade, ammunition and a bomb.

The funeral of Peadar Breslin came to Glasnevin from the Carmelite church on Whitefriar Street. On its way to the cemetery the hearse carrying his coffin was flanked by members of Cumann na mBan and the mothers and wives of republican prisoners walked behind. At the grave, in the Republican Plot, the Last Post was sounded and three volleys fired over the grave. His widow, Annie, who was pregnant, and his infant son were also present at the funeral. Annie Breslin died in 1991 and is buried in Glasnevin.[132]

11 October 1922
Joseph Claffey

National Army
ID 80, South New Chapel

Joseph Claffey, from Great Western Villas in Phibsboro, was serving as a sergeant with the National Army in Bandon, Co. Cork when he was accidentally killed following the discharge of a comrade's rifle. Before joining the National Army, he had worked as a porter with the Midland and Great Western Railway. His father, also Joseph, participated in the War of Independence and was a captain in the National Army at the time of the death of his son.[133]

13 October 1922
John Young

National Army
ID 80, South New Chapel

John Joseph Young was born in March 1902 at Warrenmount Place in Dublin. He was the only son of Jane Scullion and James Young, a member of the Dublin Metropolitan Police. The family later moved to Mabel Street in Drumcondra and then to James Street. John joined the IRA in 1918 and during the Civil War enlisted in the National Army. He joined the Criminal Investigation Department for a period and later returned to the army. He served with Dublin Guard on campaign in Kerry with the rank of captain. He was wounded through the lung on 29 September 1922 during an ambush at The Bower, between Rathmore and Barraduff. He succumbed to his injuries two weeks later. His funeral to Glasnevin was accompanied by a large number of officers of the National Army, a firing party and the band of the Dublin Guard.[134]

14 October 1922   **National Army**
James Byrne   *ID 81, South New Chapel*

James Byrne was a member of the Dublin Guard from Rathfarnham who was fatally wounded in an ambush at Duagh in Kerry. Before joining the National Army, he worked in Terenure Laundry. He had also served as a member of Fianna Éireann and the IRA during the War of Independence. On the night of his death, Byrne was part of a military escort travelling from Tralee. The escort consisted of a party of soldiers in a Crossley Tender accompanied by the armoured car *Danny Boy*. At Duagh, the party came to a barricade and stopped. Immediately they were ambushed and a short but intense burst of fire hit the National Army soldiers. The armoured car and soldiers returned fire and the attackers quickly fled into the darkness. James Byrne was shot during the first volley while in the back of the tender. He died in Abbeyfeale Hospital. Another soldier, John Brown, was also killed. James Byrne's body was badly disfigured due to dumdum or expanding bullets being used in the ambush that killed him. Due to this and a lack of material on his person that specifically identified him, his body was returned to Dublin by sea with only the name James Byrne as identification. In an attempt to identify him, adverts were placed in newspapers and a short list was made of fifty different men with the name James Byrne serving with the National Army. This effort to identify him was unsuccessful. Finally, members of the public were allowed to attend a viewing of the remains in the mortuary in Portobello Barracks. Many worried families visited, but no positive identification was made. As a result he was buried in the National Army plot in Glasnevin with no family present. In the meantime, his mother had been trying to ascertain his fate. It was some time before she eventually received official confirmation of his death and that he was buried in Glasnevin. In a letter to James Byrne's aunt, the parish priest at Duagh described that James was:

> ... mortally wounded in an ambush in this village on 13th Oct. Shortly after the attack on the troops had ceased I was summoned to attend poor James and his comrade Sergt Browne (*Sic*), who died just as I had finished anointing him. Though mortally wounded (he was shot through the abdomen) I found James perfectly conscious on reaching him. He had little or no difficulty in making his confession and after giving him absolution I anointed him and gave him the last blessing. Unfortunately I could not give him viaticum because he was bleeding internally and this made him inclined to vomit. He was naturally in great pain and said so in my asking him, but you will be glad to learn he never complained or murmured whilst I was with him ... He was removed to Abbeyfeale in a motor ambulance that night and died there about half an

hour after its arrival. Tell his dear mother that she has reason to be proud of James for he was an excellent boy as well as a most lovable character and that I'm sure he is happy. He was quite resigned to die and gladly forgave those who had so foully done him to death.[135]

15 October 1922
Andrew Furlong

Andrew Furlong was a veteran of the 1916 Rising who returned home from London to take part in the rebellion. During Easter week he was attached to the GPO garrison and was stationed at the Metropole Hotel. He later served with the IRA during the War of Independence and was interned in Ballykinlar. He was fatally wounded at Roscrea while serving as a captain with the Army Corps of Engineers on 13 October 1922 and died of his wounds two days later in the Jervis Street Hospital. An inquest in Dublin returned a verdict that Furlong had died due to 'haemorrhage following bullet wound through the lung', as no in-formation had been submitted regarding the exact circumstances in which he had been wounded. In a letter, within a pension application, his family expressed their belief that their brother '... was shot through culpable negligence in Roscrea Barracks by the Commandant's brother.' Amongst the attendees at his funeral in Glasnevin was J.J. 'Ginger' O'Connell who once had Furlong as a member of his staff.[136]

Andrew Furlong (right) during the Civil War. Courtesy of Roscrea through the ages.

17 October 1922
Patrick Collins

Patrick Collins from McDowell's Terrace, Mount Brown was accidentally shot and killed in Dundalk in October 1922. He was aged twenty-one at the time of his death. The son of Maud and James Collins, a cabinetmaker originally from Limerick, he was born in Dublin and grew up in Harold's Cross before moving to Mount Brown with his family. He worked as a carpenter before joining the National Army and was serving as a private with the 5th Northern

Division when he was killed. His funeral came to Glasnevin on 21 October from the church on James Street accompanied by his parents and siblings.[137]

19 October 1922
Michael Bailey

National Army
ID 81, South New Chapel

Michael Bailey, from Porth in the Rhondda Valley in south Wales, was killed in an ambush in Kill, Co. Kildare in October 1922. A member of the Mechanical Transport Corps he was travelling with a convoy of soldiers from Portobello Barracks to the Curragh when they were ambushed on the Naas Road at Kill. He was shot in the head, the bullet passing through his right eye. He died instantly. Both his father and two brothers also served in the National Army. It was originally intended that his body be returned to Wales for burial in Rhondda Valley, however, he was interred in the National Army plot in Glasnevin.[138]

19 October 1922
Seán O'Sullivan

National Army
ID 80, South New Chapel

Seán O'Sullivan from Glengarriff Parade was sixteen and serving as a company sergeant major in the National Army when he was shot accidentally on Corporation Street in Dublin. At 01.30 on the morning of 18 October O'Sullivan was part of a small group of National Army soldiers from Wellington Barracks who were on patrol in the Amiens Street and Corporation Street area. Having encountered a group of civilians near Shanahan's pub O'Sullivan, Comdt Owens and Sgt Clarke left their car and made their way towards the gathered crowd. According to Clarke, Owens ordered the group home but they refused and verbally insulted him. The commandant then drew his revolver and fired into the air. The bullet was described as having ricocheted off a wall and hit Seán O'Sullivan in the groin. He was brought by car to the Mater Hospital where he was operated on but died of his wounds. His mother. Kate, described that her son had, like his brothers:

> ... been a boy scout associated with the Volunteer movement and subsequently joined the National forces. He was a careful and diligent soldier and was promoted to the rank of Company sergeant major on merit alone. At the time he was killed, he had been on the Staff of Captain Patrick Ryan, who was then Quartermaster, Wellington Barracks. The circumstances of his death were detailed at the inquest

and it transpired that he was shot accidentally by Commandant Owens ... Although the evidence did not show in detail that the bullet fired from Commandant Owen's gun was a ricochet bullet, his father and myself never introduced any matter that would tend to bring the Army or any member of it into disgrace or distrust. Both of us and our children took our risks and responsibilities during the Black and Tan regime and when the Treaty was accepted the very same loyalty and service was given in trying circumstances to the Saorstat Éireann leaders, as was given to them in darker days.[139]

21 October 1922	**National Army**
John Corcoran	*ID 81, South New Chapel*

John Joseph Corcoran, a member of the Dublin Guard, was killed in an ambush in Kerry, aged twenty-nine. Corcoran was born in the home of his family on Kenmare Parade in September 1893, the son of Mary Connell and Matthew Corcoran. He enlisted in the British army in August 1914, using his mother's maiden name as an alias, and remained in the service until November 1921. Spending time in Gallipoli, Egypt and France he was wounded in August 1915 during the landing at Suvla Bay. His use of an alias during his time in the British army may have been linked to a conviction in 1912 for attempted robbery. Having returned home in 1921, John Corcoran worked for the Midland Great Western Railway before enlisting in the National Army in July 1922. He was sent to Kerry where he was killed in October. On the day of his death, Corcoran was travelling with a group of National Army soldiers from Tralee to Killarney. Near Rockfield, north of Killarney, they were ambushed. The National Army and anti-Treaty combatants exchanged fire for twenty minutes during which Corcoran was fatally wounded.[140]

21 October 1922	**National Army**
Nicholas Tobin	*ID 81, South New Chapel*

Nicholas Tobin, a staff captain in the National Army was accidentally killed during a raid on a premises, known as Breffney Mansion, on Gardiner's Place, in Dublin. Born in Cork in November 1898, Nicholas was the son of David Tobin and Mary Agnes Butler. He was also the only brother of Liam Tobin, who at the time of his death was a major general in the National Army.

Nicholas Tobin had been a member of the Irish Volunteers since 1917 and participated in the War of Independence with Dublin Brigade, IRA. He joined the National Army as a lieutenant later being promoted. He was present during the arrest of Brendan Holohan and Eamonn Hughes (*see 7 October 1922*). On 21 October 1922, Tobin took part in a raid on a bead factory that was doubling as a munitions factory. As they surrounded the property, the raiding party split into two. Staff Capt. Patrick Dalton and Capt. Seán Bolger entered at the rear of the property. Bolger described that he ran into the building shouting 'hands up'. Two men there immediately put up their hands but a third hesitated and Bolger fired a shot to one side of him. The bullet travelled through a partition wall and hit Nicholas Tobin who was on the other side, as he had entered the building with the remaining section of the raiding party. The bullet hit Tobin in the chest and entered his heart. He was taken to the Mater Hospital and from there his funeral came to Glasnevin via St Peter's church in Phibsborough. The hearse was followed by his mother, father, brother, sister and many prominent members of the National Army. He was interred in the National Army plot.[141]

23 October 1922   Civilian
Nevins Jackson   **TD 67, South New Chapel**

Nevins Aloysius Vincent Jackson was born in Roscrea, Co. Tipperary in September 1900, the son of Henry Vincent Jackson and Mary Cecilia Nevins. He was educated in Banagher College and at the time of his death resided at Clifton Lodge, Athboy, Co. Meath where he was managing the Clifton Estate. On the day of his death, Nevins travelled to Ardee in Co. Louth with his brother, William, in a car. They visited a friend and attended a theatrical show in the town hall, where she was performing. After the show, they went for a drive with their friend before bringing her back to her home near the courthouse in Ardee. By this time, it was just after 02.00 and the brothers had a problem starting their car. William left the car to help start it, which he did successfully and then got back in. Just as Nevins put the car into gear William heard a bang and turned to his brother to ask him what had happened. Nevins did not reply and the car began rolling back down the hill. As it did so William heard somebody shout 'put out the light'. He managed to stop the car and saw two soldiers approaching. It transpired that the noise of the attempts to start the engine and the bright lights of the car had drawn the attention of members of the National Army on sentry duty. Pte Farrelly and Sgt Gorman went to investigate and they later stated that they shouted halt a number of times before opening fire as they had orders to stop any passing cars. It appeared that the Jackson brothers had not heard the calls due to the noise of the engine. Nevins Jackson was shot in the neck. His funeral came to Glasnevin on 26 October and he was buried in a grave in which his mother, who died six months earlier, had been interred.[142]

23 October 1922   **National Army**
James Marum   *ID 81, South New Chapel*

James Marum, the son of James and Ellen Marum, was originally from Moneycleare in Co. Laois. He was a member of the British army for over eleven years, serving with the Leinster Regiment and Machine Gun Corps. Following his return home after the First World War, he met Isabella Fitzroy while they were both working at a house on York Terrace in Dún Laoghaire. They later married and moved to nearby Blackrock where James was employed as a gardener. He joined the National Army in May 1922 and was fatally wounded in a skirmish with the anti-Treaty IRA that October in Charleville, Co. Cork. He had two children, James and William. Both children died of separate causes within two weeks of one another in 1923 aged one year and two months respectively. Isabella Marum died in England in 1959.[143]

24 October 1922   **National Army**
Thomas O'Shea   *ID 81, South New Chapel*

Thomas O'Shea from Dublin was a member of the National Army's Volunteer Reserve and was accidentally shot dead while on duty at the Curragh Camp. O'Shea had previously been a member of the Royal Munster Fusiliers. In 1917, he married Elizabeth O'Brien and together they had two children, a son and a daughter. Before joining the National Army, he worked as a temporary labourer in the Guinness brewery. On 23 October 1922, O'Shea was stationed at a post at the Curragh Camp when, at about 16.00 he was accidentally shot by a fellow soldier. He was taken to hospital and later died of his injuries. He was buried in the National Army plot in Glasnevin on 27 October 1922. His widow Elizabeth died in 1930 at the age of forty.[144]

25 October 1922   **National Army**
Thomas Kavanagh   *ID 82, South New Chapel*

Thomas Kavanagh from Hanover Street East in Dublin was accidentally shot dead in Cork while serving with the National Army. The son of Edward and

Mary Jane Kavanagh, he worked as a plumber for Morgan and Mooney on Sir John Rogerson's Quay before joining the army. His father, Edward Kavanagh, also died while serving with the National Army – his death was the result of an accident at the North Wall in Dublin, just a few days after the death of his son. Both father and son were buried in the same grave in Glasnevin following a joint funeral at City Quay church.[145]

26 October 1922 — National Army
Joseph O'Riordan — ID 82, South New Chapel

Joseph O'Riordan (O'Reardon) from Sackville Avenue was a member of the National Army stationed at Wellington Barracks who was accidentally shot at the Telephone Exchange at Crown Alley in Dublin. A pre-Truce member of Fianna Éireann, O'Riordan was on duty early on the morning of his death. During the changing of the guard Cpl O'Neill, another member of the National Army, dropped his Webley revolver as he was handing it over to the sergeant on duty. When the gun hit the floor it fired and the bullet hit Joseph O'Riordan, who slowly slumped to the floor. He was taken by ambulance to Mercer's Hospital where he was treated, but died later that day at around 17.00.[146]

28 October 1922 — National Army
Joseph Byrne — ID 82, South New Chapel

On 3 November 1922, the funeral of a soldier identified as Joseph Byrne from 74 Rialto Buildings came to Glasnevin. According to newspaper reports Byrne, who was attached to the Dublin Guard, was killed during a successful anti-Treaty IRA attack on Clifden in Galway. The attack resulted in the capture of the barracks in a fight that lasted some ten hours. In 1924, Mary Morgan, the owner of a boarding house on Lower Gloucester Street, made an application for a pension for a Peter Byrne who was killed on 28 October 1922 serving with the Dublin Guard. Morgan claimed that she was Byrne's aunt and his foster mother as his mother had died and his father abandoned him. She believed he had been killed in Buttevant, Cork. Mary Morgan was granted a dependent's gratuity, however, in 1933 a man named Michael Hanley (Hanlon) from Church Street wrote a letter claiming that the person buried in Glasnevin was actually his son, also named Michael Hanley. He described that he was in England when he was killed and was not informed of his death. He also stated that his other children, who were living in Dublin at the time, were also unaware of his burial. Michael Hanley's application to the Army Pensions Department came too late under the terms of the Army Pensions Act and no further investigation was made into his claims.[147]

1 November 1922	**National Army**
Joseph Vincent Martin	*ID 82, South New Chapel*

Joseph Martin, from Arbour Terrace in Dublin, was accidentally shot dead while on duty with the National Army in Beresford Barracks at the Curragh. On the evening of his death Martin was one of the guard stationed at the power station in the barracks. Pte John Scully, a fellow member of the guard, accidentally fired his rifle and Martin was hit in the head being fatally injured. John Scully was exonerated from any blame in relation to the incident.[148]

4 November 1922	**National Army**
Thomas Gallagher	*ID 82, South New Chapel*

Thomas Gallagher, an eighteen-year-old medic with the National Army died of injuries received during an attack by the anti-Treaty IRA in Ballineen in Co. Cork. During the engagement, there were a number of fatalities on both sides. Gallagher was born in April 1905 in his family home on Paradise Row, Kingstown (Dún Laoghaire). He was the son of Thomas Gallagher and Mary Keegan. Thomas' father died suddenly in August 1906 so he grew up living with his aunt, Mary Jane Gallagher, a grocer in nearby Kill of the Grange. He was educated at Blackrock College and during the War of Independence had been a member of the Deansgrange Company of Fianna Éireann. He was a college student before joining the National Army. At the time of his death, he was a medic with the Army Medical Corps, attached to C Company, 15th Infantry Battalion, and stationed at Ballineen. Early on the morning of 4 November 1922 a large and concerted attack on the garrison there took place. A National Army officer described that:

> After half an hour's fighting there was a soldier named Fox wounded. Gallagher was going to his assistance when he was hit by Thompson machine-gun fire. He staggered across the road and was taken into the house of Mrs M. Sullivan, Ballineen, where he died the following day.

A doctor who tended to him in the hours before his death described his wounds as being 'terrible'. He had been shot through the lungs and the bullets had opened his chest. His remains were returned to Dublin by boat and he was buried in the National Army plot in Glasnevin on 9 November 1922.[149]

8 November 1922	Anti-Treaty Irish Republican Army
James Spain	*TK 105, St Patrick's*

James Spain was shot dead following an attack by members of the anti-Treaty Irish Republican Army on Wellington Barracks in Dublin. Aged twenty-two at the time of his death, he was born in 1900 at Harty Place in Dublin, the son of Francis Spain and Christina Kenny. He joined the Irish Volunteers in 1917 and in 1921 was made a second lieutenant while serving with A Company, 1st Battalion, Dublin Brigade. Taking the anti-Treaty side during the Civil War, he became a member of the Active Service Unit. On the day of his death, Spain was part of a group of anti-Treaty volunteers, under the command of William Roe, who attacked Wellington Barracks, where members of the National Army were stationed. They took positions at a height in houses over-looking the barracks and opened fire on the soldiers who were attending morning parade in its square. A panic ensued as the bullets rained down on the ranks and a number of soldiers were hit. The attackers dispersed quickly, some wounded in an exchange of fire, pursued by members of the National Army.

Sarah Anne Doleman, a lady in her seventies, who lived at 22 Donore Road, less than a kilometre from the barracks, was one of those who gave evidence at the inquest into Spain's death. She stated that on that morning she was feeding chickens in her garden when Spain came to her gate and pleaded with her saying 'For God's sake, let me in'. He then limped into her house, throwing himself onto a sofa. Doleman asked Spain what he was running for and he replied that he was blamed for the attack on the barracks and asked if she could see the soldiers coming. By this time members of the National Army were approaching the house and Spain exclaimed, 'Jesus, Mary and Joseph, help me, if they get me they'll shoot me. They know me'. When the soldiers entered the house, they took James Spain through the back garden as he asked them not to shoot him. He was brought onto Susan Terrace at the rear of the house and here Mary O'Byrne, who lived there, saw the National Army soldiers with James Spain in front of them. O'Byrne hurried into her house and closed the door behind her. A few minutes later, she heard shots being fired. The IRA report relating to the incident stated that before being shot Spain shouted,

'Christy, don't shoot me'. It surmised that this was Christy Clarke, a member of the National Army, formerly of Dublin Brigade, IRA. James Spain's body was brought to the Meath Hospital where it was found he had five bullet wounds to his body, two of which were to his head. A reporter who saw his body at the hospital described him as wearing:

> ... a dark tweed overcoat, a well-worn, dark grey whipcord suit, with a right-angle repaired reef in the right knee of the trousers. He wore black shoes and brown cashmere socks. He was clean shaven and had dark brown wavy hair, brushed back from the forehead. No papers were found in the clothes which contained only a fountain pen, a packet of Player's cigarettes, a box of matches and an unmarked handkerchief. There was a large wound in the back of the head near the right ear and the right leg was practically severed across above the knee torn and lacerated in a terrible manner as though the unfortunate man was caught in a burst of machine gun fire.

The inquest into his death returned an open verdict in accordance with the medical evidence that James Spain had died from 'shock and haemorrhage following laceration of the brain and multiple wounds caused by bullets'. His funeral came to Glasnevin from the Carmelite church on Whitefriar Street on 11 November 1922. A large cortege with members of Cumann na mBan marched behind the hearse and volleys fired over the grave.[150]

11 November 1922	**National Army**
Frederick Weatherup	*C 165, Garden*

Frederick Stephen Weatherup, a twenty-three-year-old member of the Military Police, was accidentally shot at Mountjoy Jail on 20 October 1922. He was born in September 1899 in a house on Emerald Street in Dublin where his parents, Maria Murphy and Frederick Weatherup, had lived as neighbours before marrying in 1895. His father, from Monkstown in Dublin, was a former member of the British army turned shipping agent and Frederick junior grew up living on North Strand Road. During the First World War he joined the British army and was sent to the Household Brigade Officer Cadet Battalion to receive training as an officer. Following this training, he was appointed as a second lieutenant in the Royal Irish Regiment in March 1918. However, he only served for a few months before being placed on the retired list and returned home to Dublin. Before enlisting in the National Army, he worked as a clerk in the Ports and Docks engineering office. On the day he was wounded, Weatherup was in a room at Mountjoy with his friend, and fellow Military Policeman, James Hamilton. A newspaper report detailed what happened next:

He (Hamilton) and deceased sat down on a bed next to the door. Deceased had a revolver in his hand. He was tricking with it. He was saying how easily it could go off. They were talking about getting a pass out that evening. Both of them stood up and witness took off his belt. While doing so he snatched at deceased's revolver, when his own went off.

Frederick Weatherup had been shot in the mouth. He was brought to the Mater Hospital where he was treated for his injuries. While there he wrote a letter stating that his wound was the result of accident and his friend James Hamilton was not to blame. He died three weeks later. His cause of death was recorded as 'meningitis following bullet wound accidentally received'.[151]

17 November 1922   Anti-Treaty Irish Republican Army
Peter Cassidy   *QD 35, South New Chapel*

Peter Cassidy was one four men executed at Kilmainham Gaol on 17 November 1922. The four were the first members of the anti-Treaty IRA to be executed following the passing of the Public Safety Act in September 1922. The act sanctioned executions, and other serious punishments, for taking up arms against the state or being in possession of guns or explosives. Those accused would face a military court, which could pass sentencing. The act was an attempt by the pro-Treaty side to end the conflict, which had fragmented into a potentially lengthy guerrilla campaign.

Peter Cassidy was born on 22 February 1901 at 18.00 in the home of his parents on Nicholas Avenue in Smithfield. He was a twin, his sister Bridget being born ten minutes after him. He was the son of Bridget Grogan and Thomas Cassidy. His parents were originally from Kildare and had married in 1889 in the pro-cathedral. His father worked as a brewery labourer and Peter and Bridget were the youngest of five children who survived into adulthood. His elder brother Thomas was killed whilst serving near Ypres with the Irish Guards. On the night of 2 July 1916 while taking part in a trench raid on German positions he was one of five men who never returned and whose bodies were never recovered.

Peter Cassidy grew up on Usher Street, off Usher's Quay, where the family had moved while he was still quite young. He worked in the electricity department of Dublin Corporation and served with the IRA during the War of Independence, being a member of the 3rd Battalion, Dublin Brigade, IRA. During the Civil War, he was serving as a section commander. Another of his brothers, James, was also a member of the same unit having joined the anti-Treaty IRA in August

The funeral of anti-Treaty IRA volunteers executed during the Civil War to Glasnevin in October 1924. This image is reproduced with the kind permission of the National Museum of Ireland. (Above and below.)

Relatives and mourners follow the coffin of an anti-Treaty volunteer as it is brought from the mortuary chapel to the Republican Plot for interment on 30 October 1924. This image is reproduced with the kind permission of the National Museum of Ireland.

1922. Peter was arrested on 27 October 1922 and was placed on trial at a military court in Wellington Barracks on 9 November 1922. He was charged with being in possession of a revolver 'without proper authority' under the Public Safety Act. He was found guilty and executed by firing squad in the stonebreakers' yard in Kilmainham Gaol eight days later, along with three other men who had been found guilty of the same offence. He was a long time friend and neighbour of John Gaffney who was also executed on the same day *(see below)*. Like others executed during the Civil War, Peter Cassidy was buried where his sentence was carried out. On 30 October 1924, the remains of John Murphy, Richard Twohig, Patrick Farrelly, Joseph Spooner, James O'Rourke, James Fisher, John Gaffney, Rory O'Connor, Erskine Childers and Peter Cassidy were interred in Glasnevin, having been exhumed from their original burial places. Their funeral was a joint one taking place at the Carmelite church on Whitefriar Street, except for Erskine Childers, before proceeding to Glasnevin in pouring rain. Just after 15.00, six lorry loads of National Army soldiers and a car with officers arrived at Glasnevin ahead of the cortege and took up positions within the cemetery alongside detectives. After the ten coffins were placed together in adjoining graves in the Republican Plot, P.J. Ruttledge delivered an oration. As the ceremony concluded,

A guard of honour at the funeral of anti-Treaty volunteers executed during the Civil War. This image is reproduced with the kind permission of the National Museum of Ireland.

The interment of anti-Treaty volunteers executed during the Civil War in the Republican Plot. Shortly after this photograph was taken shots were fired over the grave and a confrontation occurred with members of the National Army and police. This image is reproduced with the kind permission of the National Museum of Ireland.

the Last Post was sounded and then six men stepped forward and took out revolvers. A newspaper account described what happened next:

> The leader suddenly called out: 'Squad, Ready, Present, Fire'. The revolvers were jerked overhead and a volley echoed around the graveyard. A second volley was then fired and preparations for the discharge of a third had been made, when there was commotion among a group of women who ran away screaming from the scene. It was observed that a party of detectives and army officers in mufti, with drawn revolvers, were endeavouring to reach the firing squad. The last volley was hurriedly fired and the armed men quickly dispersed. The passage of the detectives was impeded by the crowd and this obstruction enabled the firing party to get rid of their arms and mingle with the gathering. Darkness was beginning to fall but the detectives succeeded in effecting an arrest. A general stampede ensued. Troops with fixed bayonets began to close in, and the spectators, in a headlong rush from the scene, trampled on and smashed to pieces the glass wreaths on the surrounding graves. More shots were fired, but in the excitement and confusion it was impossible to gather by whom. The troops held up a number of men and searched them but made no arrests ... and captured at least three revolvers, which had been discarded in the cemetery.[152]

17 November 1922	Anti-Treaty Irish Republican Army
James Fisher	*QD 36, South New Chapel*

James Fisher was born in April 1903 in 8 Bow Lane, he was the son of Thomas Fisher and Mary Jane Christian. His father, who worked as a messenger in the offices of Guinness, was born in England and his mother was from Dublin. He was the second son of Thomas and Mary Jane to be named James, the elder James having died aged nine months in 1902. The family later moved to Belview (Bellevue) Buildings and Echlin Street, off James's Street. They settled in the latter for many years and resided there in 1922. James was a volunteer with 2nd Battalion, Dublin Brigade, and was found guilty at a military court of 8 November 1922 of being in possession of revolver 'without proper authority' and sentenced to death. He was executed on the morning of 17 November 1922 in Kilmainham Gaol. In his final letter to his mother he wrote:

> Dear Mother, I am now awaiting the supreme penalty at 7 o'c in the morning. But I am perfectly happy, because I've seen the priest and I am going to die a good Catholic and a soldier of the Irish Republic. Don't worry or cry for me, but pray for the repose of my soul and my three comrades. I asked to see you, but they said they would see what they could do. Ask all my friends and comrades to pray for me and Dick and my other two comrades. Mother I would just love one look at all the faces at home, yours above all, but seemly that is denied me. I get everything I want now, which as you know is the usual stunt. Mother, my heart grieves for one look at your dear face. But please God I will meet you and them all in heaven. I picture how this will affect you, but mother

don't fret, for remember I am happy. The priest here is going to get me to hear my confession and I will receive at the altar in the morning. Lord Jesus give me courage in my last moments. If I had only got told of my sentence I would have been well prepared before now. Oh mother if I could only see you, just again. Don't fret mother because I am happy. To my mother I dearly love. Goodbye, Goodbye, Goodbye. We will meet again in heaven please God. Mother, I am to die for Ireland. God strengthen you in ordeal mother.

The death of James was one of two in a few months for the Fisher family. His sister Kate died, aged twenty-two, in January 1923 from tuberculosis.[153]

17 November 1922	**Anti-Treaty Irish Republican Army**
John Gaffney	*QD 36, South New Chapel*

John Gaffney, from Usher's Quay in Dublin, was a friend and neighbour of Peter Cassidy (*see above*). Both were executed together by firing squad, alongside two other members of the anti-Treaty IRA on 17 November 1922 in Kilmainham Gaol. He was born in November 1902 in 5 Earl Street and was the son of Helena, or Ellen, Whelan. Ellen and John had married in 1890 in Dublin. His father, John, had been a member of the British army for four years during the First World War with the Royal Irish Fusiliers and the Royal Dublin Fusiliers. He served with the 5th Battalion of the latter when it was involved in the suppression of the 1916 Rising. John Gaffney junior worked alongside his father in the electricity department of Dublin Corporation and had joined the IRA in 1921. He was arrested on 27 October 1922 and placed on trial on 9 November charged with being in possession of a revolver 'without proper authority'. His execution took place exactly a week before his twentieth birthday. Ellen Gaffney described that the death of John had '... broke his father's heart with the result he died shortly after'. His father and mother are also buried in Glasnevin Cemetery.[154]

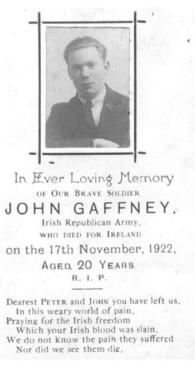

In Ever Loving Memory
OF OUR BRAVE SOLDIER
JOHN GAFFNEY.
Irish Republican Army,
WHO DIED FOR IRELAND
on the 17th November, 1922,
AGED 20 YEARS.
R. I. P.

Dearest PETER and JOHN you have left us,
In this weary world of pain,
Praying for the Irish freedom
Which your Irish blood was slain,
We do not know the pain they suffered
Nor did we see them die.

Courtesy of Kilmainham Gaol.

17 November 1922   **Anti-Treaty Irish Republican Army**

Richard Twohig   *QD 36, South New Chapel*

Richard Twohig, the fourth of those executed in Kilmainham on 17 November 1922, was aged nineteen at the time of his death. His father and grandfather were both born in India. Richard's father, James Twohig, had been born in Bangalore (Bengaluru) India when his grandfather was serving there with the British army and James had followed the same path enlisting in the Royal Artillery at the age of fifteen. He served in South Africa for a short period during the Anglo-Boer War before coming to Ireland in 1900 where he was stationed in Limerick. In 1902, he married Josephine Denihan, a local woman, and Richard was born there in December that year. Richard's mother died in October 1905, aged twenty-six, and James Twohig re-married in Dublin the following year. Mary King became Richard's step-mother and following James' discharge from the army they resided in Mary's family home, 4 St James Avenue. Mary later described that '... I reared Richard Twohig from the age of three years and looked upon him as my own son. I also gave him to Ireland.' James Twohig again served with British army during the First World War being amongst the first of its members to land in France in August 1914. Initially serving with the Army Service Corps, he later transferred to the 2nd Battalion Royal Inniskilling Fusiliers. He died on 8 December 1917 having been wounded while his battalion were trying to hold shell holes and parts of trenches in an area near a position known as Teall Cottage north of Passchendaele in Belgium.

In 1918, Richard Twohig joined Fianna Éireann before becoming a member of Dublin Brigade IRA in 1920. He also worked as a blacksmith's helper in the Inchicore Railway Works. Taking the anti-Treaty side during the Civil War, he was arrested on Hanbury Lane on 23 October 1922. He was found guilty in a military court on 8 November of being in possession of a revolver 'without proper authority' and was executed nine days later. Mary Twohig was denied a pension under the Army Pensions Act in respect of the death of Richard as the act made no accommodation for step-mothers as dependents. In a letter she noted the contrasting circumstances that led to her not being entitled to an Irish pension while receiving one from the British Ministry of Pensions to support all her children, including Richard Twohig, until he turned sixteen.[155]

19 November 1922   **Civilian**
John Crosbie   *WC 27, Garden*

John Crosbie, an employee in Jameson's Distillery on Bow Street, was shot and fatally wounded by a member of the National Army. On the night of 11 November 1922, members of the Army arrived at Queen Street and searched the house in which Crosbie resided. According to Kathleen Mooney who lived in the same house, a soldier came to Crosbie and began talking to him before returning to the army lorry. A few moments later, another soldier came back to Crosbie lifted a revolver and shot him. John Crosbie fell in to the arms of Mooney and was taken to hospital by the members of the National Army. The person who fired the shot was immediately identifiable to Kathleen Mooney as he lived on the same street. His name was George Geoghegan, a sergeant in the National Army. John Crosbie died of his injuries eight days later in the Richmond Hospital. George Geoghegan was later convicted of manslaughter by a military court. He was sentenced to two years imprisonment.[156]

20 November 1922   **National Army**
John Foley   *ID 83, South New Chapel*

John Foley from Caragh Lake in Co. Kerry was fatally injured in the Four Courts Hotel and died of his wounds in the Jervis Street Hospital. Foley worked as a farm labourer and in an iron ore works in south Wales before joining the National Army. According to his family, he also served during the War of Independence with the IRA in Kerry. On the day after his death an inquest was held in the City Morgue; it heard evidence that Foley was a member of a National Army guard at the Four Courts Hotel. On the evening that he was wounded he was in the guardroom when another member of the guard, Laurence Troy, came in having been relieved from duty. Troy was in the process of taking his revolver from its holster and placing it on the table when it accidentally discharged and hit Foley.[157]

23 November 1922   **National Army**
Francis Mullen   *ID 83, South New Chapel*

Francis Mullen from Dublin was accidentally killed in Kerry in November 1922. A carter before joining the National Army he had married Sarah Devlin just over a year prior to his death. A report into the circumstances surrounding his death stated that:

> Deceased was stationed at Lixnaw for a short period before his death. On the night of the 23rd November 1922 in company with another soldier, he proceeded from the Military Post to a public house nearby. As they were about to return from Barracks they commandeered a pony and trap, which were outside the public house door and drove to their quarters. When approaching the sentry they were ordered to halt, but whether or not they heard the challenge cannot be ascertained, at any rate they continued to drive on. Lieut Kavanagh, who was standing near the sentry fired from his revolver and shot Mullen dead. This officer took them to be irregulars and under the circumstances, no blame can be apportioned to him.

Francis Mullen was buried in the National Army plot in Glasnevin following a joint funeral with Sgt Maj. Thomas McCann *(see 24 November 1922)* at the Carmelite church on Whitefriar Street.[158]

24 November 1922	**Anti-Treaty Irish Republican Army**
Robert Erskine Childers	*QD 37, South New Chapel*

Robert Erskine Childers, known by his middle name, was born in London in June 1870, the son of Robert Caesar Childers and Anna Barton. Anna's family, the Bartons, were a well-known Anglo-Irish landed family with a large estate in Wicklow. His father died when Erskine was aged six and he moved to live with his mother's family at Glendalough House. Anna Barton died in 1883 and Erskine was educated at Haileybury School and Trinity College Cambridge before entering the civil service. In 1899, following the outbreak of the Second Anglo-Boer War, he enlisted in the City of London Imperial Volunteers and was sent to South Africa for service with the rank of driver.

Following the war, Childers came to prominence as a writer. His first book, *In the ranks of the C.I.V.* drew on his experiences during the Boer War. However, it was his second, *The Riddle of the Sands*, a fictional thriller, that brought him great success. A tale of espionage it drew on Childers own knowledge and experience and told, forebodingly, of a plan by the German Empire to mount a seaborne invasion of the United Kingdom. A pioneering piece of writing it is one of the earliest examples of spy fiction. It proved to be very popular and contributed to the debate on military preparedness in Britain in the wake of the Boer War and increasing tensions closer to home. In the same year that it was published, 1903, Childers met Molly Osgood during a visit to the United States and they married the following year. In the late 1900s, Childers turned his attention to issues of Irish nationalism and self-determination. Increasingly committed to the Irish cause it was Erskine and Molly's yacht, the *Asgard*, that was used in the Howth gun-running in July 1914. It was also his organisation and seamanship that contributed significantly to the project being a success.

A member of the Royal Naval Volunteer Reserve Childers was commissioned as an observer lieutenant the following month on the outbreak of the First World War. The varied work he carried out during the war was quite remarkable. Initially he was attached to the Royal Naval Air Service as an observer on *HMS Engadine*. During this time he was mentioned in dispatches for his role in the RNAS air raid on Zeppelin sheds near Cuxhaven on Christmas day 1914. In 1915, he served on board *HMS Ben-my-Chree* in the Dardanelles before taking up intelligence duties in 1916. It was for his service during his time on *Ben-my-Chree* that he was awarded the Distinguished Service Cross. The award of the medal was formally published in April 1917 and the citation read:

> In recognition of his services with the R.N.A.S. for the period January-May 1916. During this time he acted as an observer in many important air reconnaissances, showing remarkable aptitude for observing and for collating the results of his observation.

Amongst other work, he continued in his role as observer throughout 1916 and carried out a flight in October 1916 over the Frisian Islands, just off the coast of Germany. It is probable that Childers' knowledge of the islands, as he had demonstrated in *The Riddle of the Sands*, led to him being chosen for that particular piece of work. He was made a temporary lieutenant commander in December 1916 before being sent for duty with the Coastal Motor Boats based in the English Channel. The experimental boats were small sized vessels that were capable of carrying a torpedo but were also light enough to skim over the minefields that protected the Imperial German Navy in their bases. He was formally transferred to the RNAS in 1917 and sent to their seaplane base in Dunkirk but left service to act as a secretariat to the Irish Convention 1917. In April 1918, following the end of the convention, he returned to the British armed forces and was posted to the naval section of air intelligence at the Air Ministry. His final posting was as an intelligence officer with the Royal Air Force where he was involved in formulating plans for a bombing raid on Berlin. The plans were never implemented due to the armistice in November 1918.

Following the war, Childers moved to Ireland and his family soon followed him. He became preoccupied with Ireland and Irish independence and worked with Sinn Féin in producing and promoting propaganda to bring attention to the war in Ireland. He held the office of director of propaganda for a short period in 1921, in the absence of Desmond FitzGerald. In the same year he was elected unopposed for Sinn Féin, alongside his cousin Robert Barton, in the Kildare-Wicklow constituency and took his seat in the second Dáil. He was present at the Anglo-Irish Treaty negotiations as one of the Irish secretaries and ultimately became an outspoken critic of the agreement. Despite his work in Ireland and unwavering nationalism, Childers struggled to shed the shadow of his background and the label of a former British intelligence officer. In the Treaty debates, Arthur Griffith famously declared to Childers that 'I will not reply to any damned Englishman in this Assembly'. In response, Childers stated that '... I am not going to defend my nationality, but I would be delighted to show the President privately that I am not, in the true sense of the word, an Englishman, as he knows. He banged the table. If he had banged the table before Lloyd George in the way he banged it here, things might have been different'. Although ostensibly a member of the anti-Treaty IRA, his involvement in military matters was marginal. Charles Townshend describes that '... although the government affected to believe that he was the *éminence grise* of the anti-Treaty movement, he had no formal place in the command structure – he was described as a "staff captain". He was as he had been during the Anglo-Irish war, a propagandist.'

Erskine Childers was arrested in November 1922 at Glendalough House in Wicklow and charged with being in possession of a pistol 'without proper authority' under the Public Safety Act. As somebody who prioritised words over weapons, it is unsurprising when he was arrested that Childers was only armed with a small pistol which was a present given to him by Michael Collins before the Civil War. Regardless, he was placed on trial at Portobello Barracks on 17 November 1922, found guilty, and sentenced to death. He appealed his sentence but to no avail and was executed by firing squad at 07.00 on the morning of 24 November 1922 at Beggars Bush Barracks. He was buried there and was exhumed in 1924 when he was buried in Glasnevin in a joint funeral with others executed during the Civil War *(see 17 November 1922)*.[159]

24 November 1922   National Army
Thomas McCann   *ID 83, South New Chapel*

Thomas McCann from Francis Street in Dublin was killed, along with another member of the National Army, in a mine explosion in Cork in November 1922.

McCann was formerly a member of the Loyal North Lancashire Regiment, having served in Gallipoli from June 1915. He finished that war with the King's Liverpool Regiment as a warrant officer class *II*. He was serving as a sergeant major in the National Army at the time of his death and was engaged in trying to make a trap land mine safe on Ballyvolane Road when the mine exploded. The National Army had initially tried to explode the mine at a distance without success. The assumption was made that the mine was a dud, however, when digging beside the mine it exploded, killing McCann and another soldier. A military inquiry into his death found that '... deceased died from destruction of vital parts, caused by the explosion of a trap mine on the public highway at Ballyvolane by some persons ...' His remains were returned to Dublin on the City of Cork Steam Packet Company's ship *Bandon* and brought to Portobello Barracks before burial in Glasnevin. He left a widow and three children.[160]

26 November 1922	**Anti-Treaty Irish Republican Army**
William Graham	*HI 131, St Patrick's*

Born on 13 January 1900, William Graham was the son of William Graham and Mary Lennon. He was born in Cornmarket in Dublin and the family later moved to Ross Road where his father, an engine operator originally from Wexford, died in 1911. Born at the height of the Anglo-Boer War, Graham acquired the nickname Kruger, after the Boer leader Paul Kruger, something which was not unusual for those who associated themselves with the pro-Boer movement of the time. During the Civil War, he carried out operations as a member of 3rd Battalion, Dublin Brigade, including an attempt to blow up Oriel House on 30 October 1922. On the evening of his death in November 1922, Graham took part in an operation with his battalion. It was their intention to take arms from the members of the guard at Harcourt Street Railway Station. The operation did not go to plan and Stephen Keys, a friend of Graham and 3rd Battalion member gave an account of events that evening:

> The next engagement was sticking up an armed guard at Harcourt St. railway. This was a battalion job and mostly 'A' Company men were on it. I had another car on this occasion, an open car. They were to bring down the rifles from the railway and load them into the car. I said, 'Make sure you don't put them with the muzzles facing me!' Willie Rowe was on this job and he shot someone which disorganised the plan and spoiled the job. I drove around, thinking I would pick up some men who might be straggling around the place. In the meantime, Kruger Graham, was captured by the Free State Army in Leeson St. and they shot him dead on the street. They got a gun on him.

Following the raid, National Army soldiers had searched the area for anti-Treaty volunteers who had taken part in the attempt to take the arms. One army tender proceeded along Hatch Street and turned right onto Leeson Street towards the canal. The soldiers noticed three men on the right side of the street and stopped them. One of the soldiers stated at the inquest into Graham's death that on searching him he found a Webley revolver, that William Graham had made an attempt to take his weapon and he was shot. The only witnesses who gave specific information relating to the shooting were military. A young girl who was present on the night said she heard somebody shouting 'Put your hands up' and then saw the soldiers beginning to search a man. She heard a shot soon afterwards and Graham fall to the ground. She did not see where the shot had come from.[161]

27 November 1922	National Army
Christopher Grehan	*ID 83, South New Chapel*

Christopher James Grehan, a member of the National Army from George's Place, died of wounds having been accidentally shot. His father was a printer and Christopher followed him into the family business. Together they owned and operated the Phoenix Press on Mountjoy Square. However, they were put out of business in July 1922 when their premises was intentionally attacked and destroyed by armed men. He later joined the National Army. On 26 November 1922, some volunteers of the anti-Treaty IRA attempted to attack and disarm members of the National Army at Harcourt Street Station (*see above*). Shots were fired and confusion reigned. In the immediate aftermath, Christopher Grehan and an-

A propoganda postcard of Thomas Whelan (see 14 March 1921) printed and distributed by the Phoenix Press which was owned and operated by Christopher Grehan and his father until it was destroyed in July 1922. **Courtesy of the National Library of Ireland.**

other member of the National Army were walking nearby in plain clothes. As they passed Harcourt Street Station, one of the members of the guard there spotted that they were carrying revolvers. It was reported and as Christopher Grehan turned into Hatch Street, Pte Duggan, one of the guards, shot him. He died the following day at St Vincent's Hospital. He was aged twenty-three at the time of his death.[162]

30 November 1922	Anti-Treaty Irish Republican Army
Patrick Farrelly	*QD 36, South New Chapel*

Patrick Farrelly was born in July 1903 in 17 Chancery Lane, the son of Thomas Farrelly and Eliza Butler. His mother died in 1910 when he was aged seven and his father left Dublin in 1914 to go to England where he was engaged in munitions work in Liverpool. When Patrick's elder brother enlisted in the British army during the First World War, Patrick was the only member of his family left in Dublin. He remained living in Chancery Lane and worked as a packer and a chemist's assistant. During the War of Independence, he joined the IRA and served with the 3rd Battalion, Dublin Brigade. He took the anti-Treaty side during the Civil War and on 30 October 1922 was involved in an attack on Oriel House. On that night, an attempt was made to blow up the headquarters of the Criminal Investigation Department. Over twenty members of the anti-Treaty IRA, including six men responsible for setting and detonating the bombs, took part in the operation. It was planned that a number of bombs would be placed but as it transpired only one exploded. The attack was a dramatic one and caused significant damage but did not come close to demolishing any part of the large building. The CID suffered no fatalities during the bombing and the attackers were pursued when National Army reinforcements arrived at the scene. Patrick Farrelly was arrested on Erne Street, along with John Murphy and Joseph Spooner (*see below*). He was tried by military court on 14 November 1922 and found guilty of being in possession of a bomb 'without proper authority'. He was sentenced to death and was executed in Beggars Bush Barracks on the morning of 30 November. Originally buried where he was executed he was reinterred in Glasnevin in 1924 (*see 17 November 1922*).[163]

30 November 1922   **Anti-Treaty Irish Republican Army**
John Leo Murphy   *QD 37, South New Chapel*

John Murphy from Belview (Bellevue) Buildings was the only son of John and Margaret Murphy. A clerk for the Great Southern and Western Railway he originally joined Fianna Éireann in 1918 and then joined 3rd Battalion, Dublin Brigade, in 1921. A member of the anti-Treaty IRA during the Civil War he participated in the attack on Oriel House on 30 October 1922 (*see above*) and was arrested with Patrick Farrelly and Joseph Spooner on Erne Street in the aftermath. He was tried in a military court on 14 November 1922, charged with being in possession of two bombs 'without proper authority'. Having been found guilty, he was executed by firing squad in Beggars Bush Barracks at 08.15 on 30 November 1922.[164]

30 November 1922   **Anti-Treaty Irish Republican Army**
Joseph Spooner   *QD 35, South New Chapel*

Joseph Spooner, from McCaffrey's Estate, Mount Brown, was executed in Beggars Bush Barracks in November 1922. The son of John Spooner and Margaret Caldwell he was the eldest of seven children. He had joined Fianna Éireann before becoming a member of the IRA. Serving with 3rd Battalion, Dublin Brigade, he took the anti-Treaty side during the Civil War and was arrested alongside Patrick Farrelly and John Murphy following the attack on Oriel House in October 1922. He was placed on trial on 14 November and found guilty of being in possession of revolver 'without proper authority'.

In 1934, Francis Stuart published an account of the executions of Joseph Spooner and the other two men he had been arrested with. Patrick Hunt, who witnessed the executions, had passed the account to him. A graphic description it nonetheless gives a sense of the reality of the executions:

> They came out without hats and I noticed that Joe [Spooner] hadn't bothered to lace his boots all the way up. It must be funny putting on your boots and knowing you'll never take them off again. There was an officer with a gun in his hand walking beside them. It was very muddy in the yard. The other two boys had rosary beads hanging from their hands, but Joe had his hands in his pockets and his shoulders hunched up. The sergeant said something to him and he shook his head. Then the sergeant stepped back and took the gun out of his holster. The firing squad was standing about fifteen paces away. When the officer gave the word, they brought their rifles up to their shoulders. The two boys had their eyes shut and Joe was looking at the mud just in front of his boots. There were tears streaming down the face of one of the boys from

under his shut eyelids. There was rain on their faces too but I saw the tears. When the soldiers fired, he put his hands to his chest and tore at his coat as though he wanted to open it. He swayed forward without falling. His coat came open with the buttons ripped off and the blood ran down his hands. Then he fell on his knees with his head bowed over the other boy who had fallen sideways, his face in a pool. Joe had fallen back against the wall but his feet were still firm on the ground and he was choking with blood and spittle coming out of his mouth and his face turning dark. The other boy fell from his knees and the two boys lay across one another. The sergeant put his gun to the side of Joe's head and fired four or five shots into it. The side of his head was torn open, then he fell sideways with his shoulders slipping down along the wall.

Joseph Spooner was interred in the Republican Plot in Glasnevin in October 1924, following a joint funeral with others executed during the Civil War.[165]

8 December 1922	**Anti-Treaty Irish Republican Army**
Rory O'Connor	*QD 36, South New Chapel*

Rory O'Connor, one of the most well-known figures of the Irish Civil War, was executed in December 1922 and is buried in the Republican Plot in Glasnevin. Born in 23 Kildare Street in November 1882, Roderick (Rory) O'Connor was the son of John O'Connor, a solicitor and Julia O'Farrell. He attended St Mary's College in Dublin and Clongowes Wood College in Kildare before studying at the National University where he graduated as an engineer. In 1911, he moved to Canada where he worked for the Canadian Pacific and Canadian Northern railways. In 1915, he returned to Dublin where he took up a position with Dublin Corporation. O'Connor had been interested in nationalist politics since his time as a student and was a member of the Gaelic League and the Irish Volunteers as well as being involved with the IRB. Basing himself with the Plunkett family in Kimmage, he became increasingly involved in nationalist politics and training with the Volunteers. Before the 1916 Rising he was involved in the printing and distribution of the infamous 'Castle document'. The document was an order for the suppression of nationalist organisations, which it was claimed had been issued by Dublin Castle and was circulated by O'Connor and Joseph Plunkett in an attempt to provide the impetus for armed insurrection. Initially successful in that regard it was soon regarded by Eoin MacNeill as a forgery and he countermanded mobilisation orders that had been made to the Irish Volunteers. The order affected the numbers that turned out on Easter week. During the rebellion O'Connor was attached to the GPO garrison. Acting as an intelligence officer, he travelled to various parts of the city during the week and was wounded but evaded capture following the surrender. In the years that followed O'Connor was a prominent figure in Sinn Féin, the Irish Volunteers and later IRA. Amongst other activities, he continued to put his experience as an engineer to use acting as director of engineering, overseeing the strategy associated with the use of explosives during the War of Independence. He was also involved in the planning of prison escapes and the use of sabotage as a strategic tool for the IRA in England. In 1922, O'Connor became a figure of leadership amongst IRA officers in voicing opposition to the Anglo-Irish Treaty. Unyielding in his republican outlook, O'Connor, alongside Liam Mellows, was one of the *de facto* leaders of the anti-Treaty forces that captured strategic buildings in Dublin, including the Four Courts. The situation eventually descended into Civil War, formally marked by the pro-Treaty assault on the Four Courts and the beginning of the Battle of Dublin on 28 June 1922.

Following the fall of the Four Courts and his surrender O'Connor was arrested and imprisoned. He remained in Mountjoy Jail until December 1922. That month, following a number of executions of members of the anti-Treaty IRA, Seán Hales, the pro-Treaty TD, was assassinated. The next morning following an order by the Irish Free State government cabinet, Rory O'Connor and three others were taken from their cells and executed by firing squad in Mountjoy. These executions differed from earlier ones in that they were simply retaliatory. The men had no connection to the shooting of Hales. Neither did they benefit from the façade of a military trial under the Public Safety Act, which was adopted after their initial imprisonment. Amongst the cabinet members who assented to the executions was Kevin O'Higgins. He was a close friend of Rory O'Connor and just over a year earlier, in October 1921, O'Connor had acted as best man at his wedding in Whitefriar Street church in Dublin. Ernest Blythe later described the meeting at which the decision was made:

> After a very few minutes' discussion Mr Cosgrave proceeded to put the question round the table to ascertain whether or not those present agreed with the proposal. I was one of the first two or three to vote, Desmond Fitzgerald (*Sic*) was before me. We both agreed to the suggestion. It then came to the turn of Kevin O'Higgins ... He hesitated a little about assenting to the summary executions. He asked whether any other measure would not suffice. The answer he got from two or three was that it would not. His hesitation did not last more than a minute and he did not ask more than two or three questions. He then paused for a moment or two, apparently turning the matter over in his own mind. The rest of us waited in silence watching him, and he finally said 'Take them out and shoot them' ...[166]

11 December 1922   **National Army**
Ernest Allen   *ID 83, South New Chapel*

Ernest Joseph Allen was born on 9 October 1905 at his family home on May Street, close to Croke Park. He was the son of Joseph Allen, a law clerk, and Annie Tonsell. The Allens later moved to Ormond Quay where they were living when Ernest enlisted in the National Army. He served as a private with Dublin Brigade. On the morning of Friday, 8 December 1923, Allen and other soldiers were in the cookhouse at City Hall in Dublin. He had just had his breakfast when a Cpl Carroll came to sit down near him. As Carroll removed his revolver from its holster to place it on the table, the gun fired and Ernest Allen was hit in the chest. He was taken to Mercer's Hospital where he later died of his wounds. He had turned seventeen, two months before his death.[167]

13 December 1922   **National Army**
Thomas Mooney   *ID 84, South New Chapel*

Thomas Mooney from Spring Garden Street in Dublin was accidentally shot dead in Cork in December 1922 while serving with the National Army. It was stated that Mooney was shot on the quays in Cork when he failed to answer a sentry's order to halt on 12 December 1922. He died the following day in Mercy Hospital, Cork. He was the eldest son of Patrick and Mary Mooney.[168]

14 December 1922   **National Army**
Thomas James Fegan   *ID 84, South New Chapel*

Thomas Fegan (Fagan) from Clonliffe Road in Dublin was accidentally killed in December 1922. Born in December 1905 he had turned seventeen the day before his death. He was the son of William Fegan and Helen Allen. A member of the National Army he was stationed at a post on Alexandra Road when he was fatally injured. On that day, Pte Joseph Lynch picked up a rifle in billets and cocking the gun pointed it at three soldiers who were joking with one another. Lynch said, 'get out of this' in jest and the rifle fired. He claimed that he was not aware that the rifle was loaded. The bullet hit Fegan in the head and he was taken to the Jervis Street Hospital where he died.[169]

15 December 1922   **Civilian**
Emmet McGarry   *EI 225½, St Bridget's*

Emmet McGarry was aged seven when he died from burns received after his family home was deliberately set alight during the Civil War. His father, Seán McGarry, was a pro-Treaty TD and captain in the National Army. He was also a very prominent figure in the independence movement, a founder member of the Irish Volunteers, a veteran of the 1916 Rising, and a former president of the IRB supreme council. Emmet Thomas McGarry was born on the evening of 22 May 1915 at the home of his parents, 24 Ballybough Road. His mother Tomasina Ryan was also politically active as a member of Cumann na mBan and would later take part in the 1916 Rising and War of Independence. By 1922, the family were living on Philipsburgh Avenue and on the evening of Sunday 10 December 1922, their home was raided by a small group of men armed with revolvers. Seán McGarry was not there that night but Tomasina McGarry, her sister, mother and niece were present, along with the children of Seán and Tomasina.

According to evidence given at the inquest into the death of Emmet McGarry the raiders poured an accelerant around the house and, despite a number of warnings from the adults in the house that there were children upstairs, they then set fire to the house and closed the door as they left. The locked door prevented those who had been forced outside from immediately re-entering the house. A neighbour stated that he saw the men leaving the house and entered himself via the rear and saw Tomasina McGarry carrying her daughter down the stairs.

As the fire spread a sergeant of the Dublin Metropolitan Police who was on duty in the area heard shouts that there was a fire and made his way to the McGarry home, seeing a crowd outside. He entered the house, which was now engulfed by flames, via the roof of a scullery, having forced open an upstairs window. There he found an unconscious Emmet McGarry and brought him to a window where he passed him to a bystander. He returned to search once more but did not find anyone and having inhaled smoke and feeling unwell, he dashed to the window and threw himself out, fainting in

Courtesy of Donal King   the process. He described the house as being like a

Schoolmates of Emmet McGarry accompany his coffin as it approaches the entrance to Glasnevin. **Courtesy of Reach plc (Daily Mirror).**

furnace and he had burned himself on the metal of Emmet McGarry's bed. Emmet was brought to Temple Street Children's Hospital suffering with extensive burns to his face, neck, chest, arms, hands and thighs. He was also in shock. He fell unconscious the following day and never recovered. He died just after 01.00 on the morning of 15 December with his father at his bedside. The inquest into his death returned a verdict that he had died as a result of 'septic pneumonia and cardiac failure following extensive burns caused by the room he was in bed in being deliberately set on fire by some person or persons unknown who were guilty of murder.' His funeral came directly to Glasnevin from Temple Street Children's Hospital and was attended by a large crowd including many children from his school. His mother was unable to attend due to her own injuries. He was interred in a grave in the St Bridget's section in which his sibling, an elder sister who had died aged two days in 1912, had been previously buried.[170]

17 December 1922   **National Army**
Seán Keogh   *ID 84, South New Chapel*

Seán Keogh from Dolphin's Barn Street in Dublin was a member of the National Army and previously an employee of the Dublin United Tramway Company.

His father, Patrick Keogh, fought during the 1916 Rising. Seán Keogh was a member of Fianna Éireann during the same period and later served in the War of Independence with 4th Battalion, Dublin Brigade, IRA. During the Civil War, he had initially joined the Criminal Investigation Department before becoming a lieutenant in the National Army with the Dublin Guard. On the night of 17 December 1922, Keogh was one of a mixed group of seven CID and National Army officers travelling in a touring car through Johnstown, Co. Kildare. As they passed through the village a shot was fired and the car stopped. The occupants searched a nearby dancehall and having returned to the road they were fired at. There was a prolonged exchange of fire before the skirmish ceased and the attackers slipped away. When the pro-Treaty men returned to their car they found that Seán Keogh was missing and began a search for him. They found him lying dead beside a small stream with his revolver in his hand. An inquest returned a verdict that '… the deceased died from shock and haemorrhage, the result of a bullet wound, the bullet fired by some person or persons unknown.'[171]

19 December 1922	National Army
Patrick Mulhall	*DD 82, South New Chapel*

Patrick Mulhall from Corn Market in Dublin was aged seventeen when he was accidentally killed in 1922. Born in June 1905 in Bridge Street Cottage he worked as telegraph messenger before joining the National Army. At the time he was fatally wounded, Mulhall was part of the Dingle Garrison in Co. Kerry and was based in Temperance Hall in Dingle. A report regarding his death stated that: 'Another soldier named Lynch was about to relieve the sentry and was in the act of loading his rifle when he discharged a shot which entered Mulhall's head, causing a wound from which he died a few days later.' He was originally buried in Kerry before being exhumed and reinterred in Glasnevin in February 1924.[172]

19 December 1922	National Army
Patrick White	*ID 85, South New Chapel*

Patrick White, a sergeant in the National Army, was accidentally killed in the barracks in Portlaoise (Maryborough) when his revolver fired. Sgt John Wrafter, who was present at the time of his death, said that White was sitting at a table when he took out his revolver and began swinging it by the trigger guard. A few moments later he heard a shot being fired and White fell to the ground. He had been fatally shot in the head. Patrick White was a former member of Fianna Éireann and the IRA and was from Temple Street in Dublin.[173]

20 December 1922   Civilian
Séamus Dwyer   *UA 67, South*

Séamus (James) Dwyer (O'Dwyer) was born in November 1886 in 50 Lombard Street West, one of twin sons of William Dwyer and Margaret Walker. Educated at Blackrock College he was a grocer and shopkeeper with premises at 5 Rathmines Terrace. A member of Sinn Féin he participated in the Dáil Courts as a judge and was active during the War of Independence as an intelligence officer with 4th Battalion, Dublin Brigade, IRA. In 1921, he was elected as one of six unopposed Sinn Féin TDs for Dublin County. He worked closely with Michael Collins during the same period and supported the Treaty. In May 1922, Dwyer was secretary to the pro-Treaty delegation that participated in negotiations that attempted to avert confrontation and reunite those for and against the Treaty. He lost his seat in the 1922 general election but remained actively involved with the pro-Treaty side.

Although ostensibly a civilian during this time Dwyer's political affiliation was clear in the minds of those who opposed him and he was rumoured to have been unofficially connected with the work of the Citizen's Defence Force and Free State intelligence. Witnesses described that on 20 December 1922 he was in his shop when a man came in and asked him if he was Séamus Dwyer and he replied that he was. There were another few words between the men, then two shots were fired at close range and Dwyer fell fatally injured. A man, Walter Foley, who was in the shop at the time, gave chase as the gunman fled. Other onlookers joined him but Dwyer's assailant slipped into laneways and disappeared.

Meanwhile, Dwyer was lying behind the counter of his shop with blood flowing from his chest. The fatal bullet had exited through his right shoulder passing through his heart and lung on the way. His body was taken to the Meath Hospital where his twin brother, Luke, identified it. An inquest found that his death was due to 'shock and haemorrhage caused by a bullet fired by some person unknown and that ... the act was one of wilful murder'. The person suspected of shooting Séamus Dwyer was Bobby Bonfield, who was later killed in a reprisal (*see 29 March 1923*). Another death linked to the events on Rathmines Terrace was that of Francis Lawler, who was also killed in an extra-judicial killing nine days after the shooting of Séamus Dwyer. Lawler appears to have been shot dead on the basis of unsubstantiated suspicions linking him to the killing *(see 29 December 1922)*. Séamus Dwyer was buried in Glasnevin on 22 December 1922 and amongst those present at the funeral was W.T. Cosgrave.[174]

22 December 1922   **National Army**
Patrick Fitzgerald   *ID 84, South New Chapel*

Patrick Fitzgerald from Bolton Street in Dublin was serving as a private in the National Army when he was shot dead near his home. During the First World War Fitzgerald enlisted and served with the Royal Army Ordnance Corps. He was shot is the wrist and gas poisoned during his time with the British army and was discharged in March 1921. Fitzgerald had only joined the National Army a few days before his death and was serving with the engineers based in Beggars Bush Barracks. On the night of 22 December 1922 he was walking near his home with Arthur Devonshire, who was also a British army veteran and electrician, originally from Belfast. They walked from Bolton Street, near Fitzgerald's home, towards Granby Row. As they passed Donohue's public house two men approached from Granby Row, shouted 'Up! Up!' and then fired two shots at close range into Fitzgerald. He fell backwards and the men then ran away in the direction from which they had come. Patrick Fitzgerald was killed instantly and his body taken to the Mater Hospital. Although he was in uniform when he was killed, Patrick Fitzgerald was not armed due to the nature of his work with the army. Arthur Devonshire died in 1948 and is also buried in Glasnevin.[175]

22 December 1922   **National Army**
Frederick Hamilton Lidwell   *ID 85, South New Chapel*

Frederick Hamilton Lidwell, a captain in the National Army, was accidentally shot dead in Kilkenny Barracks. Born in Clonskeagh in September 1900, he was the son of George Lidwell and Josephine Christina Cott. His father was a solicitor, originally from Fermanagh. After early education at Belvedere College, he became a solicitor's apprentice. The family later moved to Corrig Avenue, Dún Laoghaire and during the War of Independence Lidwell joined the Dalkey Company of 6th Battalion, Dublin Brigade. He also served as registrar to the Dún Laoghaire republican court. During the Civil War, he joined the National Army and was promoted to the rank of captain, serving as assistant legal officer in Kilkenny Barracks. On the day of his death Lidwell was in the orderly room in the barracks with a number of officers when Comdt Joyce arrived and, in a jovial manner, ordered the room to be cleared of anybody not on business. Another officer fetched two members of the guard, who were not aware of the joke, and told them to clear the room. One of them Edward Murphy later stated that:

> ... I went over to the men and said 'come on get out of here'. The three men were laughing and they paused for a while, so I shoved a round up the breech of my rifle, it's a fashion I can't get rid of, and I did it mostly to frighten them more than anything else. Then the three men started to walk out of the Orderly Room, just as they got to the door one of them looked back, Lieut Harney, I shoved him with my rifle ... I had my rifle pointed upwards when the three men got out in the hallway. My sleeve got caught in the knob of the Orderly Room door, I had my finger on the trigger and the shot went off ... I had no intention of firing that shot whatever.

The bullet fired by Murphy hit Frederick Lidwell in the head and he was killed instantly. He was buried in the National Army plot in Glasnevin on 27 December 1922.[176]

25 December 1922
John Foran

National Army
MB 30, South

John Foran died on Christmas Day 1922 from wounds received in Mountjoy Jail whilst serving with the Dublin Guard earlier that year on 22 July. From Lower Clanbrassil Street, he was nineteen at the time of his death and had previously been a member of Dublin Brigade, IRA. At an inquest into his death evidence was given that on the day he was wounded Foran was in an area of Mountjoy Jail known as 'B' Basement when a rifle had been accidentally fired. In was stated that one bullet had been fired and it had ricocheted off the floor, the bullet splintered and its shards wounded three men. John Foran was badly wounded in both of his thighs and was brought to the Mater Hospital where he underwent an operation. He died a few months later of his injuries. His cause of death was formally recorded as 'heart failure following toxaemia, injuries being caused by accidental discharge of rifle'. In a letter to Frank Aiken, John Foran's mother, Kate, later claimed that the fatal wounding of her son was not an accident and that he had been shot for carrying messages to anti-Treaty IRA prisoners. She wrote that:

... I was told by a man in the N(ational) Army to warn him to keep away from the prisoners wing or else there would be an accident, it was known that he was carrying messages to the prisoners, a week later the accident happened, he had a letter to a prisoner attached to B Company 4th Battalion when it occurred but that letter was never delivered, I was not notified about that accident, it was a stranger who was visiting the ward where he was lying sent me word to go to see him. We were not notified about the inquest, on the 27th when his father went to the hospital he met the coroner coming out, he was told that the inquest was over.

John Foran was buried in a grave in the South section of the cemetery on 29 December 1922.[177]

29 December 1922	Criminal Investigation Department
Matthew Daly	*BH 190½, St Bridget's*

Matthew John Daly was born on the island of Inishark, near Inisbofin, in Galway in May 1894. He was the son of Matthew Daly senior, a constable in the Royal Irish Constabulary, and Bridget Killeen, a national schoolteacher. His father, originally from Cavan, had joined the police in 1889 and was posted to Galway where he met and married Bridget in 1896. Matthew was their second eldest son and he joined the Irish Volunteers in 1914, rising quickly in its ranks to become a section commander. He served during the 1916 Rising in Galway and took part in the occupation of Moyode Castle, near Athenry, under the command of Liam Mellows. Having been arrested, Daly was interned in Frongoch before being released later in late 1916. He returned home to Athenry where he was involved in attempting to establish the republican police in the area, he was also an active volunteer with the IRA in the military campaign. During the same time, his father was a serving member of the RIC until he was pensioned in 1921.

Following the Truce, Matthew Daly came to Dublin where he intended to join the National Army but instead joined the Criminal Investigation Department based at Oriel House. He served under Capt. Patrick Moynihan and during his time with the CID part of his work involved in the investigation of armed robberies and he became a well-known figure.

On the night of Saturday 23 December, Daly was one of a small group of CID officers who were carrying out enquiries on the quays in Dublin. At the junction with Queen Street, shots were fired at Matthew Daly and he was hit in both legs and his lower back. A number of men ran from the scene towards Haymarket and another fled up Queen Street escaping the remaining CID men. Matthew Daly was carried into a nearby public house bleeding badly from one leg. A bullet in his right thigh had hit the femoral artery and he was taken to the Richmond Hospital for treatment before being transferred to the Meath Hospital. The bullet was successfully extracted but on the afternoon of 29 December, he died of his injuries.

At an inquest into his death, the ambush on Daly was described as having been carefully planned. Before the attack, a Dublin Metropolitan Police constable who was on patrol in the area was taken to Garrison Lane at gunpoint where he was held until the shooting had taken place. The funeral of Matthew Daly came to Glasnevin on 2 January 1923 and he was buried in a grave in St Bridget's section of the cemetery. His father and mother, who died in 1938 and 1940 respectively, are also buried in the same grave.[178]

29 December 1922	**Anti-Treaty Irish Republican Army**
Francis Lawler	*LB 55, St Paul's*

On 29 December 1922, a body was found lying in a pool of blood at Milltown in Dublin. The man, Francis (Frank) Lawler, had been shot three times in the head and twice in the body. There was singeing around the wounds, suggesting he had been shot at close range. He had been abducted and killed.

Francis Mathew Lawler (Lawlor/Lalor) was born in his family home in Haddington Road in January 1894. He was the son of Mathew Lawlor, a sergeant in the Dublin Metropolitan Police and Catherine Burke. A member of the Irish Volunteers from 1917, he served with Dublin Brigade IRA during the War of Independence. During that time, he was involved in a raid on the Coastguard Station on Pigeon House Road in 1919 and other quests for arms. He also worked as an auditor for the Irish Agricultural Organisation based in Plunkett House in Merrion Square.

He took the anti-Treaty side during the Civil War and was on the run at the time of his death. On the night of Thursday 28 December 1922, Lawler was staying at the home of a friend, Thomas Ffrench, in Castlewood Avenue in Rathmines. Just before midnight, Ffrench heard a knock at the door and two men in trench coats and hats asked if Lawler was in. Ffrench called Lawler, he came to the door and asked who they were. The men didn't answer and said that he would have to come with them. Lawler resisted and they pulled him out of the house despite his attempts to resist by clinging to a clock in the hall. Lawler once again asked who was taking him and the reply of one of the men was 'the authorities'.

The following morning the Civic Guard in Dundrum received a phone call that a body was lying in a laneway in Milltown. Two workers on the nearby Milltown golf course were the first to see the body, however, they assumed that the man was dead and ignored the body carrying on their duties. It was another member of the public who later informed the police. Mathew Lawler identified the body as that of his son Francis. He had last seen him on Christmas day. Some, such as Mary Flannery Woods and James Kavanagh, later suggested that Lawler was killed as he was suspected of having been involved in the death of Seamus Dwyer (*see 20 December 1922*). Kavanagh stated that some years later he met Paddy Sheehan, then secretary of the General Prisons Board, in the street. He asked him if they had ever found the person who had shot Dwyer. He stated:

> ... he told me they had. I wondered who it was as I had seen nothing about it in the newspapers. He said he couldn't remember the fellow's name at the moment but that his body had been found in a ditch up in Milltown. The name of the man whose body had been found in a ditch in Milltown was Frank Lawlor who, from what I was told afterwards, could not have shot Seamus Dwyer for he was in another place when Dwyer was shot.

A 1933 report for pension purposes described that from confidential enquiries they were satisfied that Lawler was killed while he was still a prisoner because of his active connection with the anti-Treaty IRA. Francis Lawler was buried in a grave in the St Paul's section of the cemetery on New Year's Day 1923. His father, who died in 1939, and mother, who died in 1944 are also interred there.[179]

1923

3 January 1923   **National Army**
Patrick Acton   *CD 84, South New Chapel*

Patrick Acton was from Clarence Place in Dublin and had been a member of the IRA during the War of Independence. Before joining the National Army, he had worked for Dixon's soap and candle factory on Erne Street.

He died from injuries received when a grenade was thrown at a party of National Army soldiers carrying out a search in an area west of Mountmellick in Laois. On the day of his death, Acton was one of a number of soldiers who were searching the area around the home of a man named Patrick Kearney in Skerries, Rosenallis. Volunteers of the anti-Treaty IRA had taken billets in a barn near the Kearney home and were surrounded. Amongst them was Laurence Brady a well-known figure in the Laois IRA. As the National Army approached, Brady and his comrades attempted to escape and a grenade was thrown. A piece of shrapnel hit Acton in the head and fatally injured him. Laurence Brady and his comrades escaped. His funeral came to Glasnevin from St Andrew's church on Westland Row.[1]

6 January 1923   **National Army**
James Caffrey   *CD 85, South New Chapel*

James Caffrey was born in April 1899 in the home of his family in Golden Lane in Dublin. The son of Edward Caffrey and Mary Byrne he worked as a newspaper seller. In March 1917, he was convicted of loitering to commit a felony and enlisted in the British army the following month. A member of the Royal Irish Fusiliers, he frequently went absent without leave and a month after his enlistment his commanding officer sought to have him transferred to another battalion stating that '... he is a very good soldier but as his people live in Dublin it is a temptation to him to go absent without leave which he does.' Caffrey continued to desert and in August he joined the British army again. This was despite him being still enlisted in his previous regiment, from which he had absconded. His time with the British army ended without him ever having served in a theatre of war.

It was around this this time that he married in Glasgow, however, he was soon separated from his wife and did not remain in contact with her. In 1919 Caffrey, was sentenced to three years in Clonmel Borstal Institution having been found guilty of breaking a pane of glass. He was released on licence at the end of April 1922 and joined the National Army, serving as a private in the Dublin Guard. He was killed in an ambush in Fermoy, Co. Cork in January 1923. His funeral, from the Carmelite Church in Whitefriar Street, came to Glasnevin accompanied by a military band and a guard of honour.[2]

17 January 1923
Christopher Farrell

Civilian
GC 38, South

Christopher Farrell, a commercial traveller employed by John Power and Son whiskey distillers, was killed when the car in which he was travelling was accidentally ambushed by the anti-Treaty IRA at Kinaffe, south of Swinford in Co. Mayo. On the day of his death, Farrell was travelling in a car from Swinford to Claremorris with Edward Harris, a fellow salesman, and Michael Byrne, the driver. As they approached a bridge at Kinaffe, they found that stones from the bridge had been placed across the road as a barrier. There was a gap in the stones and the driver negotiated his way through to the other side. As the car proceeded, it came under fire and one of the first bullets hit Christopher Farrell who moaned and fell backwards dead. He had been shot just under his neck in the chest. Another shot hit Edward Harris in the shoulder and then a hail of fire was aimed at the car. The driver managed to pull the car to one side and leave it while Harris tried to lift Farrell to get a response but realised he was dead.

As the firing dissipated, Michael Byrne made his way towards the group who had ambushed the car. He explained that the men in the car were commercial travellers and they responded by asking why he did not halt. Byrne told them that there was no call to halt and he did not hear it. The body of Christopher Farrell was driven to Knock and then to Claremorris where an inquest took place. At the time of his death Farrell, who was unmarried, was living with his sister and mother on Waterloo Road in Dublin. He had been working for Powers for twenty years, mainly in the west of Ireland. His funeral took place at St Mary's on Haddington Road before burial in Glasnevin on 19 January.[3]

17 January 1923   **National Army**
Patrick Geraghty   *CD 83, South New Chapel*

Patrick Geraghty a sergeant in the Dublin Guard was killed in an ambush near Kilfeacle in Co. Tipperary. He was one of a party of four National Army members in a Ford car travelling from Dublin to Mitchelstown. As they reached Kilfeacle hill a barricade of stones had been place on the road and the men were ambushed. Patrick Geraghty and John Kelly were killed (*see below*). The two other National Army men were captured and taken prisoner. It was reported that the dead men were stripped of their weapons, ammunition and uniforms. Geraghty was born in Dublin in 1899 and in 1921 had married Julia Tuite. At the time of his death, they were living on North King Street and had one child.[4]

17 January 1923   **National Army**
John Kelly   *GK 145, St Patrick's*

John Kelly, a National Army lieutenant and member of the Dublin Guard was killed in the same ambush in which Patrick Geraghty died (*see above*). Known as Jack, he came from Caledon Road in Dublin and worked as a plater in the Dublin dockyards. He had been a member of 2nd Battalion Dublin Brigade, IRA during the War of Independence. In the Civil War, he fought in the Four Courts area during the Battle of Dublin and was promoted to lieutenant by Eoin O'Duffy before his transfer to Kerry Command. He was buried in Glasnevin on 22 January 1923.[5]

17 January 1923   **National Army**
Robert Nash   *CD 84, South New Chapel*

Robert Nash, from Great Ship Street in Dublin, enlisted in the National Army in September 1922. His father, also Robert, had died in January 1919 of an illness contracted while serving with the Cameronians (Scottish Rifles) and Royal Defence Corps during the First World War. Following the death of his father, Robert lived with his widowed mother, Elizabeth. A private attached to 4th Curragh Reserve his body was found in his quarters at Portobello Barracks on the evening of 17 January 1923. According to a later inquest, it appeared that his death was accidental. A report on that inquest stated that:

…it appeared that the deceased was a member of a patrol which had just returned from duty. The men of the patrol had all gone to their billets and were hanging up their coats and disposing of their guns and equipment. The deceased went down the room towards his bed, in a few minutes he came up again striking the butt of his rifle on the floor. There was a report, and the deceased fell, the bullet entering his breast, coming out the back of his head and lodging in the ceiling. He was immediately attended to by a doctor, who found life extinct.

Robert Nash was aged nineteen at the time of his death.[6]

18 January 1923   National Army
Joseph Foster   *CD 83, South New Chapel*

Joseph Foster was born on 26 January 1887 at the home of his parents, William Foster and Catherine McMahon (Mahon) on Peter Street in Dublin. The family later moved to Bride Street where they remained for a long period. Joseph Foster worked as a carpenter and during the War of Independence moved to Belfast. There he was described as an active member of the IRA and worked in shipyards until the Belfast riots. He returned to Dublin following the Truce and joined the National Army.

In January 1923, he was part of a contingent of men, based in Clonmel, who were taking part in search operations. The group were stopped by farm carts placed across the road at the entrance to Ninemilehouse, between Kilkenny and Clonmel. The members of the National Army then witnessed men running from the village into fields and pursued them. On reaching the centre of an open field, they came under heavy fire from machine guns and rifles. Shots were exchanged and a National Army commandant was wounded in the leg while Joseph Foster was shot through the neck. A description of his death stated that:

> He was one of a party which left Clonmel on searching operations and on arrival at the village of Nine-mile-house, which is situated about 16 miles from Clonmel, the party was attacked by Irregulars. The attack lasted about three hours and, during the fight, Private Foster received a bullet wound through the neck which severed the jugular vein and he died almost immediately.

Joseph Foster's remains were taken to Clonmel and later to Dublin where he was buried in Glasnevin Cemetery on 23 January.[7]

18 January 1923   **National Army**
George Gorman   *CD 85, South New Chapel*

Sgt George Gorman, from Cook Street in Dublin, was accidentally shot dead in St Bricin's Hospital following a tussle for a rifle between two fellow members of the National Army. A court of inquiry held at Collins Barracks found that one of these men, Pte Edward Rock, was responsible for the death of Gorman as had he not attempted to take a rifle from Pte Timoney, the fatal shot would not have been fired. Both Timoney and Rock gave conflicting accounts of the events leading to the death of Gorman. Pte Rock said that:

> I was due to go out on patrol with Pte Timoney from 6 p.m. on 18th January 1923 until 11 p.m., of the same date. Before going on patrol Timoney accompanied me around St. Bricin's Hospital. He was drunk when starting and not in a fit state to do his duty. We then started our patrol down through the long avenue to the bottom Guard Room, we turned about to go back to the Hospital Guard Room. I insisted on bringing Pte Timoney to the Guard Room and he refused and said he would go around the sentries. I then placed No. 1 Sentry in charge of him, while I went on my patrol, in the meantime the Sergt of the Guard came up to me and went as far as No. 2 Sentry to look at the wicket gate. While looking at the gate, a shot rang out. I then left Sergt Gorman and went back to Pte Timoney. On approaching Timoney, he called upon me to halt and asked 'Who is that?' I said 'It is alright it is Rock'. On going up to Timoney I heard him pull his bolt back and again shoving it forward. As soon as I heard this I asked him for his rifle and he absolutely refused. I then made an attempt to take it from him and in doing so a second shot rang out.

Pte Timoney claimed that on the night of the shooting he and Pte Rock had:

> ... met Sergt Gorman coming back from the hospital accompanied by two ladies. All five went towards No. 1 Post where I stopped and Sergt Gorman and Pte Rock accompanied by the ladies went towards No. 2 Post. After staying for a while with Pte Norton (sentry at No. 1 Post) I went back towards the Guard Room. On my way back I placed my rifle against the wall and it fell, and a shot went off. After a few minutes Pte Rock came up and made an attempt to take the rifle from me when a second shot rang out. Pte Rock and myself then sent back to the Guard Room and it was then I heard that the Sergt was shot.

George Gorman had been fatally wounded in the left lung. He left a widow, Esther, whom he had married in 1918.[8]

27 January 1923
William McGowan

Civilian
PH 243, St Bridget's

William McGowan was twenty-four at the time of his death. He had married Mary Norton in August 1919 and had one son. He worked for the Midland and Great Western Railway as a carpenter at the Broadstone Railway Works. From Upper Gardiner Street, he was shot dead in the Phoenix Park on the afternoon of 27 January 1923. It was initially surmised that a stray bullet had accidentally hit McGowan. Witnesses close to McGowan when he was shot they did not see anybody fire a gun and his wounding appeared to be a mystery.

His wife stated that he was belonged to no organisation other than his trade union and was a very quiet and reserved man who had, what she described as, a 'holy horror' of firearms. She also dismissed any possibility of his death being related to robbery as he had a reasonable sum of money on his person when he was killed which was not taken. However, an unusual inquest into his death brought to light the full details of the circumstances surrounding his death.

On the day of his death, William McGowan left work and made his way to the home of his father-in-law on Mountjoy Square. Here he met his wife, had some dinner and spent some time playing with their infant son before returning to his home on Upper Gardiner Street. There he washed, changed his clothes and left on his bicycle going towards the Phoenix Park. As he was passing the tunnel entrance of the Great Southern and Western Railway opposite the River Liffey near the park he stopped and looked down the tunnel. Members of a National Army guard that was stationed near the entrance of the tunnel waved him on and he left entering the park and going towards the Wellington Testimonial.

As he did so Sgt Greene, the sergeant of the guard at the railway tunnel, took a rifle from Pte Andrew O'Toole lifted it to his shoulder and pointing it in the direction of William McGowan fired. The members of the guard then saw him slump to the ground. The bullet had hit McGowan in the back of the head causing catastrophic injury and a large exit wound on the other side of his skull. Greene then told O'Toole to clean his rifle, to obscure the fact it had been fired, and gave him a live bullet to replace the empty cartridge that had been fired. Greene then warned the guard not to tell anybody that he had fired the fatal shot.

A number of people in the area, including two Dublin Metropolitan Police men made their way to the scene of the shooting where they found William McGowan dead. Nobody in the park had seen where the fatal shot had come from. That night Greene read of the shooting in the evening newspaper whilst in the guardroom. He once again warned the guard not to mention anything about where the shot had come from. Despite this, the other National Army soldiers on duty gave evidence at the inquest into McGowan's death regarding the actions of Greene that evening. The verdict passed stated that:

> ... William M'Gowan died on the 27th inst., from shock and laceration caused by a penetrating gunshot wound of the skull, the said shot was fired by Sergeant Greene, and that we find no justification for this act, and that we recommend the widow and child of the deceased to the kind consideration of the National Army.

At the conclusion of the inquest, the National Army placed Sgt Greene under arrest.

The death of William McGowan had a significant impact on his widow. She described herself as being unable to sleep and being in great shock in the aftermath of his killing. Her mother had also died a month earlier in December 1922. The case of his death was raised in Dáil Éireann in connection with the circumstances of his family and compensation. Alfie Byrne described that following his death his widow and son were '... now destitute and have been compelled to apply for Poor Law Relief'.[9]

29 January 1923	National Army
Charles Burke	*CD 83, South New Chapel*

Charles Francis Burke was twenty-four and serving as a lieutenant with the National Army when he was fatally wounded during an ambush at Killurin in Wexford while travelling on a train. Born at Upper Erne Street in November 1898 he was the son of Catherine Robinson and Thomas Burke. His aunt, Mary Florence, or Mollie, Burke, was politically active and was married to Robert Monteith, who landed with Roger Casement at Banna Strand in 1916. Charles was a commercial traveller and a Gaelic footballer, well known within the GAA in Dublin, and was a member of the now defunct Peadar Macken club.

On the afternoon of 27 January 1923, Burke travelled on the 16.40 mail train from Wexford to Dublin. As the train approached Killurin, it came under fire in an ambush. Lieut William Crean, who was travelling on the train with Burke, described the moments that followed:

> After leaving the tunnel at Killurin before reaching the station fire was opened on the train from both sides of the line. I asked him (Burke) where he was hit and he replied in the back. The train was in motion at the time but pulled up before we arrived at the station. The firing continued till the train pulled up. After the firing ceased some of the irregulars came to the carriage where Lieut Burke and I were and said that an

Army Officer was shot dead. They brought in about 4 of their own men from both sides and carried Lieut Burke out and placed him on the ground beside the line. They then told me to put up my hands and ordered me out of the compartment. I did so, and I saw Lieut Burke lying on the ground. I knelt beside him and said 'are you badly hit Charlie', he replied 'I am done, Billy, they got me, but the Tans never did.'

Charles Burke was removed to the County Infirmary in Wexford where he died as a result of his injuries two days later.[10]

6 February 1923	Anti-Treaty Irish Republican Army
George King	*ZK 107, St Patrick's*

On the evening of 5 February 1923, a man identified as Nicholas Murphy from Enniscorthy was brought the Meath Hospital suffering with a gunshot wound to the neck. It transpired that this man was in fact George King who was twenty-six-years-old and living at Old Mill House in Tallaght. King, from Kirkdale in Liverpool, was a veteran of the 1916 Rising and had fought with the GPO Garrison alongside his brothers, John and Patrick. All of the brothers had been born in Liverpool to Irish parents and George King had worked as a clerk before travelling to Dublin in 1916. Following the Rising he was interned in Frongoch and after his release he returned to Liverpool where he was conscripted, against his will, into the British army as a member of the King's Liverpool Regiment in November 1916. King did not sign his enlistment papers and refused to follow orders given to him and as a result was sentenced to six months detention. He was discharged in 1917 and later returned to Ireland to take part in the War of Independence. During the Civil War he opposed the Treaty while his brother, Patrick, joined the National Army. On the day he was fatally wounded King had been part of a small group who had attempted to disarm a sentry at 'Arley' the house of Michael A. Corrigan, chief state solicitor, on Leinster Road in Rathmines. That evening members of the National Army were on duty at the ruins of Corrigan's house, which had been blown up by anti-Treaty volunteers the previous month.

Four men in civilian clothes approached the soldiers. They produced revolvers and told the soldiers to put their hands up. The command was refused and there was a struggle between the men with shots being fired. At the same time the sergeant major commanding the National Army guard came to the scene of the struggle and exchanged fire with the assailants, hitting George King who fell to the ground. The three men were chased away and in the confusion King attempted to also flee but only made it a short distance before he collapsed. He

National Army soldiers stand outside the ruins of 'Arley' where George King was fatally wounded in February 1923. Author's Collection.

was brought to the Meath Hospital where he identified himself as Nicholas Murphy from Enniscorthy. He had been hit twice, once in the neck and once in the back of the left shoulder and died soon afterwards. An inquest returned a verdict that:

> Death was due to shock and haemorrhage following a wound caused by a bullet fired by a member of the National Army in the discharge of his duty.

No members of George King's family were present at the inquest and after it, his brother, John, claimed his body and arranged his funeral to Glasnevin.[11]

8 February 1923   **National Army**
James Brennan   *CD 83, South New Chapel*

Sgt Maj. James Brennan of the National Army was fatally shot in unusual circumstances in February 1923. From Mary's Abbey in Dublin, Brennan was stationed in Mountjoy Jail at the time of his death. On the evening he was killed, Brennan and three other men stationed at Mountjoy went for drinks in the Bohemian Bar before travelling to town by tram. They eventually arrived at a pub on Commons Street where they engaged in a game of ring throwing. An error in score-taking resulted in an argument and a physical fight took place between some of the party.

It was decided that they would return to barracks but on leaving the pub the argument resumed between James Brennan and a Sgt Maj. Murphy. A shot was fired and Brennan exclaimed that he was hit and accused Murphy of shooting him. He was taken to the Jervis Street Hospital where he died of his wounds. It appeared clear that Murphy had shot Brennan, however, all of the men had been searched for weapons on leaving Mountjoy and no revolver was found in the aftermath of the shooting.

At an inquest into the death it was questioned if it could '... have been possible for a man to shoot another man beside him and with whom he had spent the evening and then get rid of the revolver?' The jury ultimately disregarded James Brennan's deathbed statements that Murphy had shot him. A verdict was reached that he had died '... from shock and haemorrhage following a wound caused by a bullet fired by some person unknown'. A theory put forward in a later pension application was that Brennan had been involved in the arrest of a man who had participated in an attack on City Hall a few days before his death. It was claimed that this man had been released on 6 February and had then shot Brennan.[12]

| **14 February 1923** | **National Army** |
| *Thomas Moran* | *CD 83, South New Chapel* |

Thomas Moran, a private in the Dublin Guard, from Kimmage was shot in the thigh during an ambush at Scartaglen, south of Castleisland, Co. Kerry in January 1923. He was brought to hospital in Tralee where he was treated before being moved to Dublin. He died there on St Valentine's Day in St Bricin's Hospital. An inquest found that he had died from '... shock and haemorrhage combined with septic absorption from the wound'. He was buried in the National Army plot three days later.[13]

| **18 February 1923** | **National Army** |
| *Patrick Kilkelly* | *CD 82, South New Chapel* |

Patrick Kilkelly, an officer in the National Army from Cabra Park in Dublin, was shot at Claremorris, Co. Mayo on 11 February 1923 and died six days later in Claremorris Military Hospital. A veteran of the War of Independence, Kilkelly had served as an intelligence officer in Dublin Brigade IRA. He had previously worked for the Midland Great Western Railway. On the day he was wounded Kilkelly had gone for a walk with some other officers to visit Castlemagarret. They were not far from their barracks when Kilkelly turned and said, 'Oh I am hit'. One officer thought that he was joking and didn't believe him until he saw blood coming down his back. It was suggested that the bullet might have been fired by another group of National Army officers who had decided to go out shooting ducks on a nearby lake using their army rifles. However, no witnesses came forward to state that they had seen the fatal shot being fired and all of the officers who had been shooting at the ducks claimed that they could not have been responsible. An inquiry found that Patrick Kilkelly had died '... as a result of a bullet wound fired ... by some person unknown.'[14]

23 February 1923	Civilian
Agnes Keogh	*WJ 247, St Patrick's*

Agnes Josephine Keogh, a sixteen-year-old wigmaker's apprentice from 75 Summerhill in Dublin, was accidentally shot in her family home where she had been born in December 1906. At an inquest into her death, her brother, Thomas Keogh, stated that his sister had asked to see his revolver, which he carried as a member of the Criminal Investigation Department. On taking it out of his pocket the revolver fired and the bullet hit Agnes in the head above her right eye. Her mother, also Agnes, was present but did not witness the fatal incident. Agnes Keogh was taken to the Jervis Street Hospital where she died of her injuries. Her funeral came to Glasnevin on 27 February 1923 after mass at Gardiner Street. Agnes was buried in a grave in which her father, who died two months before her birth, was buried. A coroner's inquest into her death returned a verdict of accidental death.[15]

27 February 1923	Civilian
George Fitzhenry	*GB 52½, South*

George Fitzhenry a clerk in the Irish Railway Clearing House from Windsor Avenue, Fairview was in his sixties when the was shot in Dublin. On the evening of 27 February 1923, Fitzhenry was standing outside Yeates and Sons shop on the corner of Grafton Street and Nassau Street as a car containing members of the Criminal Investigation Department was passing by. As the car was turning onto Nassau Street, a shot was fired hitting Fitzhenry in the knee. One of the men in the car claimed to have seen a person on the street put their hand into their pocket and interpreted this as an attempt to draw a weapon. The men in the car drew their own weapons and as they did so, a revolver was accidentally fired. George Fitzhenry was taken to Mercer's Hospital where he died of his injuries that night. An inquest found he had died of 'shock and haemorrhage following a bullet wound of the right leg said injuries being caused by an Inspector of the Criminal Investigation Department in the discharge of his duty'.[16]

2 March 1923   **National Army**
John Kelly   *CD 82, South New Chapel*

John Kelly from Drumcondra was shot dead whilst on sentry duty in Barraduff, Co. Kerry. On the night of his death, Kelly was on twenty-four hour guard duty at a post guarding a junction in Barraduff where the roads led to Rathmore and Headford. Early in the morning, when Kelly was finishing his duty and leaving his post, Cpl Butler, who was in charge of the guard, picked up a rifle and pointed it at Kelly telling him in jest to return to his post. As Butler raised the rifle, it fired and John Kelly was shot in the head.[17]

6 March 1923   **National Army**
Michael Dunne   *CD 82, South New Chapel*

Michael Dunne was one of five members of the National Army who were killed in the Knocknagoshel booby trap mine explosion in March 1923. Dunne, who held the rank of captain at the time of his death, was from Dublin and had originally joined the IRA in 1918. A member of the Dublin Brigade's Active Service Unit, he joined the National Army serving with the Dublin Guard during the Civil War. On the day of his death, Dunne was with a party of National Army soldiers who were acting on intelligence received that an anti-Treaty arms dump was located in the Knocknagoshel area. On making a search, the dump was found and as the soldiers approached to inspect it a tripwire mine was detonated resulting in a large explosion, killing and injuring those in the immediate vicinity. An official report issued from Portobello Barracks stated that:

> Three officers and two other ranks were killed and one volunteer seriously wounded as the result of a mine explosion in Knocknagoshel, Co. Kerry, this morning. From details to hand it appears that intelligence was conveyed of a dump in the Knocknagoshel area, A party of troops left and located the dump in Barrinarig Wood, it contained a trap mine which exploded when disturbed ...

The remains of Michael Dunne were brought by rail and road to Dublin. His funeral to Glasnevin took place on 9 March 1923, alongside that of his friend Edward Stapleton, who was killed in the same incident. The procession to the cemetery was witnessed by many with W.T. Cosgrave, Desmond FitzGerald and Michael Hayes amongst those in attendance.

One newspaper noted that the joint funeral was possibly the largest that Dublin had seen since that of Michael Collins. Michael Dunne's surviving next-of-kin, his mother and sister, both died within a few weeks of one another in December 1924 and January 1925 respectively and are also buried in Glasnevin.[18]

6 March 1923 — National Army
Edward Joseph Stapleton — CD 82, South New Chapel

Capt. Edward Stapleton, from Lower Gloucester Street, was also killed in the Knocknagoshel explosion (*see above*) and was a friend of Michael Dunne. Born in the Rotunda Hospital in March 1893 his parents, Edward Stapleton and Julia Morris, had married in 1890. At the time of his birth, the family resided on Howth Road in Clontarf but soon moved to Gloucester Street where Edward remained for the rest of his life. His father died in 1896 with Edward being his only surviving child. In September 1916, he married Mary Tancred from Summerhill in Dublin. Their eldest child, Edward, was born in October 1918 followed by another son, Patrick, two years later. During the same period, Edward was serving as a member of Dublin Brigade IRA in the War of Independence. In November 1920, Auxiliaries from Dublin Castle under the command of Maj. William L. King raided Stapleton's home. Nothing connecting him to the IRA was found but the papers seized give some insight into his memberships and interests. Among them were membership cards for the Catholic Young Men's Society as well as documents relating to the trade union movement and a minute book and collection book for the Irish Transport and General Workers' Union. His mother, Julia, died in 1934 and widow, Mary, died in 1941. His eldest son Edward died in 1941, aged twenty-two. He was the third of three generations named Edward Stapleton to die in their twenties and thirties. All three are buried in Glasnevin.[19]

7 March 1923   **National Army**
Christopher McGrane   *CD 81, South New Chapel*

Christopher McGrane, from Railway Avenue in Inchicore, was killed during an anti-Treaty IRA attack on his post at Barraduff in Kerry on the night of 7 March 1923. Before joining the National Army, he had worked as a blacksmith's helper at the Inchicore Railway Works. His remains were returned to Dublin and following mass at Goldenbridge church were buried in the National Army plot in Glasnevin on 12 March.[20]

7 March 1923   **National Army**
William Kelly   *CD 82, South New Chapel*

William Kelly from Rutland (Parnell) Square in Dublin, a member of the 57th Infantry Battalion, was shot dead in an accident at Collins Barracks in Dublin. Before joining the National Army, he worked as a messenger in Fitzgibbon Street Police Station. John Charles, whom Kelly had known for many years and been in school with, was handling the rifle that fired the fatal shot. He later recalled the incident:

> I remember the 7th day of March 1923. I had been speaking to Pte Kelly on the platform post of the Laundry Guard about fifty minutes. He asked me to hold his rifle while he went to the lavatory. I did so and told him not to be long away. He was away for about 9 minutes. When he returned he was walking slowly and I told him to hurry as I was going on Guard at 6 p.m. He said there was no hurry 'leave the rifle down' and he then proceeded to mount the ladder. I put the rifle against the railings, it fell and I then heard a shot. I looked down and saw Pte Kelly falling back. I immediately laid hold of the rifle and threw it behind and I ran up and told the Corporal in charge of the Guard. He told me to report the matter to the Orderly Room.

According to Charles, the rifle had fallen as William Kelly ascended the ladder and discharged as the muzzle was level with his head and just eight inches away from him. He was killed instantly.[21]

13 March 1923   **Civilian**
Hugh Haughton   *LI 224, St Bridget's*

Hugh Haughton, a carpenter for the Dublin United Tramways Company, was born in October 1904 in Dolphin's Barn, the son of Mary Curran and John Haughton. His father, a cooper, died in February 1911 aged forty-one and shortly afterwards the family moved to live on Hamilton Street where they remained for many years. He had eight siblings, one of whom, also named Hugh, died in 1894 aged ten months. His brother John was a member of the British army, discharged in 1921. Another brother, Bernard, was in the National Army based in Gormanston at the time of Hugh's death. On the night of 12 March 1923, Bridget Ward, who lived near the Haughton family home on Hamilton Street, was standing at her door when she saw two people coming towards her from the opposite side of the street. One of them placed her hand on her shoulder and said, 'I am shot Mrs Ward'. It was Hugh Haughton who said he was dying and asked for a priest while also stating that a National Army officer had shot him. An ambulance was called for and when it arrived Haughton was sitting in a chair in a state of exhaustion. He was taken to the Meath Hospital where he died of his injuries early the following morning.

Haughton was shot by Comdt Patrick Griffin, barracks officer commanding at Portobello Barracks. Griffin had been a member of the Active Service Unit of Dublin Brigade, IRA during the War of Independence. He described that on the night that Hugh Haughton was shot dead he was walking in uniform from Donore Avenue to Washington Street. He stated that as he turned onto Washington Street two men approached from behind him and one said 'come on, sky them' while they both produced revolvers. Griffin then pulled out his own revolver opening fire and hitting Hugh Haughton in the abdomen and chest. He said that he then pursued his attackers and they ran into the distance along with another three men whom he believed were part of an attacking party.

A general order, signed by Liam Lynch, to shoot members of the provisional government and National Army was produced at the inquest. The direct connection to Haughton was not made clear in reports, however, the suggestion that Haughton was actively involved with the anti-Treaty IRA took his family by surprise and they denied that this was the case. Bernard Haughton stated that he was willing to swear that his brother was not a member. No additional witnesses to the shooting itself were questioned before the inquest.

The only account of the events leading to Haughton's death was given by Patrick Griffin and the inquest found that he died as a result of 'shock and haemorrhage following wounds in the lung and abdomen said injuries inflicted in self-defence'. It is difficult to ascertain Haughton's affiliation, if any, with the anti-Treaty IRA. He was buried in a grave in the St Bridget's section of the cemetery in which his brother, Hugh, and father, John, had previously been interred. Patrick Griffin died in 1935 and is buried in Glasnevin, a short distance from Hugh Haughton.[22]

13 March 1923   **Anti-Treaty Irish Republican Army**
James O'Rourke   *QD 37, South New Chapel*

James O'Rourke from Upper Gloucester Street in Dublin was executed at Beggars Bush Barracks on 13 March 1923. The eldest son in his family he was nineteen at the time of his death and had worked as a clerk for Smith's wholesale merchants on Merchants Quay. During the War of Independence, he had served with the 3rd Battalion, Dublin Brigade, IRA, and supported the anti-Treaty position during the Civil War. On 21 February 1923, O'Rourke took part in an attack on members of the National Army in Jury's Hotel on Dame Street. The hotel held a number of government offices. Following the attack a National Army official account stated that:

> At 1.30 p.m. today an attempt was made by a party of armed men to destroy Jury's Hotel, Dame St., which is being utilised as Government offices. Some of the parties took up positions on the roofs opposite the building and opened fire, under cover of which they endeavoured to rush the building. A guard of troops stationed in the building immediately replied to the fire forcing the armed party to make a hurried retreat. In a motor beside the building, which had been abandoned, the troops found three land mines, two revolvers and three tins of petrol. A revolver, with a quantity of ammunition was found on the roof of a house beside the hotel. A number of arrests have been made by the troops in connection with the affair. Beyond some glass broken in the windows, no damage was done to the building.

When James O'Rourke was captured and arrested, he was taken to a touring car belonging to National Army troops. He was described as 'bleeding from a nasty wound on the right temple, his long brown hair was terribly tousled and damp with perspiration and he appeared dazed'. He was charged with having a Webley revolver and ammunition in his possession 'without proper authority' under the Public Safety Act. He was found guilty by a military court and sentenced to death. On the evening of 12 March 1923, having been informed that he would be executed the following day, he scrawled a message on the wall of his cell on B Wing in Mountjoy Jail. It read:

> My God the news was startling. I am to be executed at 8 o'c. The angelus is ringing. If I could only see my mother, I never thought I should die for Ireland but God willed otherwise. I have only 13 more hours to live. Every minute brings another life to a finish. Death is but a release from a troublesome life. Ireland what a most unfortunate country, you have suffered.

He was executed by firing squad at 08.00 the following morning at Beggars Bush Barracks.[23]

14 March 1923
Henry Kavanagh

Henry Kavanagh from Lower Fownes Street in Dublin was shot dead at Charlemont Bridge in March 1923. A former member of the British army he had enlisted in the Leinster Regiment in August 1920, aged twenty. He was discharged a few months later and returned to Dublin where he worked as a dispatch clerk for *The Irish Times* and also a labourer before joining the National Army. On the evening of his death, he had left his home to travel to Portobello Barracks where he was stationed. It was the last time his mother saw him alive. At approximately 22.00 that night Mary J. Fitzpatrick was returning to her home at Dartmouth Place when she saw something lying on the ground near the canal. Having moved closer she noticed it was the body of a National Army soldier. She lifted his hand and found that it was cold, her subsequent screams brought a number of people to the scene. The body was taken to the Meath Hospital where it was examined and bullet wounds were found in the chest and back. There were singes also found around the entrance wounds, indicating that the shots had been fired at close range.

Mary Kavanagh identified the remains as those of her son Henry. An inquest returned a verdict that he had '... died from shock and haemorrhage, caused by bullet wounds inflicted by some person or persons unknown said person or persons in our opinion being guilty of wilful murder'. It was surmised that while returning to his barracks, after a short period of leave, the unarmed Henry Kavanagh was held up by some members of the anti-Treaty IRA and shot dead. It was suggested that the death of Thomas O'Leary (*see 23 March 1923*) was retaliation for that of Kavanagh.[24]

15 March 1923
John Nolan

John Nolan, a member of the Railway Protection and Maintenance Corps stationed at Wellington (Griffith) Barracks, was shot dead on Bride Street in Dublin. On the night of his death, Nolan was walking alone and unarmed at about 21.20 when two men approached him with revolvers. They fired at him at close range and bullets hit his chest and abdomen. The attackers quickly fled and Nolan died almost immediately. His body was carried to the Adelaide Hospital by some of those who had witnessed the shooting.

John Nolan was from New Row in Chapelizod and was married with five children under the age of seven at the time of his death. An inquest found that he had died from 'shock and haemorrhage caused by bullet wounds from shots fired by some person or persons unknown, in our opinion wilful murder'.[25]

17 March 1923	Citizens' Defence Force
Charles Cooper	*VK 108, St Patrick's*

Charles Patrick Daley Cooper was a member of the Protective Corps, Citizens' Defence Force, part of the Irish Free State intelligence apparatus, based in Oriel House. He was shot on Merrion Street in the early hours of Saturday 17 March 1923. Cooper, from South Circular Road, was with a group of CDF members who were returning to quarters when they were halted by a National Army patrol. A military rifle was accidentally fired and the bullet hit Cooper in the abdomen and pelvis. The same bullet also slightly wounded one of his colleagues. He was taken to St Vincent's Hospital where he died a few hours later.[26]

18 March 1923	National Army
John Little	*CD 80, South New Chapel*

John Little from Charlemont Mall in Portobello, Dublin was eighteen when he was accidentally shot in Collins Barracks in March 1923. Born in May 1904 in Holles Street Hospital, he was the son of James Little and Sarah Sheridan. According to his father John had been a member of D Company, 4th Battalion, Dublin Brigade, Fianna Éireann before joining the National Army. On the evening of St Patrick's Day 1923, he was shot by Robert Francis Bailey, a fellow member of the National Army. At that court of inquiry, Bailey stated:

> I had the revolver out and Clark asked me to let him have a look at it. I handed it to him and when he broke it two or three rounds slipped under the ejector. I put them in right and on closing it I must have pulled the trigger. I was absolutely certain that I had the two empty chambers next to the hammer. I had a handkerchief loosely tied around my forefinger as I had cut it slightly previous to the occurrence and it may have caught the trigger. I had no enmity against Little ...

John Little had been shot between the jaw and neck. He died in St Bricin's Hospital. Robert Bailey was later exonerated from any blame in relation to his death.[27]

22 March 1923
Michael Joseph Baker

National Army
CD 80, South New Chapel

Michael Joseph Baker was born on 8 November 1898 at his family home on Townsend Street in Dublin. The son of Andrew Baker and Evelyn Hart, he worked as a barber before enlisting in the Royal Marine Light Infantry in June 1916 at seventeen. The following year he deserted and was later arrested and returned to his unit. In April 1918, he was sent as reinforcements to the 1st Royal Marine Battalion, which was serving with the 63rd (Royal Naval) Division as infantry on the Western Front. On 29 September 1918, Baker and his battalion advanced eastwards as part of an assault against a retreating German army near Cambrai in France as part of the Hundred Days Offensive. They crossed the Canal de Saint-Quentin and gathered together to attack at 13.45 that afternoon. However, they met with heavy opposition and enfilade fire from the village of Proville, on the outskirts of Cambrai. Little progress was made but the battalion suffered sixteen men killed and 115 wounded, one of whom was Michael Baker, who had been shot through the left wrist. His wound was considered slight and he soon returned to his battalion seeing out the rest of the war and the fighting to November 1918. Baker was discharged in December 1919 and returned home to Dublin where he married Frances Eastwood in November 1920 in the pro-cathedral.

Working once again as a barber, he joined the National Army during the Civil War and served as a corporal. On the day of his death, Baker was engaged in raiding a house on Albert Road in Glenageary. The objective of the raid was to arrest members of a small anti-Treaty column, based in Dalkey, which had been actively engaged in attacks against the National Army in south Dublin. According to a National Army account given at an inquest in Dún Laoghaire, the raiding party consisted of four men under the command of Capt. Michael Kelly. They found a known anti-Treaty IRA member, Michael Meaghan, attempting to escape through a window carrying a Mauser pistol. Kelly challenged Meaghan who surrendered and the other National Army soldiers went to the back garden to arrest him.

Unknown to them was that a number of other members of the anti-Treaty column remained armed in the house and a gun battle quickly broke out. Capt. Kelly and another officer present later described that in the midst of the skirmish Patrick Thomas, an anti-Treatyite from Dalkey, who had been a member of 6th Battalion, Fianna Éireann during the War of Independence, rushed through the back door of the house. He shot at Michael Baker and hit him in the stomach, the National Army returned fire and Thomas was wounded and arrested. The fight soon ended and Baker was taken to the nearby St Michael's Hospital where he died of his injuries. One of the anti-Treaty IRA members, Michael Neary, also died of his wounds two months later. Michael Baker left a widow, Frances aged twenty-three, and two children, a boy, aged one, and girl, aged three. Frances died in 1932 aged thirty-one and is also buried in Glasnevin.[28]

23 March 1923	Anti-Treaty Irish Republican Army
Patrick O'Brien	*SD 39, South New Chapel*

National Army soldiers shot Patrick O'Brien, from Cadogan Road in Fairview, after he detonated a bomb in the Carlton Cinema on O'Connell Street in Dublin. The bombing came following the issuing of the 'amusements order' by Liam Lynch. The order was made following the recommencement of state sanctioned executions in March 1923. It declared '... that a time of national mourning be proclaimed, all sport and amusements be suspended, all picture houses and theatres and other places of public amusement be closed ... Anyone refusing this order will be treated as an enemy of the Republic.' It resulted in an anti-Treaty IRA campaign against these forms of public entertainment.

At 23.30 on the evening of Friday 23 March 1923, a National Army officer on patrol saw a flame burning at the Carlton Cinema and went towards the building. As he did so, two shots were fired at him from the ruins of a building on the opposite side of the street and then a bomb exploded knocking him to the ground. The officer ordered the patrol to follow his attacker and they pursued a man in a trench coat who ran from the ruins towards nearby Cathedral Street. As they ran the man, who was joined by another, turned and shot at the soldiers who returned fire. At this time, a sentry on Marlborough Street saw two men running towards Talbot Street and called on them to halt. One of the men fired at the sentry who, along with the patrol, fired back and one of the men fell wounded outside the Masterpiece Picture House.

A member of the National Army approached and realised that he knew the wounded man, Patrick O'Brien, who said, 'I think I am done for' before asking for a priest. O'Brien confirmed that he was a member of the anti-Treaty IRA and told the soldier that he had a revolver in his pocket. He had been wounded multiple times in the legs with the bullets hitting both his thighs and he was taken to the Jervis Street Hospital. He died soon after admission. Patrick O'Brien was in his twenties at the time of his death and had been involved in the republican movement from the age of fifteen. His brother, James, stated that 'he always intended to die as he did rather than change his principles'.[29]

23 March 1923	Anti-Treaty Irish Republican Army
Thomas O'Leary	*SD 39, South New Chapel*

Thomas Theodore Joseph O'Leary was born in March 1901 at the home of his family on Darley Street in Harold's Cross. He was the son of Thomas O'Leary, a glazier, and Jane Kavanagh. The eldest of three brothers, Thomas junior later moved with his family to nearby Armstrong Street where he lived for the rest of his life. A tram conductor for the Dublin United Tramways Company he had been a member of Fianna Éireann and later 4th Battalion, Dublin Brigade, IRA. He took the anti-Treaty side during the Civil War.

Early on the morning 18 March 1923, the O'Leary family home, on Armstrong Street in Harold's Cross, was raided by members of the National Army. Jane O'Leary later said that on this occasion one of the raiding party told her that Thomas would have until the following Wednesday to give himself up or the next time that she would see him would be in a coffin.

Another witness to the raid stated that a soldier had said 'you can say goodbye to one of your sons, there was a soldier shot at Charlemont Bridge the other night and it was he that shot him'. The soldier referred to was Henry Kavanagh (*see 14 March 1923*). The day after the raid O'Leary's brother, William, met him at the bottom of Grafton Street and told him what had happened and the threat that was made. Thomas told him that he had no intention of giving himself up. In the meantime, those seeking to catch O'Leary were getting closer to him. Unknown to them was that he had been staying at a house on John Dillon Place, the home of two brothers, Jack and Jim Harpur, officers in the National Army who were sympathetic to the anti-Treaty cause.

By this time, O'Leary had dyed his hair red. Stephen Keys, a fellow anti-Treaty volunteer recalled that '... O'Leary went back to Harper's (*Sic*) that evening and the Free State came along to raid it. They knocked at the door. One of the women was sick in bed. One of the Harpers called on O'Leary and said, "Go and get into bed". He got into the bed beside her. She was so stout and he was so small and thin that he was covered up in the bed beside her. He got away that time. He had been seen going into the house. The Free Staters passed a remark before they left the house that they "would never see O'Leary alive again".'

The following day Const. John MacLoughlin was on duty and walking on Upper Rathmines Road when he found the body of Thomas O'Leary lying in a pool of blood on the path. Ten spent bullet cartridges were found nearby. Edward Finnegan who lived in the house opposite where the body was found recalled that he was awakened early on the morning of 23 March by the sound of a motorcar followed by shots and shouts of 'Halt! Halt! Halt!' Other neighbours gave similar evidence. One stated that she had witnessed a lorry stop and about a dozen men in National Army uniforms get out before hearing the shots. The doctor that examined O'Leary's body found that he had twenty-two circular wounds to his body. Some may have been both entrance and exit wounds but he could conclude that O'Leary had been shot three times in the head, once in the heart and a number of times in the legs.

The inquest into his death returned a verdict that he died due to 'shock and haemorrhage following numerous gun shot wounds caused by armed forces unknown and the military did not give sufficient help to us in the inquiry'. Less than a week after the death of Thomas O'Leary one of his close friends, Bobby Bonfield, was also killed *(see 29 March 1923)*.[30]

24 March 1923
Thomas Jones

National Army
CD 80, South New Chapel

Thomas Jones was one of three members of the National Army who were killed by the anti-Treaty IRA at Adamstown, Co. Wexford in a summary execution. Born in August 1899, he was the son of Matthew Jones and Elizabeth Healy. Jones spent all his life living on Pleasants Street and was a member of the IRA during the War of Independence, serving with 3rd Battalion, Dublin Brigade. At the time of his death, he was serving as a lieutenant in the National Army and was in command of a small detachment that was occupying Palace East in Wexford while carrying out railway protection duty. On 23 March 1923, Jones travelled to McCabe's public house near his post and was captured by the anti-Treaty IRA. Varying accounts exist as to why Jones and his men made the journey, either to investigate an attempted armed robbery or to check on drunken soldiers. Regardless, the outcome is clear. A formal report stated that:

> At 2 p.m. on Friday 23rd inst., Vol. Keane, Sgt O'Gorman and Pte Horan left Palace East without permission. They proceeded to a public-house two miles distant from the Post. At 8 p.m. the O.C. Palace East [Thomas Jones] received a report that these three soldiers were creating a disturbance in the public-house. Lieut Jones and Vol. Croke proceeded to investigate the case, armed with revolvers. On entering the public-house they were immediately surrounded by a party of irregulars armed with rifles and

Thompson Guns. Vol. Croke attempted to draw his revolver and was fired on being wounded in the hip. Lt Jones, Sgt O'Gorman were taken to Adamstown. A local Priest was made attend them and afterwards each soldier was perforated with bullets from a Thompson Gun. Their legs and bodies were a mass of bullet marks.

The shootings were carried out by members of the South Wexford Brigade anti-Treaty IRA and appear to have been formally planned and approved. The brigade activity report notes that '... following the execution of 3 IRA by F[ree] S[tate] troops in Wexford. Div[ision] with Bde. [Brigade] officers and members of D Co[mpany] 1st bn. [Battalion] captured 4 F[ree] S[tate] troops at Ballagh, New Ross. 1 resisted and was wounded. The 3 others were taken to Adamstown and executed as a reprisal for the Wexford executions ...'

The other executions referred to took place in Wexford Jail on 13 March 1923. Thomas Jones had been shot twenty times, twelve times in the legs, four times in the chest, three times in his arms and once in his head. He was interred in the National Army plot in Glasnevin, following mass at St Kevin's church on Harrington Street, on 28 March 1923.[31]

25 March 1923   **Anti-Treaty Irish Republican Army**
William J. Walsh   *BD 96, St Paul's*

At 20.20 on the evening on 24 March 1923, a National Army Crossley Tender under the command of Sgt Joseph Cochran, with a driver and two other soldiers on board, left Gormanston Camp destined for Portobello. At Whitehall as they approached 'The Thatch' public house their vehicle came under attack. A number of shots were fired and the National Army soldiers accelerated towards Drumcondra. In the aftermath of the ambush, it was discovered that a man, seemingly a civilian, had been wounded in the area of his right groin. The man was William J. Walsh and he was brought to the Mater Hospital where he was operated on but died the following evening at 16.30. Before his death Walsh had the opportunity to give a short account of what had happened to him: '... about 9 o'clock last night I was walking along the road at Whitehall beyond where the trams stop, with a boy named Ned Doyle of Francis Street, I do not know what number, when what I believe to have been a motor car passed by and a shot rang out immediately'. Walsh said he did not know who shot him and that he did not see anybody in the vicinity. At an inquest, the bullet that was extracted from William Walsh was described as being different to those used by the National Army troops present on the day and it was assumed that it was those who had set the ambush were responsible for his death. This also lent some credence to the belief that he was a civilian caught in crossfire. The coroner passed a verdict that William Walsh had died of 'shock and haemorrhage caused by a bullet fired by a person or persons unknown'. Although it was not ascertained at the time of the inquest, Walsh was in fact a member of the anti-Treaty IRA who had ambushed the National Army vehicle that evening.

William Walsh was from Coombe Street in Dublin and worked as a wood-carver. He had also served in the part time reserve of the British army and in 1914 on the outbreak of the First World War had enlisted for service with the Royal Dublin Fusiliers at the recruiting office on Great Brunswick Street (now Pearse Street). Serving with the 5th (Reserve) Battalion of his regiment he spent much time at home and was present in Dublin during the 1916 Rising. In August 1917, he was sent to the Western Front to serve with the 8th Battalion Royal Dublin Fusiliers, part of the 16th (Irish) Division.

Somewhat unusually, it appears that Walsh had not actively served with the IRA during the War of Independence before joining the anti-Treaty IRA during the Civil War, holding the rank of staff captain. William Walsh left a widow, Alice Carolan, whom he had married in 1905 and six children. The youngest was eight months old at the time of his death. His funeral to Glasnevin took place on 28 March 1923 and he was buried in a grave in which his son, Christopher, who had died aged two a year earlier, was already interred.[32]

26 March 1923   **National Army**
Nicholas Whelan   *CD 80, South New Chapel*

Nicholas Whelan from Gordon Street, Ringsend was a member of the Railway Protection Corps who was accidentally shot dead in an incident at Kilgarvan, near Athlone. Whelan was one of a number of men tasked with guarding Kilgarvan Railway Bridge. Early on the morning of 26 March 1923, a night patrol of fellow National Army soldiers from Custume Barracks encountered the men of the Railway Protection Corps unexpectedly and an exchange of gunfire took place in which Nicholas Whelan was fatally injured. He was buried in the National Army plot in Glasnevin five days later.[33]

29 March 1923   **Anti-Treaty Irish Republican Army**
Robert Bonfield   *SD 115, St Paul's*

The body of Robert Bonfield, a twenty-year-old student who was known as Bobby, was found in a ditch at Red Cow, near Clondalkin, on Easter weekend, March 1923. His body was lying on its front with his knees drawn up and his hands clasped across his front. He had been shot a number of times in the head and chest at close range.

Robert Bonfield was born in Waterford, where his family lived on Daisy Terrace, in August 1902. He was the eldest child of John Bonfield, a customs officer, and Johanna Foley. His father originally came from Nenagh in Tipperary and his mother from Castlemaine, Kerry. While Bobby was still young, the family relocated to Bootle in England where they remained for a number of years before returning to Ireland and settling at Moyne Road in Rathmines. Here he attended school at St Mary's College and also joined Fianna Éireann in 1914.

He participated in the War of Independence as a member of 4th Battalion, Dublin Brigade, IRA during which time he also entered University College Dublin as a dental student. He took the anti-Treaty side during the Civil War, was an active officer and served in the Battle of Dublin. It was suspected that in December 1922, Bonfield shot dead the former TD, Séamus Dwyer (*see 20 December 1922*). In early March 1923, Bonfield was arrested but escaped from barracks and went on the run. Evidence was given at the inquest into his death that on 29 March 1923, Bonfield was walking on St Stephen's Green when he encountered W.T. Cosgrave who was taking part in the seven churches visitation, a Roman Catholic Lenten tradition. Cosgrave was accompanied by Joe McGrath, TD, Comdt Joseph O'Reilly and some members of the CID Protective Corps. Bonfield was recognised, and there was a struggle following which he was captured and taken away. It was the last time that he was seen alive in public.

That evening a thirteen-year-old girl from Red Cow heard six shots being fired and saw two men leaving the area where Bobby Bonfield's body was later found. The inquest into his death returned a verdict of '... murder by some person or persons unknown'. The shooting of Robert Bonfield was one of a number of similar killings in late March and early April 1923.[34]

1 April 1923
John Flynn

National Army
CD 79, South New Chapel

John Flynn, a sawyer's assistant, from Irvine Terrace in East Wall, was killed in the Devonshire Arms Hotel in Bandon while serving as a private attached to A Company, 15th Infantry Battalion, Cork Command. He was a former member of Fianna Éireann, which he had joined in October 1920, and also of 2nd Battalion, Dublin Brigade IRA. He was nineteen at the time of his death. A short description of the circumstances surrounding his death described that:

> John Flynn and a comrade, whose name cannot be ascertained but was a member of the N.A. in Bandon and a native of Dublin, had retired to a room in the upper part of the Devonshire Arms Hotel with some food. A shot was accidentally discharged by Flynn's comrade whilst removing a long Webley revolver from his pocket. The bullet entered deceased's right side, fatally wounding him.[35]

3 April 1923
Christopher Breslin

Anti-Treaty Irish Republican Army
SD 39, South New Chapel

The bodies of two men were found in Cabra on the night of 3 April 1923 after local residents heard a number of shots being fired and went to investigate. The men were later identified as Christopher Breslin and Joseph Kernan (*see below*).

Christopher Breslin was born in January 1892, the son of James Breslin and Johanna Phelan from New Street in Dublin. He was youngest of four brothers involved in the independence movement, one of whom, Peadar, had been killed a year earlier at Mountjoy Jail (*see 10 October 1922*). Christopher had served during the Easter Rising with the Irish Volunteers in the Church Street and North King Street area and had subsequently been an Intelligence Officer and later company quartermaster with Dublin Brigade IRA during the War of Independence. Like his brother Peadar, he took the anti-Treaty side during the Civil War.

At the time of his death, Christopher was living in the family home on Mount Temple Road in Arbour Hill. On the night of 3 April 1923, after 23.00 there was a knock on the door of his home. Christopher's young nephew, Thomas, opened the door and three armed men entered the house while another remained outside. They asked, 'Is this where Breslin lives?' to which Thomas replied, 'Yes' and they then went upstairs.

Here they found Christopher, who identified himself. Thomas Breslin stated that the men asked his uncle if he was a brother of Peadar Breslin, which Christopher confirmed and they replied, 'you are another good thing' before telling him to get dressed and come with them. On leaving they told Christopher's sister, Mary Margaret, that they were bringing him to Portobello Barracks and that Christopher would be '... home in the morning or you can bring him up something'. However, Mary Margaret thought this was not the intention

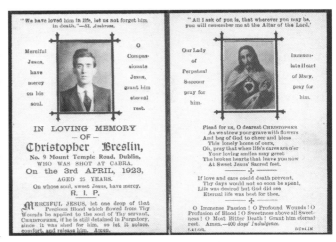

Courtesy of the Breslin Family.

of his captors. As her brother was being taken away she ran out to the street shouting for neighbours to help, as she believed her brother was to be taken away to be killed. The Breslin family also knew who had taken Christopher and Mary Margaret had stated at the inquest into his death that she could identify and name one of the armed men.

Shortly after Christopher had been taken from Mount Temple Road Michael Foley, who lived a short distance away in Cabra, heard a number of shots being fired. He rushed from his home and saw a car being driven away. Christopher Breslin lay dead on the road. He had been shot six times in the face, head and neck and six times in his body. Richard Mulcahy issued a special order four days after the shootings of Christopher Breslin and Joseph Kernan stating that an allegation had been made that they '... were murdered by persons holding positions in the Irish army. Such acts and the doers of such acts are repudiated by the army. Its record during the very difficult past demonstrates indisputably that such acts are foreign to its spirit. It is the duty of any Officer or man having information that would establish the identity of any person concerned in these

A contemporary postcard of a memorial to Christopher Breslin and Joseph Kernan. **Courtesy of the Breslin Family.**

murders to communicate without delay that information to the C.-in-C.'

Christopher Breslin's funeral came to Glasnevin on 6 April 1923 following requiem mass at Whitefriar Street church. His coffin was covered in the Tricolour and after interment in the Republican Plot prayers were recited at the grave by members of the Gaelic League.[36]

3 April 1923 — Civilian
Joseph Kernan — FG 148½, Garden

Joseph Patrick Kernan, aged nineteen, was shot dead with Christopher Breslin (*see above*) at Cabra in April 1923. Joseph was born in March 1904, the son of Margaret Magnor and Joseph Kernan. His father, who died in 1914, worked as a baker for Jacob's Biscuit Factory. At the time of his death Joseph Kernan junior was employed as a messenger for Eastman's butchers on South Great George's Street and resided at number 40 Upper Mercer Street. Just after 23.00 on the evening of 3 April, Joseph Kernan was speaking to a woman named Margaret Byrne at Redmond's Hill when a motorcar passed them. Margaret Byrne later described the car as being a green-grey touring car 'like what officers go in'. She said that after the car passed she heard somebody shout 'halt' before three men got out of the car and approached Joseph Kernan. One of the party told Kernan to come with him, and he replied, 'What?' The man told Kernan once again to come with him, hitting him in the face, before another of the men hit him with the back of a revolver and Kernan fell to the ground. He was then placed in the car and driven away north into the city. Both Margaret Byrne and another witness stated that there was a National Army patrol located at the junction of Bishop Street at the time of the incident but the car was not halted as it passed.

The description of the men in the vehicle was also similar to those who raided Christopher Breslin's home on Mount Temple Road a short time later. Two local men found the body of Joseph Kernan less than an hour after he was taken from the street. It was a short distance from Christopher Breslin. He had been shot three times in the head. Joseph Kernan does not appear to have had any formal connection with the anti-Treaty IRA. The reason he was targeted seems to have been due to his friendship with Christopher Breslin. Both men were buried in Glasnevin on the same day, with Joseph Kernan being interred in a family grave in the Garden section.[37]

10 April 1923   **National Army**
Elmer Loftus   *CD 79, South New Chapel*

Elmer Arthur Loftus was born in Cong, Co. Mayo in January 1898, the son of Ellen O'Grady and Patrick Loftus, a postman who had previously served with the British army as a member of the Connaught Rangers. The family later moved to Belfast where they lived on Panton Street. On the night of his death, Loftus was serving as a member of the National Army at New Ross, in Co. Wexford. He was in charge of a guard there. The circumstances surrounding his death were unusual. John Flanagan who was with Loftus that night described that:

> ... about 11.50 p.m. I was speaking to Corporal Loftus, the deceased. He asked me for a loan of my civilian overcoat. I asked him why he wanted it and he said he was going on a 'stunt'. I questioned him further and he said 'I am going to see if the Sentries are on the alert'. I told him it was a risky thing to do and he said he would chance it. He took down a civilian jacket and cap and put them on. He then went out wearing them. Shortly afterwards hearing a shot I went outside and found Corporal Loftus on the footpath badly wounded. We took him to hospital and on the way he said 'I am done, tell Harpur he played the soldier'.

The person referred to as Harpur was Peter Harpur, another member of the 41st Battalion, and the person who shot Loftus. He stated that:

> I was a member of the Main Guard on Outpost Duty at New Ross, Co. Wexford. At about 12.20 p.m. I was on Sentry at No. 1 Post on Friary Street. I heard Vol. Gaffney, the other Sentry on No. 1 Post, halt someone and I saw the person halted wore civilian clothes, with a grey cap down on his eyes. To approach the Sentry he came by a laneway where the wall projects and the Sentry approached also to cut off his retreat. Near the corner of the projecting wall the Sentry and the civilian met and I saw the civilian draw a revolver on the Sentry and seize the Sentry's rifle. The Sentry shouted three times for help and I covered the civilian and fired one round. The civilian fell into Vol. Gaffney's arms and Vol. Gaffney seized the revolver. I alarmed the Guard who immediately turned out and Vol. Gaffney shouted out 'It is Loftus'. This was the name of the Sergt of the Guard. We sent for the Priest and Doctor and attended the wounded man.

Elmer Loftus had been shot in the abdomen. He died two hours later at a nursing home on Mary Street in New Ross. He was buried in Glasnevin four days later.

A later report by Sgt Maj. M. Doyle described that: '... before he died I heard him say he did not blame the sentries, that they did their duty, and that it was his own fault. I was in the Barracks at the time and the general opinion was that Loftus did a very foolish thing'. Comdt James O'Hanrahan was less certain in his assessment and claimed that '... these details are only hearsay. There is no one in this unit who actually saw the incident and because of this I would not like to say whether there was any negligence or misconduct on the part of the deceased or otherwise.'[38]

16 April 1923   **National Army**
James O'Neill   *CD 79, South New Chapel*

James O'Neill, aged eighteen and the son of John O'Neill and Jane Smith from Grenville Street in Dublin, was killed during an engagement between the National Army and anti-Treaty IRA at Clashmealcon Caves on the north Kerry coast.

John O'Neill, father of James, was a member of the Irish Citizen Army who served in the St Stephen's Green area during the 1916 Rising. He was one of those who occupied the Royal College of Surgeons and was arrested following the surrender, being interned in Frongoch. He later participated in the War of Independence and during the Civil War took the anti-Treaty side fighting during the Battle of Dublin at the Hammam Hotel.

His son, James, joined the National Army late in 1922, just after his father had been released from Mountjoy where he had been interned. At this time, his father's health had begun to deteriorate. James was sent to Kerry where he was employed as an orderly at Command Headquarters. On the day of his death, he volunteered to be one of a group of men of the National Army who were sent to search cliffs and caves at Clashmealcon in Kerry. Their objective was to capture members of an anti-Treaty column. They were led to a cave within a sheer cliff falling a great distance towards the sea below. The cave provided a place of shelter for the anti-Treaty men, albeit a perilous one, only reachable via a precarious route. Early on the morning of Monday 16 April, James O'Neill with an officer, Lieut Henry Peirson, and two other men descended the cliff face towards the cave entrance. They found a small opening and O'Neill and Peirson squeezed in. They went a short distance into the cave and found a barricade, which they began to remove. As they did so they were fired at, James O'Neill was killed and Peirson was wounded. Two other National Army soldiers took shelter on the cliff face behind a rock. The National Army soldiers above threw ropes down to the men who were still under fire and they, along with the wounded Peirson, were hauled up to the top of the cliff under fire. The body of James O'Neill was thrown on to the beach and a National Army witness recorded the scene and subsequent recovery of his remains:

> The body of Volunteer O'Neill lay on the sands, face downwards with arms and legs outstretched. The morning was bright and clear and shafts of sunlight played on the green-clad form. A red patch of blood showed on the sands nearby. To the left was a moss-covered rock, crimson-stained. On this rock Lieut Pierson (*Sic*), had remained for hours, striving to staunch the flow of blood from his legs till he was finally rescued. All around one saw nothing but beetling cliffs and the sea thundered against the rocks. It was a grim forbidding spot, fit setting for the tragedy that had taken place. Standing on the cliff's edge, comrades of the dead Volunteer gazed down on the body which was already being encircled by the fast approaching tide. 'Poor Ginger' one of them muttered 'he insisted on coming out with us though he was not supposed to go out on stunts'. The tide came sweeping in and soon the body was being tossed about among the rocks, the helpless plaything of the waves. The men on the cliff were powerless to effect anything, for several efforts on the part of the Red Cross men to climb down to the beach resulted in fire being opened from the cave. And so the body remained on the beach buffeted backwards and forwards till at last the tide receded and left it lying on a jutting rock staring with unseeing eyes at the heavens ... at noon on Tuesday, two Medical Orderlies, Volunteers [Edward] Brophy and [Christopher] Mulready, pluckily offered to go down and fetch it up. 'We will take our chances' they decided and began the dangerous journey, carrying a Red Cross flag. They advanced slowly and warily along the slippery path, one false step and they were precipitated a hundred feet below on the sands. A tense silence reigned on the cliffs as the two men drew nearer and nearer the beach. Every moment we expected a burst of fire from the cave but they met with no opposition. The Irregulars at this time were in another cave the location of which prevented them from firing on the Red Cross men. A rope was flung down to the beach and the body of the dead Volunteer was brought up. The two Orderlies directed the course of the body thus preventing it from striking against the rocks on the way up. They finally clambered up, breathless after their exertions.

In the meantime the National Army, with reinforcements, lay siege to the small cave in which the anti-Treaty combatants had remained. They attempted to smoke, bomb and shoot them out but the anti-Treaty men remained resolute for a number of days before surrendering. Three of their number died while another three were later executed at Ballymullen Barracks. The body of James O'Neill was returned to Dublin where his funeral took place on 20 April. He was interred in the National Army plot in the cemetery. James' father died later the same year in the psychiatric hospital in Grangegorman. His mother died in 1962. Both are also buried in Glasnevin.[39]

17 April 1923   **Anti-Treaty Irish Republican Army**
James Tierney   *KD 116, St Paul's*

On Tuesday 17 April 1923 just before 21.00 James Tierney entered a tobacconists and newsagents at 81 Lower Dorset Street along with another man. One of the men produced a revolver and told Patrick Rooney who was standing in the shop to put up his hands. The raiders then asked Miss Dowling, the shop assistant, if there was anybody else inside the building and she replied 'no'. Soon afterwards, a struggle broke out between Rooney and the men as they fought for control of the revolver when Rooney had refused an order to go into a back room of the shop. A shot was fired at Rooney that missed him and the men tumbled out onto the pathway as they fought. Patrick Rooney later stated that:

> I then got free and held on to the revolver. All the time while struggling with the men one of the other men kept boxing me about the head but when he saw I had possession of the gun he ran away towards Healy's Corner. I then fired a shot at him and he fell.

The man was James Tierney. He had only made it a few yards before Patrick Rooney fired at him. Rooney stated that he had never previously held a gun. He pointed it towards Tierney and pulled the trigger without knowing if it would go off. The bullet hit Tierney through the chest, entering his lung and his heart. The other man who accompanied Tierney escaped towards Drumcondra. The city coroner attributed the motive for the incident to simple robbery, however Tierney was an active volunteer with the anti-Treaty IRA who was acting under orders at the time of his death. The intention of the raid was to capture Criminal Investigation Department communications that were held in the building. Following his death Tierney's parents received a letter from his unit stating:

> A chara, I have been instructed by the Staff and Officers of the 1st Batt. to convey to you their deepest sympathy on the death of your son. For many years he has been a trustworthy soldier of the Irish Republican Army and his death will be a big loss to the 1st Batt. I take this opportunity of myself tendering to you my own deepest sympathy.

John Tierney, father of James, stated that his son had been a Volunteer since 1917 and that his brothers were also active in the movement. John opposed the nature of the press reports in relation to the death of his son and was assured that a different account of his death would be published in *Éire – The Irish Nation*, a weekly Republican publication.[40]

23 April 1923   **National Army**
James Montgomery   *DD 79, South New Chapel*

Sgt James Montgomery, from Belfast, was serving with Mechanical Transport based in the Curragh Camp when he was killed in 1923. He was accidentally shot by Pte William Jones while taking part in a search of the grounds of Moore Abbey in Monasterevin. The search, by a group of sixteen National Army soldiers, followed reports that a group of eight or nine civilians had been seen on the grounds of the Abbey the previous night. William Jones later recalled events leading to the death of James Montgomery:

> On the 23rd of April 1923 at about 12.30p.m. we were on the square at the A.S.C. Barracks and were just dismissed when Lieut Chandler ordered everybody to get their dinner quickly. After dinner about 2 o'clock Lieut Doogan fell us in the square. He ordered everybody who had not fired a course to get back to their billets. Lieut Doogan asked me if I had fired a course. I said I had fired a course at Beresford Barracks because I was anxious to go with the party on whatever duty they were going on. I joined Lieut Chandler's party and we proceeded by motor lorry. In the lorry about half a mile from camp somebody said 'lets load up' and we all loaded our rifles. Lieut Chandler did not give us any order to load, nor did he see or hear us load as far as I know. I put five rounds in the magazine and applied the 'cut off'. When we got to Moore Abbey I was with Sgt Montgomery and Private Furlong searching the Park. I asked the Sergeant what we were searching for and he replied 'that there were 8 or 9 irregulars whom we were searching for'. I passed the remark 'we'll put one up the breech' and the Sergeant said 'we might as well, because it looks like a place for an ambush'. I put a round up the breech and the Sergeant saw me do it and passed no remarks. I then put the safety catch in the safe position. Later at the Abbey we met the other party and we started off to continue the search after a rest. I was alongside Sgt Montgomery who was on my left hand side. I was holding the rifle with my two hands, my right was horizontally across the body. Suddenly a shot rang out. I don't remember that I had my finger on the trigger. I don't remember interfering with the safety catch. I saw the smoke coming from the muzzle of my rifle and I saw the Sergeant doubling up and falling crying 'I'm shot, I'm shot'. Somebody took the rifle from me then and I knew I had shot the Sergeant.

Jones also explained that he was nineteen years old and that he actually knew nothing about the mechanism of a rifle. His only experience was two or three lectures and that, as he worked in the cook house, he had never fired a shot in his life before. The bullet had hit James Montgomery on his right side above his hip, travelled through his stomach and exited on his left. The rifle, a Short Magazine Lee–Enfield Mk I, that fired the fatal shot was found to have a defective safety catch. The court of inquiry exploring the death of James

Montgomery also noted that William Jones had suffered severe psychological issues following the incident.[41]

25 April 1923   National Army
Michael Behan   *DD 79, South New Chapel*

Michael Behan, from Prices Row, off Robert Street, Dublin was killed in an ambush in Kerry while serving with the National Army in 1923. A mill packer, who worked at Halligan's Flour Mills, on Usher's Island, Behan was a member of D Company, 1st Battalion, Dublin Brigade, IRA, from 1918. During the War of Independence, he participated in an attack on an armoured car in Phibsborough and operations at Kingsbridge (later Heuston) Station, amongst other actions. He was arrested and interned in April 1921. Having joined the National Army he was made a lieutenant, attached initially to the 19th Infantry Battalion, and later posted to Castleisland in Kerry. On the day of his death, Behan was travelling in a car from Currow to Castleisland with Lieut Jeremiah Gaffney, who was later executed for murder in 1924, and two members of the Civic Guard. Outside Castleisland, they encountered a barrier blocking the road and left their car to attempt to move it. When they did, they were ambushed and placed under heavy fire. The two officers, who were armed with revolvers, returned fire. In the exchange, Michael Behan was killed. Jeremiah Gaffney succeeded in escaping back to Castleisland. The Civic Guards, who were captured, were stripped of their uniforms and subsequently released.[42]

8 May 1923   National Army
Francis McGinley   *DD 79, South New Chapel*

Francis McGinley from Millbrae, Buncrana, Co. Donegal was accidentally shot at Bonniconlon in Mayo while serving with the National Army. Early on the morning of 7 May 1923, McGinley was shot by Pte R. Moore, a member of the Machine Gun Company, 61st Infantry Battalion. On the day that McGinley was fatally wounded, Moore returned to his room after a patrol in Bonniconlon. He later stated that on arrival there he began to unload his rifle:

> ... I was perfect sure everything was quite clear. I pulled the bolt of the rifle back several times, then pulling the trigger, a shot rang out. I was surprised to hear it, immediately I heard a man moaning, dropping my rifle I ran into the next room where the wounded man was kneeling. I saw Corporal Whelan on his knee stripping the wounded man,

he called for a field dressing. I returned to my own room, for my own field dressing and gave it to Corpl Whelan.

Francis McGinley died of his wounds the following day in St Bricin's Hospital in Dublin. [43]

Endnotes

Endnotes are given in full in the first instance and abbreviated in further citations. See
BIBLIOGRAPHY for commonly used abbreviations.

1919

1 General Register Office [*GRO*], Irish Genealogy (civilrecords.irishgenealogy.ie); *Irish Independent [II]*, 12 Sep. 1919; 8 Aug. 1919; 11 Sep. 1919; 'Dublin Metropolitan Police and Civic Guard personnel registers indexes' (Garda Museum and Archives), 'Shooting "the dog"', *History Ireland*, vol. 27 no. 4 (2019), pp. 40–43; 'Bureau of Military History witness statements James Slattery', 1951 (Military Archives, Dublin, WS445).

1920

1 *Freeman's Journal [FJ]*, 23 Mar. 1920; *Evening Herald [EH]*, 15 Apr. 1920; II, 3 Apr. 1920; GRO; Riot, Dublin, HC Deb 1920 vol. 127 cc259–60; 'First World War Other ranks service papers', 1914–20 (National Archives, London [*TNA*], War Office Registered Papers, WO363); Database, Commonwealth War Graves Commission (cwgc.org).

2 *Dublin Evening Telegraph [DET]*, 10 May 1920; *FJ*, 10 May 1920; GRO; 'Prosecution of civilians: A2 2302 – 2379', 1920–22 (*TNA*, War Office Registered Papers, WO 35/111)

3 *FJ*, 2 Jun. 1920; *Belfast Telegraph [BT]*, 29 May 1920; *The Irish Times [IT]*, 6 Mar. 1920; *Derry Journal [DJ]*, 2 Jun. 1920; *GRO*; O'Reilly, Terence (ed.), *Our Struggle for Independence* (Cork, 2009), pp. 85–91; 'Royal Irish Constabulary general register' (*TNA*, Home Office Registered Papers, HO 184/44).

4 *Kerryman [K]*, 31 Oct. 1970; *II*, 27 Jun. 1949; *Irish Press*, 28 Jan. 1949; 27 Jun. 1949; *GRO; TNA* WO363, WO329; 'Connaught Rangers Mutiny' (http://www.irishmedals.ie/Connaught-Rangers-Mutiny.php); 'Bureau of Military History witness statements Joseph Hawes', 1949 (Military Archives, Dublin, WS262).

5 *GRO; TNA* WO363, WO329.

6 *GRO; Cork Examiner [CE]*, 14 Aug. 1920; *EH*, 11 Aug. 1920, 13 Aug. 1920; *Dublin Evening Telegraph [DET]*, 17 Aug. 1920; *II*, 18 Aug. 1920; 'Shooting of Thomas Farrelly in August 1920' (https://comeheretome.com/2016/11/28/shooting-of-thomas-farrelly-in-august-1920/).

7 *GRO*; 'Military service pensions collection Neill Kerr', 1916–23 (Military Archives, Dublin, DP7713); *DET*, 9 Sep. 1920; *Dundee Evening Telegraph*, 7 Sep. 1920; BMH WS814 (Patrick G. Daly).

8 *GRO; NAI*, 1901 census, 1911 census; *II*, 2 Oct. 1920, 4 Oct. 1920, 5 Oct. 1920, 13 Oct. 1920; *CE*, 5 Oct. 1920; *BN*, 2 Oct. 1920; TNA WO363, WO 372, WO 339/98391; BMH WS 1278 (John P. Brennan).

9 *GRO; EH*, 15 Oct. 1920; *FJ*, 23 Oct. 1920; *Belfast Newsletter [BL]*, 16 Oct. 1920.

10 *EH*, 16 Oct. 1920, 19 Oct. 1920; *II*, 19 Oct. 1920; *FJ*, 18 Oct. 1921; BMH WS380 (David Neligan), WS594, WS 314 (Liam O'Carroll); *GRO*.

11 *FJ*, 16 Oct. 1920; *EH*, 21 Oct. 1920; *BN*, 16 Oct. 1920; *GRO; TNA* WO364.

12 *FJ*, 19 October 1920; *MSPC* DP6240; BMH WS503 (James Cahill).

13 *FJ*, 25 Oct. 1920; *Ibid.*, 30 Oct. 1920; *GRO; MSPC* MSP34REF60517..

14 BMH WS1043 (Joseph V. Lawless); *GRO; Drogheda Independent [DI]*, 6 Nov. 1920; *FJ*, 1 Nov. 1920; *II*, 1 Nov. 1920; 'Courts of inquiry in lieu of inquest individual cases', 1920–22 (*TNA*, War Office Registered Papers, WO 35/145).

15 *II*, 12 Oct. 1920, 30 Oct. 1920; *FJ*, 21 Oct. 1920; BMH WS434 (Charles Dalton), WS1043 (Joseph V. Lawless); *GRO*; 'Dublin Metropolitan Police D Division. Superintendents Journal And Letter Book', 1921 (*TNA*, Home Office Registered Papers, HO 184/71); *TNA* HO 184/11; *CWGC; Dublin's fighting story, 1916–21* (Cork 2009), pp. 257–270.

16 *GRO*; *CE*, 3 Nov. 1920; *EH*, 8 Nov. 1920; *FJ*, 6 Nov. 1920; *Ibid.*, 5 Nov. 1920; BMH WS493 (Seamus Kavanagh); 'Kevin Barry papers court martial documents', 1920 (UCD Archives, Dublin, P 93/20); Richard Hawkins. 'Barry, Kevin Gerard'. *Dictionary of Irish Biography* (ed.) James McGuire, James Quinn. (Cambridge University Press, 2009) (http://dib.cambridge. org/viewReadPage.do?articleId=a0451).

17 GRO; *EH*, 22 Nov. 1920; *II*, 30 Nov. 1920; *FJ*, 26 Nov. 1920; 'Courts of inquiry in lieu of inquest individual cases', 1920–22 (*TNA* London, War Office Registered Papers, WO 35/88B); English Parliamentary Labour Party, *Report of the Labour Commission to Ireland 1921* (London, 1921); Michael Foley, *The Bloodied Field* (Dublin, 2014), p. 82.

18 *GRO*; *II*, 26 Nov. 1920; *Ibid.*, 27 Nov. 1920; *EH*, 22 Dec. 1915; 'Courts of inquiry in lieu of inquest individual cases', 1920–22 (*TNA*, War Office Registered Papers, WO 35/88B); 'Admiralty Royal Marines attestation forms', 1790–1925 (*TNA*), records of the Admiralty, ADM 157/3430/29); 'Compensation claim for M. Feery Croke Park', 1921 (*TNA*, War Office Registered Papers, WO 35/41); TNA WO363, WO364; 'Mountjoy Prison registers', 1900–1922 (*NA* Dublin); *CWGC*.

19 *TNA*, HO 184/37; GRO; BMH WS1299 (Christopher Carroll); *II*, 25 Nov. 1920; *FJ*, 3 Mar. 1924; *The Nationalist*, 19 Jan. 1924; *Weekly Irish Times [WIT]*, 10 Nov. 1917; *IT*, 9 Mar. 1921; MSPC 34REF5714; *TNA* WO 35/159B, WO 329; 'Royal Air Force officers' service records' Michael Joseph Carroll, 1918–19 (*TNA*, Air Ministry records, AIR 76/162/170); Anne Dolan, 'Killing and Bloody Sunday, November 1920', *The Historical Journal*, Vol. 49, No. 3, 2006, pp. 789–810; A. J. L. Scott, *Sixty Squadron R.A.F. 1916–1919* (London, 1920).

20 GRO; *II*, 23 Nov. 1920; *IT*, 13 Aug. 2016; *TNA* WO 35/88.

21 *Connaught Telegraph [CT]*, 25 Dec. 1909, 3 Apr. 1920, 4 Dec. 1920; *GRO*; *TNA* WO35/159B; May Moran, *Executed for Ireland the Patrick Moran story* (Cork, 2010) pp.72–79; *MSPC* 24SP11341; BMH WS503 (James Cahill); Anne Dolan, 'Killing and Bloody Sunday November 1920', *The Historical Journal*, 49, 3 (2006), pp.789–810.

22 *GRO*; *II*, 25 Nov. 1920; *EH*, 24 Nov. 1920; *TNA* WO 35/88.

23 *GRO*; *II*, 29 Jun. 1921; *FJ*, 29 Jun. 1921; *TNA* WO 35/88; MSPC 24SP2327.

24 *GRO*; *CE*, 26 Nov. 1920; TNA WO 35/88; MSPC DP7168.

25 *GRO*; *TNA* WO 35/149A; 'Dublin District raid and search reports', 1920–21 (*TNA* War Office Registered Papers, WO 35/81).

26 *TNA* WO364/4679, WO35/159B, WO372; *The Times [TT]*, 18 Feb. 1919; 23 Nov. 1920; Foreign Office, *The Foreign Office List and Diplomatic and Consular Year Book for 1917* (London, 1917), p. 50; *MSPC* MSP34REF57114, 24SO6860, MSP34REF1549; BMH WS503 (James Cahill).

27 GRO; *II*,. 26 Nov. 1920, 24 Nov. 1920; *FJ*, 27 Nov. 1920; *TNA* WO 35/162; 'Dublin District claims for damages', 1920–21 (*TNA*, War Office Registered Papers, WO 35/166); BMH WS511 (Michael Lynch); MSPC 1D412; Pauric J. Dempsey. 'Clancy, Peadar'. *Dictionary of Irish Biography*. (http://dib.cambridge.org/viewReadPage.do?articleId=a1679).

28 *GRO*; *II*,. 26 Nov. 1920, 24 Nov. 1920; *FJ*, 27 Nov. 1920; *TNA* WO 35/162, WO 35/166); BMH WS511 (Michael Lynch); *MSPC* DP23324; Marie Coleman, 'McKee, Dick (Richard)'. *Dictionary of Irish Biography*. (http://dib.cambridge.org/viewReadPage.do?articleId=a5715).

29 *GRO*; *II*, 23 Nov. 1920; *TNA* WO 35/157A.

30 *GRO*; *TNA* WO 35/149A; *FJ*, 27 Nov. 1920.

31 *GRO*; *EH*, 25 Nov. 1920; *TNA* WO 35/88B; *TNA* AIR 76/78/23.

32 *GRO*; *EH*, 29 Nov. 1920; *II*, 26 Nov. 1920; *FJ*, 27 Nov. 1920; *TNA* WO 35/149A; *MSPC* DP1364.

33 *GRO*; *II*, 17 Dec. 1920; *BN*, 17 Dec. 1920; *Connacht Tribune [CTrib]*, 27 Nov. 1920; *TNA* WO 35/148.

34 'Royal Irish Constabulary officers' register', 1920 (*TNA* Home Office Registered Papers, HO 184/47); *GRO*; *EH*, 7 Mar. 1921; *Skibbereen Eagle [SE]*, 1 Jan. 1921; *Southern Star [SS]*, 30 Dec. 1989; *TNA* WO 35/157A; BMH WS547 (Joseph Leonard).

1921

1 *II*, 12 Jan 1921; TNA HO 184/71, WO 35/208, HO 184/38; GRO.

2 *GRO*; *FJ*, 14 Jan. 1921, 15 Jan. 1921, 18 Jan. 1921, 3 Feb. 1921; *EH*, 9 Mar. 1921; *The Liberator*, 15 Jan. 1921; *TNA* WO 35/154.

3 *TNA* HO 184/31, HO 184/47; *GRO*; *FJ*, 21 January 1921; *CE*, 25 Jan. 1921; *Northern Whig*, 25 Jan. 1921; *TNA* WO 35/157A; BMH WS1123 (Cornelius Brosnan).

4 *GRO*; *EH*, 18 January 1921; *TNA* WO 35/153B, WO 35/76; BMH WS508 (Dermot O'Sullivan), WS 1687 (Harry Colley); *MSPC* 1D73.

5 *GRO*; *CE*, 2 Feb. 1921; *TNA* WO 35/154, HO 184/30; BMH WS1121 (Martin Fallon), WS 954 (Seán Leavy), WS 661 (Luke Duffy).

6 *GRO*; Col. J. M. MacCarthy (ed.), *Limerick's Fighting Story* (Kerry, 1973), pp. 126–128; *TNA* HO 184/44, WO 35/149A, WO 329; BMH WS891 (Maurice Meade), WS737 (Seán Meade).

7 *GRO*; *II*, 11 Mar. 1921, 13 Apr. 1921, 16 Apr. 1921; *FJ*, 22 Feb. 1921, 18 Mar. 1921, 13 Apr. 1921, 15 Apr. 1921, 16 Apr. 1921; *TNA* WO 35/136, WO 35/82, HO 184/30.

8 *MSPC* 24SP323; BMH WS 1399 (Thomas Peppard); *TNA* WO 35/153A, HO 184/57; *GRO*.

9 *II*, 24 Feb. 1921, 28 Feb. 1921; *TNA* WO 35/151A; HO 184/35; *GRO*; BMH WS423 (Vincent Byrne), WS477 (Edward J. Kelliher), WS 631 (Bernard C. Byrne), WS 822 (William J. Stapleton).

10 *II*, 7 Mar. 1921, 10 Mar. 1921; *FJ*, 7 Mar. 1921; *TNA* WO 35/157A; *GRO* 'Australian Imperial Forces personnel dossiers', 1914–20 (National Archives of Australia, B2455/ 7998443).

11 *MSPC* 1D142; *GRO*; Tim Carey, *Hanged for Ireland* (Dublin, 2001), pp.100–133; *EH*, 22 Feb. 1921, 12 Mar. 1921; *FJ*, 15 Mar. 1921; *II*, 2 Mar. 1921; 15 Mar. 1921.

12 *MSPC* 1D26; *GRO*; Carey, pp. 96–133.

13 *TNA* WO 35/150; *FJ*, 18 Mar. 1921; *II*, 17 Mar. 1921; *MSPC* 1D320; Caoimhe Nic Dháibhéid, *Seán MacBride: A Republican Life 1904–46* (Oxford, 2011), pp. 44–47; BMH WS626 (John Donnelly).

14 *MSPC* 24SP13201, 24SP1409, 24SP1550, 24SP2302); *GRO*; Seán Kearns. 'Flood, Francis Xavier ("Frank")', *Dictionary of Irish Biography* (http://dib.cambridge.org/viewReadPage. do?articleId=a3293).

15 *II*, 17 Mar. 1921, 19 Mar. 1921 *FJ*, 17 Mar. 1921, 18 Mar. 1921; *EH*, 17 Mar. 1921; *TNA* WO 35/152); *GRO*; BMH WS889 (Seamus Ua Camhanaigh).

16 *EH*, 15 Mar. 1921; *FJ*, 16 Feb. 1921, 2. Mar. 1921, 10 Mar. 1921, 15 Mar. 1921; *II*, 17 Feb. 1921, 7 Mar. 1921, 12 Mar. 1921, 15 Mar. 1921; Moran, p. 88; *MSPC* DP7559; *GRO*; *TNA* WO35/147B, WO35/135.

17 *GRO*; *II*, 15 Mar. 1921, 24 Mar. 1921; *TNA* WO 35/141; *MSPC* 1D131.

18 *MSPC* 1D125; BMH WS707 (Michael Noyk); *GRO*; *TNA* WO35/72/3; Carey, pp. 56–67.

19 *II*, 23 Mar. 1921; *FJ*, 22 Mar. 1921; TNA WO 35/157A); *GRO*; *MSPC* 1D364); BMH WS266 (Charles Walker).

20 *II*, 29 Mar. 1921; *FJ*, 29 Mar. 1921; *TNA* WO 35/162, WO363; *GRO*; *MSPC* MSP34REF19315; *MSPC*, 24SP6360; 'Imperial Yeomanry Soldiers Documents', 1899–1902 (*TNA*, War Office Registered Papers, WO 128/102); 'Air Ministry Airmen's Records', 1918–28 (*TNA*, Air Ministry Records, AIR 79/2584).

21 *TNA* WO 35/151A, HO 184/31; *MSPC* 24SP4864; *GRO*; BMH WS813 (Patrick O'Connor); *II*, 1 April 1921.

22 *TNA* HO 184/71; *TNA* WO 35/147A; *GRO*; *II*, 5 April 1921.

23 *GRO*; *II*, 8 April 1921; *FJ*, 7 April 1921, 11 April 1921; *TNA* WO 35/148; *MSPC* 1D193.

24 *II*, 28 Mar. 1921; *FJ*, 28 Mar. 1921, 13 Apr. 1921; *TNA* WO 35/159A; *GRO*.

25 *GRO*; *TNA* WO 35/159A; R. R. Lycette (ed.), *Being an account by Ernest Lycette of his life as a young man and soldier in the years between 1911 and 1921* (New Zealand, 2007), p. 216; 'Ernest Lycette' (http://theauxiliaries.com/men-alphabetical/men-l/lycett-e/lycett-e.html).

26 *GRO*; *II*, 20 April 1921; *EH*, 9 July 1921; TNA WO 35/159B, WO 35/153B, HO 184/30; *MSPC* 1D450; BMH WS 1395 (James Crenigan).

27 *TNA* WO 35/150); *GRO*; *FJ*, 25 April 1921; *II*, 26 April 1921; *MSPC* 1D134; BMH WS157 (Joseph O'Connor); 'General Courts Martial Civilian Thomas Traynor', 1921 (*TNA*, War Office Registered Papers, WO 71/366).

28 *II*, 9 May 1921; *SI*, 8 May 1921; *GRO*; *MSPC* 24SP1695; *TNA* WO35/148..

29 *GRO*; *FJ*, 14 Jan. 1921, 15 Jan. 1921; *BN*, 14 Jan. 1921; *TNA* WO 35/156.

30 *TNA* HO 184/30; *GRO*; BMH WS1456 (John Kelleher).

31 *TNA* HO 184/40, WO 329, WO 363, 'Irish Constabulary records Auxiliary Division', 1921 (*TNA*, Home Office Registered Papers, HO 184/50); *GRO*; 'Irish Republican Army Dublin Brigade general orders', 1918–21 (*NLI*, MS 901/121).

32 *CE*, 18 May 1921; II, 18 May 1921, 21 May 1921; *TNA* WO 35/163; GRO.

33 *GRO*; *FJ*, 23 May 1921; *TNA* WO 35/162; BMH WS 813 (Pádraig Ó Conchubhair), WS 956 (George White).

34 *TNA* WO 35/166, WO 35/85; *GRO*; *EH*, 26 May 1921; *II*, 26 May 1921; BMH WS340 (Oscar Traynor), WS1411 (Daniel McAleese); 'General Courts Martial Civilian Thomas Traynor', 1921 (*TNA*, War Office Registered Papers, WO 71/366).

35 TNA WO 35/166; GRO; *EH*, 26 May 1921, 30 May 1921; *II*, 26 May 1921.

36 *GRO*; *II*, 28 May 1921, 30 May 1921; *TNA* WO 35/158; *MSPC* 1D186; BMH WS1687 (Harry Colley).

37 *GRO*; *II*, 28 May 1921, 30 May 1921; *TNA* WO 35/158; MSPC 1D186.

38 *FJ*, 16 May 1921; *II*, 30 May 1921; *TNA* WO 35/148; GRO.

39 *EH*, 3 Jun. 1921; *FJ*, 2 Jun. 1921, 3 Jun. 1921; *MSPC* 1D27; BMH WS445 (James J. Slattery); *GRO*; *TNA* WO35/149A/50; 'Sean Doyle 'Sad Quest for a dying Squad Man' (customhouse commemoration.com/2016/12/16/sad-quest-for-a-missing-squad-man-sean-doyle-custom-house-burning/).

40 *FJ*, 30 May 1921; *TNA* WO 35/163, HO 184/51), HO 184/42; *GRO*.

41 *TNA* WO 35/157A; *GRO*; *II*, 6 Jun 1921.

42 *GRO*; *FJ*, 8 Jul. 1921; *CE*, 25 Sep. 1920, 25 Oct. 1919; *II*, 22 May 1919; *TNA* WO 35/136; BMH WS597 (Edmond O'Brien); *MSPC* 1D279.

43 *FJ*, 9 June 1921; *EH*, 8 June 1921; *TNA* WO 35/163, WO 35/150; *GRO*.

44 *TNA* WO 35/150 *FJ*, 9 June 1921; *EH*, 8 June 1921; *GRO*.

45 *TNA* WO 35/157A, WO363; *FJ*, 21 June 1921; *MSPC* MSP34REF59866; BMH WS434 (Charles Dalton); *GRO*.

46 *TNA* WO 35/163; *GRO*; *FJ*, 20 Jun. 1921; *Sunday Independent [SI]*, 19 Jun. 1921.

47 *GRO*; *SS*, 23 Dec. 1922; *Evening Echo [EE]*, 16 Dec. 1922, 19 Nov. 1920; *II*, 10 Nov. 1919; *FJ*, 7 Aug. 1920; *TNA* WO 35/149B, WO 35/72, WO 35/79, 'Claims for damages 1922' (WO 35/166); *MSPC* 1D188.

48 *TNA* WO 35/155A; *GRO*; *FJ*, 20 Jun. 1921; SI, 19 Jun. 1921.

49 *TNA* WO 35/155A; *GRO*; *FJ*, 20 Jun. 1921, 19 Aug. 1921; 'The death of Bessie O'Brien' (theirishstory.com/2021/06/21/today-in-irish-history-the-death-of-bessie-obrien-dublin-21-june-1921)

50 *TNA* WO 35/149A; *GRO*; 'Catholic Parish Registers, St Catherine's Dublin', 1873 (*NLI*, 07139/06).

51 *GRO*; *FJ*, 5 Jul. 1921, 6 Jul. 1921, 7 Jul. 1921, 19 Aug. 1921; *II*, 19 Aug. 1921; *EH*, 18 Aug. 1921; *TNA* WO35/163.

52 *MSPC* 3P313; *CE* 23 Dec. 2019; *EH*, 12 Jul. 1921, 14 Jul. 1921; *II*, 13 Jul. 1921, 15 Jul. 1921; *FJ*, 11 Jul. 1921, 14 Jul. 1921, 15 Jul. 1921; *NAI*, 1911 census; *GRO*.

53 *TNA* WO 35/149A; *GRO*; *MSPC* MSP1D306; *EH*, 10 Sep. 1921.

54 *GRO*; *II*, 12 Nov. 1921; *FJ*, 16 Nov. 1921; *MSPC* 1D206.

1922

1 *EH*, 4 Feb. 1922; *FJ*, 3 Mar. 1922; *II*, 4 Feb. 1922, 7 Feb. 1922; *GRO*.

2 *EH*, 6 Mar. 1922; *CE*, 3 Mar. 1922; *II*, 3 Mar. 1922; *FJ*, 4 Mar. 1922; *GRO*; BMH WS1475 (Patrick Kinnane); *TNA* HO184.

3 *EH*, 7 Apr. 1922, 12 Jun. 1922, 1 Aug. 1922; *FJ*, 4 Mar. 1922, 6 Mar. 1922, 14 Mar. 1922, 13 Jun. 1922, 8 Dec. 1922, 22 Dec. 1922; *CE*, 4 Mar. 1922, 13 Jun. 1922; *II*, 4 Mar. 1922, 6 Mar. 1922, 6 Apr. 1922; *IT*, 26 Sep. 2015; Pádraig Yeates, *A City in Civil War Dublin 1921–4* (Dublin, 2015), pp. 22–4; *GRO*; *TNA* HO144/10308; BMH WS731 (Katherine Barry-Moloney); 'Civil Engineer Membership Forms', 1818–1930 (London, 7568).

4 *CE*, 11 Apr. 1922; *II*, 11 Apr. 1922; *GRO*; *MSPC* DP8615.

5 *EH*, 10 Apr. 1922; *II*, 12 Apr. 1922; *GRO*; *MSPC* 2D131.

6 *FJ*, 11 Apr. 1922, 13 Apr. 1922, 17 Apr. 1922; *II*, 12 Apr. 1922, 11 Apr. 1922, 15 Apr. 1922; *EE*, 14 Apr. 1922; *TNA* WO95/1279; CWGC; *MSPC* DP6152; BMH WS607 (Joseph McGuinness), WS596 (George Nolan).

7 *MSPC* DP4008; *CE* 31 May 1922, 1 Jun. 1922; *FJ*, 31 May 1922; *GRO*.

8 *EH*, 27 Jun. 1922; *II*, 27 Jun. 1922; *GRO*; *MSPC* DP23657.

9 *GRO*; *NAI*, 1911 census.

10 *GRO*; *FJ*, 8 Jul. 1922.

11 *GRO*; *FJ*, 8 Jul. 1922; *EH*, 29 Jun. 1922;

12 *EH*, 1 Jul. 1922; *II*, 29 Jun. 1922; *FJ*, 8 Jul. 1922; *GRO*.

13 *GRO*; *II*, 29 June 1922.

14 *EH*, 28 Jun 1922; *GRO*.

15 *II*, 29 Jun. 1922, 5 Jul. 1922, 6 Jul. 1922; *TNA* ADM 196/70/453; Dorney, pp. 259–60; *GRO*.

16 *GRO*; *II*, 29 June 1922.

17 *GRO*; *BN*, 30 June 1922.

18 *II*, 29 Jun. 1922, 5 Jul. 1922, 6 Jul. 1922; *MSPC* 2D156; BMH WS707 (Michael Noyk).

19 *MSPC* DP1665, MD2272.

20 *MSPC* 2D231; Dorney, pp. 169–70.

21 *FJ*, 8 Jul. 1922; *EH*, 11 Oct. 1922; GRO; *NAI*, 1911 census.

22 *GRO*; *II*, 4 Jul. 1922.

23 *GRO*, *IT* 4 Jul. 1922; *II*, 4 Jul. 1922.

24 *GRO*, *II*, 4 Jul. 1922; *MSPC* DP3949

25 *IT*, 1 Jul. 1922; *FJ*, 8 Jul. 1922; *II*, 4 Jul. 1922.

26 *TNA* WO372; *MSPC* 2D381.

27 *EH*, 1 Jul. 1922; *FJ*, 8 Jul. 1922; *MSPC* 2D370; *GRO*.

28 *GRO*; *MSPC* 2D452. Date of death is recorded both as 29 and 30 June.

29 *II*, 1 Jul. 1922, 5 Jul. 1922; *GRO*; *MSPC* DP6739.

30 *II*, 30 Jun. 1922, 4 Jul. 1922; *MSPC* 2D464.

31 *MSPC* 2D10; *TNA* WO329, WO372; *GRO*.

32 *II*, 4 Jul. 1922, 7 Jul. 1922; *GRO*.

33 *Ibid.*

34 *MSPC* 2D142; *GRO*.

35 *II*, 7 Jul. 1922; *MSPC* 2D228; *GRO*.

36 *FJ*, 11 Jul. 1922; *GRO*; *MSPC* 2D196.

37 *FJ*, 8 Jul. 1922; *GRO*; *NGA*, *Last Post*, p. 43; Dorney, p. 109.

38 *FJ*, 6 Jul. 1922; *II*, 6 Jul. 1922; *TNA* WO372; 'Mountjoy Prison Registers' (NAI).

39 *FJ*, 8 Jul. 1922; *II*, 8 Jul. 1922; *GRO*; *MSPC* 2D419.

40 *FJ*, 7 Jul. 1922; *II*, 8 Jul. 1922; *GRO*; *MSPC* 2D81.

41 *GRO*; *EH*, 8 Jul. 1922; *FJ*, 10 Jul. 1922; *TNA* WO329.

42 *EH*, 10 Jul. 1922; *FJ*, 8 Jul. 1922; *GRO*; BMH WS404 (Linda Kearns); dib.ie/biography/brugha-cathal-a1077; Fergus O'Farrell, *Cathal Brugha* (Dublin 2018).

43 *FJ*, 12 Jul. 1922; *MSPC* 2D409; *GRO*.

44 *EH*, 10 Jul. 1922; *FJ*, 13 Jul. 1922; *MSPC* 3D17; *GRO*.

45 *EH*, 10 Jul. 1922; *FJ*, 11 Jul. 1922, 12 Jul. 1922; *MSPC* 2D364.

46 *FJ*, 12 Jul. 1922, 14 Jul. 1922; *CE* 12 Jul. 1922; *MSPC* 2D333; *GRO*.

47 *GRO*; *EH*, 10 Jul. 1922; *FJ*, 11 Jul. 1922.

48 *EH*, 11 Jul. 1922; *FJ*, 14 Jul. 1922; BMH WS805 (Annie O'Brien); *MSPC* DP2196; GRO; wexfordcivilwar archaeology.com/2018/10/24/shot-dead-at-enniscorthy-post-office-july-1922/; theirishstory.com/2018/10/16/the-killurin-ambush-1922-and-the-civil-war-in-wexford.

49 *GRO*; *EH*, 21 Jul. 1922; *FJ*, 22 Jul. 1922; *IT* 22 Jul. 1922.

50 *FJ*, 24 Jul. 1922; *MSPC* 2D134; *GRO*.

51 *II*, 25 Jul. 1922; *GRO*; *MSPC* 3D242.

52 *EH*, 24 Jul. 1922; *II*, 25 Jul. 1922; *GRO*; *MSPC* 2D108.

53 *FJ*, 25 Jul. 1922, 26 Jul. 1922; *II*, 26 Jul. 1922, 3 Aug. 1922; *MSPC* 2D180; *TNA* WO372, WO329; theirishstory.com /2018/10/16/the-killurin-ambush-1922-and-the-civil-war-in-wexford.

54 *FJ*, 26 Jul. 1922; *MSPC* 2D417; *GRO*.

55 *FJ*, 25 Jul. 1922, 26 Jul. 1922, 28 Jul. 1922; *II*, 26 Jul. 1922, 3 Aug. 1922; *GRO*; *MSPC* 2D137; *TNA* BT350; NAI, Mountjoy Prison Registers.

56 *FJ*, 25 Jul. 1922, 26 Jul. 1922; *II*, 26 Jul. 1922, 3 Aug. 1922; *GRO*; *MSPC* 2D417.

57 *FJ*, 4 Aug. 1922; *II*, 31 Jul. 1922; *GRO*; *MSPC* 2D43.

58 *FJ*, 4 Aug. 1922; *II*, 31 Jul. 1922; *TNA* WO372; *NAI*, Mountjoy Prison Registers.

59 *II*, 3 Aug. 1922; *The Nationalist [TN]*, 9 Aug. 1922; *MSPC* 2D395.

60 *EH*, 31 July 1922; 1 Aug. 1922; *FJ*, 1 Aug. 1922; *II*, 3 Aug. 1922, 5 Aug. 1922; *GRO*; BMH WS369 (William Whelan); dib.ie/biography/boland-harry-a10060.

61 *GRO*; *EH*, 4 Aug. 1922; *IT*, 5 Aug. 1922.

62 *GRO*; *II*, 7 Aug. 1922; *EH*, 7 Aug. 1922, 8 Aug. 1922; *MSPC* 2D343.

63 *GRO*; *II*, 7 Aug. 1922; *EH*, 7 Aug. 1922, 8 Aug. 1922; *MSPC* 2D242); *TNA* WO 329, WO364.

64 *GRO*; *II*, 7 Aug. 1922; *EH*, 7 Aug. 1922, 8 Aug. 1922; *MSPC* 2D315; Tom Doyle, *The Summer Campaign in Kerry* (Cork, 2010).

65 *GRO*; *II*, 7 Aug. 1922; *EH*, 7 Aug. 1922, 8 Aug. 1922; *MSPC* 2D293.

66 *GRO*; *II*, 7 Aug. 1922; *EH*, 7 Aug. 1922, 8 Aug. 1922; *MSPC* 2D322.

67 *GRO*; *II*, 7 Aug. 1922; *EH*, 7 Aug. 1922, 8 Aug. 1922; *MSPC* 2D83; 'Enlistment book of the Royal Dublin Fusiliers', 1920–1922 (National Army Museum, London, 7077005-7077322).

68 *GRO*; *II*, 7 Aug. 1922; *EH*, 7 Aug. 1922, 8 Aug. 1922; *MSPC* 2D86.

69 *GRO*; *II*, 7 Aug. 1922; *EH*, 7 Aug. 1922, 8 Aug. 1922; *MSPC* 2D316.

70 *GRO*; *II*, 7 Aug. 1922; *EH*, 7 Aug. 1922, 8 Aug. 1922; *MSPC* 2D342.

71 *EH*, 5 Aug. 1922; *II*, 9 Aug. 1922; *SI* 6 Aug. 1922; *GRO*.

72 *EH*, 10 Aug. 1922; *CT*, 12 Aug. 1922; *Kerry People [KP]*, 12 Aug. 1922; *GRO*; *MSPC* 2D74; BMH WS387 (Paddy O'Daly).

73 *EH*, 10 Aug. 1922; *CE* 14 Aug. 1922; *MSPC* 2D25.

74 *II*, 15 Aug. 1922; *CE*, 17 Aug. 1922; *EH*, 14 Aug. 1922; *MSPC* 2D371.

75 *EH*, 14 Aug. 1922; *TNA* AIR76; *GRO*; Alex Thom & Co. Ltd., *Thom's official directory for the year 1928*; *NAI*, 1911 census.

76 *EH*, 14 Aug. 1922; *GRO*; *NAI*, 1911 census.

77 *EH*, 14 Aug. 1922.

78 *EH*, 14 Aug. 1922; *MSPC* 2D17

79 *EH*, 14 Aug. 1922; *TNA* WO372; *CWGC*; *GRO*; *MSPC* 2D133.

80 *EH*, 14 Aug. 1922; *GRO*; *MSPC* 2D450.

81 *GRO*; *II*, 11 Aug. 1922; *IT*, 11 Aug. 1922; *MSPC* 2D459; *TNA* WO 372.

82 *GRO*; *MSPC* 2D93; *CE*, 22 Aug. 1922; *FJ*, 10 Aug. 1922.

83 *II*, 15 Aug. 1922; *CE*, 17 Aug. 1922; *NAI*, 1911 census; MSPC 2D40; 'Files of the Canadian Expeditionary Force', 1914–1918 (Library and Archives Canada, RG150).

84 *MSPC* 2D396; *TNA* WO372.

85 *EH*, 22 Aug. 1922; *GRO*; Dorney, p. 163; *NGA*, *Last Post*, p. 77; *MSPC* MD6732.

86 *EH*, 25 Aug. 1922; *MSPC* 2D130; GRO; *NAI*, 1911 census.

87 *II*, 23 Aug. 1922; *TN*, 23 Aug. 1922; *MSPC* 2D352, 2D23, 24SP1302; 'South Tipperary Brigade

activity report', 1922 (Military Archives, Dublin, A14).

88 *EH*, 31 Aug. 1922, 2 Sep. 1922; *FJ*, 31 Aug. 1922, 2 Sep. 1922; *II*, 1 Sep. 1922; *Westmeath Independent [WI]*, 2 Sep. 1922; *GRO*; Anne Dolan, William Murphy, *Michael Collins: The man and the Revolution* (Dublin, 2018); Piaras Béaslaí, *Michael Collins and the making of a new Ireland* (Dublin, 1930); dib.ie/biography/collins-michael-a1860; youtube.com/watch?v=SLrGnImYCwU

89 MSPC 2D361.

90 *EH*, 29 Aug. 1922, 30 Aug. 1922; *II*, 28 Aug. 1922, 30 Aug. 1922; *FJ*, 31 Aug. 1922; *IT*, 30 Sep. 1922; *WIT*, 2 Sep. 1922; *GRO*; *MSPC* DP3749, MSP34REF609; Dorney, pp. 177–78.

91 *Ibid.*

92 *EE*, 28 Aug. 1922, 30 Aug. 1922; *CE*, 30 Aug. 1922; *MSPC* 2D378; *TNA* WO339/96676, WO363.

93 *WI*, 2 Sep. 1922; *FJ*, 1 Sep. 1922; *MSPC* 2D365.

94 *EH*, 1 Sep. 1922; *CE*, 30 Aug. 1922, 2 Sep. 1922; *II*, 30 Aug. 1922, 2 Sep. 1922; *SI*, 3 Sep. 1922; *MSPC* 2D477; *TNA* WO363; *NAI*, 1911 census.

95 *MSPC* 2D190; *GRO*.

96 *GRO*; *FJ*, 1 Sep. 1922; *EH*, 30 Aug. 1922; *TNA* WO329.

97 *Kilkenny People [KP]*, 2 Sep. 1922; *MSPC* 2D34; *GRO*; *TNA* 1911 census.

98 *FJ*, 6 Sep. 1922; *EH*, 5 Sep. 1922; *MSPC* 2D300; *TNA* WO329.

99 *EH*, 27 Apr. 1923; *II*, 28 Apr. 1923, 1 May 1923; *MSPC* 3D224.

100 *FJ*, 4 Sep. 1922; *GRO*; *NAI*, 1911 census; *MSPC* 2D172; *NAI*, Mountjoy Prison Registers.

101 *MSPC* 2D260; *GRO*.

102 *FJ*, 4 Sep. 1922; *CE*, 2 Sep. 1922.

103 *EH*, 6 Sep. 1922; *MSPC* 2D235; GRO.

104 *EH*, 5 Sep. 1922; *FJ*, 12 Jul. 1922, 6 Sep. 1922; *II*, 11 Sep. 1922; *GRO*; *MSPC* DP5759.

105 *EE*, 25 Sep. 1922; *FJ*, 25 Sep. 1922; *CT*, 30 Sep. 1922; *MSPC* 2D91; *GRO*.

106 *MSPC* 2D444; *GRO*; *TNA* WO363.

107 *II*, 13 Sep. 1922, 14 Sep. 1922; *FJ*, 14 Sep. 1922; *Poblacht na h-Éireann War News*, 16 Sep. 1922; *GRO*; *MSPC* 34REF301.:

108 *EH*, 16 Sep. 1922, 18 Sep. 1922; *GRO*; *MSPC* 2D309.

109 *EH*, 14 Sep. 1922; *MSPC* 2D217; *GRO*.

110 *MSPC* 2D208; *GRO*.

111 *MSPC* 2D397; *GRO*; *CE*, 15 Sep. 1922; *EE*, 15 Sep. 1922.

112 *EH*, 21 Sep. 1922; *FJ*, 22 Sep. 1922; *II*, 19 Sep. 1922; *MSPC* 2D36, 24SP11467; *GRO*; *TNA* ADM188/799; Thomas Langan 'Civil War in Mayo: The battle of Glenamoy 1922', *North Mayo Historical Journal*, 2 (1) (1987/8).

113 *MSPC* 2D335; *CE*, 18 Sep. 1922; *EE*, 18 Sep. 1922; *FJ*, 18 Sep. 1922, 21 Sep. 1922; *II*, 19 Sep. 1922, 20 Sep. 1922; *EH*, 20 Sep. 1922.

114 *FJ*, 18 Sep. 1922; *GRO*; *MSPC* 2D120.

115 *MSPC* 2D438; *CE*, 18 Sep. 1922; *EE*, 18 Sep. 1922; *FJ*, 18 Sep. 1922, 21 Sep. 1922.

116 *CE*, 21 Sep. 1922; *FJ*, 18 Sep. 1922, 20 Sep. 1922; *EE*, 19 Sep. 1922, 21 Sep. 1922; *EH*, 19 Sep. 1922; *NAI*, Mountjoy Prison Registers; dib.ie/biography/odea-denis-a6674

117 GRO; *CE* 21 Sep. 1922; *EH*, 19 Sep. 1922; *II*, 20 Sep. 1922; *CT*, 23 Sep. 1922.

118 *FJ*, 20 Sep. 1922, 21 Sep. 1922; *II*, 20 Sep. 1922, 21 Sep. 1922; *Nenagh Guardian*, 23 Sep. 1922; *MSPC* 2D92.

119 *CE*, 21 Sep. 1922; *MSPC* 2D289; *GRO*.

120 *EH*, 25 Sep. 1922; *FJ*, 26 Sep. 1922; *II*, 26 Sep. 1922; *MSPC* 2D366; *GRO*; *TNA* BT350.

121 *II*, 27 Sep. 1922; *GRO*; *MSPC* 2D455.

122 *EH*, 27 Sep. 1922; *FJ*, 27 Sep. 1922, 28 Sep. 1922; Brian McCarthy, *The Civic Guard Mutiny* (Cork, 2012); *GRO*.

123 *EH*, 29 Sep. 1922, *II*, 30 Sep. 1922, *MSPC* 2D367; *TNA* WO372.

124 *EH*, 29 Sep. 1922; *EE*, 30 Sep. 1922; *MSPC* 2D401.

125 *CE*, 30 Sep. 1922; *EE*, 30 Sep. 1922; *II*, 2 Oct. 1922; *TNA* WO372; *MSPC* 2D349.

126 *EH*, 4 Oct. 1922; *FJ*, 5 Oct. 1922; *MSPC* 2D357.

127 *CE*, 10 Oct. 1922; *EE*, 10 Oct. 1922; *FJ*, 10 Oct. 1922; *MSPC* 2D189; *GRO*.

128 *II*, 9 Oct. 1922; 12 Oct. 1922; *EH*, 9 Oct. 1922; 16 Oct. 1922; 18 Oct. 1922; *FJ*, 10 Oct. 1922, 14 Oct. 1922; 16 Nov. 1922; *SI*, 8 Oct. 1922; GRO; *NAI*, 1911 census; *MSPC* DP4496; theirishstory.com/2017/11/22/revisiting-the-red-cow-murders-october-7-1922

129 *Ibid.*

130 *MSPC* 2D391, 24SP913; Anne Dolan, 'Killing and Bloody Sunday November 1920', *The Historical Journal*, 49, 3 (2006), p. 789.

131 *BN*, 14 Oct. 1922; *II*, 14 Oct. 1922; *GRO*; *MSPC* 2D298.

132 *II*, 12 Oct. 1922; *FJ*, 12 Oct. 1922; *CE*, 12 Oct. 1922; *NGA, Last Post*, p.88; *MSPC* DP2138; *GRO*.

133 *MSPC* 2D216, 24SP3860.

134 *MSPC* 2D270; GRO; *FJ*, 16 Oct. 1922, 18 Oct. 1922; *EH*, 17 Oct. 1922.

135 *MSPC* 2D22.

136 *MSPC* 2D177; *EH*, 16 Oct. 1922, 18 Oct. 1922; *FJ*, 18 Oct. 1922, 19 Oct. 1922.

137 *MSPC* 2D266; *II*, 28 Oct. 1922; *FJ*, 23 Oct. 1922.

138 *FJ*, 21 Oct. 1922; 23 Oct. 1922; *II*, 21 Oct. 1922; *MSPC* 2D6.

139 *MSPC* 2D317; 23 Oct. 1922; *GRO*.

140 *EE*, 23 Oct. 1922; *TNA* WO372; *NAI*, 1911 census; *GRO*; *MSPC* 2D412; *NAI*, Mountjoy Prison Registers.

141 *FJ*, 23 Oct. 1922, 24 Oct. 1922, 25 Oct. 1922; *II*, 23 Oct. 1922; *EH*, 21 Oct. 1922; *SI* 22 Oct. 1922; *GRO*.

142 *FJ*, 26 Oct. 1922; *II*, 28 Oct. 1922; *Democrat and Peoples Journal*, 28 Oct. 1922; GRO.

143 *EH*, 28 Oct. 1922; *FJ*, 28 Oct. 1922; *GRO*; *MSPC* 2D218.

144 *MSPC* 2D375; *GRO*.

145 *CE*, 2 Nov. 1922; *II*, 1 Nov. 1922; *MSPC* 2D344, 2D344A.

146 *EH*, 8 Mar. 1923; *II*, 9 Mar. 1923; *MSPC* 3D121.

147 *EH*, 3 Nov. 1922; *II*, 2 Nov. 1922, 3 Nov. 1922; *FJ*, 1 Nov. 1922; *MSPC* 2D320.

148 *MSPC* 2D109; *GRO*.

149 *CE*, 7 Nov. 1922, 10 Nov. 1922; *EE*, 7 Nov. 1922; *GRO*; *MSPC* 2D329, MD5283.

150 *GRO*; *FJ*, 10 Nov. 1923; *EH*, 8 Nov. 1922; *II*, 13 Nov. 1922; *IT*, 10 Nov. 1922; *MSPC* DP5763.

151 *MSPC* 2D310; *GRO*; *II*, 15 Nov. 1922; *CE*, 16 Nov. 1922; *EH*, 14 Nov. 1922; *London Gazette [LG]*, 16 Apr. 1918; *TNA* WO97/4120, BT350; WO372.

152 *FJ*, 18 Nov. 1922, 21 Nov. 1922, 20 Oct. 1924, 31 Oct. 1924; *II*, 18 Nov. 1922, 21 Nov. 1922; *TNA* WO 95/1220; *MSPC* DP1616, MD31236; *CWGC*; *GRO*; BMH WS1751 (Cahir Davitt).

153 *FJ*, 18 Nov. 1922, 21 Nov. 1922, 20 Oct. 1924, 31 Oct. 1924; *II*, 18 Nov. 1922, 21 Nov. 1922; guinness-storehouse.com/en/archives

154 *FJ*, 18 Nov. 1922, 21 Nov. 1922, 20 Oct. 1924, 31 Oct. 1924; *II*, 18 Nov. 1922, 21 Nov. 1922; *MSPC* DP305; *GRO*; *NAI*, 1911 census; *TNA* WO363.

155 *FJ*, 18 Nov. 1922, 21 Nov. 1922, 20 Oct. 1924, 31 Oct. 1924; *II*, 18 Nov. 1922, 21 Nov. 1922; *GRO*; *CWGC*; *NAI*, 1911 census; *TNA* WO97, WO95/2397; *MSPC* DP5824.

156 *FJ*, 23 Nov. 1922, 21 Nov. 1922; *II*, 21 Nov. 1922; *GRO*; *NAI*, Mountjoy Prison Registers.

157 *MSPC* 2D57.

158 *MSPC* 2D346; *II*, 29 Nov. 1922.

159 *FJ*, 25 Nov. 1922; *IT*, 11 Dec. 2015; *LG*, 16 Feb. 1915, 30 Jan. 1917, 24 Apr. 1917, 27 Nov. 1917; dib.ie/biography/childers-robert-erskine-a1649; 'Private papers of Lieutenant Commander R. E. Childers D.S.C. R.N.V.R.' 1914–18 (Imperial War Museum, London, Documents.471); *TNA* AIR76; ADM337; WO100; oireachtas.ie/en/debates/debate/dail/1922-01-10/

160 *MSPC* 2D351; *FJ*, 29 Nov. 1922.

161 *GRO*; *FJ*, 28 Nov. 1922; BMH WS1209 (Stephen Kay).

162 *EH*, 27 Nov. 1922; *FJ*, 29 Jul. 1922; *II*, 28 Nov. 1922; *GRO*; *MSPC* 2D294.

163 *EH*, 31 Oct. 1922; *FJ*, 1 Nov. 1922; *II*, 1 Nov. 1922, 1 Dec. 1922; *MSPC* DP1230; *GRO*; Dorney, pp. 170–1.

164 *EH*, 31 Oct. 1922; *FJ*, 1 Nov. 1922; *II*, 1 Nov. 1922, 1 Dec. 1922; *MSPC* DP8262.

165 *EH*, 31 Oct. 1922; *FJ*, 1 Nov. 1922; *II*, 1 Nov. 1922, 1 Dec. 1922; *MSPC* DP5774; *NAI*, 1911 census; *GRO*; Francis Stuart, *Things to live for: notes for an autobiography* (London, 1934), pp. 219–21.

166 *FJ*, 9 Dec. 1922; BMH WS939 (Ernest Blythe); *GRO*; dib.ie/biography/oconnor-roderick-rory-a6614; theirishstory.com/2016/06/27/to-cost-you-in-blood-rory-oconnors-1916-rising-and-aftermath.

167 *MSPC* 2D3; *GRO*; *NAI*, 1911 census.

168 *MSPC* 2D296; *NAI*, 1911 census; *GRO*.

169 *MSPC* 2D55; *GRO*.

170 *FJ*, 16 Dec. 1922, 18 Dec. 1922, 19 Dec. 1922; *II*, 16 Dec. 1922; *GRO*; *MSPC* 24SP5125; MSP34REF60225; dib.ie/biography/mcgarry-sean-a5663.

171 *MSPC* 2D84, 24SD9684.

172 *MSPC* 2D339; *GRO*.

173 *EH*, 22 Dec. 1922; *Nationalist and Leinster Times [NLT]*, 23 Dec. 1922; *MSPC* 2D161.

174 *EH*, 22 Dec. 1922; *FJ*, 22 Dec. 1922; *II*, 22 Dec. 1922, 23 Dec. 1922; *GRO*; theirishstory. com/2013/09/02/who-was-seamus-dwyer.

175 *EH*, 23 Dec. 1922; *FJ*, 27 Dec. 1922; *MSPC* 2D434; *GRO*.

176 *KP*, 30 Dec. 1922; *MSPC* 2D90; *GRO*.

177 *FJ*, 28 Dec. 1922; *MSPC* 2D58.

178 *EH*, 26 Dec. 1922; *FJ*, 30 Dec. 1922; *II*, 27 Dec. 1922; *SI* 31 Dec. 1922; *GRO*; *NAI*, 1911 census.

179 *FJ*, 30 Dec. 1922; SI 31 Dec. 1922; *GRO*; theirishstory.com/2010/05/25/who-shot-frank-lawlor-encounters-with-the-irish-civil-war/; *MSPC* DP5250; BMH WS889 (James Kavanagh); BMH WS624 (Mary Flannery-Woods).

1923

1 *EH*, 6 Jan. 1923; *II*, 8 Jan. 1923; *FJ*, 6 Jan. 1923; *GRO*; *MSPC* 3D138.

2 *EH*, 11 Jan. 1923; *II*, 12 Jan. 1923; *MSPC* 3D99; *TNA* WO 363; *NAI*, Mountjoy Prison Registers.

3 *II*, 19 Jan. 1923; *GRO*

4 *FJ*, 23 Jan. 1923; *CE* 19 Jan. 1923; *The Nationalist*, 20 Jan. 1923; *MSPC* 3D239; *GRO*.

5 *MSPC* 3D250.

6 *GRO*; *MSPC* 3D220; *CWGC*.

7 *MSPC* 3D261; *GRO*; *EH*, 23 Jan. 1923. His date of death is recorded by the cemetery as 18 January, however, contemporary newspaper reports show that he was killed on 19 January.

8 *MSPC* 3D219; *GRO*.

9 *EH*, 29 Jan. 1923; *FJ*, 30 Jan. 1923; *SI*, 28 Jan. 1923; *GRO*; oireachtas.ie/en/debates/debate/dail/1923-03-27/13/.

10 *MSPC* 3D145; *EH*, 30 Jan. 1923; *FJ*, 31 Jan. 1923.

11 *GRO*; *FJ*, 6 Feb. 1923; *EH*, 7 Feb. 1923; *II*, 8 Feb. 1923; *Liverpool Echo*, 30 Mar. 2016; Wren, Jimmy, *The GPO Garrison Easter Week 1916* (Dublin 2015), pp. 154–5.

12 *EH*, 12 Feb. 1923; *EH*, 12 Feb. 1923; *GRO*; *MSPC* 3D228.

13 *MSPC* 3D52.

14 *FJ*, 22 Feb. 1923; *MSPC* 3D127.

15 *GRO*; *FJ*, 26 Feb. 1923; 27 Feb. 1923; *CE*, 27 Feb. 1923.

16 *EH*, 28 Feb. 1923; *II*, 28 Feb. 1923; *FJ*, 28 Feb. 1923; *GRO*.

17 *MSPC* 33APB30; *NAI*, 1911 census.

18 *CE*, 9 Mar. 1923; *FJ*, 7 Mar. 1923, 8 Mar. 1923; *EH*, 9 Mar. 1923; *II*, 10 Mar. 1923; *MSPC* 3D164.

19 *CE*, 9 Mar. 1923; *FJ*, 7 Mar. 1923, 8 Mar. 1923; *EH*, 9 Mar. 1923; *II*, 10 Mar. 1923; *MSPC* 3D70; *GRO*; *TNA* WO35.

20 *FJ*, 13 Mar. 1923; *MSPC* 3D256.

21 *EH*, 8 Mar. 1923; *II*, 9 Mar. 1923; *MSPC* 3D121.

22 *EH*, 13 Mar. 1923, 14 Mar. 1923; *FJ*, 14 Mar. 1923, 15 Mar. 1923; *GRO*; *MSPC* 24SP1549.

23 *II*, 22 Feb. 1923; *MSPC* DP2903; James Adam & Son Auctioneers, 800 years of Irish history auction catalogue (Dublin, 2013).

24 *MSPC* 3D33; *FJ*, 17 Mar. 1923; *CE*, 17 Mar. 1923; *GRO*.

25 *EH*, 19 Mar. 1923; *FJ*, 17 Mar. 1923; *II*, 16 Mar. 1923; *MSPC* 3D55.

26 *GRO*; *II*, 19 Mar. 1923.

27 *GRO*; *MSPC* 3D38.

28 *GRO*; *TNA* WO363, WO372; *MSPC* 3D213; *FJ*, 23 Mar. 1923; *EH*, 22 Mar. 1923; *II*, 23 Mar. 1923.

29 *EH*, 26 Mar. 1923; *FJ*, 26 Mar. 1923; *GRO*; theirishstory.com/2018/01/28/the-iras-war-on-public-entertainment-the-amusements-order-of-1923.

30 *EH*, 24 Mar. 1923; *II*, 26 Mar. 1923; *CE*, 28 Mar. 1923; *BN*, 26 Mar. 1923; *GRO*; *MSPC* DP2719; Dorney, pp. 249–50.

31 *EH*, 28 Mar. 1923; *FJ*, 27 Mar. 1923; *II*, 26 Mar. 1923; *MSPC* 3D125, MD9951; *GRO*; militarypensions.wordpress.com/2020/04/03/execution-of-national-forces-adamstown-wexford-march-1923.

32 *FJ*, 28 Mar. 1923, 25 Mar. 1923; *II*, 26 Mar. 1923; *MSPC* DP4702; *GRO*; *TNA* WO363, WO372.

33 *MSPC* 3D37.

34 *FJ*, 10 Apr. 1923; *II*, 4 Apr. 1923; *MSPC* DP2399; *GRO*; theirishstory.com/2013/09/02/who-was-seamus-dwyer.

35 *GRO*; *MSPC* 3D307.

36 *II*, 5 Apr. 1923, 7 Apr. 1923; *FJ*, 6 Apr. 1923; *EH*, 6 Apr. 1923; *CE*, 7 Apr. 1923; *GRO*; *NAI*, 1901 census, 1911 census; *MSPC* DP496.

37 *II*, 5 Apr. 1923, 7 Apr. 1923; *FJ*, 6 Apr. 1923; *EH*, 6 Apr. 1923; *CE*, 7 Apr. 1923; *GRO*; *NAI*, 1901 census, 1911 census; csu1916.wordpress.com/3-lower-kevin-st/no-3-kevin-st/children/joseph-patrick-kernan/.

38 *MSPC* 3D281; *NAI*, 1911 census; *GRO*.

39 *FJ*, 18 Apr. 1923; *An tÓglách*, 16 Jun. 1923; *MSPC* DP11294, 3D233

40 *FJ*, 19 Apr. 1923; *II*, 19 Apr. 1923; *MSPC* DP3998.

41 *GRO*; *MSPC* 3D51.

42 *MSPC* 3D224; *EH*, 27 Apr. 1923; *II*, 28 Apr. 1923, 1 May 1923.

43 *MSPC* 3D93.

Bibliography

Primary Sources

Dublin Cemeteries Committee Archive
Dublin Cemeteries Committee General Committee Minute Books GTA/MB/1
Dublin Cemeteries Committee Rotation Committee Minute Books GTA/MB/2
Dublin Cemeteries Committee Visiting Committee Minute Books GTA/MB/3
Dublin Cemeteries Committee Special Sub Committee Minute Books GTA/MB/4
Dublin Cemeteries Committee Letter Books GTA/MB/LB
Interment Registers General Ground Prospect Cemetery, GTA/RI/PC/1
Interment Registers Poor Ground Prospect Cemetery, GTA/RI/PC/2
Prospect Cemetery Grant Books, GTA/PC/GB
Prospect Cemetery Interment Orders, GTA/PC/IO

Dublin City Library and Archives

Deansgrange Cemetery burial registers, 906131-32
Mount Jerome Cemetery burial registers, 910612-14

Imperial War Museum

Private papers of Lieutenant Commander R. E. Childers D.S.C. R.N.V.R.

Institution of Civil Engineers Library

Civil Engineer Membership Forms

Library and Archives Canada

Files of the Canadian Expeditionary Force, 1914–1918, RG 150

Military Archives

Brigade Activity Reports
Bureau of Military History witness statements (*BMH*)
Military service pensions collection (*MSPC*)
National Army Census 1922

National Archives of Australia

Australian Imperial Forces personnel dossiers

National Archives Ireland (*NAI*)

1901/1911 Census
Chief Secretary's Office Registered Papers CSO/RP

Kevin Barry: proposed reinterment in republican plot Glasnevin, DT/98/6/268

The National Archives U.K. (*TNA*)

Burial plots for ex-members of Royal Irish Constabulary, HO 45/19233
Campaign medal rolls 1914-20, WO 329
Dublin District claims for damages, WO 35
Dublin District raid and search reports, WO 35
Dublin Metropolitan Police D Division. Superintendents Journal, HO 184/71
First World War war diaries, WO 95
General courts martial civilians WO 71
Home Office Supplementary Registered Papers HO144
Imperial Yeomanry soldiers documents' WO 128
Officers' services personal files, WO 339 & WO 374
Prosecution of civilians: A2 2302 – 2379, WO 35/111
Records of the army in Ireland, courts of enquiry in lieu of inquest, WO 35
Registry of shipping and seaman, BT350
Royal Air Force officers' service records, AIR 76
Royal Irish Constabulary records Auxiliary Division HO 184
Royal Irish Constabulary general register, HO 184
Royal Irish Constabulary officers' register HO 184
Royal Marines attestation forms, ADM 157
Royal Naval Volunteer Reserve records of service, ADM337
Service medal and award rolls index, First World War, WO 372
Soldiers other ranks pension papers, WO 364
Soldiers other ranks service papers, WO 363

National Army Museum, London

Enlistment books of the Irish regiments

National Library of Ireland (*NLI*)

Catholic Parish Registers
Grangegorman Military Cemetery burial registers, POS 9488
Irish National Aid and Volunteer Dependents' Fund papers, MS 24,320-392
John Devoy papers', MS 18,000-18,157
Roger Casement papers, MS 13,073-13,092

University College Dublin Archives

Papers of Éamon de Valera, IE UCDA P150
Papers of Richard Mulcahy, IE UCDA P7
Papers of Sighle Humphreys, IE UCDA P106
Papers of Kevin Barry IE UCDA P93

Newspapers and periodicals

An tÓglach

Belfast Newsletter (BN)
Belfast Telegraph (BT)
Connacht Tribune (CTrib)
Connaught Telegraph (CT)
Cork Examiner (IE)
Democrat and Peoples Journal
Derry Journal
Drogheda Independent
Dublin Evening Telegraph (DET)
Dundee Evening Telegraph
Evening Echo (EE)
Evening Herald (EH)
Freeman's Journal (FJ)
Irish Independent (II)
Irish Press (IP)
Irish Times (IT)
Kerry People
Kerryman
Kilkenny People
Liverpool Echo
London Gazette
Morning Chronicle
Nationalist and Leinster Times
Nenagh Guardian
Northern Whig
Poblacht na h-Éireann War News
Skibbereen Eagle
Southern Star (SS)
Sunday Independent (SI)
The Irish Volunteer
The Liberator (TL)
The Nationalist
The Times
Weekly Irish Times (WIT)
Westmeath Independent
Thom, Alex & Co. Ltd., *Thom's official directory for the year 1928* (Dublin, 1928)

Secondary Sources

Abbott, Richard, *Police Casualties in Ireland, 1919–22* (Cork, 2019)
Andrews, C.S., *Dublin Made Me* (Cork/Dublin 1979)
Anon. *Dublin's fighting story, 1916–21* (Cork, 2009)
Babbington, Anthony, *The Devil to Pay: The Mutiny of the Connaught Rangers, India, July 1920* (London, 1991)
Barry, James, *Glasnevin Cemetery: A short history of the famous Catholic necropolis* (Dublin, 1932)
Béaslaí, Piaras, *Michael Collins and the making of a new Ireland* (Dublin, 1930)

Borgonovo, John, *The battle for Cork, July–August 1922* (Cork, 2011)

Boyne, Seán, *Emmet Dalton: Somme soldier, Irish General, film pioneer* (Dublin, 2015)

Carey, Tim, *Hanged for Ireland* (Dublin, 2001)

Connell, Carmel, *Glasnevin Cemetery, Dublin 1832–1900* (Dublin, 2004)

Crowley, John, Donal Ó Drisceoil and John Borgonovo (ed.), *Atlas of the Irish Revolution* (Cork, 2017)

Daly, Mary E., *Dublin the deposed capital. A social and economic history 1860–1914* (Cork, 1984)

D'Arcy, Fergus, *Remembering the War Dead* (Dublin, 2007)

Dickson, David, *Dublin: The Making of a Capital City* (Dublin, 2014)

Dodd, Conor, "Glasnevin Cemetery's 'Patriot Plot' after 1916", in *1916–18 Changed Utterly, Ireland after the Rising History Ireland* (2017)

Dolan, Anne, "Killing and Bloody Sunday, November 1920" in *The Historical Journal*, vol.?? 49, no. 3 (2006)

Dolan, Anne & Murphy, William, *Michael Collins: The man and the Revolution* (Dublin, 2018)

Donnelly, Mary, *The last post – Glasnevin Cemetery being a record of Ireland's heroic dead in Dublin city and county also places of historic interest* (Dublin, n.d.)

Doyle, Tom, *The Civil War in Kerry* (Cork, 2008)

—— *The Summer Campaign in Kerry* (Cork, 2010).

Dorney, John, *The Civil War in Dublin* (Kildare, 2019)

Dublin Cemeteries Committee, *A guide through Glasnevin* (Dublin, 1879)

—— *Extracts from the bye-laws of the Dublin Cemeteries*, Committee for the management and maintenance of the cemeteries at Prospect (Glasnevin) and Golden Bridge (Dublin, 1906)

Durney, James, *The Civil War in Kildare* (Cork, 2011)

Dwyer, T. Ryle, *Tans Terror and Trouble, Kerry's Real Fighting Story 1913–23* (Cork, 2001)

English Parliamentary Labour Party, *Report of the Labour Commission to Ireland 1921* (London, 1921)

Fitzpatrick, David (ed.), *Terror in Ireland 1916–23* (Dublin, 2012)

Fitzpatrick, William John, *History of the Dublin Catholic Cemeteries* (Dublin, 1900)

Foley, Michael, *The Bloodied Field* (Dublin, 2014)

Foreign Office, *The Foreign Office List and Diplomatic and Consular Year Book for 1917* (London, 1917)

Gillis, Liz, *The Fall of Dublin* (Cork, 2011)

Griffith, Lisa Marie and Ciarán Wallace (ed.), *Grave matters: Death and dying in Dublin 1500 to the present* (Dublin, Ireland, 2016)

Herlihy, Jim, *Royal Irish Constabulary officers: A biographical dictionary and genealogical guide 1816–922* (Dublin, 2005)

—— *The Black & Tans, 1920–21: A complete alphabetical list, short history and genealogical guide* (Dublin, 2021)

—— *The Dublin Metropolitan Police: A short history and genealogical guide* (Dublin, 2001)

—— *The Royal Irish Constabulary* (Dublin, 1997)

Hopkinson, Michael, *Green Against Green: The Irish Civil War* (Dublin, 2004)

Igoe, Vivien, *Dublin burial grounds and graveyards* (Dublin, 2001)

Jalland, Pat, *Death in war and peace* (Oxford, 2012)

Kautt, W.H., *Ground Truths: British Army Operations in the Irish War of Independence* (Dublin, 2013)

Kelly, James (ed.), *The Cambridge history of Ireland* (Cambridge, 2018)

Langan, Thomas 'Civil War in Mayo: The battle of Glenamoy 1922', *North Mayo Historical Journal,* 2 (1) (1987/8)

Lycette, R. R. (ed.), *Being an account by Ernest Lycette of his life as a young man and soldier in the years between 1911 and 1921* (New Zealand, 2007)

McCarthy, Brian, *The Civic Guard Mutiny* (Cork, 2012)

MacCarthy, J. M. Col. (ed.), *Limerick's Fighting Story* (Kerry, 1973)

MacThomáis, Shane, *Glasnevin Ireland's necropolis* (Dublin, 2010)

—— *Dead Interesting: stories from the graveyards of Dublin* (Dublin, 2012)

Milne, Ida, *Stacking the coffins* (Manchester, 2018)

Molyneux, Derek & Kelly, Darren, *Killing at its very extreme: Dublin October 1917–November 1920* (Cork, 2020)

Molyneux, Derek & Kelly, Darren, *Someone has to die for this: Dublin November 1920–July 1921* (Cork, 2021)

Moran, May, *Executed for Ireland the Patrick Moran story* (Cork, 2010)

Moran, Jamie, *Dean's Grange Cemetery* (Dublin, 2009)

Neligan, David, *The Spy in the Castle* (London, 1968)

Ní Rathaille, Bláthnaid, 'A complicated patch of land: the evolution of the republican plot in Glasnevin Cemetery 1916-30', in *Dublin Historical Record,* 69 (2) (2016)

Nic Dháibhéid, Caoimhe, *Seán MacBride: A Republican Life 1904–46* (Oxford, 2011)

O'Duffy, Richard J., *Historic graves in Glasnevin* (Dublin, 1915)

O'Farrell, Fergus, *Cathal Brugha* (Dublin 2018)

O'Malley, Cormac & Dolan, Anne (ed.), *No Surrender Here!: The Civil War Papers of Ernie O'Malley* (Dublin, 2007)

O'Malley, Ernie, *On Another Man's Wound* (Cork, 2013)

—— Raids and Rallies (Dublin, 1982)

O'Reilly, Terence (ed.), *Our Struggle for Independence* (Cork, 2009)

Ó'Ruairc, Pádraig Óg, *Truce: Murder, Myth and the Last Days of the Irish War of Independence* (Cork, 2016)

Price, Dominic, *The Flame and the Candle: War in Mayo 1919–24* (Cork, 2012)

Ryan, Salvador (ed.), *Death and the Irish: a miscellany* (Dublin, 2016)

Ryan, Seán, 'Shooting "the dog"' in *History Ireland,* vol. 27, no. 4 (2019)

Scott, A.J.L., *Sixty Squadron R.A.F. 1916–1919* (London, 1920)

Stuart, Francis, *Things to live for: notes for an autobiography* (London, 1934)

Thom, Alex & Co. Ltd., *Thom's official directory for the year 1928* (Dublin, 1928)

Townshend, Charles, *The Republic: The Fight for Irish Independence, 1918–23* (London, 2014)

Wren, Jimmy, *The GPO Garrison Easter Week 1916* (Dublin, 2015)

Yeates, Pádraig, *Dublin 1914–1918 A City in Wartime* (Dublin, 2011)

—— *Dublin 1919–1921 A City in Turmoil* (Dublin, 2012)

—— *Dublin 1921–24 A City in Civil War* (Dublin, 2015)

Websites

Catholic Parish Registers at the NLI (www.registers.nli.ie)

Census of Ireland 1901/1911 (www.census.nationalarchives.ie)

Ancestry (www.ancestry.co.uk)

Come Here To Me (www.comeheretome.com)
Commonwealth War Graves Commission (www.cwgc.org)
Dictionary of Irish Biography (www.dib.ie)
Findmypast (www.findmypast.ie)
Guinness Archives (www.guinness-storehouse.com/en/archives)
Houses of the Oireachtas debates (www.oireachtas.ie/en/debates/)
Irish Genealogy, General Register Office (www.irishgenealogy.ie) (GRO)
Irish Medals (www.irishmedals.ie)
Irish Newspaper Archives (www.irishnewsarchive.com)
Military Archives (www.militaryarchives.ie)
Military Service Pensions Collection, Stories from the Collection (www.militarypensions.wordpress.com)
The Archaeology of Conflict: Wexford in the Civil War (www.wexfordcivilwararchaeology.com)
The Auxiliary Division of the Royal Irish Constabulary (www.theauxiliaries.com)
The British Newspaper Archive (www.britishnewspaperarchive.co.uk)
The Clock is Still Going (www.customhousecommemoration.com)
The Irish Revolution Project (www.ucc.ie/en/theirishrevolution/)
The Irish Story (www.theirishstory.com)
Workers & Rebels: Jacob's Factory 1913–16 (www.csu1916.wordpress.com)

INDEX

Ryan, Capt. Patrick   246
Ryan, Michael   152
Ryan, Sgt Richard   138
Ryan, Thomas   59, 60

S

Sandwith Street   99, 117, 138, 169
Saunders, William   180
Scott, John William   60
Scully, Liam   78, 79
Scully, Pte John   251
Sears, Peter   21, 22, 23, 24
Seville, Annie   108, 113
Sex, Patrick   109, 113
Sheehan, Jack   79
Sheehan, Paddy   280
Shenton, John   90
Sheppard, Annie   212
Sherlock, Joseph   231
Shine, James   163
Ship Street Barracks   17, 234
Sinn Féin   27, 35, 101, 140, 143, 176, 189,
    208, 263, 264, 270, 275
Sir Patrick Dun's Hospital   118, 139, 143,
    148
Skerries   189
Slattery, James   13, 133
Sligo   28
Smith, Charles Humphrey   108
Smith, Lieut J.A.   25
Smith, Pte   23, 45
Smythe, Patrick   22, 24
Smyth, Maj. George O.S.   41, 43
Smyth, Patrick   12, 13, 14, 24
Smyth, Sgt Patrick   231
Soloheadbeg   30, 136
Somers, William   222, 223
South Circular Road   145, 171, 224
Spain, James   252, 253
Sparrow, Temp. Cadet   126
Spillane, Maurice   182
Spooner, Joseph   256, 267, 268, 269
Squad, the   13, 43, 55, 63, 66, 73, 91, 124,
    125, 140, 210, 229, 258
SS Lady Wicklow   191, 193, 198
Staines, Michael   34, 104

St Andrew's Catholic Hall   98
Stapleton, Capt.   204
Stapleton, Edward   293
Staunton, Sect. Comdt   44
St Bricin's Hospital   285, 290, 298, 315
Steele, Lieut Alan D.S.   140
Stewart, Joseph   171
St Mary's Place   110
St Michael's Hospital   300
Straw, William [Jack]   38, 39, 40
Strokestown   83, 84
St Stephen's Green   29, 134, 135, 154,
    230, 305, 310
St Vincent's Hospital   135, 158, 163, 184,
    187, 190, 219, 231, 232, 267, 298
St Vincent's Industrial School   186
Suffolk Street   156, 157
Sweeney, Michael   156, 157
Swords   39, 40, 90, 91, 115, 116, 148, 178

T

Talbot Street   30, 31, 32, 63, 87, 88, 89,
    300
Taylor, Lieut R.V.   134
Teeling, Frank   89, 181, 240, 241
Temple Street Children's Hospital   273
Thomas, Patrick   299, 300
Thornton, Frank   206, 207, 217
Thornton, Hugh   207, 216, 217
Tierney, James   312
Timmins brothers   51, 157
Timoney, Pte   285
Tipperary   41, 43, 50, 53, 59, 69, 103, 105,
    109, 111, 136, 151, 152, 167, 188,
    206, 232, 248, 283
Tobin, Maj.-Gen. Liam   33, 239, 247
Tobin, Nicholas   239, 247, 248
Tomkins, Matthew   168
Townley, Ernest   119
Tralee   190, 191, 192, 193, 194, 195, 197,
    206, 223, 224, 244, 247, 290
Traynor, Oscar   124, 145, 157
Traynor, Thomas   99, 116, 117, 118
Treacy, Seán   30, 31, 32, 35, 40, 41, 42, 43,
    136, 137, 138, 140
Trinity College   28, 54, 117, 149, 152